*f*P

HEART
LIKE
WATER

surviving katrina
and life in its disaster zone

JOSHUA CLARK

FREE PRESS
New York London Toronto Sydney

FREE PRESS
A Division of Simon & Schuster, Inc.
1230 Avenue of the Americas
New York, NY 10020

Some names and identifying characteristics have been changed.

Copyright © 2007 by Joshua Clark

All rights reserved, including the right to reproduce this book or portions thereof
in any form whatsoever. For information address Free Press Subsidiary Rights Department,
1230 Avenue of the Americas, New York, NY 10020

First Free Press hardcover edition August 2007

FREE PRESS and colophon are trademarks of Simon & Schuster, Inc.

DESIGNED BY ERICH HOBBING

Manufactured in the United States of America

1   3   5   7   9   10   8   6   4   2

Library of Congress Control Number: 2007005157

ISBN-13: 978-1-4165-3763-2
ISBN-10: 1-4165-3763-5

For information about special discounts for bulk purchases,
please contact Simon & Schuster Special Sales at 1-800-456-6798
or business@simonandschuster.com

for all those whose bodies remain here,
but whose voices water silenced

and for a time when we first whooshed,
far away from here

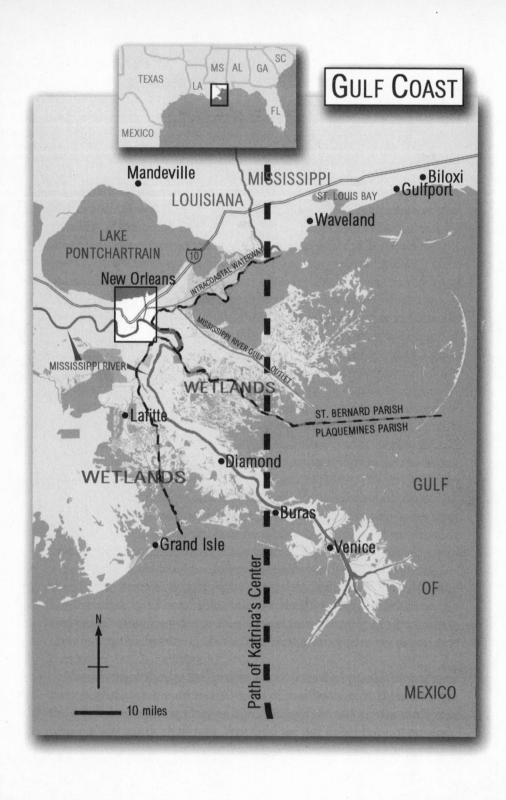

GULF COAST

SC
MS AL GA
TEXAS
LA
FL
MEXICO

Mandeville   MISSISSIPPI   •Biloxi
                                                •Gulfport
LOUISIANA   ST. LOUIS BAY

LAKE   •Waveland
PONTCHARTRAIN

New Orleans

INTRACOASTAL WATERWAY

MISSISSIPPI RIVER GULF OUTLET

MISSISSIPPI RIVER   WETLANDS

                                        ST. BERNARD PARISH
•Lafitte   PLAQUEMINES PARISH

WETLANDS   •Diamond   GULF

                        •Buras
                                    •Venice   OF
•Grand Isle

N   MEXICO

10 miles

NEW ORLEANS

LAKE PONTCHARTRAIN

University of New Orleans

West End Marina

LAKEVIEW

NEW ORLEANS EAST

17th Street Canal

Orleans Avenue Canal

London Avenue Canal

Industrial Canal

CITY PARK

Paris Avenue

10

10

Intracoastal Waterway

METAIRIE

New Orleans Museum of Art

Fairgrounds

Esplanade Avenue

JEFFERSON PARISH

ORLEANS PARISH

Canal Street

Claiborne Avenue

St. Claude Avenue

MARIGNY

BYWATER

Poland Avenue

LOWER 9th WARD

ST. BERNARD PARISH

Poydras Street

A.J.'s

FRENCH QUARTER

Superdome

Hyatt

CENTRAL BUSINESS DISTRICT

Harrah's

ALGIERS

Oak Street

RIVERBEND

St. Charles Avenue

Convention Center

UPTOWN

WAREHOUSE DISTRICT

Magazine Street

GARDEN DISTRICT

MISSISSIPPI RIVER

WEST BANK

N

1 mile   Flooded Areas on September 1, 2005

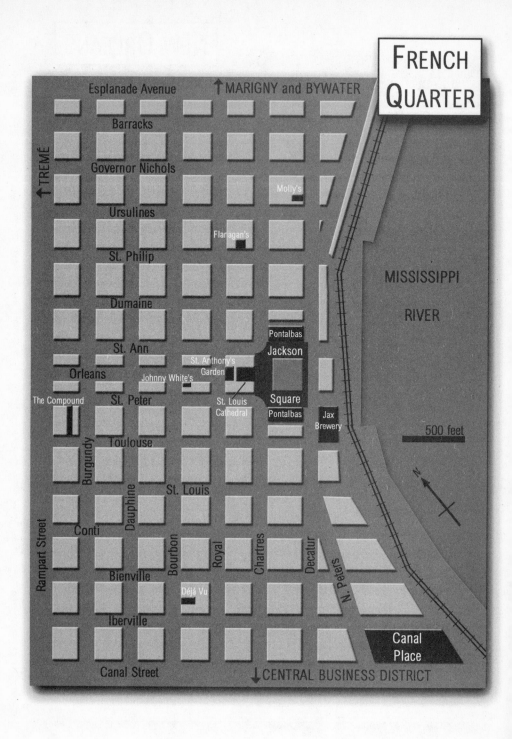

... when I awake, I awake in the grip of everydayness. Every-dayness is the enemy. No search is possible. Perhaps there was a time when everydayness was not too strong and one could break its grip by brute strength. Now nothing breaks it—but disaster.

—WALKER PERCY, *The Moviegoer*

This land which man has deswamped and denuded and derivered ... The people who have destroyed it will accomplish its revenge.

—WILLIAM FAULKNER, *Go Down Moses*

It is better to live in New Orleans in sackcloth and ashes than the entire state of Ohio.

—LAFCADIO HEARN

1

. . . and America returns whispering this time.

A tick, air-conditioning, falling, soft, a tock, the ceiling fan beginning to turn, stirring it in, a closet light suddenly spilling an absurd yellow line past its open door, across this bed, my eyes, pulling the plug on some dream.

So, that's all there is to it?

Huh.

My pores curl in, close. I climb under the covers, silver silk cold like silver, wrench them over my head, curl my knees into my chest, close my eyes, and grope frantically for sleep that's not there not anywhere, and her. My fingertips finding sweat. Still there. Warm outline of a body.

Open my eyes. Peek out. See the air-conditioning's digital monitor, the desired temperature 71.2 degrees, the actual temperature beside it 93.1 . . . 92.8 . . . 92.4 . . . 92.0 . . . 91.7 . . . twin streams, warm as August sun, down my cheeks for the first time since I was nine, the age I stopped crying no matter how hard I tried, no matter who died. The clock changes to 10:19 A.M., Monday, September 26, 2005, and I can feel the city shivering with fire alarms, and this first place that loved me is now burning. By 10:20 I can't squeeze another drop from my eyes and I'm left whimpering, panting like some spoiled thirsty dog into the sweat beside me fading cool against my cheek, and I begin laughing at how pathetic it is until that too fades into half-coughs . . . 84.9 . . . 84.5 . . . 84.1 . . . 83.8 . . .

It struggles for a while around 72, kicks on and off several times. Yesterday, the radio told me the mayor wants 250,000 people back in the city by Friday. When at last the two numbers match at 71.2 degrees, cold hint of sweat slipping through my fingertips, I throw the cover off. I slip on my bathing suit, walk into the kitchen, a floor cold under my feet for the first time in four weeks, flip open cabinet after cabinet, and it's pretty obvious this person, whoever it is used to live in this apartment, didn't live here much, like so many others who have condos in the French Quarter.

There's an open package of chocolate-chocolate-chip sugarfree cookies, sugarfree Hershey's syrup, and a can of chicken vegetable soup and that's it. I don't even glance at refrigerators anymore. The cookies are soft like I like them. I open the soup, dip a cookie in it, then drink the rest out of the can. I can feel them already, the evacuees flooding in, fluttering to the electricity, to the lights like moths that for twenty-eight nights now drowned in the wax around our candles. On the second-to-last cold gulp, soup rolling off my chin onto my toes, I notice the blinking clock on the microwave, feel kind of stupid.

The alarm goes off as I exit the apartment, walk through the courtyard, along the cleanest pool in the Quarter, piles of cans we never needed to open, skillets, kindling, the grill, beads and clothes hanging from trees, a table with too much liquor, coolers holding too much food, military rations, first aid kits, flashlights, bug repellents, shovels, brooms, tiki torches, blue-and-red candle wax splattered on the patio bricks, and I leave it all right where it is, walk the width of the French Quarter, six blocks down toward the river, past fellow holdouts struck dumb with electricity's onslaught, their glares fractured into *Whoa Wow Shit Cool Hell Okay Well No Fuck Huh Whoa . . .* and evacuees already returning, clean and smiling, some of them friends who don't recognize me at first, some chasm now opened between us into which I futilely throw a few sugar-free cookies and a story or two, maybe what it's like to have to suck your blood back out of mosquitoes, what it was like to be one of the hundred or so in the Quarter who never left, then keep walking while Decatur Street's distant alarms, awed with sudden power, rage closer and closer, and at last I am past the St. Louis Cathedral, through rows of Humvees and state police cars from New York, New Mexico, and Oregon parked upon the stones of Jackson Square we've swept, take a right, the first door on Decatur off the square, through my entryway's strobe alarm light, to the third floor, my own apartment, where I suppose I'll start getting normal again.

Flies and gnats swarm excitedly down the hallway from my kitchen to greet me. Outside, New Orleans is going off like a thousand newborns kicking and screaming and crying into light now. Across the street, the Ripley's *Believe It or Not!* Museum finally cranks up its own siren. The smell of rot wafts up along with the alarm from the restaurant below me. I stand in front of my floor-to-ceiling window, in the sunlight—the only thing that hardly changed this whole time—between the heat outside and the air-conditioning inside.

A container ship named *Ocean Favour* plows a crescent bulge of water down the Mississippi. There is no wake there, around its bow, as there is behind the ship. The water simply lifts up into a soft hill, the height of a man, casting aside the creole color of its river to catch flecks of blinding September sun that lead to the Gulf of Mexico. The river's settled back into its man-made grooves. I suppose I can be put back in mine alongside it. The ship tilts to port as it rounds the river bend, slides past hills of smoldered bricks where warehouses stood a few weeks ago and for the first time I can no longer smell a million burning bananas simply by looking over there.

The television's on, MSNBC, and, just like when the power went off a month ago, there they are, still raging about Katrina, only the alarms have drowned even whatsherass out now. In fact, it's my own fire alarm that's really drowning her out. It's not the kind where you can simply unplug the battery. It's wired into my wall. I find my hammer, swing wildly at my alarm until it slows—*whack!*—dawdles—*whack!*—moans—*whack! whack! whack! goddammit!*—dies. In its place is an advertisement for some plastic cylinder that removes women's facial hair, no prescription required, 19.95 with shipping and handling. *Call now.*

And I sink to the couch, appalled, think back to the last time I saw a commercial, thirty days ago, the Saturday before She came. It was Uptown in Parker Junior's house and the Professor was trying to get his pod back from the pod people.

2

"My spleen just changed colors. Can you feel it? This is what happens when I am wholly consumed with low-to-moderate-scale burning righteous fury." Smoke poured forth from the Professor into his cell phone. "I *am* very, very calm. I've had three verbal assurances—three—from your employees that they would bring the pod this afternoon. Now this. PODS equals Portable On Demand Storage, correct? Well, sir, you are on demand. I need to move into my new house this afternoon, right now, and everything I own is in that pod. Everything that is valuable to me. My stuff. What on God's green Earth I ask you can I do without my stuff? How would you like it if I took all *your* stuff? What could you do? What? No, that is not a threat. Listen, I've got an entire workforce waiting here to help me move my stuff into my new place." He waved his pipe at Parker Junior and me—the workforce—as we opened a couple of Heinekens that the Professor, in all his telenegotiations, had neglected to put in Junior's refrigerator. He was living on Junior's futon until he could move into his place.

I flipped on the television. It asked me if I were swimming in a pool of credit-card debt. The Professor yanked the remote out of my hand, turned it off, and said into the phone, "My workforce, they—my God, man, they have nothing to do but sit here and watch the commercials. In exchange for—no, now it is *your* turn to listen to *me*—for helping me move I was going to treat them to a barbecue. Now, you have to understand, I already bought all the stuff for the barbecue, so it's too late, we need the pod. And you are making my spleen hurt, sir."

He plunged the pipe back into his beard, crossed his legs, and stared into his plumes of smoke wafting up into Junior's overhead fan. The Professor came down from Columbia University to teach political science at Tulane a few semesters back, decided he'd stay, and finally bought a house for real last week after several housewarming parties in places he never actually closed on.

My girlfriend Katherine and I met him and each other at his third such housewarming party. The three of us stood in the corner talking since we didn't know anybody there, including each other. He had no idea who'd invited these people. No one invited me, I told him. He said he could never buy the house now because it was too much like civilization, always full of people he didn't know. Thirty-one hours later Katherine and I were still awake, sitting in her Maxima in the Audubon Zoo parking lot, holding hands over the console between us, while it rained and dawn opened the sky, feeling sleep come on, still growing our eyes at each other, hers spanning like wings to her long thin nose, their ends falling slightly down over her cheekbones, the bottoms falling out of her depthless green irises, and only a train blaring its way along the bottom of the levee.

I flipped on Parker Junior's television again. For some small fee I could have Gwen Stefani singing, "B-A-N-A-N-A-S, Bananas!" every time someone called me. Right now, no one was calling me because they couldn't, nor could I call them, all circuits busy all day. Everyone was calling everyone until no one could call no one, same as last year before

Hurricane Ivan missed us. The Professor had the last working cell phone in New Orleans that we knew of. Apparently, while I was working this morning he'd spent a couple of hours on the phone with the energy company and made enough of the right threats to enough of the right people that, against all odds, someone drove out on a Saturday and turned his power on at his new house a couple of miles away in Lakeview. And he was not about to let some possibly impending Hurricane Katrina backhand his batting average down to .500 this afternoon.

"Yes, yes, okay, hurricane." The Professor plunged the pipe into his beard where the side of his mouth must have been, closed his eyes, and continued into his cell phone, "Do you realize that you are in Kenner where the swamp used to be? You are on the low ground. So, you need to bring my stuff to Lakeview so it will be safe and so I can move into my— Hello? Hello? Hello?" He hung the phone up. "I will mutilate them. Throw the steaks on the grill, you sods."

They weren't really steaks at all but gray slabs of steak-flavored soy protein. By the time the corn was finished boiling they'd turned beige and shrunk to half their size. We ate on Parker Junior's mismatched furniture while we flipped through the commercials. A giant troll walked across the television while a girl in the foreground told us she believes *anything's* possible, "A world without spyware, identification theft, and viruses. I believe. Earthlink." When the commercials took breaks, we'd watch weathermen's eyes bulge and their forehead veins pulse as they beat doomsday drums: Hurricane Katrina *could* increase to a Category 4, *could* come to New Orleans, assuming this and that and that and this. They showed the cars driving on both sides of the highway one way out of town, "contraflow," they called it. The latest satellite image came on.

"Where'd the Gulf go?" asked Parker Junior. There was no *could* about that part. Sometime that afternoon, on the weatherman's map at least, the storm's red had mostly eclipsed the Gulf of Mexico's blue, over six hundred miles across. Then it was back to the ring tone commercials.

As I put a couple beers in the freezer, I told the Professor the only thing worse than Heineken was warm Heineken. Then I turned and slammed my knee into an old bookcase with glass doors Junior had apparently begun using as a pantry.

Junior was a wiry giant who, like many tall people, would contract his neck and spine down into his body like a tortoise into its shell, so that he fooled the unsuspecting into believing he was just a *little* taller than the rest of us. He taught English composition at the University of New Orleans, wrote fiction, painted, played bass in a gospel band called the Number Wonders, had three testicles and several holes in his fingers from the time he went back to the frame shop he worked in after our ten-cent-martini lunch and attempted to drill small screws into massive frames. He moved here from D.C. a couple of years ago and I fell in love with him when he told me over a $1.50 twenty-ounce Miller High Life draft one night, "D.C. has some of the greatest art in the world—the National Gallery, the Library of Congress, theater, music, everything you could possibly want for inspiration, you know? Yet somehow it's all dulled by the glass cases, those metal detectors at the door, the security guards—art's something to be protected and viewed from a safe distance. In New Orleans, art's something you eat and breathe, man. Everything from the streamers on your bicycle to the way you pronounce the street names is art. Like, in D.C. if I had dragged home furniture from the neighbor's garbage, my girlfriend wouldn't let me back into the house. Here, she says, 'Put that in the kitchen.' "

We put on jackets, piled into Junior's car, and crashed the Children's Museum fundraiser where Katherine was volunteering. Apparently most of the $150 ticketholders had hightailed it. This left the children's interactive exhibits largely open. I kissed Katherine hello and, while she picked corn out of my teeth, tried to tell her how stunning she looked, completely true even though the only makeup she wore was some subtle lavender stuff with sparkles in it over her eyes.

Junior, the Professor, and I roamed the Children's Museum wildly, grabbing appetizers from the city's greatest chefs standing lonely behind their serving stations until we found a faux news studio for kids. We stood in front of the green board, watched ourselves on the monitors as fake warm and cold fronts swirled behind us while we imitated the subdued hysteria of our favorite weathermen an hour earlier. Junior shrank his spine down to fit in front of the green board, pushed us aside, and looked into the camera as his image bisected all the surrounding monitors and held up a chocolate éclair.

"You see, now let's say this is the Gulf Coast, okay?" he said. "You know, if it was a chocolate éclair. Now here's Hurricane Katrina down in the Gulf." With his other hand he began spinning a clear Chinese rice noodle like a lasso, his hips gyrating right along. The few people who were still at the party gathered around to watch him in his jeans, them in their tuxedos and evening gowns.

"As the hurricane approaches it could push up a tidal surge—Hey, sprinkle some of that Tabasco on this thing will you, man? So, you can now see the coast has Tabasco on it, which is just like the muddy sediment-filled waters that the Mississippi River kicks out south of the Mississippi Gulf Coast. Except that it's Tabasco. And as the winds get closer the noodle wraps around the coast and it gets devoured. And it tastes, wow, not bad at all . . ."

Everyone clapped. Junior crammed the rest of the éclair into his mouth, slurped on his cocktail, and continued, "Now, lucky for us, New Orleans is not on the coast holy shit that's starting to burn." He lifted up another noodle. "To get to us this noodle has to spin through God help me I can't feel my mouth fifty miles of swamp, which is kind of like this bowl of chunky seafood marinara sauce here, and that marinara, boy does it slow it down. Of course, keep in mind this bowl was full not too long ago, there's a lot less marinara now than there used to be because we've eroded hell out of it, someone get me some milk or I'll die. Of course, we may not even get the noodle. In fact, I think I lost it in the marinara here. No here it is. So now if it starts spinning toward us." As the sauce flew, people fled, giggling. "Oh, God, help me, I'm burning," said Junior. "Why would I eat that? Why? We can't let this happen!" He handed me the rice noodle and fled downstairs to the bar.

I stood there holding the limp noodle, marinara dripping onto my sneakers, staring at Katherine who was the only person left standing there, stone cold. She had seen the noodle in real life, twice, and maybe it wasn't so funny for her. She was a child when Hurricanes Betsy and Camille came in the late sixties. She knew them, their destruction, how they transformed the Mississippi Coast—where all four of her grandparents had lived—then lined with some of the oldest homes in the country, and a history within which her first senses of family and summer and nostalgia were forged, into what was now a twenty-mile-long strip mall spattered with Waffle Houses, gaudy casinos, and Wal-Mart-sized "surf" shops that sell overpriced fluorescent bathing suits. Betsy and Camille were memories of the impossible, simply part of the Gulf Coast's skeleton, zero moments that it was taken for granted, despite prophecies of a future hurricane sinking us, we newcomers would never see and never ever understand.

We were not from here, since there is no way to be from New Orleans unless you first came into the light here. If you are birthed in Baton Rouge, say, and move here when you're two weeks old and stay here until you die at the age of 100, your obituary will state, "Originally from Baton Rouge, So-and-So moved to New Orleans where he attended . . ." Katherine was *from* here. Betsy and Camille were her noodles. She had grown up staring into the Mississippi and, after a decade away, given up tenure at a university back east to come back and be able to stare into it again every day for the rest of her life and, fortunately for me, the first party she wandered into after her return was the Professor's third housewarming party next door to her.

"Here," I said, dangling the noodle humbly toward her. "You can have it." She just glared at me, those eyes going shallow. The noodle slipped through my fingers and landed on my left Adidas. "That violet skirt looks gorgeous," I said. "Is that silk?"

I finally caught up to her downstairs at the bar. We drank two cups of water each—hydrating our hearts, we called it, because the human heart is 80 percent water, more than any other organ—then showed the bartender how to make our invented drink of the month, Elle in August: rocks, couple ounces vodka, soda, splash of cranberry, two limes, and Katherine took one and the Professor and Junior and I took three apiece and we all headed across the French Quarter into the Marigny to Mimi's bar where a friend was having a going away party, not for the hurricane but for good. This too was fairly empty, just empty enough to make the $500 party bar tab go real, real far for the several of us there.

Katherine and I ducked out onto the balcony with our Elle in Augusts, happily alone with Mars piercing the city sky's lavender din above us all by itself. Because of my deadlines, it was the first time in a week we'd really been awake together. We wrapped our arms around each other and held tight and talked excitedly as always about things we would never remember between the silences in which we grew our eyes by simply staring at each other nose to nose, her long thin nose to my ordinary one and her eyes the water over Nova Scotia.

Nova Scotia, for me, was a sandbar in Cape Cod Bay. My family would spend summers in a small cottage just down the street from the one my father was born in, in the same town six generations of fathers before him had been born in. I was the first son born in the New World outside Cape Cod, in the northwest section of Washington, D.C., a segregated section of a segregated city with all the cultures of the world and no culture of its own, the antithesis of New Orleans.

The tide in Cape Cod Bay went out farther than anywhere in the world, that's what my father said, anyway. When it was halfway out, we would go in a little dinghy with a four-horsepower motor to the farthest sandbar from our beach. I still have no idea why it was called Nova Scotia, maybe because it seemed as far away as that. It was about a mile from the coast with a deep channel separating it from all the other flats which, at low tide, ran together back to the beach. We'd fish for a couple of hours, casting into the channel.

At first, there would be just a few inches of clear green water splaying strings of light over the ribbed sand. The water's rippled, sun-flecked surface and the strings of light upon the bottom seemed to move independently of one another, even in different directions, unconnected. It

was impossible for me to tell the depth between the two simply by looking. This was how Katherine's eyes could get. And it is what I saw that
morning I woke in her car in the Audubon Zoo parking lot, thirty-one
hours after the Professor's party, and she was still awake watching me
and she suggested we walk down to the river in the rain, and it is what
still shook me two years later, the striations in her green eyes wavering
like those strings of light over Nova Scotia, depthless below the surface.

They would became a mere echo of one another only for a flash
before sand broke through at low tide. The sand would be ribbed and
white and it would get hard and dry and hot in the sun like the bones of
waves, like something dead. And I would wait for the water to creep back
in and clothe its bones. I would sit there in the sand while the tide came
back in around me. When it got to my shoulders, the strings of light on
the sand went away and I would stand up. We would get in the boat and
I would look over the side and see exactly how deep it was, the two surfaces again seemed connected, as they were in most people's eyes.

Water for me was something you swam in, something you could see
through, something that stretched to the horizon. Something that came
and went predictably and benevolently. And then this. Mississippi. Roiling and black as outer space inches below its surface. Finally held in place
weakly by two centuries of engineering and the world's largest human
creations—its levees. Before that it had roamed at will. Every bit of the last
1,300 miles of old Mississippi River which La Salle first floated down in
a canoe 324 years ago was solid, dry land now. Mark Twain judged it the
longest river in the world, though it has shortened by several hundred
miles since then, due to man and the river itself cutting some of its
near 180-degree curves. Beginning from the head of the Missouri, its
largest tributary, it is now a close third. Unlike the other great rivers of the
world, instead of widening toward its mouth, it grows narrower and
deeper, more violent and unpredictable, as it winds through southern
Louisiana, land made wholly from sediment carried down the continen-
tal shelf by the river's tributaries. From the Montana Rockies to the
Appalachians, the Dakota plains down through the Ozarks, the deserts of
New Mexico to the Great Lakes, we live on tiny pieces of every landscape
in America.

I suppose I'd spent the last eight years in New Orleans inching my way
closer to the river until it was my front yard. Right now, standing on the
bar's balcony with Katherine, it was just over some warehouses a couple
of blocks to the south. We grew our eyes until our drinks were done and
we finally and stupidly went inside for more drinks and the party was
just small enough to suck us in, and we were forced to share ourselves.

All the talk was of staying or going. Of course I was staying, I said. "Unless someday a Category Five comes straight for us—I may be stupid but I'm not crazy—I'm always staying during hurricanes. Besides, I got two books on deadline that my company's publishing and a travel piece for the *L.A. Times* and thousands of other little things and I can't afford to waste a couple of days stuck in traffic trying to get out of the city, only to come back in the next day, the way everyone did last year when Ivan missed us, could I please have another with a little less cranberry?"

The bartender reminded me to fill my bathtub up if we were going to stay because you never knew if the water might get cut off. It was decided the Professor and Parker Junior would crash at my place tomorrow if Katrina headed near us. I extended the invite to the dozen or so others there too. Sure, I told them, the television was hyping the possibility of twenty feet of water in the Quarter but my place was forty feet above Decatur Street, the highest street in New Orleans, in the oldest apartment building in America, the Pontalba Apartments had seen 160 years or something like that of hurricanes, they took up a whole city block, a veritable goddamn fortress, the brick sumo of apartment buildings on the highest ground in the city. Just bring water and wine, I told them. At least half of them agreed to crash at my place and three Elle in Augusts and seven waters and scattered shots of Maker's Mark later and the bartender again reminding us to fill the bathtub up if we were going to stay, we left with more drinks, and next thing I knew I was lying on my mattress, arms, legs tangled in Katherine's, something beginning half in sleep, when her phone started going off Sunday morning.

Obviously, I'd forgotten to ask her to make sure it was turned off before we went to sleep. I knew my own cell phone was off because it was part of the four F's: lock the Front door, turn the cell Fone off, landline Fone off, and the Fan on which provided white noise in the rare occurrence that one of my neighbors should walk down the entryway in high heels. Of course, the outdoor buzzer and intercom were disconnected, and my windows were locked (I checked them every night despite not having opened them in weeks). I always knew I would wake to find these things done because my routine was like God for some people—it was just there. But I'd forgotten about Katherine's phone and I couldn't believe it and I was pissed at myself, really pissed. I wanted to find the phone wherever it was within the previous evening's clothes and turn it off, but I wasn't about to untangle myself from what we had begun.

The fifth time or so it started ringing, Katherine now sleeping again, I unwound myself from us and crawled out of bed just to find out who the hell it is thinks they can call me before 9 A.M. on this Sunday when it was the first day I was taking off in a month. I managed to get my arms and head out of the bed before calling it quits. I laid my head down on the pinewood floor and dreamt of the time Katherine and I were in Cuba birdwatching and she said she had spotted the smallest bird in the world, the bee hummingbird, and I was a bit upset at her because she always noticed everything around us before I did, and I asked where it was and she pointed to it sticking out of her eye, its wings still beating into a blur around its red neck glittery like sequins, clouds of blood blooming in Katherine's eye, washing over her emerald iris and she was laughing, saying, "If you can choose, it's not love, don't you know? Some poet said that to me," and then the hummingbird's wings were ringing again and goddamnit this time I made it all the way out of bed and crawled around trying to find the phone because I just needed to know *who* it was thought they could call this early. It stopped and I curled up into Katherine's violet skirt, used my pin-striped pants as a pillow and almost went to sleep before it went off again and stopped again before I could find it.

I rose, defeated, walked into the kitchen, dropped a packet of Tangerine Emergen-C into a plastic go cup, filled it with water, slumped onto the futon in my living room, and flipped on CNN. A series of red spirals, hurricane symbols, each marked with a 5 in its center, arched through a diagram of the Gulf straight into where I was sitting.

"Whoa," I muttered. "Wow. Shit. Cool. Hell. Okay. Well. No. Fuck. Huh. Whoa . . ."

We were in the path of something very important, and everything else was lost.

Katherine walked in checking her messages, all of them from friends saying the same thing CNN was, how Katrina, now a Category Five hurricane, one of the strongest ever recorded, was supposed to make landfall here early tomorrow morning, and we had until this evening to leave the city under the first-ever mandatory evacuation. I checked my own messages. Friends were on the road halfway somewhere already: Houston, Austin, Pensacola, Missouri, and the rest just west to Baton Rouge. The Professor had enjoyed his newfound power sleeping on his new linoleum kitchen floor for about an hour last night before he bolted podless to Baton Rouge at four in the morning. We had no idea how he or anyone else got through, because neither Katherine nor I could return the calls, or make any others, all networks still being busy. But my land line worked and I tried to call my friends and tell them to get back here, dammit, but I just got busy signals.

I looked out the window at Jax Brewery, the palm trees on its roof standing tall in breeze, the stores on its ground level already boarded up, their signs still hanging out front, idling from their chains, the Mississippi past them fighting its fall as ever downstream. "Well, suppose I better go fill the bathtub up," I said.

I knelt beside the tub as it was filling and prayed every single prayer I knew to every God I knew, and some I made up, that lives and property would be spared. I was still praying when the bathtub overflowed.

Part of me felt that, like every hurricane for the last decade, it would not really arrive. History, for me, never had. The rest of me knew that if it did, Katherine and I would make it though this. And I was not going to miss it.

Yet I did not choose to say. I could not choose.

3

We spent the afternoon at Katherine's apartment uptown, rummaging around in her neighbors' trash to find enough plywood, planks, crates, driftwood, old signs, anything to effectively seal her house from all sunlight. We moved most of her stuff away from her windows, then tripped all over it gathering up some clothes, jewelry, and shrimp gumbo to take back to my place. After driving back downtown and parking our cars high up in the Canal Place shopping-center garage, we scurried back to my apartment through deepest blue dusk as the first feathery outer rain band of Katrina tickled our faces.

Pressure was getting sucked out of the air, allowing the faintest electric gust to lift wrappers and shopping bags from gutters and overfilled trash cans, a single Mardi Gras purple ribbon dancing a tango with a plastic shopping bag four stories high between Jax Brewery and the Pontalba Apartments. The Quarter was swept clean of people, cars, lights, noises, routines, and, already, an aloneness more vast than lying down in the vastest desert swallowed us whole. There was a terrifying comfort in being so alone in a place where you always, always saw so many people, a place that people probably had not left this empty since its birth three hundred years ago. Static in the air shuffled electrons through our bone marrow and gave us hot goose bumps. Along with the floating garbage, the potential for anything at all now hung weightless above us.

A police car eased toward us in the distance. Aware of curfew and mandatory evacuation we slipped into my entryway. We walked onto my balcony to see gray clouds racing frantically away from what was in the Gulf as the cop car rolled out of view. "I'm sure lots of people are staying," I said to Katherine.

"Yeah."

She gazed down empty Decatur Street along the endless slanting wrought iron balconies to the business district's skyline six blocks to our right, then over to the Marigny neighborhood seven blocks to our left, and between them the Old U.S. Mint; the last down and dirty bars of lower Decatur; Central Grocery, "Home of the Original Muffuletta"; Café du Monde; Jackson Square; Jax Brewery; Tipitina's; the House of Blues; countless twenty-four-hour bars and daiquiri cafés and Cajun/ Creole restaurants and t-shirt and hot-sauce tourist schlock shops connecting them, every one now sleeping behind plywood. We looked ahead of us, past the train tracks, over the levee into the Mississippi about 150 feet from my front door, my view of it sandwiched between a giant oak and the Jax Brewery shopping mall directly across the street from me, the Ripley's sign creaking on its chains out front, palms poking the sky on the mall's top. The clouds got faster, darker, and I suddenly realized what it was that was so terrifying about it all. It was not the disappearance of the immediate sounds. It was the susurrus of a city, gone.

The days here were usually buses, beer-delivery trucks, calliope on the riverboat, zydeco blaring out of tourist shops, accordion of a gutterpunk in cowboy boots and striped tights on the corner competing with a tuba and trumpet on the next corner, train's horn as it slows along the bottom of the levee, steamboat blasting its call, the eight million tourists a year we had to weave through to get anywhere. This was all you could hear in the day, each noise upon the other endlessly.

Late at night and into morning they slowed—the ships blowing horns, the occasional car, siren, the Nina Simone songs the homeless listen to on Jackson Square to keep themselves awake so they won't get arrested, a guttural yawp every few minutes whose emotional provenance I could never discern between laughter or surprise or fright or agony or rapture or just for the sake of letting it out before its owner had to go home—and there was space between these immediate sounds. And what lay in these spaces in the night was the susurrus of a city. It is something you do not listen to, just something you know. People are always doing things that make noise, even sleeping. In a city, there is enough thousands of them that they make a whispering. A city person knows, consciously or not, that the breath of a city is missing when they travel to a place without thousands of people. It was missing now. And it was terrifying.

We walked back inside, closed the two windows, locked the inside shutters, looped belts around them, nailed crutches across one set and a half-painted door we'd been planning to make into a dinner table for a year now across the other. We left ourselves a vantage by only closing, not nailing or even belting, the top shutters of one window which were just over our heads, but could be opened and peeked out if we stood on the futon.

That was the only room with windows. I got everything in my office at least three feet off the ground, then did the same in the bedroom. Katherine heated the gumbo and I filled every cup I had with water and placed it in the freezer, enough to keep our hearts hydrated for a few days, then walked into my laundry room, the room deepest into the massive building, the room where come tomorrow morning I figured we'd be standing huddled together, cowering on top of the dryer hoping the water stops at our shoulders because it would have to.

We ate the gumbo and watched every television station go so nuts over Katrina that they provided enough actual content that we avoided having to watch commercials just by flipping back and forth through channels while little patches of rain pitter-pattered the windows. "An environmental disaster of biblical proportions, one that could leave more than one million people homeless . . ." they said. It could turn New Orleans into "a vast cesspool tainted with toxic chemicals, human waste, and even coffins released from the city's legendary cemeteries." The mayor told us to get an ax to chop our way out through the roof after the water traps us in the attic, in case we're still alive at that point. One channel showed a clip of the mayor of Grand Isle, Louisiana's only inhabited barrier island, trying to convince an old family friend named Riley Lasseigne to leave. Riley was on his four-wheeler saying, "When it's your time to die, it's gonna be your time to die. I was on a metal fishing boat for Camille. We were scared. I don't care where yat, when the storm hits you gonna be scared. *But*—I'm still staying." And that was that.

Then came incessant shots of traffic. Contraflow had ended, but evacuation had not, and the cars fell along my screen, out of the city like water from a faucet. Most of these people had locked their pets in the kitchen with a couple of days of food and water and newspaper, then packed a few shirts and shorts and looked forward to a couple of days off work. Hurricane Ivan, this time last year, had been the dress rehearsal. They'd sat in ten hours of traffic to get seventy miles west to Baton Rouge, fleeing the ship that never sank. And we who stayed smirked at them as they spent another ten hours coming back the next day. But even those who'd smirked after Ivan were now driving across my television screen. And, as I weeks later found out, so too was Riley Lasseigne who, upon realizing he'd be the only person left in all of Grand Isle, rode his four-wheeler into the bed of his Dodge pickup and left like the others, taking my confidence carload by carload with them.

We decided to cheer ouselves up by watching *Silence of the Lambs* when my cell phone rang for the first time all day. It was Get off the Babysitter, a friend from Biloxi, Mississippi, who earned his name by marrying his boss's babysitter. "Where are you?" he asked.

"Here."

"Where? Baton Rouge? Houston?"

"At my place," I said.

"You fucking idiot, are you out of your fucking mind?"

"There's other people staying, too."

"Who? How many?"

"Well, there's Katherine and me and like this one other girl I know who lives on Orleans Street and I think there's this guy uptown."

"There's titties everywhere."

"Where?"

"In Birmingham. I Googled for the nearest Hooters convention."

"Where's your wife? Your baby?"

"They're right here. Well, it's not really a convention, but it's Hooters. Little Nigel loves the titties and the titties love him. He wants the milk! Don't you little Nigel? Little Ni-gee love that milk, baby want the milky milk milk milky milk, yes he does. I can't hear you."

"I didn't say anything."

"I'm sorry you're going to die. Baby want some milky milk, baby want some—" And the signal faded.

Hours went by. Every time we checked the news, cars were still running down I-10. I searched for a blank cassette tape, but couldn't find one. After rummaging through old tapes, I found an interview I did with this guy whose nineteenth-century French Quarter home had been made uninhabitable by Bourbon Street's subwoofers:

Those things will go thru lead, man. You walk down Bourbon any night after twelve o'clock, it's like an Orwellian generator. Pat O's plays Say-leen Deeeee-on until four AM! If the people who make this a neighborhood can't live here, it's just going to be one t-shirt shop after another and people are gonna say what the hell do we wanna go to New Orleans for?

Amen.

I dug out an old school RadioShack recorder I'd been meaning to return, the kind that's almost the size and shape of a shoe box with the buttons sticking out like teeth on one end and a big speaker on the other, popped the tape in, tested it, and left it on the living-room coffee table, just in case there was actually something worth recording tomorrow.

Midnight came, went, and it was now the last Monday in August, still and always the greatest month because it used to be summer vacation's final roar and that's all that mattered no matter how hot it was. Outside was the rain and thunder burst of any other summer day, strange only because it rarely rains at night in New Orleans. We swallowed over-the-counter sleeping pills and lay in my bed.

Uncertainty eased into me as the day eased out of me and my head lost the ability to override logic. I knew fuck-all about how safe I was. I knew fuck-all about this building and this hurricane. I knew fuck-all about any buildings and any hurricanes. I knew sleep and I felt myself slipping into that closet, locking the door, peering out the keyhole for the beast that was coming, hoping it wouldn't find me, knowing I could not wake from it if it did, but *to* it.

"Do you think we'll ever really get to walk on the bottom of the Mississippi?"

I came up out of it, back into consciousness. We were naked on our backs beside one another, still holding hands between our hips. "What?" I asked.

"Remember how you used to say we'd do that someday," said Katherine. "Walk the bottom?"

"I'd still like to. I know a river pilot. Maybe he'd have an idea who we could talk to. It would be pretty cool, huh? I bet more people have climbed Everest than walked on the bottom of the Mississippi."

"And we'd be the only people to have ever done it together. We'd have the only's. That's what I used to think about when we were going to sleep, walking on the bottom, holding hands like this, like we were in a womb, two hundred feet below, all senses gone. But sound. I would imagine nothing but the sound and darkness and it would put me to sleep when I couldn't sleep."

I turned the lamp on beside my bed, walked across the room, rifled through the bottom drawer of my bureau until I found my miniature boom box. I flipped through commercials, changed it to AM, then ran through channels starting on the bottom frequency. "Let's see if we can find it," I said.

"It's on the radio?" she asked.

I switched slowly higher and higher through frequencies shallow with static until I hit 1460. This frequency was different, deeper, it filled the room, like many different layers of static tumbling over and over themselves. "There," said Katherine. "I think I can sleep in that."

The thunder outside washed below 1460 AM and I lay back on the bed, put my fingers through hers again. When I felt the first twitch of her hand, her fingers squeezing my own suddenly and then relaxing, I leaned over, kissed her cheek, felt the soft sleeping breath.

I woke with a start. I slowly pulled my hand from Katherine's, walked out of the static-filled bedroom, down the hall into the living room, and picked up the tape recorder.

Monday, August 29, 3:28 AM. Thought I heard wind howling. Only air conditioning kicking on. Peaking outside. Like real bad rainstorm outside. Going back to bed.

5:25 AM. Gotten a bit worse. I can hear pressure of wind knocking the windows. All news channels are covering it. CNN says the storm took a slight turn to east, good for us. They say it'll make landfall around Empire down in Plaquemines Parish in a half hour. It's about seventy miles south of us, going fifteen miles per hour.

6:37 AM. Just lost power. Opening the shutters. Invisible sun came up maybe five minutes ago making everything a little gray but mostly still dark. All trees outside are bent. Debris flying. Newspaper machine just blew into street. Rain's cutting off visibility. Can't see Mississippi River across the street. Trees swept around like twigs. Palm trees on top Jax Brewery bent over parallel to ground, their leaves swept around like a woman's hair in wind. Going to go lay down beside Katherine, try to sleep.

8:39 AM. Building just shook for the second time. Saw Mississippi for a couple seconds during split second break in rain. Swells roaring upriver just like when the previous storms came near, but white caps this time. Three birds—pigeons?—shooting past window, hurled down into ground. Small one—sparrow or starling—gone in blink of an eye. Now the palm trees on top Jax Brewery standing straight up like nothing happening, but leaves, branches shooting straight down to the ground like they don't know where to go. It's as if the wind is trying to split the trees from the top down.

9 AM. Palm trees gone. Wind shouting. Listen to it . . .

9:13 AM. Called mom with land-line phone which is miraculously still working back in the kitchen, told her everything's cool. Still have water. Wind shooting through my apartment, like trying to find a voice, something out of a bad horror film. Heavy, heavy rain. Leaves everywhere. Trees down in middle of Decatur street. Katherine sleeping in all that static white noise. God bless this place and I hope it stays the one I love.

9:29 AM. Amazing rainstorms outside. Little tornadoes of rain. Wind banging, barging on windows and door, screaming, trying to break in. Blown away by amount of wind coming up under entryway door back by the kitchen despite three stories high and deep into the building. Okay, opening door—[loud crash] [garbled] Fuck! [garbled]—my ass. Just got knocked onto my—[garbled] Shit. Can't get the door closed. Bastard. There. Got ya. Hey baby. Good morning. Sorry. Sleep well?

4

Anemic light spilled around Katherine, naked, drained itself upon her muscular shoulders, shoulder blades like anchor palms jutting from the shank of her spine, shadows outlining her back muscles which even now warped the darkness in the room to every finger's twitch, playing in the candlelight like colliding conflicting currents in the river we could no longer see for the rain. She closed the living-room window's top shutters, the light withdrawing from the room, her, me, us now left in the flicker of three candles on the mantel. Wind still filled the darkness, still inhaling and exhaling, still trying to find words.

"It's something you don't see so much as hear," she said. We listened, naked next to one another, our knees, shoulders, hands inches apart as the wind rose over us into a banshee's wail, then subsided again, whispered through my front door, sucked at my windows, and the city she was born in died.

"Want some oatmeal?" I asked.

"No."

I filled a bowl with dry oatmeal, chopped up half a banana, added a scoop of vanilla protein powder, some nutmeg, water, stuck it in the microwave and felt kind of stupid. I took it out, stirred it up as air whipped around and around me, desperately trying to find its way back outside, and I brought the cold oatmeal to the living room and spoon-fed Katherine half of it and ate the rest myself. Something loud hit the side of the building. Katherine shivered, then stood up on the futon again, opened the top shutters.

"What is it?" I asked.

"The oak. The one you wanted to kill."

"No. The giant one? That blocked my view of the river bend?"

"Some of it anyway."

I got up on the futon, stood beside her, leaned against the lower shutters and peered out the top of the window. And there it was, through a fleeting break in the rain and the few half-broken branches still remaining on the oak's trunk: the reason three hundred years ago Bienville chose this strategic spot to found *La Nouvelle-Orléans*, a 110-degree bend where the river digs down 240 feet—the deepest spot of once the longest river in the world—before hurling itself to the right toward the Gulf, laid out plain for me.

"Pruned hell out of that oak," I said, and stepped off the futon. "Now, I'll have a real view. We should get away from the window. All it takes is one piece of debris and that's the end of us."

She did not move. Stormlight tangled in her blond hair which came down her back like the wet sun-stained wood that the river coughs up onto its banks here after shaping it for a thousand miles, striations flowing in waves until they ended in splinters just over her tailbone.

"Maybe we could make love," I said, "while we listen to it all."

"I don't think I've seen a single drop of rain hit this window," she said.

"No," I said. "Never mind." I reached up, touched her extra rib. She had a thirteenth rib on her left side only, a lumbar rib, a little half rib that reached barely around to her side. There was a time when we would lie together, before we were intimate, and do nothing but grow our eyes while it trembled beneath my fingertips. It was warm and still. "But, please, c'mon, it's not worth it. Stay away from that window. We'll listen."

And we did, on opposite ends of the futon, the tape recorder lying between us, wind whistling through the dancing candlelight until it blew out, the only movement in the room, not daring to look at each other for fear something would break, until the gusts became more and more sporadic and the rain, while still whipping hard, thinned.

At half past eleven, I walked back into the kitchen and called my mother again and told her not to worry. We dressed in windbreakers, shorts, and sneakers and walked down the three dark flights and opened the street entrance and almost knocked over an old man with a cane. He stood below the Pontalba's balcony in soiled plaid pants, flip-flops, T-shirt, and three days' worth of white beard, smiling at us, impossibly dry.

"Excuse me, sir, ma'am," he said through a single black tooth. "Would y'all happen to have a cigarette?"

We were speechless.

"Oh, no, no, no," he said. "Don't worry, don't worry." He reached into his pocket, held out a quarter. "I'll pay for it."

"Don't smoke," I said. "I'm very sorry."

He hobbled along. We walked over to the daiquiri bar on my corner. The dozen or so ceiling-high windowed doors that had surrounded the entire place were lying broken in the street, one now perfectly framing a fire hydrant on the opposite sidewalk. Customer-signed dollar bills, stapled to the wall, flapped wildly in the wind, like dry leaves in some place that has autumn, above the inert daiquiri machines every color of the rainbow and some nature never intended. Thirty-foot-long streamers swam in the air from the ceiling out over us to Walgreens on the other side of the street, then snapped free as a sudden gust ballooned our jackets, swept rain up our shorts, and we clutched each other around a drainpipe.

The sun had been shut down like I'd never seen before in New Orleans. The sky was white drizzle, the air just cold enough to be cold. Rain in New Orleans was supposed to come with thunderous billowing black-bellied clouds and vanish within the hour into a sky cast with humbling purple and pink and gold and orange and blue and every other color of daiquiri, even the seemingly unnatural ones, but for the first time, the air and sky were drab as a rainy day somewhere else in America. It took Katrina to do that.

And now I would see what it had done to Jackson Square, the solar plexus of the city. About two-thirds of it was down. Trees from the park had been blown into lumber upon the pedestrian mall that framed the square. Where there were no branches or trees, wet green leaves covered every last stone beneath our feet. Lining opposite sides of the square, the Pontalba Apartments looked unscathed, as did the Cabildo, the seat of the Spanish government centuries ago and where the Louisiana Purchase was signed, with only a couple of windows blown out, as did the St. Louis Cathedral, the oldest active cathedral in the country, its first incarnation destroyed by a hurricane in 1772, brick fortresses that they all are. In the center of the square, Andrew Jackson reared back, hat raised in oblivious triumph, upon his veined horse. And, above it all, the cathedral's clock had frozen at 6:37.

Another gust swept Katherine into my arms. We fell against a piece of plywood declaring, WE DON'T RUN FROM HURRICANES, WE DRINK THEM! HURRICANE PARTY INSIDE! in red spray paint. It was over the door of an abandoned restaurant, some tourist trap where they shoveled jambalaya and syrupy "N'awlins" punches into foreigners from Texas to Tasmania, the first place I bartended in New Orleans when I moved here eight years ago, and the first place I quit.

"Looks like someone took them up on their offer," she said. She pointed below the HURRICANE PARTY sign, which was just high enough for a person to crawl under. One of the doors behind the plywood sign was ajar. I wondered if they were still in there.

We walked to Royal Street as the wind lessened. "You know how it is when you wake up after a real long sleep and feel like hell and realize you have the flu?" she said. "That's what this is, what it feels like. But, it's everything else that's sick, of course. We're fine, I guess."

People began slowly emerging, cocktails in hand. We passed the Cornstalk Fence Hotel, handed pieces of the only copyrighted, not-legally photographable iron fence to the owner who was otherwise happy as hell that they'd made it through okay, his face like everyone else's filled with *Whoa Wow Shit Cool Hell Okay Well No Fuck Huh Whoa.*

Roof flashing was everywhere like copper tinfoil wrapped around whatever had stopped it from flying into eternity—fire hydrants, parking meters, stop signs, cars. And still more cocktails, almost full now. We were getting warmer. We rounded St. Philip Street, saw someone slip into Flanagan's Pub. Big black spray paint on the plywood-laden door declared

WE WILL NOT DIE SOBER!

These guys, unlike the bar on Jackson Square, were apparently serious. We slipped into the darkness sprinkled with candles, flickering tattooed and pierced faces exuding cool indifference around the bar. Strangely, this was the second bar I tended in New Orleans, this one for a year and a half after I quit the first one on Jackson Square, and I still knew it with my eyes closed, a good thing now because it was almost that dark. The place prided itself on not having a lock on the front door. The new owner, Andy, dug out a couple of the last cold Budweisers he had, told us everything's on the house, "This is a shelter now, not a bar," then crawled onto an air mattress on the pool table and started snoring.

We walked around the square bar in the pub's center, to the back where there were two free stools. We exchanged our story with the sunken figures across the bar, wavering candlelight forming great jittery shadows looming nervously behind them. They'd been here all night, they said, and they had plenty of guns in case they needed them. "This whole thing's like one real bad hangover that needs real bad nursing, ya know?" said one of the women as she passed us the bong. We declined, passed it around. She had red tears tattooed down both cheeks. "Wanna hear my joke?" she asked.

"Sure."

"There once was a red widow spider who asked an alligator for a ride across the Mississippi. So, the alligator says, 'No way man, you'll sting me and then I'll be stunned enough to drown!' The spider replies, 'Dude, if I sting you we're both dead because I can't swim.' So the alligator thinks on this, then lets the spider crawl up on his back. Halfway across the river—"

"I know this already," I interrupted. "He stings him and while they're both drowning the alligator asks the spider why he did that and the spider says—"

" 'Because it's my nature,' says the spider. Now just wait," the girl told me. "Then these two Cajun guys Boudreaux and Thibodaux row up in their pirogue and pull them up onto the shore. Boudreaux breaks a branch off this cypress tree and pokes the alligator for a bit 'til it coughs up water and starts breathing, then Boudreaux takes him by the snout, flips him over, and pushes him back to the river. Thibodaux catches the spider by a leg as it's crawling away, and dangles it in the air for a bit, just having a look-see, then puts it on the cypress tree, and walks off. The alligator crawls back onto the shore, looks up at the spider and screams, 'What in fucking hell was that?!' The spider replies, 'The surest sign that God has gone completely goddamn nuts.' And then he jumps into the river and drowns." She winked across the small darkness between us and slurped down the last of her drink. It was the first humor we'd heard since I went to sleep Saturday night.

"Why aren't you laughing?" she asked. Before I could answer she shouted, "Andy, drink me, dammit!"

Andy sprang to life off the air mattress and got her another beer. We showed him how to fix Elle in Augusts and took a couple to go, tipped him fifteen dollars, and slid back down Chartres Street.

The Ursuline Convent, the oldest building in the Mississippi Valley and residence of Our Lady of Prompt Succor, to whom the nuns pray before impending disaster that the convent and the city be spared, appeared unharmed but for one shattered chimney whose bricks were now fused into a crater on the massive slate roof like someone had dropped a bomb there. A squat Asian man with a body and face so soft and indistinct he seemed to be a series of brown marshmallows strung together walked out of the convent's parking lot, said he was just checking on his car, the nuns had let him keep it there during the storm. "I didn't evac because I got six young children to take care of," he proudly explained to us. I suggested he could have taken them with him. Pointing to his house next door, he said, "Well, this building's been here for a hundred fifty years," shrugged, and walked off.

Esplanade Avenue was a mess of a rain forest. The street's median had had more trees than anywhere else near the French Quarter. We weaved through the splintered trunks, their branches, their leaves still glistening with Katrina's last rain band, and thanked God they were in the street, not the houses. A white-haired mustachioed man stood in his plaid bathrobe and bunny-rabbit slippers between two fallen trees, his hands outstretched in exasperation. "Hey," he shouted at us, "where's my paper?!"

Across the street, someone somehow had neglected before the storm to put away the single tallest ladder I'd ever seen. Over seventy feet high from the ground to the roof, it was still leaning against the gigantic Old U.S. Mint. An oak tree had bent it like straw on its way into the building. A good $50,000 worth of copper roof flashing from the Mint had wrapped itself in a gravity-defying heap around the top of a single No Parking sign like a cabbage on a toothpick.

Lower Decatur Street's bars, squirreled far as possible away from Bourbon's slop, were at this Monday noon hour usually occupied by sunken figures comforting each other in their loneliness in stale darkness that only a fuzzy television scratched at and Tom Waits groaned out of every jukebox and you were asked to kindly fuck off if you ordered bottled water. These were the spaces in which people ignored many a previous storm, but now each last one of them was nailed shut.

A couple of blocks to the right, a couple to the left, and we were standing toe to toe with Christ upon a fallen oak tree, scraps of bark still clinging to its naked trunk like scabs, in St. Anthony's Garden behind the St. Louis Cathedral. Christ, affectionately dubbed Touchdown Jesus, because of the life-sized statue's high- and wide-stretched arms, stood triumphant in the end zone above a congregation of debris and two fallen 300-year-old trees turned to scrap at his pedestal, parting Orleans street

and the entire Quarter down its center. But something was missing. A finger. It was his left thumb, and it was the only damage the cathedral had
taken. We wondered where it was in all the mess, if it would ever be
found. "And He will say to those at His left hand, 'You that are accursed,
depart from me into the eternal fire prepared for the devil and his
angels,' " I said. "Had to write a paper about the Last Judgment once."

One block up Orleans Street, where it cuts through Bourbon at the
dead center heart of the Quarter, Johnny White's Sports Pub was the
place. "There's two things you need to know here," said an old wild-eyed
man with a long white beard that yellowed at its wispy ends, who'd
managed to claim a seat along the tiny L-shaped bar as we tried to get the
busy bartender's attention. "The first is that the bartender's name is
Bob. The second's that you should tip him heavily," he told us. "Because
I don't."

A couple dozen people were crammed into the small pub. All drinks
were half price. We got cold Bud Light drafts, moseyed over to the far
end of the bar, between the restroom and a video-poker machine, the
only comfortable standing room, next to a middle-aged man with a
salt-and-pepper ponytail. I nodded to him, asked how he was doing.

"Awwww, you know, same shit, different day," he said.

"A hurricane just hit us," I said.

"Hell, I got two or three hurricanes hit me every week, romantic life
I got."

It took us ten minutes to get the busy bartender's attention and grab
another couple of drafts. There was a vague underlying sense of disap-
pointment in the bar. People had gone to sleep last night with a distant
hope that they would wake up inside an important piece of history. But
this was all there was to it. Some roof flashing and trees and a couple of
broken windows and a white sky.

We walked back to my place, stepped over the busted Ripley's *Believe
It or Not!* sign and entered the dark of my entryway. The sign was half the
size of one of the Ripley's kids who two days before had stood on the
sidewalk across the street. Those kids were what got me about life. The
museum never seemed to do any business and so the kids who worked
there would lean against the building out front, dawdling away their nine-
to-five's, ticking away life's seconds gazing vacantly at drifting clumps of
lost tourists, their youth quietly washed clean with routine. No matter
how hard I tried, I couldn't stop looking at them. So, I'd while my own
days away watching them while they watched the tourists who seemed to
lack the free will to do anything but ogle whatever corporate honky-tonk
fanfare was put in their path around the street mimes and musicians and

clowns, wondering if anyone was watching me. It made me sorry for these tourists and sorry for this neighborhood, for this world so full of Ripley's kids, and myself in it. It would all be back soon now.

I turned to see the closing door eclipse Katherine's silhouette, reached for her hand but couldn't find her, moved down the stone corridor, her footsteps a beat behind my own, up through the winding stairs, so long the route of my own rote routine, my eyes closed as though it made any difference, and felt my way home for the first time.

5

"I think the batteries died," said Katherine when I tried to turn the boom box radio on. "That's when I woke up this morning, when it went off."

In a box in the back of my closet I finally found the matchbook-sized battery-operated radio I'd bought so I could listen to the news nonstop in the days after 9/11. We spent an hour on my bed, heads together, sharing a pair of earphones, listening to the only radio station left, WWL, usually 870 AM, but now it had taken over numerous frequencies on both AM and FM. The broadcast was out of Baton Rouge and all they could do was take call-ins: a man surrounded by water, trapped on his rooftop, a dead dog floating by him; reports of a floating body; the Industrial Canal levee may have been breached, but where and on which side no one seemed sure; twenty thousand people had looked straight up and watched a chunk of the Superdome roof fly off early this morning; someone staying at the Hyatt next to the Superdome watched the piece of roof fly into his side of the building; looting at the Winn-Dixie just above the Quarter; and *Whoa Wow Shit Cool Hell Okay Well No Fuck Huh Whoa* and here we were lying in the same positions as when we went to sleep last night and I tasted the fears and doubts that had slid into my mind then and Christ—we really had survived. We had survived. That was all there was to think about it right now.

We walked up the middle of Decatur Street trying to hitch a ride to

Katherine's place uptown, since we had no idea what we'd do with our own cars if we got them out of the parking garage, or if we could even get them at all, or if we could even get uptown at all.

A white Volvo station wagon with Oregon plates soon pulled up alongside us and we told the thin, thirty-something, pony-tailed guy we were headed uptown, as far as he could take us. He wanted to see what had become of Uptown, too, so we shot through the business district, barreling over streets and sidewalks covered in glass shards from down-town windows, past cars with their windows blown out and some flat-tened with brick walls in them, into the labyrinth of fallen trees and power lines that was now Uptown, in a matter of minutes. Besides some big puddles, there was no flooding anywhere we could see. Our driver had just moved here a couple of weeks ago to bus tables while completing a definitive book on the 1919 influenza outbreak.

No traffic lights were working, of course, so he just continued barrel-ing through every intersection around fallen trees, through trees where possible, stopping and reversing and spinning around at whiplash veloc-ities where not possible, weaving back and forth across St. Charles Avenue, yesterday the most beautiful street in America with its expansive neutral ground lined with street-car rails and centuries-old oaks and monstrous palm trees now snapped clean in half, farther and farther uptown until we got to Louisiana Avenue. There, no matter what side streets we tried, it was all impenetrable, impossible to get further upriver. We handed him five dollars for gas money, though all the stations had looked pretty much closed.

Katherine and I got out and walked over trees and under power lines a dozen battered blocks, some roofs and windows missing, but mostly everything intact except for the sporadic and seemingly random houses that were now piles of sticks and stones.

"Tornados," said Katherine as we walked by one such pile. "A hurri-cane spits out little tornados called microbursts that destroy everything below them in the blink of an eye then disappear just as fast."

Most fences were gone or partly gone and we saw for the first time what Uptown really looked like. The homes shrank from Corinthian-columned mansions down into trailers then up into sagging century-old shotgun houses within a single block. We saw what Katrina had left mysteriously unmoved on their porches, in their windows, bronze shih tzus, half-full whiskey bottles, crayon drawings, porcelain Jesuses, where the paint was missing, what colors had once shone now hidden below new surfaces, which lawns were worn with children's footsteps, which were not, which porch steps sagged from feet after work and bottoms during family cookouts. We waved at a black couple we'd never seen before, sipping 24-ounce Icehouse cans on their porch, now in full view of the street, and rounded the corner into Katherine's block, a typical Uptown smorgasbord of medium-sized houses, their porches slanting toward the sidewalk at different angles, whose only sense of design seemed to be to clash greatest with their neighbors.

From the outside, her apartment looked fine, thank God. I removed the planks from her front door, opened it. Something black came swooping out of the darkness at my face. I flinched, reeled back, flailing wildly, until I realized it was just a dragonfly. It was the largest one I'd ever seen. It paused in the fresh white light between Katherine and me, turned to her then me, then dropped down to our waist level, knee level, finally gliding onto the Oriental rug between us. It twitched its wings twice, then stayed still. Katherine broke past me into her place, frantically scanning for damage. I crouched down over the dragonfly. Its black body was as thick as my forefinger and a little longer. Its wings fluttered weakly as I nudged its tail until it was in the palm of my hand. I placed it on the side of Katherine's front step, its body shedding its darkness into an emerald green so bright it was obscene. It lifted into the air a few inches then came to rest again in the same spot. "Damn," said Katherine. "These windows."

There was water on the floor below two windows in her library. When I removed the patchwork of sopping wet wood, we saw that a few terra-cotta tiles from her neighbor's roof had flown through her porch and shattered the windows. We taped garbage bags over them, nailed dry boards back up, then removed the hodgepodge of wood from the rest. I pried the last board from her last window as the sky grew grey again and the sun sank into a pool of wild canary-yellow light, and so we made that color with chilled Stoli Limon vodka and pineapple and mango juice and drank it on her porch and toasted the sun's dying return and it made us feel a little better, I guess.

We took what we could—a cooler of food, more clothes in paper shopping bags, her laptop—and transferred all her essentials into her burgundy leather purse, the pearl-trimmed image of a lavender dragonfly stitched into it, that her great-grandfather had brought back from their ancestral village of La Ferté-St. Aubin, France, after he fought in World War I and had given to her great-grandmother soon as they were reunited in New Orleans. (As Katherine tells it, the purse was so beautiful that her great-grandmother didn't notice her husband was missing his left arm until they got home from the train station and she tried to hand him a cup of tea, which fell onto their Oriental rug, now Katherine's Oriental rug, giving it the stain just inside her doorway that I was standing on now as I held her cooler.)

The dragonfly lay upon her front step where I had left it, its emerald faded, vanished into black now. I asked Katherine to get a box or something. She came out with an empty cigar box from Cuba, made a sad face when she saw the thing in my hand. I placed the dragonfly in the box, put it in the cooler. In twilight's last azure glimmer I boarded her front door back up to dissuade any would-be looters.

There was no life anywhere—no people, distant cars, dogs barking, bird calls, crickets—and as we used her sole flashlight to navigate through puddles and electrical lines and trees I wondered which of those would be first to return and claim this silence. By the time we got to St. Charles Avenue, which would lead us straight back to the Quarter, it was dead moonless night.

I somehow always figured that light pollution was like other kinds of pollution—just because you stopped polluting all of a sudden one day doesn't mean all the previous pollution magically vanishes—like there'd be some kind of lingering lavender haze still blocking the stars out even if you cut a city's lights entirely. But, now that no one had any power, the universe raged.

Out of the mess of it came Vega, blue, straight overhead, that first note you can't hear the beginning of because it's just there suddenly as though it always was. Then constellations, Lyre and Northern Cross, Big Dipper and Bear, Swan and Eagle and the Herdsman sat upon the western horizon and Hercules in the middle began pounding away with his club, faint at first, his body arrested in forward charging motion, then louder, pounding boom and thunder into the tiny empty darkness below him, beating black out of the sky. And it was not the people or distant cars or dogs barking or bird calls or crickets after all that would ever return to claim this silence, this time. It was they who had it just as they had it in time before Earth was place, and they fell down into the silence upon one another until they became one deafening harmonious mess, a single omnidirectional timbre, the wordless groan of our whole tiny universe so piercing it shivered into silence. But silence, too, of course, has volume and voice. And I was listening.

I was listening as the Archer fired a shot screaming into the southern horizon through the cat's moaning eye, red Anteres, backbone of the Scorpion, its tail unwinding, gristle creaking, below the shadow of some St. Charles Avenue mansion. And that, too, subsided into murmuring silence behind us as Andromeda rose straight ahead of us, chained to a rock for her mother's pride, left there to be devoured by Poseidon's sea creature, so that he should spare their coast; Andromeda's knight in shining armor Perseus not yet visible, his Pegasus above her saddled but empty, only the water constellations there; the Water Carrier shimmering faint, foreshadowing the fall, a last cymbal soft as the last drops of rain this morning, and I was still listening.

But I was not listening to Katherine, who I suddenly realized was asking me what I was laughing about, and as I said, "Huh?" I tripped over a power line and, while trying to catch my balance, slammed my shin into a fallen palm tree and her cooler and everything in it went flying into the darkness as did I, screaming, catching another power line in my armpit on the way into the roots of a fallen elm. As I attempted to stand, I hit my head on a broken tree, spun around, tripped backwards over a telephone pole, and wound up with my ass in the branches of another tree and my left elbow in Katherine's homemade cilantro guacamole. It took a long time to make it the dozen blocks back to Louisiana Avenue.

We hoped to grab another ride there because, far as we knew, that was the furthest cars could get uptown. We were still the only life anywhere. Then a couple of cop cars rolled slowly by. We'd heard there was a strictly enforced curfew, but we weren't really sure when it was, nor what time it was right now. No matter. We tried to flag them down, but none would stop.

We carried Katherine's stuff until our shoulders got numb from the pain then began burning all over again and we collapsed on the side of the road. My face was bleeding from falling into the branches. A patrol car finally stopped. We explained we were just trying to get back to safety in the French Quarter and might they be able to give us a ride even part of the way since they were headed that direction? "Liable to get robbed sitting there," said the officer before driving off.

A few minutes later a black Land Rover stopped, or rather had to stop because we were splayed across the road at this point and it looked like I had already been run over, and we piled in next to this couple, Jorge and Julia, all four of us in the front seats, Katherine's few belongings piled on top of all theirs in the back, my bleeding face out the window so I wouldn't get anything on the seats. They drove us all the way through Uptown, the business district, into the Quarter to my front door, said they were going to spend the night back in the Hyatt.

We drained the bathtub since the water had stayed on and, after a cold shower which made my face look a lot better, had my birthday dinner. My thirtieth birthday wasn't for a week but there was talk of days without electricity and so we ate a whole package of smoked salmon with cream cheese, spring greens, capers, a splash of lemon, on candle-toasted

French bread, then had fresh jumbo Gulf shrimp for dessert. We took a couple of Elle in Augusts out on my balcony and listened to Patsy Cline on Katherine's iPod in our pajamas under the stars while passing red and blue police lights bounded off Jax Brewery and we smiled at the reality of us living together these next couple of days. Though we spent most nights at each other's apartments, we still needed those apartments, those spaces, for our own reasons—my work, and Katherine's recent, long marriage, which ended just before she moved here, home. When the iPod battery died she pulled her shirt above her belly button, just above her extra rib. "That was before I got to see the rest," I said.

She laughed. "You used to beg me, after a date, before you went home, to show this rib to you."

"And you'd make me tell you something about me I had never told anyone else ever before."

"That was the deal."

"Hell of a deal."

"Tell me something now," she said.

"You know it all, baby. There's nothing left to me."

"A little something? Please?"

"You know me better than anyone in the world."

"That's a big something. Is that true?"

"Sometimes I think you know me better than I do."

"I know how much you used to want to touch this rib."

"To touch it, I had to promise to keep my shorts on."

"Which was an even harder challenge, huh?"

"No. No, it wasn't. I always meant it when I said I'd stick with you even if we never got naked together. Really."

We decided to have our own French Quarter pajama party. We got up in our bathrobes and sandals to roam the curfewed night, see if anything was open, who was out, what they were saying. But Katherine's purse, the one her great-grandfather had brought back from France. We couldn't find it. Using her sole flashlight, only allowing us to see an agonizing square foot at a time, we ransacked my apartment, even tore through Saturday night's clothes still strewn about over my bedroom floor. It had her everything—wallet, keys, camera, phone, birth control, you name it, and it was nowhere. We'd left it in the Land Rover. The irony of making it through a Category Five unscathed only to leave Katherine's purse in the back of a car did not amuse us.

The Land Rover was supposedly at the Hyatt, and all we knew was that the Hyatt was somewhere next to the Superdome in the middle of the business district. So, we walked the length of Decatur Street back out of the Quarter, our calves and thighs still weak from the hike back from Katherine's apartment uptown, crossed Canal Street, the widest street in America, into the business district, again the only ones anywhere. Everything was dark and foreign. Stars lit street signs and showed us the way through this strange forest the city had become.

"That's it," I said.

"What? The Hyatt? I thought that was further up."

"No. It is. But this is the corner."

"Which corner?" Katherine asked. "We need to get my purse."

"Where I finally got the balls up to kiss you for the first time."

"Is it?"

"This is it. Let's find the lamppost."

"Let's find my purse."

"C'mon, take a second." And I pulled her along. "You were the assistant for that actor who was staying at this hotel—see, it's the Windsor Court right there. And you kept him waiting for you in the lobby while we were wobbling down the street together on my '56 Schwinn?" We came to the Windsor Court, once voted "Best Hotel in the World" by *Condé Nast Traveler* readers, and there were the lampposts all lined up. I couldn't remember which one it was that we stopped beside that day. "It's this one here," I lied, "and I asked if I could first."

"You asked me would I smack you if you tried to kiss me."

I kissed her and it was tentative and slight as that first kiss, slight not out of shyness and heart flutters like one year nine months nineteen days four hours three minutes and thirty-nine seconds earlier, but out of preoccupation.

"And then came the rib," she said.

"Yeah. This was before even that. How long ago. Okay," I said, and wanted to say I never had any idea I was capable of loving someone this much despite how stupid it sounded, "your purse."

We turned right on Poydras Street which runs from the river into the heart of the business district, skyscrapers hulking shoulder to shoulder above us, lining our path, looming black into the galaxy overhead. And we walked upon their windows—all those high-up tinted office windows, the ones you always wondered what was happening on the other side of—in pieces, each shard holding a star's reflection, constellations' rhythms scattered and twinkling and crunching beneath us, occasionally cutting through our flip-flops, and we'd pause to lean on each other, pull the stars out of the soles of our bleeding feet.

A cop car rolled past us every five minutes as we walked toward the Superdome. "What?!" I yelled after the fifth one that ignored my extended thumb. "Just cause I'm in my flip-flops and bathrobe doesn't mean I'm not out looting! Damn! Well, I guess we should just put on our jammies next time we want to rob a liquor store."

"And be white," said Katherine.

"Shit."

The blue BellSouth sign was lit at the top of its building above us, the only sign of power anywhere. I guess they were trying to make some kind of statement, and so long as they kept my land line going, the only working phone in New Orleans we knew of, I was all for it.

"You know, this is very likely the only time two people have had all of downtown—well, Poydras Street anyway—all to themselves," I said. "It's probably the only time since it was first paved. Who else has had this, done this in this city? In any city anywhere?"

"We've got the only's, babe," said Katherine. "Let's enjoy them while we got them."

Six more blocks or so up Poydras the Superdome came into view like a giant white rock. I wondered how many were trapped inside it. We knew they were there but not what was becoming of them. And we could see no one and nothing outside it but Poseidon's sea monster above it swallowing Mars on its way to Andromeda in the sky.

Sure enough, to our left was the Hyatt, most of its south-side windows cracked or gone, gaping black in the bright white starlight. We felt our way through the cars parked twelve-wide the whole way down the long covered driveway to the Hyatt's entrance. Across from the entrance, the very last car, was the black Land Rover. And there was Katherine's great-grandmother's purse behind the passenger-side front seat. The doors were locked, of course.

"What was his name?" Katherine asked.

"Julio. Something like that."

"Julio," said Katherine. "That's it."

It took us fifteen minutes of crocodile tears over her "medication" which we'd left in Julio's car for the security to let us into the hotel, and another fifteen of pure hysteria to get an escort to the third floor ballroom where we were assured everyone was sleeping, everyone but the mayor and the governor and the press who were squirreled away on some upper floor.

The air in the cavernous ballroom was the stale hot breath of some beast that's lain in the back of its cave for as long as it can remember and, despite its high ceiling, the darkness and warmth imbued the mass bedroom with stifling closeness. Dim fluorescent lights cast sallow green pall over the shifting bodies strewn about the floor beneath white sheets, huddled together, gasping, in couples and families, all eyes open and fol-lowing us as we scrutinized each silent one of them, whispering "Julio? Julio? Julio. . . ."

No dice. After three rounds we gave up, went back outside to their car and left notes tucked in every door and on the windshield for them to call my land line. It was excruciatingly frustrating to be inches from the purse and yet to have to leave it there and walk all the way back to my apartment. But at least we knew where it was now.

On the way back down Poydras I wondered if we had time, in between the patrol cars that refused to stop for us, to make love in the middle of street, to consummate our only's. As I opened my mouth to suggest it, another cop car cruised by, so I looked up, saw something I had only once before seen in my life, the newly blossomed Andromeda Nebula, a galaxy like our own off Andromeda's knee, the most distant object man by himself may see, its hundred billion suns shining light 2.7 million years old. It left a taste like peanut brittle in my mouth. We moved toward the Quarter and into Bourbon Street.

Bourbon. Imagine it: Disneyland for grown-ups, g-string-clad bot-tomless dancers and bead-and-boa-wearing middle-American house-wives singing "Hotel California" karaoke throwing down three-for-one cocktails and hurricanes and hand grenades and subwoofing Orwellian generators cranking out of every open doorway, every step a different smell—sweat, smoke, sex, cigars, seafood and sausage gumbo, puke, pizza, piss, seafood gumbo again—more bars and clubs side by side than anywhere in the world, and suddenly it had all become a shamble of shadows. There was not one noise, not one cigarette's ember glowing, not anything, not even a smell. Bourbon's buildings now were shallow cliffs rising to either side of us, the Milky Way's river washing straight ahead, as it had down St. Charles Avenue earlier. Our city in a new light, no light, starlight. And us. The only's.

After ten or fifteen minutes we saw an orange glow like campfire spilling from shutters ahead. I didn't know where we were until I saw Touchdown Jesus white in the night at the end of the street to our right. Orleans Street. Johnny White's Sports Pub. Inside, a half-dozen patrons exchanged candlelit whispers in air so thick and hot we had to push our way into it. I slurped down a burning-cold can of Bud Light, then ordered another before the bartender had gotten my change and Kather-ine's water. I wanted to join the handful of people crowded around the bar, to drape my own uncertainty with their insouciance, share this space out of time with them. I tried and tried but I couldn't decipher their whispers, the air too thick for them to get to me, too thick for me

to move to them. They were way ahead of me, too late to catch up and
Katherine was tired, so we made our way back out, past Christ, through
the forest that Jackson Square had become and into my bed. Before I
knew it, a phone was going off again, wrestling me from another dream.
It was morning. Soaked in sweat, I flew to my land line in the kitchen
hoping it was Julio with Katherine's purse. But it was National Public
Radio in Washington, D.C. They wanted to know what I'd been eating.

"Stars," I said. "A whole lot of stars."

6

I held the phone in one hand, listening to the National Public Radio producer tell me how amazed she was to have reached somebody in New
Orleans, while I examined a piece of glass sticking in my heel with the
other hand. She couldn't believe my landline was still working a day after
Katrina. I finally got the shard with the tweezers, slid it out of my heel. It
was the size of a fingernail clipping and whatever star it held last night
was gone.

While the producer told me Neal Conan wanted to do a live interview
on his *Talk of the Nation* show in an hour, I thought about how when I
was little I stepped on a glass Christmas ornament of Christ. My mother
pulled the pieces out of my foot but, for another month, it hurt. Eventually, we went to the doctor and he cut the last piece out. It was just clear
glass. I told him it had had Jesus' left hand on it. He laughed, said my
body had eaten a piece of Jesus.

I agreed to do a live interview on *Talk of the Nation* in an hour, hung
the phone up, and wondered who it was that used to look down on the
city through this piece of window, if I had ever been one of the ants they
glanced over, and I wondered what town they were in now, what news
channel was granting them another, still more distant vantage.

I swung the freezer open, grabbed a cup, slammed it shut fast. At least
it was still slush. I drank half, poured the rest over the back of my neck,
then put the glass shard in the cigar box with the dragonfly we had

found waiting for us in Katherine's apartment uptown yesterday. I left the cigar box on the refrigerator and, not wanting to wake Katherine, tip-toed into the living room, into one of the strips of blinding copper morning falling through the two open floor-to-ceiling windows, stared into the empty Mississippi, the sunlit floor no warmer into the cuts in my feet than the stifling heat elsewhere in my apartment. For the first time, the river was empty of ships, its currents contorting, colliding, alone. The water level had receded to about its usual level now. Before the storm it had been extremely low. I wondered how many that had saved.

"They're saying—"

"Jesus!" I said. Katherine was sitting right beside me, between the windows. The sun was so bright it had cast the rest of the room into darkness, her in it. "Scared hell out of me, baby."

"They're saying no electricity for four weeks," she said. "Four weeks."

"Is this for sure?" I threw my hand toward the sun, trying to get it out of my eyes. She was listening to the radio with earphones, her back against the wall between the two windows, her hand on my ankle. How long had her hand been there?

"How should I know," she said, removing one earphone. "It's not a joke, I know that. New Orleans would be shut down as a functioning city."

"Was it ever one?"

"Every company, every office, every store, every university, every court, everything."

"Well, if that's really true, if that's really going to happen, we'll go somewhere." I sat beside her against the wall, out of the sun, my eyes inches from hers, hers narrow and swollen. "We'll go to my grandmother's old place in Maine, wait for the leaves to turn."

"Really?" she said and she smiled and her eyes opened a bit for the first time in two days.

"Sure," I said. "Have you heard of a radio show called *Talk of the Nation*?"

"Of course."

She handed me the other earphone. It was WWL again, broadcasting from Baton Rouge. They'd taken over every frequency. The broadcaster stated that Uptown had become one big "shootout." There were carjackings going on everywhere up there, apparently. Katherine and I had missed that part when we walked through it yesterday. Then, he told someone from the Red Cross how low the death toll from the hurricane itself was, how it was horrible that three people died from a tree falling in Mississippi but it could have been so much worse. Then, more reports of flooding trickled in. Some flooding. A lot of flooding? No one seemed to know how much, nor exactly where it was going, nor exactly where it was coming from: The river? The lake? The swamp? Another canal? A few canals? Which ones? Were the levees breached? Or overtopped? Or both? Or what?

I cupped a handful of sun from the window beside me, let it pour through my fingers, played their long shadows upon the floor, then removed my earphone, swung around into the day again. From where I sat all was dry, hot, bright, and happily empty of tourists. I opened my mouth, swallowed the heat, reached out to Katherine's shoulder, her neck, how hot it was, hotter than the sun. And quiet, true silence for the first morning ever in the Quarter. Until the landline rang back in the kitchen again.

It was the Professor.

"So, are you on the roof?" he asked.

"I'm in my kitchen."

"You mean you're above the water?"

"There is no water," I said.

"Dammit, man, don't tell me that. There's water all over my television. All over it! I'm looking at it right now."

"Where are you?"

"Washington, this symposium. I understand there's alligators that are swimming around the city and they're going to eat you. I was very sorry to hear that."

"That's okay. How's your pod?" I asked.

"Airtight. Best thing that ever happened to me. Thank God I didn't let them deliver it."

"Listen, I have to go because we're waiting for a call about Katherine's purse."

"She lost her purse in the storm?"

"No. It's in a Land Rover."

"You lost a Land Rover in the storm? What are you doing with a Land Rover, for God's sake? Just because everyone else down there is car-jacking doesn't make it right. Is it underwater with the sharks? They say there's sharks swimming down Williams Boulevard. Just remember, you need to hit them in the nose when they come at you."

"Maybe the alligators will get them first."

"There's alligators, too?"

"I'm hanging up," I said.

"Do you think you'd have the time to get me one?"

"An alligator?"

"Land Rover."

I hung up. The phone rang again.

"Are you in the toxic soup?"

"What soup?" I asked. "Who is this?"

"It's Babysitter, you fool. New Orleans is a bowl and it's filling up with toxic gumbo. Get on your roof!"

"How's your house, Babysitter?"

"Don't know, haven't been back. We can't go back supposedly. We're in Pensacola. They told us all about the toxic gumbo on the news. Just go to your roof and flag down a boat or something."

"What's in Pensacola?"

"Hooters. Three of them. Brunch, lunch, dinner. Walking in here with a kid is so damn cool. You really should try it. I'd let you borrow him sometime if you weren't going to drown in the toxic gumbo. You have no idea the attention little Nigel's getting. He keeps trying to grab all the boobies to get the milk out of them. They think it's so funny."

"We're waiting on a call. I'm hanging up."

I got another few calls from cousins and friends, assured them we were okay, despite whatever they were seeing on the television. Eventually, it was National Public Radio again. We talked for ten minutes about what the storm was like and the day since then. Then I found Katherine on my bed, lay down and listened to WWL with her.

Along with water, words were rising in New Orleans. And it was too soon to sift fiction from fact. All Katherine and I knew for sure was what we could see and hear here in the French Quarter. Unlike any other section of New Orleans, the Quarter was an insulated, small, treeless, perfect rectangle, all the streets parallel or perpendicular and dead straight. If there was fire, flood, looting, anything, we, and the police, would see it from at least six blocks away. This had long been a neighborhood that sheltered tourists from the realities of the surrounding city, and now it was sheltering us.

A desperate man came on the radio. He was trapped on his roof on Desire Street, the 800 block I thought I heard him say, surrounded by twelve feet of water, dead cats floating by. "Oh, my God," I said. "Taylor. Leigh."

The 800 block of Desire was only a mile or two out of the Quarter, in the Bywater, a diverse working class neighborhood of sagging Creole cottages and shotgun houses, small corner groceries and bars. It was a place to which many artists fled from the Quarter's rising rents and where some of the people closest to me in this world lived and I didn't know where most of them were, in particular Taylor and his mother, Leigh, who both lived out on Poland Street at the very end of it, right next to the Industrial Canal. Their family had been in New Orleans for several generations, but on the opposite side of town from Katherine's family, one which I hadn't frequented much since we'd been going out. I grabbed some more old tapes filled with old interviews, threw my tape recorder in my shoulder bag along with a T-shirt, and went out in a bathing suit and sandals, Katherine in the same and a tank top.

We hardly got ten feet when Ty and Ashley came cruising up to us on their flamed low-rider bicycles. Ty and Ashley—TnA—were some of those people that you connect suddenly and intensely with at a mutual friend's party (in this case Parker Junior, who worked in Ashley's frame shop) and you all decide you need to hang out a whole bunch and then never get around to it, but act as though you do, when you only see each other in passing once every few months. So, we acted that way and got all excited to see each other even though we hardly knew each other. Ty, like me, was wearing a bathing suit and was shirtless, Ashley in Daisy Dukes and a bikini top, each a couple inches shorter than us and whole lot tanner. I took out the recorder, asked what their plans were. Ty rested his elbows on his handlebars, tilted his lean shoulders in toward the recorder.

Ty: Well, our kayaks are on the second floor. We figure if the water gets that high, we'll just sit in them, wait 'til it lifts us off. We'll see if Johnny White's Sports Pub is still open, or if they've moved up to the second floor or whatever. Maybe canoe from balcony to balcony and see if they're any parties going on.

Katherine: We're hearing it might be four weeks without electricity.

Ty: Well, we have survival gear, we have these high-end pump water filters for camping, life jackets, Christ's finger, all that stuff. We're good.

Christ's finger?

Ty: Right after the storm, we noticed the fence to the garden behind the Cathedral was down so we climbed in. There was old Touchdown Jesus, the trees fallen around Him. As it turned out, one hit Him. A limb came down across the hand and broke His thumb off and ya know, us being the first ones there, there it lay.

Ashley: Jesus gave us the finger.

Ty: There will come a point in time where that's the huge question: "Where is the finger?"

Ashley: I had it in my pocket yesterday when there was still 150 mile an hour gusts and the rain was just like pelting down. Having Jesus' finger in my pocket was reassuring. I was like, this feels good, this feels really good.

You jealous, Ty? Your girl having another man's finger in her crotch?

Ty: Well, you know, if it were anybody but Christ, I might have an issue with it.

What else you seen?

Ty: This is one of the stupidest things I've ever seen, and I've seen some pretty stupid stuff. Soon as the hurricane's over, Ashley and I and two of our neighbors were walking past the fire station down on Decatur after we got the finger, and there were fireman everywhere, standing out front. This neighbor we're with, Petrovski, he picks up a dead pigeon lying there and just being dumb throws it up in the air and it comes down right on the hood of this fire truck in front of all these firemen who braved the storm there.

Ashley: They didn't even look mad, just real disappointed.

Ty: The way they looked at us. That hurt.

Ashley: We knew it was coming when we saw Petrovski sipping on the Windex.

Ty: He drank Windex in protest to us hiding the rum from him. Windex'll make you throw pigeons every time. Especially dead ones.

Ashley: It's funny, the pigeons that did make it okay, they're like these gangs of them swaggering down the middle of the streets with their heads held high, their leader strutting out in front, claiming his territory.

Ty: Even the pigeons won't go near Canal.

What do you mean?

Ty: They're tearing the whole street up. We were just there. The looting's gotten out of control. Cops won't even go down there now. You don't even want to go blocks near there, it smells so bad of piss and shit and stuff.

Katherine: Our cars are in Canal Place.

Ty: If they're even still there, I'd leave them be for now.

Shit.

Katherine: Damn.

Well, that's that. We're going to walk as far as we can into the Bywater, see where the water starts, see how bad it is.

Ty: Wow. Check out Conan.

A man was walking toward us on otherwise empty Decatur Street, a big man, forearms heaped with tattoos, wearing a full green canvas duffle bag the size of a regular man like a backpack, carrying a bottle of Budweiser in one hand and a Louisville Slugger in the other, his eyes glazed with determined oblivion. I had a vague notion of standing behind the bar years ago, serving him a Budweiser bottle, like the one he was now holding, in graying predawn light after he'd plugged "Freebird" into the juke box and the just-off-work strippers he'd walked in with were dancing with each other. He stopped beside us, swept his long sweat-clotted hair off his neck, glared at the recorder in my hands.

Name's Edgar.

Where you coming from, Edgar?

Edgar: When the water got to three feet in my place I started walking. Passed a body back on Magazine Street, 1900 block. Shot in the brain. That's when I decided to get this thing. The Slugger. Walked by the Rite Aid on St. Charles. Cops were just sitting there across the street watching people go in there. Bout the only thing left when I got there was prune juice and prescriptions. That's what's in this bag. Well, not the prune juice. Here, help me get this thing off, it's tearing through my shoulders.

Jesus Christ. Must weigh a hundred pounds.

Edgar: Yup, every kind of anything a body could want. Selling them cheap, too.

Thanks, man, I think we're okay though.

Edgar: Stopped feeling the pain a while ago. Took some of these here.

I think that's speed.

Edgar: Well, can't concentrate on the pain long enough for it to hurt. Oh well. Plenty of other satisfied customers. Think I'll just rest here a while.

We left him leaning on the end of his Louisville Slugger like a cane that'd carried him across continents, sipping his beer, wads and wads of crumpled cash poking out of his pockets, staring through us into something too close for his eyes to focus on. Ty and Ashley headed toward Bourbon Street and Katherine and I continued down Decatur toward the Bywater, not a person or car anywhere. All of lower Decatur's bars were boarded up except for Molly's at the Market, where we'd passed

Hurricane Ivan the year before, or Ivan passed us. Molly's was typically the cleanest, most well-lit, and busiest of lower Decatur's bars, its hodge-podge of pictures and memorabilia and polished wood tables and stools and gold-railed bar bathed in gold light, imbuing it with warmth. "Uh-uh," said the bartender, wagging a finger at me. "You gotta put a shirt on you come in here."

When I realized she wasn't kidding, I complied and followed Katherine into the bar. Daylight barely entered the place, despite the doors and windows being wide open, like it too was half-naked and not allowed in. The only one sitting at the bar was Matt Gone. He had all his belongings, all $56,000 worth, right there with him. He'd made every cent of that money from washing dishes and cooking at the restaurant next door at Coop's Place, and spent it on tattoos until he was one of the very few people in the world to have his entire body covered. "I've seen people lose everything they have," he once told me, the day after he tattooed his own face with vegetable oil so that checkers would glow across it in black light. "I have one thing they can't take away. No matter what happens, no one can take this from me." The storm had taken his apartment from him, but here he was, still him, alone with his $56,000 skin, worrying about his artist friends in the Bywater because he too had heard it was washed out.

A pickup truck filled with ice screeched to a halt out front. Jim Monaghan II, the owner of Molly's, came running out to unload it before any passers-by had a chance to wonder where it was coming from. But the only passers-by were two men hunched under the weight of tripled-up white kitchen garbage bags slung over their shoulders, walking from the direction of the Bywater. They set their bags down on the sidewalk outside Molly's, caught their breath, wiped sweat from their faces with their t-shirts and motioned for Matt and Katherine and me to come out and have a look. There were a couple dozen bottles of cheap champagne in each man's bag. They said they'd sell us a whole bag for fifty dollars, both for seventy-five dollars.

"You see, they were in my refrigerator. Had to clean it out," explained the older one. "My house is on Egania Street, 9th Ward, other side of the Industrial Canal. Got about twenty foot of water. We were downstairs, then we gotta go upstairs, we were up to our waist up there. Coast Guard brought us to the levee. You see them National Guard trucks came past here? They're bringing the people off the levees. You got twelve hundred people in line at the St. Claude bridge over there waiting to be picked up. So, we just walked. Fifty bucks."

"You headed to a shelter?"

"Yeah. Ain got no house no more. I'm going to the naval base across the river. Dome's full up and it's flooding up on Canal they say. Seventy-five for both, what you say, dude?"

"All you rescued from your home is that champagne?"

He motioned to his partner, slung his bag over his shoulder, and off they walked toward downtown, strange Santa Clauses. And Katherine and I walked in the other direction toward the Bywater.

We made it out of the Quarter into the Marigny neighborhood, all of it dry, over the railroad tracks, past Mimi's bar where the party was last Saturday, and, just before we got into the Bywater, there was Taylor Grewe bent over in the middle of Chartres Street, puking up gasoline.

"Tayl. Shit. What are you doing here, man?" I asked. "Your house out on Poland, your mom's place, they all gone?"

He looked up at me, opened his mouth to say something, then retched. He wiped his chin with the back of his hand, eyes red, tears streaming down his cheeks, smiling. "Well, hey, man," he said. "Whatcha up to?"

"Your homes? Is Poland Street underwater? That's what we were on our way to, to check on you guys."

He removed the hose from the gas tank of the pickup truck beside us. "What are you talking about? We didn't get an inch of water, man. Not an inch," he said. He screwed the funnel onto his gas can, walked across the street with it, and began filling his Bronco. "Friends here left. Said to come get their gasoline," he explained, nodding to the truck from which he'd just liberated the gas.

Three years ago I helped Tayl rip the back roof off his '79 Bronco and install a bench seat in the bed. A crazed looking wiry red-headed devil with a eight-inch horned goatee and little match-tip eyes sat on the Bronco's tailgate glaring at us.

"Josh, this is T," said Tayl. "Rowed my pirogue up to his place yesterday morning, got him. He's only about four, five blocks from me, that's where the flooding was, the other side of St. Claude. But Bywater's dry. Y'all grab a couple beers."

T handed Katherine and me a couple of ice-cold sixteen-ounce cans of Busch out of Tayl's cooler.

"All of it?" I asked. "The Bywater? It's all dry? We just heard this guy on the radio, said he's trapped on his roof on the 800 block of Desire."

"They might have gotten a foot or so in some spots, but it's gone now. All of it." Tayl took a sip from a bottle of water, gargled, spat, guzzled the rest.

"Huh," I said.

The beer burned cold and sweet down my throat. The Toyota pickup he'd taken the gas from was the only other vehicle on the block. And it had the only tree on the block in it. The young oak had wrapped the truck's hood around its base, its top branches fallen into the crumpled windshield, still whole, but white and flaky and strange as snow. Chartres Street was empty of anything but sun and heat and a silence you expected at any moment to fill with the bird's call that unfailingly swoons into the quietest pockets of the world. But it wasn't there yet. There wasn't even an insect. It was unnerving, just standing there, hearing every movement, every creak of bone, every swallow, breathing in pulses of silence, while we gazed vacantly over sagging pastel shotgun houses.

Katherine was not swallowing, not moving, just holding her perspiring beer as its coldness flattened her olive veins, slowly up and up her wrist, withering the slim shadows the veins cast as they slanted into the muscles of her long arms like tributaries into a valley. "By the way, this is Katherine," I said. "Sorry, baby. Didn't realize you hadn't—I haven't seen him in that long."

7

"Thought they were mannequins," said T as he wiped foam from his Busch tallboy down into the fiery wisps at his goatee's end. "Looked just like mannequins floating out in front my house. Then one of them turned over and I saw the fingertips all puckered. There was two, a kid and a woman. That kid, he was this kid I'd pay five bucks to mow my lawn every Thursday."

His eyes went thin as razor slits over little match-tip pupils as he turned his freckled, sallow face into the sun, toward Katherine, then me, said, "I live at the thirteen hundred block of Kentucky, just the other side of St. Claude from the Bywater. Had three foot of water inside my house, which is five feet up so about eight foot total there. Had everything ruined. You know, when it started flooding, I just figured all the drains are clogged. I put on my waders, went out there into the street, felt along the gutters. There wasn't a thing in the drains. They'd turned the water pumps off. The city'd turned the pumps off. Then I bumped up against the woman floating there. Her left hand touched me. Them puckered fingertips."

"So, is it down now? The water?" I asked.

"It's going up," said Tayl. "Water's arcing through the city from the 17th Street Canal levee breach. That's where they think it's coming from. What is it now, Dago?"

A skinny old man wearing boxers and flip-flops was suddenly standing behind me in the empty street. He had a couple of tattoos long ago turned to green splotches on his chest, his skin brown and taut and smooth. "Hey, where yat, Tayl? Yo, yall got an extra brewski for me? Do ya please?"

"I told you, don't ask that," said Tayl. "There's no such thing as an extra beer. Every beer shall be drank, every cigarette smoked, whether we give you one or not."

T handed him a beer. I asked Dago where he was when it hit yesterday.

"I was right around the corner in my place. My old lady, she said, 'Why the house movin?' I told her, 'Tie your ass down, bitch, we gettin ready to fly!' " He smiled proudly down into his beer. "Yall been to Robért's supermarket up on Elysian yet?"

"What? It's open?" asked Tayl.

"You can go over there and they're letting you take anything you want!"

"Let's go!" said T.

"You better go there. Everything's free!" said Dago. "It's not looting—it's open. You can take all you want!"

"We're just talking now," said Tayl.

He and T got into his Bronco, and Katherine and I crawled up into the uncovered bench seat in the back and held onto the roll bar, leaving Dago standing there in the middle of the street sucking on his beer, gazing at our taillights.

There were only six other vehicles in the Robért's parking lot, but people of every color and age were spilling out of the grocery. The few who'd scored shopping carts were pushing ungodly masses of food, the others carrying loads in whatever makeshift containers they could find, some just kicking all the stuff they could through the parking lot.

The grocery store was cavernous, cloudy liquid creeping over our flip-flops, our eyes trying to make sense of all the dark, and darker shapes within it, scurrying, colliding. There were no police, no store managers, no officials, nobody overseeing anything. I grabbed the latest *Atlantic* off the magazine rack, something on the cover about how Arafat ruined Palestine. We felt our way past the cash registers, through shifting figures, all groping the dank black space around them, pierced only with the flicker and glimmer of matches and lighters and a flashlight or two deeper into the store. "We need a flashlight," I said.

"Yeah, in the truck," said T, and he and Tayl headed out.

I grabbed for Katherine's hand behind me. "Katherine?"

Nothing.

"Katherine?!"

"I'm here."

But I had no idea where here was.

"Goddammit. Katherine!"

The man next to me dropped his match into the liquid on the floor. It hissed, he swore, jabbed me with an elbow, then pushed through two other figures while he flailed and sloshed toward the exit. Those two other figures stopped moving beside me. We stood silently facing each other, breathing in sweat. I could feel their stillness, hulking, their eyes, the frailty to the calm, the latent fear we all had of each other. Then the darkness began shifting around them again as they went back to loading their trays with soda cans. I wanted to scream for Katherine, but was too afraid it would shatter this fragile civility, give voice to questions: Who is it that's just behind me, bumping their ass into mine? Who just hit me with their elbows? Who just splashed me, knocked my tray over, took the last Sunny D, even though he already had eleven of them? The place was waiting for the first drop of panic, and I wasn't about to let it out.

"Katherine," I whispered with all the rage and volume whisper can carry.

Nothing.

I felt my way back through the cash registers and caught up with T and Tayl outside. T pulled the largest flashlight I'd ever seen out from under the back seat of the Bronco. It was rectangular, the size and shape of a large shoebox. It was so big it had three smaller, regular-sized flashlights that came out of the body of the main one. "Use it for alligator hunting," said T, storming back toward the entrance with us in tow. "Sun got nothing on this baby."

He was right. When we got back into the heat of the place T turned it on and everything in front of us became blinding noon. "Boom," he said. People who'd been groping the dark could now see what was in front of their faces, their feet sloshing through the light's glare off the inch-deep colorless muck. As his pupils shrank to pinpricks, the man next to us said, "Oh, *hell*, no! Thought these was Rolos," and dropped the dozens of loose tampons he'd had piled up in his arms like they were biting him. "Where the candy is?"

People started to follow us, scrambling to get into the light, push each other out of it. But none of them was Katherine. T shut it off. Light vanished and whispers crowded around us, the air too close to hear them as we made our way further into the place. Then T flipped up a panel on the flashlight's top that emitted just enough of a glow for us to follow him and not bump into anything or anyone. "Katherine?" I whispered as we made our way to the beer section. "Katherine?"

Matches lit dark faces all around. T hit the light just long enough to see that only three dented cans of Milwaukee's Best were left. No beer and no Katherine. We stood shoulder to shoulder, crestfallen, in the glow of the flashlight's top panel.

Then Tayl tapped me, pointed behind me, "Look."

"Oh, my God," I said.

"Jesus," he said.

"Jesus Christ," said T.

"Jesus fucking Christ," I said. "No."

"I cannot fucking believe this," said Tayl. "They haven't touched the imports."

"Look what I found," said Katherine. She handed each of us a Big Shot Soda display shelf to use as carrying trays. I was too angry for words. I just took my shelf and started grabbing beer.

The first few six-packs we picked up broke from all the slop they'd been sitting in and the bottles slid onto the floor, smashed, and added to the sludge. We picked the rest up from the bottom, loaded up our Barq's trays, and the four of us headed back to the Bronco with about forty beers each: Dos Equis, Dos Equis Amber, St. Pauli Girl, Foster's, Becks, Blue Moon, Bavarian, Bass, Boddingtons, Harp, Red Stripe, Corona, Corona Light, Negro Modelo, Newcastle, and Guinness. The Heineken was gone.

As we walked back inside, a teenage girl, her lips and cheeks pierced, concentric circles tattooed around her right eye, pushed past us on her way out with what looked like an industrial-sized laundry cart loaded with enough food to fill a smaller grocery store. A girl with a pink mohawk poked her head out of the top of the cart between bags of Fritos and asked me what time it was.

"Three-thirty, something like that," I said.

"Good. We all need to get outta here, because at four they're going to blow the river levee to save the French Quarter," she informed us. "Doesn't that suck?" Then she disappeared back into the Fritos.

We just laughed at her. I suppose it was a cunning ploy to rid the area of competing looters. Disregarding the fact that the river had, after Katrina, only reached a normal depth, thus posing no threat, we were only blocks out of the French Quarter anyway. Canal levee breaches were one thing, and catastrophic enough, but if the Mississippi spilled unhindered into New Orleans, that would be the end of the city, forever.

Back inside, we hit every aisle one at a time. We'd stand behind T at the beginning of each one as he illuminated it for about two seconds, before anyone else had a chance to see anything, then we'd scramble in the dark, fumbling around for what we'd seen that we wanted, trying to remember where it was, darkness so close it seemed to press my own sweat back into my pores. It was about fifty-fifty hit or miss.

While we walked out for the third time, little flickering matches going out one by one around us, the edges of the piled-high Barq's trays slicing into our fingers, a kid who couldn't have been older than thirteen, wearing a red bandana pulled high over his nose and mouth, heaved a large black safe, the size of him, out of the manager's office just inside the entrance, picked up a sledgehammer, and started going at it. We shimmied around him into the light.

On my own tray I had salted and unsalted peanuts, almonds, macadamias, cashews, roasted walnuts, red beans, white beans, white rice, brown rice, long-grain rice, wild rice, saffron rice, dirty rice, basmati rice, broccoli-and-cheese couscous, three boxes of white chocolate sugar-free Jell-O instant pudding mix and three liters of prune juice that I'd thought was Cran-Raspberry Cocktail. I heaped it all on top of the already foot-deep pile in the Bronco after Katherine and Tayl had dumped theirs. T had meant to load up on Cheetos and instead walked out with ten bags of sun-dried tomato vegetarian chips cooked in olive oil which left an aftertaste like a pencil eraser in my mouth as we walked back in again. The kid was still going at the safe, really getting into it now. We agreed this would be our last trip in. And it was time for liquor.

And every ounce of it was gone. Only the schnapps were left. I grabbed some Cactus Juice and Spearmint Schnapps, figured that'd work if we ran out of mouthwash. T hit the light one last time to see what was in the darkness just past the liquor. "Boom," he said.

There must have been hundreds of different types of wine, every shelf full up and untouched. We probably weren't getting ice anytime soon, so reds it was. We didn't waste time looking at the brands, only the prices in the dim glow of the flashlight's top panel, grabbing anything over ten dollars. The sledgehammer made a deep crash somewhere behind us, then shifted into a more tinny, piercing ring with every blow like it had struck another level of the safe.

When we'd loaded a dozen bottles on each of our trays, we headed out, T leading and me in the rear, taking little steps, shuffling through the sludge now well over our toes. As I tried to walk by the kid his sledge-hammer came down beside me. I flinched. Two bottles of wine rolled off my tray, smashed onto the ground between me and him. The kid stopped, framed by the exit, silhouetted with the day, and looked at the wine, burgundy swirling into the cloudy sludge around his boots, then up at me. He stood between me and the exit. The whites of his eyes above his bandana caught some spark of light in the darkness behind me. In ringing silence, the place roared, chaos building without the rhythm of his sledgehammer. He looked at the wine, then me, shifted his man-sized fingers around the shaft, his silhouette taking on three dimensions, muscles twitching, shining ribs heaving, white boxers sweat-soaked. The safe below him didn't appear to have a single scratch in it. A bead of sweat fell from the bandana's tip. Then another. And another. He smelled sweet, of tangerines and strawberry-banana yogurt. "I will kill you," I said.

His eyes smiled. He began chuckling. It was high-pitched, maybe what my laugh sounded like when I was that small. I pushed by him. That smell, yogurt and tangerines, seeped past me into the parking lot as the sludge crept toward Tayl's Bronco, seeking low ground. People stood there guarding enormous quantities of food heaped on the asphalt before them, unsure what to do next. There was still silence behind me, ringing with the kid's laughter. Then, at last, just as I reached Tayl's truck, the sledgehammer came down again and I began breathing again.

Tayl had the truck running. I dumped my wine on top of the food in the back seat, tossed the Barq's shelf in after it, then grabbed a bottle of a Cabernet-Shiraz blend from southern Australia. I told Tayl we'd walk, meet them back at his place in the Bywater, the car was too full as it was. He told us to round up anyone who was hungry, said he'd have a couple dozen lamb chops going on the grill by the time we got there.

As he pulled out an old man, white hair and white beard, walked up to Katherine and me and held out an opened bag of cookies. "Would you all like some shortbreads?" he asked.

"We don't really need them," I said.

"Well, okay then, but what am I going to do with all them?" he asked us. His skin was barely a shade lighter than his black polyester shirt which hung loose over his sunken frame. "I only wanted a couple," he said. "I just couldn't resist having a couple shortbreads. I was going to put the rest back inside, but, now, well it looks like it's getting a little scarier in there now and maybe that's not a good idea. But what do I do with them? I can't just let them waste."

"Do you need anything else?" I asked him. "Any food or water or anything?"

"No, no," he said.

"You come with us," said Katherine. "We have plenty where we're going. It's not far. We'll have a barbecue. We can get your family. Do you have family left here? Some friends?"

"No, no, that's okay," he said. "I only wanted a couple shortbreads. You see, I got me a sweet tooth."

We left him there looking down at the cookies in his hand, extended in offering to the people scattering around us, away from him and away from the building with all the food they could hold. And then there were the ones with garbage bags slung over their shoulders, the ones paying no attention to the old man or us or even Robért's, walking along St. Claude Avenue in the opposite direction, ones who'd apparently given up waiting on the Industrial Canal levee for the National Guard and had already walked through the entire Bywater on their way toward the Superdome.

Across the street, on the other side of St. Claude, was water, the first flooding we'd actually seen. Just a few brown inches at first, then deeper and deeper and darker into the distance until it swallowed cars. It was as still as though it had always been there. Like many major streets in New Orleans, St. Claude had a raised, grass-covered median, or "neutral ground," between opposite directions of traffic, below which lay water pumps. Rainwater had to be pumped up over the levees, out of the city into the lake or the river. They were clearly not working, and this was clearly more than rainwater.

A heap of mannequins lay piled in the avenue's dry neutral ground, torsos, arms, legs, heads scratched and mutilated, all of them absurdly white and lifeless amongst the black people walking by. I sifted through the mannequins, broke the thumb off one. I picked up a brick from the crumbled wall of a building, put the wine down on the sidewalk, held the mannequin finger, its tip pointing down on top of the cork, and pounded the broken top end lightly with the brick. Wine flew up into my face as I knocked the cork into the bottle. I sat beside Katherine on the curb, took a sip, handed her the bottle.

On the other side of the French Quarter, St. Charles Avenue shot uptown through the Garden District, lined with those palm trees, elms, streetcar lines, and Corinthian-columned mansions we'd walked through the day before. This, here, St. Claude Avenue, ran out the other end of the Quarter into the Bywater, St. Charles' antonym—Po'boy sandwiches, used furniture, corner markets, a Super 10 where nothing was over ten dollars, bars over all their windows and little above two stories high, all of it boarded up now.

A couple about our age with backpacks and dreadlocks and silver-ringed holes in their ears big enough to fit a broom stick through stopped beside us, asked if we'd heard the news: "They just shot some girl dead in the back of Robért's over there," said the girl. "Just a couple minutes ago. Some white chick who'd gotten lost from her friends. They shot her for cheese. Fucking animals. We were gonna go over there until we heard about that. One package. American cheese. Apparently she's still lying back there and there's blood seeping out of the place now. Some crazy fucking shit, man. We're getting the hell out of here."

She started to walk away. The guy stood still, holding her hand, pulled her back to his side. "You know, you should really come with us," he said, standing above us on the sidewalk. "Really. People like you shouldn't be here anymore. We're meeting this one other couple, they have a van up on Magazine Street, but we gotta get there before curfew. We can get you to Baton Rouge."

"What time is it?" Katherine asked him.

"Quarter to four."

"Here," said Katherine, holding the wine up to them. "You all take a sip. Then you better get going, fast. Don't you know? They're blowing the levee in a few minutes."

He looked at the bottle, a few splotches of blood on the white label from where the Barq's trays had cut our fingers, and took it. When the girl handed the bottle back to us we said farewell, walked in opposite directions, each pair holding hands, them toward downtown, us into the Bywater, toward the Industrial Canal, bleeding fingers entwined, our sandals squeaking as the muck from the floor in Robért's crept up into every cut on the bottom of our feet. The water stayed just to our left, the Bywater dry to our right, both within touch. Women dragged their children past us in the opposite direction toward the Superdome, fathers and husbands and brothers hunched beneath the weight of what was left heaped into green garbage bags over their shoulders, stumbling, so dehydrated they were no longer sweating. We walked slow, knowing we had too long until the light died, until we wouldn't have to see T's house a few blocks up from Tayl's, and what were not mannequins, while we ate those lamb chops and searched the sky for the stars we had in our feet.

8

Like the streets that divide them, New Orleans' major neighborhoods branch out of the Mississippi one by one, from Katherine's house at one end of the city uptown, to Tayl's downriver in the Bywater, my place in the French Quarter somewhere in the middle. Like the Quarter, the Bywater is six blocks deep, from St. Claude to the river, but about twice as long. In general, rent gets lower and the yards bigger and the residents more diverse the further downriver you go. At the very end of the Bywater, at the Industrial Canal, is Tayl's home, right across the street from his mother's, where he grew up. His mother, a poet, was one of the first artists to flee the Quarter for the Bywater. Her house is a living, breathing museum and on the walls in her guest bedroom in which I've often napped are Daniel Finnegan's paintings. And there stood Daniel in the middle of Dauphine Street, six-foot-four, shirtless, a string of tattoos running from his heart to his belly button, red bandana pulled low over his brow, calm in his soft voice. He was happy to see us. He took a couple of healthy pulls from the bottle, handed it back to me, as day softened around us.

Daniel: Our power went off about eight Sunday night. Way before the storm, just because this neighborhood is so fucked up. So, we didn't know the hurricane was here until we were outside watching the storm Monday morning. It was great. The way the winds were going, once the storm passed us you could visibly see the wind change directions a hundred eighty degrees, and the real shit was—you wanna see something, look at this. We sat on our balcony right there and watched the shingles pop off this roof, all these shingles we're standing on right here. It'd be like one, two, three, and then, *boom* the whole roof came right at us. That's when we went in for a bit. Before that we were just sitting outside watching it. Listen man, how many time you going to go through something like this? And, meanwhile, you got four feet of water here. And every block you went away from the river, away from the levee, it was another foot. So it's four foot here,

and five foot there, and six a couple blocks away by St. Claude
Avenue. Course it's gone away now, Bywater's dry now, most of it
always was, but one block up, the flooding is still there. St. Claude's
where all the refugees are, right over there. They're bringing them from
the Lower 9th. Everyday, they've been bringing like caravans of fifty at
a time, these Forestry and Wildlife guys are bringing them. But I'm
staying. No matter what. I don't have a choice. I got sixty bucks in my
wallet, three cats and a dog and no car. I've slept an hour in the last
fifty hours from stress. I can't sleep at all. Man, if you get a hook-up for
beer, let me know.

Funny you should ask.

Daniel, Katherine, and I walked the few blocks to Tayl's place on
Poland. The closer we got to the Industrial Canal, the deeper into the
Bywater, the more people there were, sitting on their stoops and porches,
casting smiles at us over fallen trees, the streets littered with pieces of
their roofs. The *Whoa Wow Shit Cool Hell Okay Well No Fuck Huh Whoa*
was falling from their faces into just *Huh*, a *Huh* that hung in the void
until they could get a hold on any sort of real understanding of what was
going on in the city around them and what was in store for their neighborhood, a dim awareness of how just the other side of the Industrial
Canal, a few hundred feet from them, in a section of New Orleans
unknown to tourists and most residents alike, there was a lot of water.
And like a good portion of other people we saw that day, a whole lot of
them had busted faces. Getting around in the dark, up and down thin,
winding, sagging staircases in some of New Orleans' oldest houses after
finishing off all your warm beer wasn't so easy. Sweat made their blood
and bruises glisten and sparkle gruesomely in the sun.

The stuff from Robért's market was laying out wall to wall on Tayl's
living room floor by the time we got there. I handed Daniel a six-pack
and three bottles of wine and he went back to his animals. Tayl and T
walked in, soaking from the waist down, with two coolers full of ice.

"Boom," said T. "Ka-boom goddammit! Got touched again." We
started throwing beer in the coolers. "Waded up to my place to get the ice
and coolers and dammit I didn't see her because she was just under the
water, then them puckered fingertips were all over me. Boom. Let's
open up a bottle of wine."

"Each," said Tayl. We did and we sat out on the steps of his shotgun,
across from his mother's Victorian house, alone on the street, the Industrial Canal to our back right behind Tayl's backyard. I pulled out the tape
recorder.

John Doe (JD): Is everyone happy with their selection?

The other Does: Yes indeed!

JD: Well it's Tuesday, 5:47 P.M. John Doe here. I'm with Jim Doe, Jerome Doe, and Jane Doe. We were up at Robért's earlier.

Jim Doe (JD): Where's Jack Doe?

Jerome Doe (JD): Jack Doe's still breaking into the safe.

JD: So, tell us what happened, Jim Doe.

JD: We heard Robért's was open for business, and we moseyed on down there in Jack Doe's Bronco, license plate #IEM 5—

JD: Fuck off!

JD: And we were like boom, boom, boom!

JD: All I wanted was some ice cream. But it was all melted.

JD: Dude, turn that thing off. Story'll get better if you drink. Let's record it later.

Jane Doe (JD): We're not going to be alive later. They're going to blow the levee to save the French Quarter at four o'clock.

JD: So, which one's Jim Doe?

JD: You are.

JD: No, I'm Jerome Doe.

JD: There is no Jerome Doe. You're Jack Doe.

JD: So, what's the T for anyway?

JD: T?

JD: Why do they call you T?

JD: It's short for John Doe.

JD: Really.

JD: Turn that thing off, I'll tell you.

JD: It stands for Trey.

JD: Boom! What the hell, dude?!

JD: Trey. You know, that's the same amount of syllables. People should just call you Trey.

JD: Let's get the grill going. I'm going to cut some veggies.

JD: What's on the menu this evening?

JD: Pork chops, lamb chops, steaks, and chicken. Brought them back from Trey's place—

JD: Whoa!

JD: Boom!

JD: Sorry. Sorry, brought them back from Jerome Doe's place just now.

JD: I need something to cut the veggies on. Let me have your knife, Josh.

JD: Boom!

JD: Don't say my name on the recording, honey, please.

JD: I meant Josh Doe. Is that Big Shot tray nasty?

JD: Trey Nasty? Big Shot Trey Nasty!

JD: Is it?

JD: Big Shot Trey Nasty!

JD: It is? The tray's nasty? Well, I need something to cut the veggies on.

JD: Trey's Nasty! T-Nasty! Big Shot T-Nasty! You got a new name, T!

JD: This tray, dammit. Is it dirty?

JD: Hell, yeah, he's dirty. Hose him down.

JD: Least I ain been puking up gasoline.

JD: Least I haven't been touching dead people.

JD: I wanna get hosed too.

JD: Big Shot T-Nasty!

JD: Wanna get hosed!

JD: I just want to cut some damn vegetables.

After we'd showered in the middle of the street with Tayl's garden hose, cold enough to make us feel cool and clean and refreshed for a few minutes, almost, Tayl pulled out his crank television, set it on his stoop. The thing was about the size of a normal thirteen-inch TV but with a black-and-white screen slightly larger than the palm of my hand. There was only one local channel and, like the radio, it was running out of Baton Rouge. As the mosquitoes started in on us, we saw the first images of the Mississippi Gulf Coast. It looked as though almost everything along the beach had disappeared in the tidal surge. This was far worse than Betsy and Camille, the hurricanes that had vanquished the family homes that Katherine grew up with.

Supposedly the water was rising in New Orleans. All we were hearing was the 17th Street Canal levee had breached. I had no idea where the

17th Street Canal was, except that it was somewhere far away, somewhere near the Jefferson Parish line, and yet supposedly the water was arcing through the lower parts of the city for miles. But, again, we knew only what we could see and touch.

And that was an unhealthy amount of chicken and lamb chops and ribs and steaks and hamburgers on Tayl's grill. We ate with our hands, gave food to anyone who came by. Big Shot T-Nasty hooked his stereo up to a car battery and danced wild-eyed in the street. The owner of BJ's bar on the corner—closed now, of course, like everything else in the city but Johnny White's Sports Pub and Molly's—traded Tayl the keys to the bar for his Bronco but only if the Bronco had a full tank and Tayl went about siphoning gas while I walked down to a pay phone that was supposedly working a couple of blocks away to call my mom again, let her know all was still well. It was black night now.

Just as I got my mother on the phone, a couple guys came up with a hammer and some plastic bags and began banging away at the padlock on an ice locker outside the corner grocery. Within ten seconds a militia of residents rounded the corner, their leader with an automatic assault rifle the size of a small person strapped over his shoulder. Daniel, the painter we'd given beer to earlier, holding a handgun, was next to him and was the first to yell, "Martial law! We will kill looters!"

The would-be ice thieves bolted. The militia just stood there across the street, staring at me. I didn't think Daniel recognized me in the starlight. "We will kill you!" said the leader.

"Hold on one sec, Mom," I said. "Just using the phone here, guys!"

"It's martial law, motherfucker!" Others with smaller machine guns flanked him.

"Yup," I said. "Just using the phone. Talking to mom."

"Martial law!"

"Talking to mom!"

"Martial law!"

"Mom!"

They argued for a bit about whether to shoot a few rounds in the air, eventually decided against it, and dispersed. My mom was happy I called. I called all the Bywater friends whose numbers I knew, including Tayl's mother, who'd never before left for a hurricane, and told them their houses were dry and that it was all bullshit that the neighborhood was underwater. They wouldn't believe me until I informed them I was calling from the pay phone across from Leo's Bar.

I got back to the barbecue, made myself a vodka and prune juice, picked up a steak off the grill in the other hand and ate it like a candy bar, then had another. There was some obese woman on the television screaming, "It's *hot*. And I've got no *gasoline*!" Tayl walked up, drenched in sweat and gasoline, and puked gas into the middle of the street. The transfer—the Bronco for the keys to BJ's bar—had been successful. T asked me where Katherine was. I realized I hadn't seen her in an hour or so. We called her name a few times. Nothing. Then I went inside to fix myself another vodka and prune juice and heard her.

I stumbled through the black corridors further and further back into Tayl's shotgun house until I could feel her lying crumpled upon a couch in his living room, crying softly. It was her purse. She'd never get it back now, she said. Now she had nothing—no money, nothing. It made no difference when I assured her she would soon get it back, that anyone wealthy enough to own a brand-new Land Cruiser and kind enough to drive us all the way back to my apartment on a night like that, was not going to steal her purse. And it made no difference when I explained that this was probably the best possible time ever to lose a purse because there was no way to spend any money now and none of our phones worked anyway. And it really made no difference when I explained that we were all in this together and we'd all taken losses and T was standing outside with a smile on his face dancing to his tunes in the middle of the street, a bottle of wine in one hand, pork chop in the other, even though his home and everything in it just had been destroyed yesterday, and the kid who mowed his lawn was still floating face down a few blocks away.

So, we left. Tayl lent us two bikes and I packed eight bottles of wine in my basket and biked through the black, star-freckled night, holding a single flashlight, weaving through trees and downed wires, through the entire Bywater, then Marigny then into the Quarter. Our city had become an obstacle course, and I wiped out three times, smashing a bottle of wine each time. All was darkness, the darkness of true night, the darkness of the power lines that clotheslined me, the darkness of my entryway as I hauled the five bottles up my winding stairs, the darkness in my living room that morning between the two windows, how long ago, the heat of Katherine's shoulder then, her neck, eyes closed-down listening to the radio, the darkness of good sleep, and the thought of leaving, fading unnoticed.

9

Next morning, dreams were incessantly interrupted by the phone that we couldn't turn off because Katherine was still waiting to hear from Julio about her purse. But he never called. Instead it was relatives and friends from the world over wondering if we were okay and what they could do for us and what the hell were we thinking? NPR called for updates a couple of times, said they'd put me on the air again later that day. WWL was still the only channel we could get. It told us there were twenty-two thousand people in the Superdome, waiting to be taken to Houston's Astrodome, and more wandering the interstate like castaways. They had figured it was safe because it was high ground, but now they were trapped and dropping from dehydration without water or food and, meanwhile, the rest of the city was filling with water.

But outside my living room window there it was again. Summer. Hotter than hell but bright and beautiful. Fallen leaves on my balcony, soaking with Katrina two days ago, now crumbled to my touch.

"I was just down there," said Katherine, coming up behind me as I stood, letting the pieces of leaf fall onto my balcony. "The river. A dream, but so real. I was down there, beneath all that, all that tumult like a storm forever, water tumbling over and over itself, all those currents and undertows that can yank a ship a hundred feet straight down and defy all that engineering that works on the other rivers of the world." She wrapped her arms around my stomach, looked into the river over my shoulder. "I was down there, a hundred seventy feet below sea level, where the river has no reason to flow at all. The bottom was soft, it rolled through me like wind until I settled into it up to my waist and my toes finally found firm ground. And I laid upon the end to the river, beneath the sediment rolling like wind over me."

"Was I there?"

"No. You were in here when I woke." She smiled, squeezed my chest tight. "We should do that every morning."

"What? Take a shower?"

"The sunrise like that. Making love in the sunrise. By the window so we could breathe it."

"Funny, had a dream like that. Forgot that." I laughed. "Yeah, it was beautiful. What, you mean you had the same dream too?"

"Dream," she said. "Silly."

"Remember how when we were apart we used to say we'd meet in our dreams. We'd pick some spot that we both knew. Like that first lamppost."

"Silly." She let go of me. She pointed to the floor just inside the window. "Right there."

"That was a dream, baby."

"No dream."

"Yes, it was," I said. "Your eyes were zipped shut like with a zipper and I tried to wake myself up but I couldn't until we both woke up literally suffocating in the heat, and we took a cold shower and lay back down on all the sweat which was still warm."

"I don't know what you're talking about," she said. "You're not making sense."

"And the water stopped when we were in the shower. I think the city lost water."

She ran into the bathroom, turned the faucet on. A few drops gurgled out. Then nothing. She tried the bath. Nothing. She left them on, stepped into the empty bathtub, sat down, curled her knees into her chest. "Please, would you close the door," she said. "Just please close the door."

I closed the door. I shoved a couple of small duffle bags into my shoulder bag and went out to search for water. I found a man wandering dazed around Jackson Square. He said his wife and kid were back at some B&B, they were on vacation from Nashville and got trapped here. Now they had no food, no water. I took him with me, walked further into the Quarter. An inch of water, not enough to get over the curb onto the sidewalk, had crept half a block away from Bourbon Street. We found Steve, the owner of the Nellie Deli, sitting on a stool outside his store. He said he'd heard they'd stopped the water flowing into the city and supposedly had found some way to drain it. He told us he didn't have much left, but to take what we could find. He brought enormous cans of tuna and yams out of the back for the Nashville guy. I loaded up on all the Guinness and Gatorade I could. There was almost no food left, no water at all. On the way out, my bags loaded, I asked Steve what I could do in return. "Just don't forget us," he said.

When I got back to the apartment, Katherine was on the phone, saying, "There's one road out? Which road? Which one?"

When I walked into the kitchen, she handed me the phone. There were four empty cups on the counter, the ones that had been filled with water in the freezer. It was the Professor. He was at some foreign-policy conference in London. I assured him we were okay and recounted the previous day's activities.

"Well, I must commend you," he said. "I'm sure you secured plenty of water and batteries at Robért's. There's certainly nothing wrong with that."

Shit. "I knew we forgot something."

"Well, no matter. There's armed gangs of marauding looters armed with Uzis and they're marauding and looting and they're headed toward your place. They're on the TV right now. Listen, do you think you can go check on my pod? I just found out the roof was torn off of the warehouse and they had severe flooding in that area."

"Check on it? In Kenner? What good is that going to do?"

"It's going to stop my spleen from hurting."

"What if I get marauded?"

"Be a man, you sod. You know, I heard you on NPR yesterday. You sounded like an asshole."

"Look, dude, listen, I need you to call all your friends who live in the Quarter wherever they are now, ask them if they have spare keys somewhere we can find them, or if it's easy to break into their place or something so we can get their water and their batteries and use any disposable food that's going to go to waste by the time they get back anyway."

"I'll get right on it." And he hung up. The phone rang again immediately. It was the Professor.

"I need to know if you have spare keys somewhere," he said. "I have a friend who needs to break into your place to use any water that's going to go to waste anyway."

"C'mon, man, I was serious."

"So am I," said the Professor. "You are all the friends I have in the Quarter."

I hung up. The phone rang again immediately. "Now *you're* being the asshole," I said.

"Joshua?"

"Yeah?"

"It's *Talk of the Nation*."

"Oh."

"We're going to put you on in two minutes."

"Okay."

At the end of the interview I told Neal Conan I wasn't leaving until people were allowed to return to the city and he wished us luck. I put the four empty cups in the sink. Katherine was standing by the door. "I need to try to find that guy at the Hyatt," she said.

"Honey, we're running out of water, you can't be drinking four cups every morning."

"I was trying to hydrate. My heart feels dry and itchy," she said. "Now I'm going to the Hyatt."

I threw my tape recorder and a disposable camera into my shoulder bag and ran after her. We biked down to Canal Street. Canal's large median strip, making it the widest avenue in America, was crawling with law enforcement vehicles and a couple of the first media campers where once there were streetcars. There were a few inches of rank brown water in the street as far as I could see. The Foot Action shoe store was burning. The looting, at least near the Quarter, appeared to have subsided, leaving only gaping, shattered store fronts, the last remains of their inventory scattered about the sidewalks. This was where Katherine's parents would take her walking every Sunday. These were the buildings where her school clothes came from, her prom dress, her Christmas and birthday presents—the stuff of her childhood. Katherine's eyes flooded. She made no move to cover them. She gestured to all that was in front of me. And I just stood there, trying to take it in myself, separate from her.

It was as though all New Orleans, up to now, had only been a movie set, all its characters and facades in place only until that final big scene a couple of days ago. And now that it was over, and the actors moved on, it was all coming down. In its absence was loneliness and defeat. I tried to think about how we'd fix it, make it like before. And somehow, standing there, I knew it would all be okay someday. That's all I could do, think everything would be okay someday.

A woman had waded out into the water and was now making a live report for some news station. All this, it was too much to be squashed into pixels, stuck on two flat axes on a television or computer screen, a front page, a sound bite just before we cut to our sponsors, the funnies, supper. The world would see New Orleans every morning now in pictures. But how could they know how it sounds, tastes, smells, and feels to head and heart and hand alike, to move through the light, let alone the darkness? I tossed my disposable camera into the trash can beside me, then led Katherine up Canal Street, new tears glistening down her cheeks.

The water got deeper the further we got into the business district and away from the river, until we had to get off our bikes, push them through the oil-slicked water up to our hips. We tried to stay on the sidewalks where it was a little shallower. We could see our knees but not our feet. Women towed their babies in plastic bins through the water in the opposite direction, escaping the Superdome for the convention center, men alongside them hunched beneath those same green garbage bags that were over their shoulders yesterday on their way out of the Lower 9th Ward. There was no hurry in their pace, no anguish in their faces. It was just the way it was.

We finally trudged into the Hyatt's deep, dark, covered driveway. All the cars were gone. Some residue of the day seeped down into the shadow there, just enough to outline the sole policeman sitting on a bar stool outside the entrance with a small rifle on his knee. Generators wrenched the air as we came up out of the water toward him. I watched Katherine plead with him, almost bring herself to fake tears again, but I could not hear any of it. There was only the generators. Eventually he waved us inside. This time we didn't wait for the escort, but flew up the emergency stairway when no one was looking to the third floor.

The air and light were sour. What little could, dribbled in through some high up windows somewhere, down the thirty-two-floor atrium. Hundreds of people were milling about in surprisingly good spirits. We roamed the same ballroom we had the first night after the storm. People were laying around in groups, some playing cards, some watching a hazy basketball game on a television, some dozing in the dank and still air, most just watching us silently as we searched for Julio.

We snuck up to the twelfth floor, still searching for Julio, and looked out the windows, and there was the Superdome with a patch of its roof missing and thousands of people in scattered lines waiting for something outside. But still, Julio was nowhere.

We discovered they'd be serving dinner at four, in about twenty minutes, and everyone in the hotel would be there because it was the only way they were getting fed. We were the first ones to file into the dining room. After grabbing our paper plates and plastic spoons we were served half a stale pretzel. Peter, a Dixie beer brewer who belonged to my old running group, stood in an apron, ready to dish out something brown. He served Katherine, then looked up at me. "Josh?! Shit, how are you? It's Chicken Creole today!" he said as he slopped a spoonful onto my plate. "Just stay here. They're getting us out of here. They're taking us to Houston, they'll get us to Houston."

I asked if he was joking.

"No, no, they'll get us there," he assured me. "Just stay here."

"Nah, man, I'm heading down to Molly's for a beer in a few minutes," I said.

"Sure." He laughed. "Next."

"Have you seen the Quarter?" I asked him.

He chuckled.

"Peter, I'm not joking."

He froze, brown stuff dripping from his serving spoon onto someone's waiting plate. "Molly's?"

"Yeah."

"That's not funny, man," he said.

"I'm serious."

"Fuck you," said the bald guy in line next to me, still holding his plate beneath Peter's spoon. "Molly's is open? Son of a—screw this, I'm outta this shit." He put his plate down and headed for the exit.

Peter watched him go, but still held the spoon out, dripping onto the tablecloth now. "Molly's. . . ." I could hear him murmuring to himself as we moved down the line. We got our six ounces of warm soda, sat, and tried to eat it all with a plastic spoon while keeping an eye on the door as the ridiculously long line curled into the dining room. Others joined our table. We realized why they all were in such good spirits. They thought they were the lucky ones, that the rest of the city was dying. And maybe they were, maybe it was. The mayor was still living in a room upstairs, they said. A young guy about our age named Jacques sat across the table. He tried to cut off a piece of chicken with his plastic spoon, but it snapped in half. So he tore the chicken apart with his hands, smiling triumphantly.

Jacques: Me, I'm in the corner of the twenty-eighth floor. They made us all come down here about ten Sunday evening, everyone in the hotel, about eight hours before it actually hit, and we could only go back to our rooms if we signed a waiver. So, I went back to my room and about six in the morning I was woken up when all the windows blew out. I ran down here with everybody else and then all of a sudden the power went out and we heard glass shatter and rain, the wind gushing out against this opening back there and the walls started leaking, and the pool, which was on the eighth floor above us, started flooding down here. People were afraid the pool was going to fall in over us.

I've been staying in my room since then. There's glass, debris, pieces of insulation all over it, but it's twenty-eight floors up so at least the breeze is nice. My curtain's somewhere in the Superdome, I think. I'm keeping it on the lowdown, don't want them to know I'm in my room. I'd rather be in a room that has broken windows than be down here. I have a view looking down at the Superdome, so I can see the military keeping all the people together. Reminds me of that movie *Red Dawn*, you know? Except it's not the Russians. All the people are walking out there like it's a big jail, but, it's weird, it's the American military out there keeping them there.

Anyway, I guess I've been here for three days or four days now, some-thing like that. We're getting enough to survive here, not three meals but just enough. They're not charging anything anymore. Initially I was like, "Why'd I have to choose the hotel where all the windows busted out?" But they're really taking care of us compared to all these other hotels. I would recommend the Hyatt for any kind of disaster.

When we'd washed the last of our stale pretzels down with our warm Sprite, Katherine and I scoured the dining room, walked up and down the hundreds-long line four times before we gave up on Julio. The front desk absolutely refused to divulge his whereabouts, so we pushed our bikes back into Poydras Street. Where once there were stars on that first night after Katrina, now there was just murky water, little pieces of debris tickling our ankles, and the dribblings of an exodus, people car-rying and pushing all they could down to the convention center on the river, more babies floating in plastic bins as we thought about drinking a couple of cold ones, and I wondered what separated us from them. We had almost no money, and quite a few of the people camping out in the Quarter were now homeless too.

One of them was the bald guy who'd been in the dinner line behind us at the Hyatt. He was now lying in the middle of the street outside Molly's, legs and arms splayed, holding a bottle of Newcastle Brown Ale on his chest, pouring a Miller Lite over his face. We got a couple of beers ourselves. Monaghan, the owner, was standing out front. Despite his thin arms and slight paunch, the man held weight in any room he walked into, he tipped the scales right over. He was a bearded ex-construction worker who took the bar over when his father passed and once told me he would have no problem hitting a man with glasses on.

"Can you believe this? Did you hear about this?" he asked with blood-shot eyes straining to break out of their sockets. "Dennis Hastert, Speaker of the House, he just said the city should be bulldozed. I'm going to send him an e-mail: 'I'll bulldoze your mother-*fucking* face!' "

His voice switched from gravelly rage to gentle, measured counte-nance when I asked him where he was for the hurricane.

Monaghan: I was at Molly's for the whole thing. The night of the storm we closed at seven o'clock. It was the first time we closed for a hurricane and I'm glad we did. I didn't want people to get drunk and get crazy and go home and do something stupid or get caught up in the storm. We opened up Monday at four in the afternoon. Had the street cleaned up, swept up. About a dozen people came in. We'll continue to open at ten, go until six, curfew. Once we get the power back on and get some employees back in town we'll be fine.

I'm not leaving. There's going to have to be somebody from the city come to me with a gun and say you have to go. We just heard the good news now, they'll have this thing in hand by Friday, in two days. It's going to get better. My only concern I have right now is that we get these marauding bands of kids off the street, get this looting stopped. I talked to one of my employees, the bartender who's working right now, she lives on Magazine street, and she said it's like a war up there, she's on the nineteen hundred block, she said there was a dead body in front of her door, and she was going to try and drag it to a church on the way to work tomorrow.

There's something in this city that's missing as far as self-respect and people disrespecting each other. I don't know where the fault lies, but for Christ's sake we gotta get past all this bullshit. I don't think four days is out of line for asking people to behave themselves, and to act like human beings, to really reach out to each other and to really help each other.

A few more people drifted into Molly's. I would like to say it felt like normal times, maybe like a slow weekday, standing outside the bar where little cocktail tables were built around the balcony supports. But it felt like we were the only people left in the world, trying in whatever feeble way to come to terms with this fact, still flinging the day's hearsay around as always. A couple different people told the same story, about a resident who caught a burglar in his house two blocks away. The resident held the unarmed burglar at gunpoint outside until a police car drove by. Then the police held the burglar down and told the resident to shoot him. There wasn't any place to put prisoners, and they didn't want the bullet traced to them. Debbie and Philipe, writers who run the Kitchen Witch, a cookbook store, walked up with one of their dogs.

"We hunkered down Sunday night," said Philipe. "Six animals and us two, underneath mattresses. It was like something surrounding you. It was just fucking everywhere. It was like a train would come this way, something would fall from above, you'd feel something from the apartment next to you. Then you look out at a break and you see the roof gone off of your neighbor's house."

"You seen any looting?" I asked.

"Sure," Philipe said. "What they do is wait for the police to go by, then somebody keeps a lookout, then somebody else picks up the USA Today dispenser and just rams it into the door. And it's like Dressed to Kill, that leather shop, over on Dauphine Street, they looted that the first day. The broke the windows and took high heels and leather boots."

"So you see twelve-year-old boys walking around with stripper clothes, you know," said Debbie. "Someone told us there were cops in uniform behind the Marriott with their police cars, trying on Reeboks. 'Business as usual,' they said. You need a drink?"

The ice ran out, the beer got warmer, and the afternoon fell away. As Monaghan closed the bar TnA came rolling up and invited Katherine and me to dinner at their place just up Dumaine Street. They'd stretched their red beans and rice last night by adding everything from hash browns, green peppers, sausage, tomatoes, you name it, until they had too much. We slipped in there just before the six o'clock curfew.

They had a plethora of top-shelf liquor, the plastic bar pourer spouts still in the tops. These were courtesy of Windex-drinking and pigeon-throwing Petrovski. The bottles had magically appeared the morning after Katrina, Petrovski's attempt to return himself to TnA's good graces after embarrassing them in front of the New Orleans Fire Department. He had since made other slip-ups, which accounted for the piles of mouthwash and Kleenex and tampons that lay around the apartment, and now toothpaste piled around two bottles of Korbel that had just materialized on the coffee table this morning after he'd used their potable water to flush the toilet last night when the water was still working. Of course, their hammer, screwdriver, and crowbar had been missing for a few days.

On their mantel was a small jewelry box. Ty told me to open it. Inside, wrapped in tissue, was Jesus' thumb. It had broken clean off the statue behind the cathedral. It was only a little larger than one of my own, smooth, almost white. We finished the red beans, ate hot sausage patties with our hands, and drank warm Grey Goose screwdrivers, just the four of us, sitting on their balcony as night rose and the stars fell. Even in the candlelight, Ty had a face that immediately made you both like him and respect him—thin mouth over a thin goatee in a thin face that framed eyes large and brown as pennies, a few white hairs breaking into his sharp widow's peak that cut into his forehead so handsomely you couldn't imagine him without the receding hairline. Ashley was the fire to his water, with the hair and stare of Medusa if Medusa were drop-dead hot, her hair falling in blonde and brown waves like dangling snakes, the tiny piercing in a nose that looked like it could breathe flames.

"I thought this would be a great opportunity to quit smoking," said Ty. "It's one of the reasons I stayed, but the first day some friends came back from a bar, they'd emptied out a cigarette machine, and they had forty packs. But they'll run out eventually, and I'll just pretend like I was going to quit that particular day anyway."

There were suddenly thunderous footsteps through their apartment behind us. "They're all over the place!" someone screeched in a thin Russian accent. "All over! Oh God!"

"What? What's all over the place, Petrovski?" asked Ty.

"The frogs! They came back. Where are you?!"

"Out here on the balcony. What's going on?"

"There's frogs in my apartment again," said Petrovski. He was a stout kid with a shaved head and eyes just barely creased in the corners with a drop of Mongol. "The hurricane brought frogs. They're all over the place!"

He scurried back into the apartment, thundered around for a bit. "I need to make a jelly sandwich. I need jelly. Jelly!" He grabbed the last slice of Wonder Bread, rifled through the condiments piled on their kitchen counter, finally settling on a fancy-looking jar of champagne jelly.

"Petrovski, watch it. That stuff's expensive," said Ashley.

He pried the top off and dumped the whole jar onto the counter over the one slice of white bread. "No problem," he said, and scooped up a handful, yellow jelly running through his fingers, and plunked it back in the jar and screwed the top back on. "No problem." He peeled the bread up from underneath the remaining mound of jelly, folded it over like a taco, and shoved the whole thing into his mouth.

Ashley returned to the balcony. "We wake up every morning with flies all over whatever mess he's left," she said. "Got to the point where I'd follow him around with Windex. Only problem was he would try to drink it."

"Hurricane Petrovski," said Ty. "Category 7."

Petrovski poked his head out the window. "Can I stay with you all from now on?" he asked through a mouthful of jelly. "Because there's frogs in my apartment."

"According to you there's been frogs down there for three days now," said Ashley. "And you've already been staying here so why are you even asking?"

"Petrovski, where's that summer sausage we've been saving?" asked Ty.

"What summer sausage?"

"The one that's like almost two feet long."

"Oh, I used it."

"You *used* it?"

"For bread."

"We don't have any bread, you just ate the last slice."

"Right. Exactly. You didn't have any bread and I was hungry this morning and all you had was some Swiss cheese but no bread so I sliced the sausage down the middle and stuck the Swiss cheese in like a sandwich and ate it. Sorry about eating all the Swiss cheese without asking."

"That sausage would have lasted us for weeks."

"What? What did you expect me to do? I used it for bread."

Ty flicked his cigarette off the balcony into the blackness below. "Well, there goes my last cigarette, thank God."

Petrovski ran out of the apartment, leaving a thin trail of jelly juice.

Ashley sighed. "Bet when we wake up tomorrow that whole coffee table's full of cigarettes."

"Anyone need a cigarette?" said a guy in a leather cowboy hat as he joined us on the balcony. He had two cartons of Camels under his arm, a bottle of Macallan Scotch in one hand, and a guitar in the other. "Name's Derek," he said to Katherine and me. He worked with Ty, shipping art, and looked like Tom Berenger in *Platoon*, even had almost the same scar on his face, which seemed to be an extension of his grin, sweeping through his stubble right up into the corner of his eye where a person's real smile lies. The scar is what he got for standing on a French Quarter balcony with Ty when it decided to give way after a hundred years. They both wound up in the hospital for two months.

Ty swore, took a pack of cigarettes. "I'm staying until I can quit," he said. "What do you guys say we go roam?"

Derek threw his guitar over his back and we piled warm Miller Lites into a small trash can and took turns carrying it while passing around Derek's bottle of Macallan 12-year, all the while keeping our steps quiet and our eyes and ears open for both the bad guys who would rob us and the good guys who would arrest us. We made it to Jackson Square without seeing another soul or hearing so much as the creak of a sagging house, and climbed up the massive steps to the Washington Artillery Park above and between the square and the river. A cannon built in 1861 loomed over us on its pedestal. We all gazed into the quiet sky, trying not to make a sound.

"The police threw Coca-Cola at me!" It was Petrovski. He was running up the long handicap ramp toward us with a bottle of Diet Coke in his hand. "They're out there guarding Walgreens and I tried to walk up to them and they pointed their guns and one of them lobbed what I thought was a grenade at me or at least tear gas but it was just this Coca-Cola. Hey, Derek, man, start playing." Derek sat beneath the cannon and started strumming the guitar. Pete began singing, making up lyrics about cops throwing Diet Coke at people. He shocked the hell out of me with how good his voice was. Katherine and Ashley's silhouettes danced together on top of the massive cannon against stars, the Cathedral hulking white in the starlit distance.

Ty and I leaned over the railing gazing into the universe shivering on the river, draining Miller Lites, talking about whether or not we should start carrying weapons. Though I had access to them, guns were out of the question for me. I just didn't do guns, but I'd probably have to start wearing my survival knife. Ty agreed, said he had a pretty big filet knife he would carry around from now on. It wouldn't be much if we had assault rifles in our faces, but we figured they were going for easy targets, and that wouldn't be us.

After what seemed like hours—time, like the cathedral's clock, had ceased to function—Petrovski ran out of lyrics and we all went down to the Riverwalk, down the steps in its center and sat on the last step and put our feet in the river, into swirling contorted constellations. The river had receded to as low as it had been before the storm, the lowest I could remember it ever being.

The tape recorder was on the whole time, but words melded into one indecipherable chant and washed away beneath the lapping Mississippi and breeze, a town washed clean of its sounds, the susurrus of a city, and Ty tai chi-ed on the top step beneath the gristle of the universe as it creaked through its own ancient movements until Derek brought it all to a halt with his guitar. He played for a long time before his voice rose into it with the lyrics of Robert Earl Keene, his mouth pulling that scar down his cheek, dragging the corner of his eye with it, a voice like Johnny Cash might have sounded if he'd actually done time in Folsom, a voice coarse as the leather of his black cowboy hat, heavy and bottomless as the river . . .

> You say you're clearing out, the devil's in your eyes
> No time to walk, no time to talk, no time for long goodbyes.
> The ticket's in your hand, you've made that final call,
> The hard words flying by like punches in a barroom brawl.
>
> I'm only what I am, I won't apologize
> But if you go you'll surely know you'll have to come to realize
> Love don't walk away, only people do
> So if you go or if you stay you know I'll still be loving you.
>
> We've made the hard time sing, we've made the miles roll by,
> We've broken both our wings and still we've had the will to fly.
> I've read a thousand books, I've been behind the wheel,
> I've known you all my life but still I can't feel how you feel.

We've made a mess of things,
It makes no difference now, let's chalk it all up to the blues.
Little girl, think it over one time
Before you break in your walking shoes. . . .

And I wondered who'd be the first to break in their walking shoes.

10

September 1 and Katherine's eyes won't grow. It had taken our first month to get them open, and from there on, for the last twenty-two months I had curled into them to sleep and stretched out from them when I woke as the little freckles came out across the bridge of her nose and tops of her cheeks in the white morning light that dribbled into both our bedrooms. I would often wake, open my eyes, to find her already looking at me, eyes wide open, inches from mine.

In the midst of sleepless night we had felt it a couple of times since the storm—bodies locked together, glide of hot skin, sweet sweat—but in waking life we became two people groping only and desperately for knowledge of what was really happening around us, trying to avoid danger, securing food and water and, after that, something to make us smile. Our city needed our hearts now. Desire for each other would have to wait. So, we waited, unsure it would wait for us.

And we groaned through our new reality, pushing our bodies through the dense heat of my apartment. The dozens of cups of water we had frozen had long since melted, turned murky and taken on the odor of the rotting food around them. We threw it all out, scrubbed the freezer and refrigerator with bleach, propped their doors open. We laid out anything edible on the counter—a few cans of tuna, some crackers, and a whole bunch of pasta and rice and beans we had no way of cooking here. Though we knew we had more than enough back at Tayl's. We had one five-gallon jug of bath water left and that was it.

The police had broken into the Walgreens on the corner below me for supplies and now had three officers guarding it throughout the day. I offered them use of my land line—some hadn't been able to call their families in days—in return for five bags of Snyder's Jalapeño pretzel bits and the last *Times-Picayune* that had been printed, the headline: KATRINA TAKES AIM. Then we walked up to my apartment, onto the balcony, waited until the officers were looking the other way down the street, and crawled around the ironwork separating my neighbor's balcony from my own. Their balcony wrapped around the corner of St. Peter and Decatur four stories up, the only vantage in the city where the cathedral, all of Jackson Square, and the river were laid out. Here was the very heart of New Orleans, and three of its major landmarks, stretched out before us. It occurred to me that this city was little by little, in a very real way, becoming ours.

We found an unlocked window, then clipped the wire that held the inside shutters together and roamed the massive apartment. I had no idea who lived there because, like many apartments in my building, it was unoccupied for most of the year. It looked like a maid spent more time in there than anyone else. There was wonder and awe and freedom and even power in roaming through the place, the coolness of the polished wood furniture, the silk bed covers, the dying tulips on the mantel, it all became ours. And on the kitchen counter were two shopping bags full of hurricane supplies—Gatorade, sparkling water, Luna bars, individual cereal boxes, and assorted canned food. No doubt, like much of New Orleans, this person was planning on weathering the storm before it got big and bad. I had never broken into anyone's place and stolen things before. Not only was it kind of cool, but neither of us felt the slightest remorse. It was necessary. That was all there was to it. There was, of course, no one there to stop us from taking anything we wanted. But all we wanted was food and water.

As we made our way back onto the balcony, the mess Jackson Square had become opened up below me. For seven years, it had been my front yard. Now, it was a pile of trees and branches and leaves. How the hell was anyone going to clean that up? *Who* was going clean it all up? When? The police didn't look up as we scaled the balcony railing back to my place with our goods.

The radio confirmed what the police had told us. We were surrounded by water. The governor claimed there was only one way in or out and that route was needed solely to get aid in. A steady stream of friends continued to call. In some ways, it was harder for them, not being here, relying only on the doom on the news, than it was for us who were here and knew what was in front of our faces, but little else. I would tell people how well we were getting along. Katherine would tell them about the heat and the mosquitoes and the gunshots and the lack of water. A dear friend, K.K., who was now at her family's ranch in Missouri, gave me the gate access code to the condominium complex she helped manage.

Five minutes later I lay on the bottom of her pool upon branches and dirt and roof tiles, gazing up at the sun breaking through all the leaves floating above me, splaying light into wavering strings around me like it would over Nova Scotia, my fingers through them, and I was tempted to breathe it all in, Katherine swimming above me like a mermaid with her legs together, back and forth four times, end to end, before breaking the surface for air. She had been a competitive swimmer in college, her long arms and legs, wide shoulders, thin hips, every curve where it should be, tight and tall enough to be a model for Ralph Lauren at the same time, and none of it had changed in the years since.

I turned over a couple of chaise longues, and we lay there, wet leaves stuck all over us, marveling at our goose bumps. For the first time in my life, I'd jimmied a lock—with my library card—to get in here. Without electricity the access code had been useless. The complex, a scattering of old slaves' quarters and Creole cottages and some newer condominiums, ran the width of the entire block, from St. Peter to Toulouse Street. There was a large garage and a long deep courtyard toward the back of which was the pool. There were, of course, branches and leaves and shingles everywhere. We did not care. The luxury of bathing was heaven.

After we broke into K.K.'s apartment, and found her keys to the other units in the complex, it took us two trips, gagging, to haul the gray slop that had become of the meat in her freezer out to a Dumpster on Rampart Street, which had become so rank it seemed to be killing the flies near it. I heard a gunshot just down the street as I tossed the last bag in the dumpster.

We biked along the river into the Bywater toward Tayl's. The town had emptied, yet there was still the giddiness, the feeling that around every corner lay another situation or sight that you would likely never experience again. One massive warehouse had spraypaint all over it saying, YOU LOOT, WE SHOOT! It was AJ's wholesale produce. Outside the entrance a man sat on the curb beside large wicker baskets of assorted fruit. He told us to take a basket each and we did, barely managing to balance them on the bikes between our legs. There were oranges, peaches, apples, bananas, and mangoes. We stopped a few times to unload some of it on the few families we passed, usually dragging some sort of cart or wheelbarrow, scavenging for whatever they could find. They were the few who believed that this was better than what they'd get in the Superdome, and word had spread that the convention center was out of control. But you could see it in their eyes, their posture, their listless gait, they wouldn't be here long, they were hanging on to their neighborhood, their home, by a thread. Still, they were the lucky ones. Like us, their homes were dry. It mattered not whether you were rich or poor, black or white. There was only wet or dry. We were dry. And we had friends who were dry. We still had our shelter. For this, we were the luckiest people in the world. And never did we take it for granted. We were all too aware things could change in a matter of minutes. All there was to do was to survive in the now, to make sure those close around you were surviving, and to try to keep smiling to soothe the frustration that we did not know how we could help those who needed it, and that we were not helping them. And so there again were Tayl and Big Shot T-Nasty, sitting on his steps, sipping on St. Pauli Girls. T-Nasty had rescued forty pounds of shrimp from his freezer.

As they got the grill ready I walked down to the pay phone and called my mom. There was no longer any sign of a militia, or anyone at all. I asked her to check my messages for me, since I couldn't for some reason. There were dozens, all from friends wondering how I'm doing or if I'm alive. The Professor had called a number of times.

"Have you started eating babies?" he asked when I called him back.

"What the shit?"

"I know all about the cannibalism down there. It's okay. Listen, it's important, after you eat the babies, if you have to eat yourself, eat your butt first. I'm sure it'll be fine with Tabasco."

"I'm about to eat forty pounds of shrimp."

"I thought you needed food."

"Right now what we really need is water. We're running out. And there's no supplies coming into the city."

"Take it out of your hot water heater."

"My hot water heater? That's potable water?"

"Of course it is. There should be a tap at the bottom of it. Most of them hold about forty gallons."

"Jesus. How come none of us thought of that?"

"Because you people have no sense whatsoever. Now, if you don't mind, I need to get some more rest, I'm going punting on the Thames at dawn."

Sure enough, there was a small tap on the bottom of Tayl's hot water heater. We all felt a lot better. While we grilled the shrimp we traded the day's rumors: postal trucks hijacked by gangs trying to escape the city, mass riots in the city jail, hundreds of prisoners killed, their bodies tossed into the water. Katherine and I made a new drink for the new month: root beer and rum with a splash of prune juice, garnished with an orange. The Bum Runner.

This night the cops were still outside Walgreens when Katherine and I got back. For the first time, we slept with some small sense of security. I had no idea what had been stopping people from robbing the boutiques, restaurants, and apartments below me, then finding their way up to my own apartment. Even with the police, we could only dream of daylight. And when daylight came, we dreamt of water. We had still not seen any sign whatsoever that any relief was coming into the city. But at least we had my hot water heater now.

I hadn't changed clothes in days. There was really no reason to. All I wore was my olive green bathing suit and, when I went out, I slipped on Aqua Socks, dropped my tape recorder in my shoulder bag and I was good to go. Today, I added an eight-inch survival knife to my apparel. I slid a cotton web belt through the sheath and fastened it around my waist. Katherine's uniform had become a tank top, Daisy Dukes, and a pair of women's Aqua Socks she'd found at Tayl's place.

When we biked by AJ's produce warehouse that afternoon the same guy was standing outside in cutoffs and flip-flops, his flesh tan and sun-beaten as old leather, sagging over his thin frame, a frazzled sun-bleached ponytail knotted down his back. He was gesticulating with an Uzi. He had some kid sitting out front in a beach chair with a pistol, just flipping it around between his legs like it was a toy. Their eyes were glazed and bloodshot. He explained someone had tried to break into an office there last night, gave us two baskets, waved toward the massive warehouse entrance with his Uzi, and told us to go take anything we wanted. There were myriad piles of fruits and vegetables just inside. We took oranges and strawberries and peaches and nectarines and bananas and onions and peppers and garlic and tomatoes.

"All we need now is a watermelon," I joked.

"I don't have time for this shit," he said. "Go get it yourselves. Third cooler on the left."

My mini-Maglite hardly made a dent in the vast cold labyrinthine darkness. There were massive cooler doors on all sides. We walked into one that was open, through the clear plastic flaps that hung down over the entrance. There must have been ten thousand bananas in there. We couldn't believe it. They were all slightly green and piled into cardboard containers stacked ten feet high. We went to the next cooler. Same thing. And the next cooler too. And the next and the next and the next and the next. Then pineapples, then mangos, tomatoes, then baby tomatoes, and on and on. We couldn't hear any generators and had no idea how the coolers could stay so cold. We found whole other sections of the warehouse that ran off the first section, again overstocked with vegetables and fruit. But no watermelons.

Eventually we found our way back out into the heat and light outside. The guy's Uzi was in my basket on top of the bananas. I set it on a pile of tomatoes, thanked him, and off we wobbled just like the day before, trying to balance our baskets on the bicycle bars between our legs.

Far as we could see, there was no sign of life in the Bywater now. I wondered how many people were still holed up here, hiding inside, some afraid of looters, others afraid of the police. But, once again, there were Tayl and Big Shot T-Nasty sitting on the steps to Tayl's shotgun house, sipping from a chilled bottle of Finlandia vodka they'd shoved dried blueberries into. We added the basket to the rest of the food and TnA joined us about an hour later—we'd told them earlier where Tayl's place was because they'd never met him before—and we barbecued the rest of Big Shot's shrimp along with peppers and onions and tomatoes on skewers and all the remaining hot dogs as night fell over us and we tossed this day's rumors around. Big Shot had heard they were sticking all would-be prisoners on Huey Long Bridge—a bridge practically too narrow for the two lanes of cars that wobbled crazily over the thin grille that separated them from a thousand-foot drop into the Mississippi—leaving the men to fend for themselves, and if they went crazy in the heat and started throwing each other off the bridge, that was their own problem. "Sounds pretty fair to me," said Katherine. "I think anyone caught looting should be made to clean all the fridges in New Orleans and then kicked out of the city permanently."

"You know, this would be a hell of a time to be vegetarian," said Ty, chewing on a hot dog. "It's like a mad dash to eat all the beef you can. An apple or tomato isn't gonna do it."

"What's for dessert?" asked Ashley.

"Ring Dings, of course," said Tayl. "Courtesy of Robért's supermarket."

"America is indeed the land of plenty," said Ty.

While we ate our Ring Dings, we listened to the radio until an ad came on for New Orleans Daiquiris. That was just plain cruel, so we cranked up the television and watched CBS kick out the worst of the worst. FEMA—the Federal Emergency Management Agency—was apparently nowhere. People still trapped on various sections of the interstate overpass were dropping from dehydration. T-Nasty, his belly full and sipping on his own bottle of wine, blocks from his own flooded home, asked, "Are we really that insane? I mean, is there something wrong with *us*?"

"I ask myself that question every ten minutes," I said.

Ty suggested we form a clean-up crew tomorrow, try to look official. "If the cops drive by and see a bunch of people in the same T-shirts and see us all picking up limbs and stacking them in a real organized fashion, and getting garbage together, we'd probably be the last people they'd tell to evacuate," he said. "And when they do, we might even have a bit of leverage. Hell, we'll go rescue people, whatever we gotta do. Like a grass-roots homeland security."

He bit the tip off another hot dog and said, "I wouldn't be surprised if, down the line, the mayor gave us some sort of commendation for it." Just then, the mayor came on the radio for a phone interview with Garland Robinette. It was the first time we'd heard his voice since the storm.

Mayor Nagin: I tell you, man, Garland, I keep hearing that it's coming. This is coming, that is coming. And my answer to that is B.S.—where is the beef? Because there's no beef in the city, there's no beef anywhere in southeast Louisiana. And these goddamned ships that are coming, I don't see them . . . They don't have a clue what's going on down here. They flew down here one time two days after the doggone event was over with TV cameras, AP reporters, all kind of goddamn—excuse my French everybody in America, but I am pissed.

Robinette: Did you say to the President of the United States, "I need the military in here"?

Nagin: I said, "I need everything." They're thinking small, man. And this is a major, major, major deal. And I can't emphasize it enough, man. This is crazy. I've got fifteen thousand to twenty thousand people over at the convention center. It's bursting at the seams. It's awful down here, man.

Robinette: Do you believe that the president is seeing this, holding a news conference on it, but can't do anything until the Governor requested him to do it? And do you know whether or not she has made that request?

Nagin: I have no idea what they're doing. But I will tell you this: You know, God is looking down on all this, and if they are not doing everything in their power to save people, they are going to pay the price. Because every day that we delay, people are dying and they're dying by the hundreds. . . . You know what really upsets me, Garland? We told everybody the importance of the 17th Street Canal issue. We said, "Please, please take care of this. We don't care what you do. Figure it out."

Robinette: Who'd you say that to?

Nagin: Everybody . . .

Robinette: If some of the public called and they're right, that there's a law that the president, that the federal government can't do anything without local or state requests, would you request martial law?

Nagin: I've already called for martial law in the city of New Orleans. We did that a few days ago.

Robinette: Did the governor do that, too?

Nagin: I don't know. I don't think so. But we called for martial law when we realized that the looting was getting out of control . . . I'm not sure if we can do that another night with the current resources. Most people are looking to try and survive. You have drug addicts that are now walking around this city looking for a fix. They're looking for something to take the edge off of their jones, if you will. And they've probably found guns. So what you're seeing is drug-starving crazy addicts, drug addicts, that are wreaking havoc. And we don't have the manpower to adequately deal with it . . .

Robinette: Apparently there's a section of our citizenry out there that thinks because of a law that says the federal government can't come in unless requested by the proper people . . .

Nagin: Really? Well, did the tsunami victims request? Did it go through a formal process to request? You know, did the Iraqi people request that we go in there? Did they ask us to go in there? What is more important?

We authorized $8 billion to go to Iraq lickety-quick. After 9/11, we gave the president unprecedented powers lickety-quick to take care of New York and other places. Now, you mean to tell me that a place where most of your oil is coming through, a place that is so unique when you mention New Orleans anywhere around the world, everybody's eyes light up—you mean to tell me that a place where you probably have thousands of people that have died and thousands more that are dying every day, that we can't figure out a way to authorize the resources that we need? Come on, man. You know, I'm not one of those drug addicts. I am thinking very clearly.

And I don't know whose problem it is. I don't know whether it's the Governor's problem. I don't know whether it's the President's problem, but somebody needs to get their ass on a plane and sit down, the two of them, and figure this out right now. I don't want to see anybody do any more goddamn press conferences . . . Now get off your asses and do something, and let's fix the biggest goddamn crisis in the history of this country. I am just—I'm at the point now where it don't matter. People are dying. They don't have homes. They don't have jobs. The city of New Orleans will never be the same in this time.

We hooted and hollered and jumped up and down and swung our fists in the air. We had never felt what it was like to actually be proud of a politician before. Nagin had imbued our frustration and confusion with voice. And we hoped the world was listening. "Lickety-quick! Lickety-quick! Boom!" screamed T-Nasty joyously. "He said 'lickety-quick'! I love that!"

Just then, we heard what sounded like a bus rounding the corner, then a spotlight came over us, an engine grinding closer and closer. We shielded our eyes and jumped out of the street, out of its way. It ground to a halt beside us. It was a tank. About eight soldiers in full gear, machine guns in hand sat perched on its top, staring down at us. We started screaming and jumping around again. Tayl just stood there clapping respectfully.

"Lickety-quick!" shouted T-Nasty, shaking his bottle of wine in the air. "Now *that* is lickety-quick! Boom-boom-boom!"

I saw now that it was not in fact a tank, but an armored personnel carrier, what looked to me like a tank with wheels rather than treads. The soldiers just sat atop it, looking down at us, visibly baffled, unsure of what to say to six people drinking beer and wine and cheering amidst the debris of a massive barbecue, the grill still going. Finally one spoke up, "Ummmm. . . . Are you guys okay? Do you need help?"

"Yeah," said Tayl. "You want to help us get rid of these shrimp?" He held up two large Ziploc bags of barbecued shrimp.

"Shrimp?" said the soldier. He looked over to another soldier who shook his head. "No. We already ate, I guess. Yeah. You all be safe." And, with that, the vehicle kicked back to life and they rolled off down the street.

In honor of the mayor's tirade, which we were convinced had caused the army to instantly appear before us, Ty decided our clean-up crew should be called the Krewe of Nagin—the word *Krewe* being a play on Mardi Gras Krewes. We decided to start cleaning up Jackson Square at seven tomorrow morning. I told Tayl and T-Nasty about the pool we now had access to, told them to meet us there around noon tomorrow.

TnA and Katherine and I biked back through the no-man's-land the Bywater had become, Ty and I talking real loud about the big guns we had in redneck accents the whole time. TnA split off from us at Dumaine

Street, and Katherine and I headed home with all the leftover shrimp for the police outside Walgreens. It was the nights alone that really got us. Total darkness filled with the monsters of every rumor you told yourself wasn't true, every creak of the building a footstep, every gunshot sounded like it was at your front door, literally praying for daylight, whatever bit of knowledge and certainty it might bring. Our only consolation was the police outside Walgreens for the last day. Hostile as some of them were toward us—twice they'd pointed their guns at us and made us walk across the street when we passed—at least we had them there. But they weren't there tonight. There was no one anywhere. I tossed the bag of shrimp on the curb.

The heat in my apartment slugged us in the belly, swallowed us whole. We pulled the futon over to the open window in the living room, lay down on our backs with our feet sticking out the window, held hands between us and stayed very, very still until sweating stopped and sleep came. But it never held long. The fright, our vulnerability, caused every sound, both in dreams and in the apartment, to make my heart race. Seeing one armored personnel carrier wasn't going to cut it. Every finger's twitch by Katherine made me bolt upright, and it was always a good while before my heart slowed and sweating stopped again and I'd squeeze in as many dreams as I could until the next thing.

It went on like this until we thought our building was blowing up at 4:35 A.M. The explosion came like a hundred bolts of thunder crashing at once, rattling our hearts and heads and the futon. We sprung upright into the open window and saw the entire AJ's warehouse shoot into the sky in flames. It seemed to hang there, grope at something impossibly high above the Quarter, at last exhaling black smoke into the stars, then the blaze cascaded back down like water shot up from a geyser falling back to earth, and settled over the entire foundation in another crash, its glow burning over our cheeks. Though it must have been at least half a mile downriver from us, the sound and sight were what big explosions in big movies can only hint at. The warehouse next to it went up, too, in a similar, slightly smaller, explosion and mushroom cloud. I did not feel the terror I had at every sound throughout the night. I was simply resigned. I figured this was our fate, that building after building would be blown up and that was that and there was not a damn thing I could do but burn when my time came. And then more, smaller explosions came out of the second warehouse. With each one, white flames rocketed into the sky with the whine and whistle and arc of the annual Independence Day fireworks over the river, only much wider and brighter. One after another, for five minutes they shot out of the massive warehouse.

We lay back, held hands between us again, the staccato white flashes ricocheting and booming over us, feeling our pulses slow in each other's wrists.

"Just realized it's my birthday," I said. And so it was. September third. But Katherine was already asleep.

11

Day did come. I left Katherine sleeping, motionless and silent as ever, her empty hand still stretched out for me on the futon's black mattress, and walked down to the river with my five-gallon bucket. Black smoke billowed into the air from the charred ruins of AJ's, drifted over me toward the cathedral. I was the only human being on the river. A double-prop Chinook helicopter came in low. I waved. The pilot gave me a thumbs-up. Then I stepped deeper into the cold dark water, got in up to my waist, and dunked my head under, scrubbed my underarms and everything else.

I brought the full, fifty-pound bucket back upstairs, placed it by the toilet as I had the last two days. It was 7 A.M. Katherine had not moved. I went down to Jackson Square.

By the time TnA showed up an hour later with brooms, smoking the cigarettes they'd found on their coffee table this morning, I'd gotten a fair portion of the trees and major branches on the St. Peter side of the square into a heap about ten feet high and forty long. Ty and I got the rest on that side of the square as Ashley swept the leaves. We could not, of course, get into the actual locked park, so we used my survival knife to saw off the protruding and twisted branches of the trees that had been uprooted inside the park and thrown by the winds onto the iron fence. When we got done with all the timber on that side of the square, we started sweeping up the inches-deep layer of leaves with Ashley. But two skimpy brooms between us wasn't going to cut it.

Then, an apparition appeared, wielding two large industrial floor sweeps with two-foot brushes. He was clad in a vintage fireman's shirt and black leather motorcycle pants with a silver-studded belt, a long red-

and-black tribal tattoo that ran down his left arm to his wrist, and hair halfway down his back, Cheyenne black and straight. He simply handed the brooms to Ashley, turned, and disappeared from the square. I asked her who the hell that was.

"Think his name's Rod," she said. "He lives near the frame shop over by Johnny White's. No one really knows much about him."

Katherine came down and brought us all various red T-shirts which we turned inside out for uniforms and four of my lanyards with plastic ID holders which we stuck our driver's licenses into against the logo of whatever book festival they had come from. Now, we were official. And when the first news crew found out we were just residents cleaning up, they were all over us. I had to throw an armful of leaves on the cameraman at one point, because he wouldn't get out of the way. Regardless, we managed to sweep up the entire St. Peter side of Jackson Square before noon rolled around.

Exhausted, exhilarated, covered in dirt-caked sweat, proud that we had begun to make order, however small, out of the chaos the storm had tossed our surroundings into, we walked up to meet Tayl and T-Nasty at the condo complex for a swim break. The manager from AJ's passed us in a forklift. He told me four policemen came over to the warehouse at three in the morning, took his Uzi away, beat him up, then took him off in handcuffs. About an hour later, someone broke in, robbed and torched the place. Then the warehouse next to it, full of solvent containers and propane tanks, caught fire. These were the white rockets we'd fallen asleep to. As usual he had on only a pair of jean cutoffs and sandals. I could see no scratches or bruises on him.

An old Dodge pickup rolled by us. A kid sat in the bed, wearing a bullet-proof vest, his hat bearing the insignia of some sheriff's department, a machine gun across his lap, and a disposable camera in his hand, snapping pictures of the Quarter.

T-Nasty opened the gate for us with bleeding elbows and a .44 Magnum strapped around his chest. Apparently they'd wanted to get in the pool so bad he had scaled the gate, crawled between the iron hooks on its top about ten feet up, then fallen down into the courtyard. He told us that on the way over here they had watched the police drag some would-be hijacker out of a city bus and squash his face to the ground with a gun.

Ty found the leaf net and started scooping debris out of the pool. The rest of us used our brooms to sweep leaves and sticks and branches into piles in the corners of the long patio. We flipped the radio on. We couldn't decide which was worse, being misinformed by our neighbors about what was right around the corner just out of reach, like dying for American cheese, being misinformed by the national media like the rest of the country, or having the local media feeding us a hybrid of the two. Someone on the radio described how the convention center had become a war zone. I opened another bottle of wine. A gunshot went off around the corner. It dawned on me we should have my birthday party here tonight.

An ambulance almost hit us on the way back to Jackson Square. We spent another couple of hours cleaning the square, then I sat on my balcony waiting for NPR to call, watching helicopters drop balloons of water onto the still-smoking warehouses just downriver. A family across the street was pushing a wheeled soda cooler—one of those waist-high cylindrical ones that sits near the register packed with ice and single cans—as their youngest daughter trailed behind, wiggling every door handle and piece of plywood along the way in case anything was loose. She tried to get her little fingers between the plywood over the Ripley's *Believe It or Not!* Museum's doors, but couldn't. It was all so casual, routine, now. They did not see me. It was the most memorable image I would take away from this entire catastrophe.

I thought about Nagin's tirade last night. I tried to remember one piece of advice, or assurance, or guidance he had given us, his citizens who, as he pointed out, were in such distress. And I could not. I tried to remember one specific solution or plan he had detailed to help fix some part of the city. Again, I could not. I wasn't quite sure what state's rights—a law decreeing that the governor had to officially ask for federal assistance before the feds could step in—had to do with giving Indonesia aid for the tsunami, nor the war in Iraq. (Later, I'd find out Governor Blanco had requested this two days before the storm came, which only made the mayor seem more ill-informed.) All I could remember was him blaming others.

T-Nasty came tearing up on a Vespa and yelled up to me, "I found cold beer! Boom ka-*boom*!" I tossed him a key. He came up and tossed us a couple of slightly cool Miller High Life ponies. "I found 'em at 2256 St. Claude. It's that karaoke bar, I do believe. I grabbed five ponies and headed this way and almost got hit twice by the same ambulance and it was flying down Elysian Fields and then I see it just take the back end off a truck full of cops. *Booooooom.* It spun the thing in a three-sixty. *Boom!* And you smell gas and all of that. And the EMS guy's trying to talk to the cops who are all laying out on the ground, he's like 'I'm asking you, are you okay?!' and there was no response. I said I'd go radio somebody and let them know. That ambulance ripped the whole tailgate off. Damn, wow, look at that, those balloons of water they're dropping on them warehouses over there, they're so small. They must be afraid of picking up a scuba diver."

The phone rang in the kitchen. It was NPR. I spent ten minutes updating Neal Conan about everything we'd seen over the past few days, about the Krewe of Nagin, and our frustration that there were no supplies coming in for those people who needed them, how water was so scarce we were washing our hands with vodka. While I was on the phone, TnA, then Derek, came into my apartment. They were standing around me in the kitchen drinking my Guinness, passing Derek's new bottle of Scotch around. After Neal ended the interview by wishing me happy birthday, Derek told me he had spent a couple of days uptown helping out an elderly couple too scared to leave their homes. The Scotch came from an uptown Rite Aid, which he'd roamed trying to help someone, who turned out to be Huey Long's grandson, find something to treat the cuts on his arm. All the first-aid stuff was gone. "I kept telling him," said Derek, "I was like there's the vodka, that works for that. But he wouldn't touch the vodka, absolutely refused, said it just wouldn't be right. But he did get himself a nice day planner."

The phone rang. I guess that's how long it takes to find someone's number. A woman who'd just heard me on NPR needed me to go check on the mule barn on Rampart Street. She used to drive buggies through the French Quarter and was sure no one was there taking care of them. She was afraid they'd drowned. She wished me a happy birthday. The next caller, through her sobs, also wished me happy birthday, then asked me to rescue her cat. The next one, also crying, wanted me to feed a dog way uptown which was virtually impossible. The next to check on a retirement home just outside of the Quarter, this woman's grandmother and others were trapped there, and no one knew about them. They passed the Scotch around me as I scribbled it all down frantically, frustrated that I wouldn't be able to do much before curfew today. I promised them all I would do what I could tomorrow.

An NAACP official from California called to reprimand me for going on about how well my friends and I were doing when the poor people at the Superdome were suffering, and that there were a disproportionate amount of blacks being disenfranchised, and he scolded me for saying they were waiting for a handout. I clarified what I had said, which was not that they were waiting for a handout, but rather that no one in the Quarter had their "hands out," and explained that people of all classes and races were here in the Quarter getting along well, and some of the people standing beside me in my kitchen did not have a dime in the world, nor even any belongings anymore, and how the hell do you know what's going on down here?

"Look, Mr. Clark, let's discuss the real matter at hand," he replied. "Iraq."

"Huh?" I said. "No, no, the matter at hand is my use of the words 'hands out,' and I'm sensitive to that." I wanted to get off the phone because I didn't have call waiting and others were probably calling about things I could do to help them. I assured him I did in fact understand his concerns, and agreed with him about my improper word usage, and genuinely promised to rectify my mistake should NPR have me back on, and so we ended cordially with him calling me "a gentleman and a scholar."

I made a short list of things I could do for the few desperate people who got through until the phone stopped ringing. T-Nasty had left to find Tayl. On my balcony, Derek was still recounting his long trek back from Uptown today. "Turned my ankle somewhere on Tchoupitoulas, last four miles hurt like hell. I walked by the convention center and the helicopters were getting thicker and thicker and I realized they're using it as like a staging area now. And from what I heard it was like a full on military assault on the convention center, the way the cops and the media and everyone's making it out. But it looks the same as it always did. It's not burned and there's not bullet holes or bodies hanging out of the windows. And then past that, the military presence gets heavier and heavier. Humvees are all right alongside each other taking the roads up, I kept expecting the guys with M-16's sitting on each to stop me, but I just waved at them and kept walking. Then there were more trucks, like the Texas Parks and Wildlife people are here, some Georgia sheriff's department is here. But FEMA can't find us on the map, I guess."

"Do we need to send them smoke signals?" Ty said, gesturing to the gray-and-black fire clouds consuming the sky on either side of the Quarter. The fire that started at AJ's last night was now spreading warehouse by warehouse toward us. And it looked like the aquarium was burning at the base of Canal Street. "Might have to go commandeer us a shark or two so we have us some meat to stick in those taco shells," he said.

I asked Derek about all the looting and gunfire we'd heard about uptown.

"Haven't seen any of that at all. Strangest thing up there really is that there's a couple places along Napoleon Avenue where people have cleaned up all the sticks and stuff from their yard and so it's odd, this perfectly green lawn like nothing ever happened with all the devastation around it."

He passed the Scotch to me. It was Macallan Single Highland Malt. I could see him perfectly well limping eight miles through the city, past the convention center and the military, sipping on eighteen-year-old Scotch, waving hi to everyone he passed. "It'll make you sound Scottish. All the top shelf in that Rite Aid was untouched, except for the Crown Royal," he said, his smile pushing the scar up his face where it caught the corner of his eye. "Same thing with Sav-A-Center. I got some Estonian vodka. All the wine was untouched too. And all the Chimay. Grabbed six bottles. All I had was my lighter so I was looking at the good beer."

"We know all about the imports," I said.

"Winn-Dixie too," he said. "The only thing left was like Guinness and Harp. Until then I'd been drinking warm Bud Light and Coors Light—you do what you gotta do in times of emergency."

"We gotta get the fuck outta here!!" It was T-Nasty, he was tearing up Decatur Street toward us, yelling up at the balcony, wearing nothing but his .44 Magnum and cutoff camo cargo pants, long red hair and eight-inch goatee shooting behind him in the wind. "Right now! There's these squads of guys with machine guns and they're forcing people to the convention center. See y'all at the Compound!"

"Convention center?" said Derek as he shuffled out the door behind TnA. "Haven't heard about any convention I need to attend."

While Katherine grabbed some food and stuff for the evening, I threw my seersucker suit on over my bathing suit. Labor Day was in two days, so there was a good possibility this would be my last chance to wear the suit until Easter next year. I didn't bother with a shirt or shoes, just the Aqua Socks, my only accessory the survival knife fastened to my waist.

By the time Katherine and I reached the Compound, the rest of the crew—TnA, Tayl and T-Nasty, Petrovski and Derek—was already there, safe and sound. T-Nasty was tossing bottles of beer and white wine into the pool. I took seven cans of Labatt's and stabbed quarter-sized holes in their sides with my knife, handed one to everyone, made a toast to this place which henceforth would be known as "The Compound Commune," cracked the top, and sucked the beer out of the bottom in two seconds flat.

New friends José and Anna showed up bearing the hurricane nutritional pyramid: a bottle of Johnnie Walker, a ten-pound chunk of cured ham sealed in foil (prosciutto), and a package of cheese puffs. Apparently the owner of Central Grocery had let José have at his stock before he evacuated. A few others showed up, too, until we figured we had a good percentage of the people left in the Quarter.

We found a large grill and a couple of packages of charcoal in the garage, and a skillet inside one of the apartments. We threw the skillet on the grill, cooked up two cans of chunky chili with beef, one can of spicy chili without beef, a can of corn, and assorted vegetables from AJ's. Then we barbecued hot dogs and Boca Burgers. A few more people, friends we'd made in the last few days, joined the party. We swam and drank and ate and danced and swam some more for beers at the bottom and all the while Derek and Petrovski traded turns at the guitar, making up songs.

Katherine explored the units we had keys to, and discovered the land line was working in 109 on the ground floor by the pool. I called my mother in Washington, D.C., who before the storm had been planning on coming to New Orleans, the first time in five years, to see me for my birthday. She had my younger brother on the other line, a Marine lieutenant serving his second tour in Iraq (the poor woman—one son in Katrina, one in Baghdad). She put us on three-way, then let me talk alone with my brother for a while. I hadn't spoken to him since last Christmas. He said he was coming home next week and was going to fly to Baton Rouge, buy all the guns he could at Wal-Mart and get me out himself and was I out of my goddamn mind for staying? Petrovski came running into the room to show me how he'd just learned to bite a chunk out of a beer can. He ripped the thing in half and blood gushed out the corner of his lip. As he ran back outside screaming, leaving spurts of blood on the floor I would have to clean, I assured my brother we were okay, that what he was seeing on the news was not the French Quarter.

We all jammed out until Petrovski, then Derek lost the ability to form words or chords and we dropped off around the pool one by one, couple by couple, in the flicker and flutter of moths' shadows, falling away from the heat and the water and the hurricane for the first time.

12

I woke in a pall of sweat and insect repellent, gasping for air in the dark and heat, arms and legs burning with mosquito bites. I was in a bed. There was noise. Someone had left a radio on, static. I could feel Katherine looking at me in the darkness. "Where are we?" I asked.

"The bottom of the river."

"Really."

"Listen to it."

"Really."

"217," she said.

I remembered now finding the door to this unit unlocked, sneaking away from the rest by the pool. She laid her head down on my shoulder. Two mosquitoes vied for my left ear. I let the victor have it, leaving only the static, heavy and tumbling over itself. "I found it on the radio that was in here," she said. "But I don't think it's 1460 AM. It's almost every channel now. The world's gone now."

"Is it day?" I asked.

"I don't know. I've been listening to it for a long time. You were talking in your sleep."

"What did I say?"

"It wasn't making sense," she said. "I asked Tayl about it last night, walking on the bottom of the river, because he used to be a river pilot. You knew that, I guess. He says that there's catfish bigger than humans down there and whole trees shooting down toward the Gulf. But I told him how that guy Eads did it back in the nineteenth century in a forty-gallon whiskey barrel. How after his wife died he'd go down to salvage ships, and walk the bottom alone with his sorrow dark as space—" She slammed her hand down onto my chest.

"Jesus!" I said.

"I heard a mosquito there. Sorry. Where are you going?"

"The door, it's to the left here, right?" I asked. "I just want to see what time it is. And I need to use the little boys' room. And I need to blow the candles out by the pool. Shit. Ouch. That's a wall. And, shit, that's not the door. Wait, there it is. Here. Try to sleep, baby, please. You need to. I'll be right back."

"I wish you would. Be right back."

I felt my way down the hallway, knocking things over, the static falling behind me, until I came into the living room, still blacker than night. I found the door, opened it, then pushed the large shutters out onto a balcony. New sun tickled the roof of the slave quarters across from me. Sleeping bodies were strewn around the pool below me, candles melted, moths and mosquitoes and flies perfectly preserved in large dried wax puddles every color of the rainbow. I walked down the stairs to the patio, from the cobalt predawn air into the deep end of the turquoise swimming pool, hardly less wet, and lay at the cool bottom between bottles of Sauvignon Blanc until my hundred mosquito bites stopped burning. I bumped my head on a beer on the way up, cracked it open, took a small sip.

Tayl woke, stood up from a chair covered in Mardi Gras beads, and loomed over me, stretching. Then he looked perplexed. "What was I going to do?" he said. "Damn . . . I know I had something to do today."

He looked all around him.

"Oh yeah: sit down."

And he sat back down.

"While you all have been sleeping I've been plotting methods to establish my dominance," he said. "Make myself the Lord of the Flies, if you will."

"So, your methods, what are they?" I asked.

"I'd show you right now. But I don't feel like standing back up."

"I bet that's your first one," I said.

Derek picked up his hat and guitar. "Well, I guess I better get going," he said.

"Oh, you gotta get to work?" said Tayl.

Derek paused, cocked his head, squinted at Tayl, then me, looked down at his feet, scratched the back of his head. "Oh. Yeah. That's right." And got into the pool.

I carved some thin slices of prosciutto, crammed them into a couple whole wheat tortillas with some Grey Poupon and leftover grilled onions and peppers and a dab of cold chili. I handed one to Tayl and ate the other myself. Petrovski was saying something but I couldn't hear a word of it because there was another Black Hawk overhead.

"Sky rage," said Tayl, as the chopper's thunder rolled away. "You know, like road rage. The way these helicopters are killing conversation, we're all going to develop sky rage."

"—and there's bodies all around my place, man, oh wow, oh *boom*, man," said T-Nasty into his phone hammering the air for emphasis with his free hand as he emerged from the garage. His cell phone alone had started working.

Tayl suggested we ride the rest of this mess out on his sailboat on Lake Pontchartrain. It had a generator and plenty of space and, most important, it was probably miles from any police. We just needed to find a relatively dry route to get us and our supplies there. T-Nasty threw his orange reflecting vest on over his bare chest, .44 Magnum dangling out of it, hopped on the scooter, tooted the horn a couple of times and took off on a recon mission. I went back up to 217, followed the sound of the radio into the bedroom without bumping into anything. Katherine was asleep. I kissed her cheek. I could hear the mosquitoes through the static all over her naked body.

I went to check on the retirement home in the Central Business District, one of the many tasks I'd agreed to the day before. Everyone was accounted for and nearly evacuated. On my way back, I passed media trailers camped almost bumper to bumper along Canal Street's dry neutral ground as far as I could see. A couple of reporters were standing in the ankle-deep water in the street doing broadcasts. One guy was wearing a wet suit. Trucks and cars ranging from heavily tinted Suburbans to old Corollas poured into the Quarter past me. They simply had TV taped across their doors and windshields in various colors. I found the house on Orleans Street where I was supposed to rescue a cat from the kitchen. Its owner had told me yesterday that the only way to get in was to climb on top of the garage, then down into the garden on the other side. The garage roof was about twenty feet high. I walked down to Johnny White's, busy as ever, and asked the bartender if they had a ladder.

"They don't have a ladder!" said some red-faced ponytailed man beside me.

I asked the bartender again. He replied that he didn't think they had a ladder.

"I told you, goddammit, they don't have a ladder!" said the red-faced man. "Why do you have to ask again?!"

I asked the bartender if he knew where I could find one.

"Goddammit! You just did it again! You ask again and I'll—"

"You know, you're the first pissed-off dude I've seen since the storm," I said. "Good for you."

The bartender told me to go ask some guy named Señor Petucci, who was sitting on the step outside, holding his cane in one hand, a Miller High Life in the other. He was wearing a tank top undershirt tight over his sagging chest and shoulders, tucked into navy blue slacks, dress shoes, big glasses, and perfectly coiffed white hair. He had a teddy bear droop to his cheeks that made his face one you had to be a real asshole not to love immediately. He asked me which house it was. I told him the address, pointed down the street.

"Oh yes, Martha," he said as I helped him up. He had no accent yet he was more meticulous in his speech than a native speaker would ever care to be. "I know everyone on this street," he said, measuring his words perfectly before pouring them gently into my ears. "Please, call me Perkins. I am Perkins Petucci. This is where I live. How is she?"

"She's in Atlanta and she's crying about her cat."

"Well, let's go get that ladder, Joshua. I have a forty-foot ladder. But I'm not going to climb it. I have the vertigo. How old do you think I am?"

"About sixty?"

"I'm eighty-one."

"That's okay. I'll climb it."

"And I'll hold it."

And so he did. I hated heights. But I made it up onto the garage roof, then hauled the forty-foot ladder after me, dragged it across the roof, lowered it into the courtyard and descended. The shutter doors were already open, the cat door unobstructed and the cat was nowhere to be seen. I cleaned two ashtrays and filled them with water from the bottle I had in my bag.

I found Ashley and Derek and Petrovski in Jackson Square wearing red shirts, sweeping leaves, while Ty was being interviewed by NBC, saying, "It's our neighborhood and we're set on food and water, so we gotta do something, so we're cleaning up. Jackson Square here is like the heart of the city. Tomorrow we'll start on Bourbon Street. We're called the Krewe of Nagin. Jesus Christ, watch out—"

T-Nasty almost ran over the cameraman on his scooter, his vest flying back like a small fluorescent cape, his Magnum big as a third arm. He screeched to a halt beside us.

"Krewe of Nagin, yeah, *boom*, yeah, fuck, we're totally trapped! I was trying to find a way to Tayl's boat, couldn't get ten blocks lakeside of the Quarter in any direction. Some places, okay, in some places the water's receding, and it's leaving bodies in its wake, one was still sitting upright in his wheelchair. It's receding but it's not enough. It's not enough."

He zoomed off. NBC took off in the other direction. "It's getting to the point where we can't work because every time we look up there's a microphone or camera in our face," said Ty. "Soon as CBS was done, these NBC guys hit us. We need a PR person—" An Apache helicopter cut off whatever else he was going to say.

"I'm not quite understanding why there's so many helicopters and no relief drops on the ground," said Derek, when it was gone. "I'm sure there's some reason. I just don't know what it is."

A resident walked by and told us he was going to get his costume because the Decadence parade was on for two o'clock and people were meeting at Johnny White's. We'd forgotten this was normally Southern Decadence weekend, a gay and lesbian celebration that draws tens of thousands from around the world, culminating in a Sunday parade. I headed back to my place to get costumes.

"There's still no water," Katherine was saying in the kitchen, on the phone, practically in a whisper. "Everything is gone. I can't really talk now."

I walked into the kitchen with my box of costumes as she was hanging the phone up. "Do you want the pink wig or the Santa one?" I asked.

There was a car parked outside Johnny White's, one I'd seen often since the hurricane. It was a small blue Ford Escort station wagon with a doughnut tire and several gas canisters and shovels bungeed to its top and Red Cross symbols made with magic markers on typing paper taped to its windows. Inside was an ungodly amount of medical supplies and a sleeping American Indian, the same one who brought us the big brooms just when we needed them yesterday.

While we were leaning against the station wagon in our coconut bras, sarongs, and wigs, waiting for the parade to start, a huge, bronze-skinned Greek came stumbling into the bar, bleeding all over the place, saying he'd just been beaten by three guys with two-by-fours on Canal Street for five dollars. His left ear was hanging off and the skin was punctured all down his left side, from his shoulder to his hip.

The Indian awoke, sent Bartender Bart to get a sewing needle and some fishing line. Bart returned, gave the man a shot of Jack, shoved a wooden spoon in his mouth and held him in a headlock while the Indian reconnected the pieces of his ear with a single stitch. I asked the Greek what his name was. "Vasilios, brah. Just call me V. Holy God!" The spoon splintered then broke in his teeth and he passed out. The Indian tied the thread together. The parade started.

We didn't make it around the corner before the NOPD shouted through bullhorns and told all two dozen of us to get to our homes or to the convention center right now. Katherine and I wound up on the sidewalk in front of Molly's in our coconut bras, drinking warm cran-berry and vodkas, munching on Special K, while the owner, Monaghan, eyes going glossy, told us that in addition to the fires in a furniture store on St. Claude Avenue and in Saks in Canal Place, the warehouse fires had still not been contained, and now they had spread across the street from his house in the Marigny. "I spent four years building that house," he said, fighting back tears. "I don't want to build it again."

"You know damn well they're not going to let the fire come into the Quarter," said Jelly when Monaghan went inside. Jelly was one of the attractions of Molly's.

"And how they going to stop it?" asked the guy beside her. "There's no water in the hydrants. And last I checked there's no space between any buildings in the Quarter. Soon as first one goes up, which shouldn't be long, we'll burn like we did in 1788 and 1794 and all those other times."

Jelly took a sip of her gin martini. "We'll see," she said. "Right now, I'm more worried about people than I am fire. You know, someone tried to kick my apartment door in this morning. I was going to chase him out and shoot him down the street so I don't have to step over him whenever I go out, but he took off before I had the chance."

"It's back on!" screamed two slender boys wearing Speedos with silver glitter and big silver swirly things on their heads. One was sitting on the bicycle seat with his legs out while the other one pedaled down Decatur Street. "It's back on!"

People sprang out of the bar. "Holy shit—electricity?!" shouted someone.

"Decadence!" said the bicyclist, who then hit a fallen branch and they both went head over heels, smashing their head gear, heads, and noses.

We gave them napkins and sent them up to the Indian, then joined the parade along with TnA, who'd been off getting some Gatorade for an elderly lady who refused to leave. Ty was wearing a colonial tricornered Minuteman hat, Ashley a bikini, carrying a parasol. We were all chucking Mardi Gras beads and condoms, unloading them upon the few people who came out of their homes. Military helicopters took turns swooping in low above us, close enough to see them giving us thumbs-up. "Thank God we don't live in America," said a girl swinging an umbrella through the air beside me. The next time I turned around, TnA had disappeared. I didn't see them until an hour or so later when we were cleaning up Jackson Square. Everyone was there this time. Tayl and I found a thirty-foot-long piece of copper roof flashing and used it to sweep wide sections of the debris into piles, while the others went behind us with brooms and Petrovski and Derek pulled trees out of Café Du Monde across the street.

"When the parade went by the voodoo place, Ashley and I stopped to speak to the voodoo priestess," said Ty. "She brought us inside and gave us a voodoo marriage, blessed us, anointed us with incense, candles, everything. It's the one thing we didn't have, that I didn't realize we were missing."

Before we knew it, what had seemed a bottomless mess covering every last stone of the square was now in massive but neat piles at every corner, and Jackson Square was cleaner than we'd ever seen it. Curfew was approaching. Katherine needed to go back to my apartment, she said she'd left something there, wouldn't tell me what, turned, and walked off. I told her to wait, but a helicopter came overhead, and it was as good an excuse as any not to follow her.

On the way to the Compound, we passed four policemen camped outside the A&P. This and the Walgreens below my apartment were the only two major sources of necessities in the Quarter. The cops said it was cool what we were doing, cleaning the neighborhood up, and warned us to stay away from the convention center. They called it "a war zone," told us to stay inside because it was so close, only a couple blocks out of the Quarter. "It's awful. It's like Baghdad," one said. Several times I'd heard police ascribe that word to various parts of the city in the last couple of days, to describe the burden they were under. And I remembered talking to my brother in Iraq last night, how he told me about the first Marines who got to the site of a suicide explosion would play a game to see who could find the bomber's penis first. That, the face, and the toes, were typically the only things left whole, usually very far apart from one another. Of course, I was not my brother, nor was I one of those police who were very likely under duress hitherto unseen by any American police force, so who was I? A guy in a bathing suit and aqua socks with a broom and a big knife I knew I would never have to use, thankful for his gourmet jalapeño pretzel bits.

Further down St. Peter, a couple of reporters from the *Miami Herald* joined us. They'd interviewed Ty earlier and asked if they could spend the night in the Compound to do a story. As we were approaching the gate, an armored personnel carrier with a police truck in tow roared up to us: "Get to the convention center! Right now!" screamed the guy hanging from the APC's door, pointing in that general direction. He looked military, but it was hard to tell the difference between soldiers and cops anymore. "The army is going to be kicking down every door! You must leave. Right now!"

I said yes, of course, we're only going to get our belongings. I wanted to pretend we were walking further up St. Peter, not to give away the location of our domicile, but there were other men with helmets and vests and machine guns just ahead of us going door to door making sure no one was left. So, we walked inside the Compound, went to the back of the patio by the pool, huddled together real quiet and out of sight of the street, nervous and sad. No one knew what to say. The reporters just sat there with us. It seemed this was the end. Their story, tonight's barbecue, the Compound, was over.

We stayed that way for fifteen minutes. A truck pulled up to the gate, screeched to a halt. Doors opened and closed. Everyone froze even stiffer, wide-eyed, held their breath. There was banging at the gate. Shit. More banging. Ty and I simultaneously mouthed the word "Fuck."

Then, Katherine's voice calling for me. I sprinted up to the gate. Katherine waved to what looked like a father and son, civilians apparently, in a blue pickup truck. She thanked them for the ride. Then, without a word, she strode past me into the Compound, past all the others still huddled together, walked upstairs, opened the shutters to 217, went inside, and slammed them behind her. "Think I fucked up," I whispered as I regrouped with the rest.

When twilight fell, Ty and I crept up to the gate. We poked our heads through the iron fence beside it, and looked both ways down the street. There was no one there. We turned around, looked back at the courtyard. The place looked too nice. Any casual passerby could see someone had clearly been living here since the hurricane. Even in the half of the courtyard closest to the street, which we never really used, leaves and branches were in piles, patio tables were upright, their chairs placed perfectly around them. So, we knocked them all over again, spread some debris around that half of the patio nearest the gate. We took big banana tree leaves and weaved them haphazardly through the fence to hinder the view into the courtyard. Then we took two of the large green umbrellas that extended from the center of the tables, opened them and lay them on their sides so that the back half of the patio, where the pool and barbecue were, was effectively hidden from the street. We lit candles behind stairs and trees and flower pots, so they couldn't be seen from the gate. T-Nasty opened the Cactus Juice and passed it around, Derek picked up his guitar, stretched that scar down his face as he started singing, and the party was on.

We decided this is what happens at dusk. We made a pact to be inside the Compound at least an hour before curfew every night. I poured some whiskey for Vince, the *Miami Herald* reporter, and grabbed a beer out of the pool for the photographer, Travis. They kept asking us if we were sure we could spare it. "Let's just say that, at all times, there's a stupid amount of liquor in this town," I told them. "And without the tourists upchucking it on Bourbon Street, we're left with plenty."

Ty boiled some rice pilaf. Not sure how it happened, especially since, before the hurricane, I rarely touched red meat, but somehow I got assigned the task of slicing the prosciutto. I pulled the chunk of cured ham out of the thick gold foil. It was the size of a small child, thick and greasy beyond belief, like trying to cut rubber soggy with Crisco. I whittled away at large chunks of white fat to get at the meat. But it was worth it. Damn was it good. And it was the only real protein we had. I'd hardly put a dent in the thing by the time Ty told me that was enough, so I shoved the rest of it back into the foil. It was going to last us a long time.

While Travis walked around the pool taking photos of us swimming and cooking and talking, Vince drew us out one by one, scratching notes in his pad, breaking only for the occasional nip. "It's reaffirmed my faith in people," Derek told him. "It's extraordinary. I've never seen anything like this. We're all going to walk away better people."

Turned out Vince had been here since the Saturday before the hurricane, Travis since Wednesday, four days ago. "We didn't have lights so I saw myself in the mirror for the first time yesterday and realized I had a beard," said Vince. He was dark-skinned, good looking, thirtyish, with a kind face. Both were living in the Hyatt. I sat with them on some steps near the grill as Tayl lit the charcoal.

Travis: You know, I was over in Iraq in 2003. Body parts would be lay-ing out on the streets after a firebomb. You just accepted that as a fact of life over there. So, then I come here, and I've never been here before, and it's just a city with a reputation for celebration. The first day I was here there's bodies laying out on the street in front of the convention center. People started bringing them there. And the next day bodies floating in the Carrollton neighborhood. They just left them there. It seemed surreal because, it just doesn't happen here, you know? It didn't feel like America.

Vince: I'm thinking about doing a story about this, where you as a jour-nalist felt the need to put down your camera, in my case my notepad, and just help somebody. And I think all of us at one point—you know, I helped a little girl bring her bags to the Superdome, carried a baby—there's some points where I just say I can't be a journalist right now, I have to help these people. The best thing I can do is help them by telling their stories, but you know when it's right there in front of me, it's hard.

I helped this black veteran guy carry his stuff to the Superdome. When we get there he says, "Don't go anywhere, I'm going to go into the dome to find my family, please stay here by my stuff." So he disappears for at least an hour. I finally just gave up waiting, I couldn't stay there, and left his belongings there. I knew that second people were already looting it all. That's when it hits you, you know? I should have stayed. I didn't. I didn't and I was lacking and I've known this since that time, last Wednesday. It's like every man for himself. And that just sucks, because that's not the best way. I'll tell you what attracted me here to you guys tonight. Your sharing resources, food, camaraderie.

Travis: You know, maybe the thing that will stick with me most out of all this was this guy laying out dead in front of the convention center. And people were saying that he was shot by a cop the night before and they just left him. And all us photographers, we all took pictures of it. And at one point, we saw these police all decked out with full armor and machine guns, they stopped and took pictures of it too.

I grabbed the whiskey, filled Vince's glass back up, looked up at the closed shutters to 217, wished Katherine would come out and join us. The warm glow of candles wavered and bounded back down at us from the canopy of trees overhead, a shallow shelter from helicopters' searchlights sweeping the night above. No matter how much we drank, our beer and liquor supply never seemed to diminish. Travis couldn't believe we kept pulling beers out of the pool for him. For dinner, we made jambalaya from two boxes of rice pilaf, one box of Spanish rice, my finely chopped prosciutto, chunks of fresh tomato from AJ's, a bottle of Guinness (two crates of it had magically appeared on the bottom of the pool this morning), some white and red wine, Tabasco, and a couple shots of Scotch. For a side, we rolled up thinly sliced potatoes and garlic in tin foil, and threw that on the grill. As we were arranging the food so that people could serve themselves, Vince asked me to top off his drink. I informed him that he was holding the Planter's Peanuts can. Vince informed me that he did not care. I informed him it was half full of peanuts. Vince informed me that he did not care. I filled the peanut can. The peanuts and whiskey were gone by the time Vince sat down to eat on a set of stairs leading up to one of the balconies. He asked for another refill, then wolfed down a plateful, then got another one, said he'd hardly eaten the last few days, and certainly hadn't had anything anywhere near this good. He sat back down, finished his second plate, and promptly threw it up all over himself, the peanuts too, then fell asleep with his head between his knees, the food still steaming all over his legs and feet. I couldn't wake him up.

"What a waste," said T-Nasty, "he'll miss dessert." We sliced a bunch of apples thin, smothered them in cranberry apple sauce from an MRE— "Meal Ready to Eat" that we'd gotten from the military—sprinkled on crumbled pecans and a touch of brandy, wrapped them in tin foil, and grilled them for the time it took T-Nasty to smoke two cigarettes.

Across the pool, up in 217, Katherine and Ashley were sitting on a couch in the living room, a candle on each of the small tables on either side of them. When she saw me in the doorway, Ashley walked out, silent. Derek and Petrovski were singing "Have You Ever Seen the Rain?" on the other side of the pool behind me. "Baby," I said. "I've been trying to make sure everything's going okay out there tonight. I feel kind of responsible for this whole place, I'm the one that has the keys, I'm the one K.K. told could use it. I'm sorry. I wish you'd join us."

"You abandoned me," she said.

"I know. I never should have let you walk alone so close to curfew. I wasn't thinking. I had no idea they'd be doing a sweep, trying to get everyone out of the city tonight. I'm sorry about that."

"I've just been sitting here all night and you wouldn't come in. We need to talk."

"Okay." I sat beside her. "So talk."

We sat in silence. T-Nasty was gyrating to the music below us. Tayl had resumed occupancy of his beaded throne. TnA were smoking a joint. I put my hand on Katherine's belly. She took it in her hand, moved it off her stomach, held it between us. "My tummy," she said.

"What is it?"

"Nothing. I'll be okay."

"How long have you been sick?"

"It'll be fine."

Silence.

"The only's," she said. "Remember the only's?"

"Of course. And we've still got them. We're just sharing them a bit."

"I'm not so sure I want them anymore. The only's are lonely. That sounds funny."

"Baby, listen. Go back and lay down and I'll be in in just a bit. Turn the static on. I just need to make sure everyone has a place to sleep and everything."

I kissed her on the cheek and her eyes gaped at me. But it was only because she was about to cry. And that pissed me off. I walked out and closed the door behind me.

I opened unit 109, the one with the working landline, told Travis he could sleep on one of the beds, let T-Nasty have the other, and Tayl took one of the couches. TnA were curled up on a pool mattress they'd laid on top of a chaise longue. Before I could stop them, Derek and Petrovski walked out of the gate, yodeling something awful at the top of their lungs, and took off down St. Peter. Ashley looked up at me as I blew the last candle out, Derek and Petrovski's serenade dying in the distant night. I wondered what gifts they'd bring back. "You know, society would have to choose what they valued if they considered getting rid of Petrovski and Derek," she said. "Music and supplies and chaos. Or the alternative."

I finally roused Vince sufficiently to get him out of his vomit and to lay down on the landing at the top of the stairs. I wiped the vomit off him as best as I could with a towel, then rolled another one up and put it under his head. We read his article weeks later. The headline: COMMUNE ONE OF FEW BRIGHT SPOTS IN NEW ORLEANS. He caught the evening perfectly. Halfway through his article was the sentence, "Their commune will likely not last long; the city is under a mandatory evacuation order."

13

Sunrise found Travis gone, Vince, too, his footprints in his own vomit dried and crusted to the stairs where he'd slept. And Tayl, on the phone, trying to find a way out of the city and the same with T-Nasty, as though they were just calling a cab to go out for a while.

Derek pulled up to the gate in Ty's white Volvo station wagon. With all their belongings in there, there simply wasn't enough room for Tayl and T as well. And so Derek and Petrovski set off alone and that was that. "On to plan D," said Tayl, and he returned to his throne and began another round of phone calls. Ty and Ashley were the only ones who weren't trying to find a way out.

Katherine and I went to Canal Place to get my car. She still had no purse, no keys. The whole shopping center, its stores all falling somewhere between Gucci and Banana Republic, was ringed with National Guard. Two soldiers from Oklahoma escorted us up the ramps into the garage. They told us the press had made this thing out to be like Hiroshima, but all they ever did was sit around bored off their asses in this insane heat, looking forward to lunch time when they'd stand in line outside Harrah's Casino, now central command, and wait to drown their shitty hamburgers in enough ketchup to make them edible. They warned us that we would see a dead pit bull up on the sixth story. It took us forever to find my car, we were totally lost walking up eight stories through the whole winding garage. "You can't miss it," I kept saying. "It's an '86 Monte Carlo Super Sport with T-tops and huge flames painted all over it and SEXY BEAST written in purple over the trunk."

Finally, we found both our cars. Like most others, they were covered in paint that the storm had shaken from the ceilings, but that was it. We took the Sexy Beast—what Katherine had named it after we painted the flames on—and headed up St. Charles Avenue for the first time since the day after the storm. The road itself was abandoned and clean. Large piles of debris had been swept to the neutral ground. In the shadow of the interstate overpass was the trash of thousands, no doubt they had camped there to stay out of the heat. The further uptown we got, the more debris we saw. Cars were all driving down the wrong side of the road. There was a scattered police presence. The radio told us the police had done a sweep of the convention center.

We made it as close to Katherine's house as we could, a couple of blocks away, until fallen trees and power lines impeded us. There were about thirty soldiers standing on a nearby corner. We walked through a foot of water in the street to get to Katherine's. I pried the boards off her front door. Some of her books were wet. She lifted each one like it was a child, separated its pages and propped them open. We cleaned and scrubbed her refrigerator, threw out most of her food, put the rest in shopping bags to take back.

After my last NPR report, a woman had pleaded with me to rescue her dog, which was only about fifteen blocks from us now. We flew there minutes before curfew, Katherine protesting all the while. I found the black Lab alive, frothing at the mouth, and ready to bite my head off. I talked it down, poured it two boxes of Honey Nut Cheerios—all I could find—and some water and we tore back to the Quarter.

I had a sinking feeling as the Compound gate swung shut behind us at the moment of curfew. I knew they were gone. There was nothing but a note from Tayl, tiny, written on the inside of a matchbook, telling us the spare key to his house was under the plastic frog in his backyard. They'd left everything for us, food and beer and wine and candles and even T's two coolers. TnA came in a couple of minutes later. Ashley had called her brother in Houston. He worked for a trucking company, could come get her at noon the day after tomorrow with some police he knew. She would only go if Katherine wanted to go.

I said nothing. I had gone only eight different days in the last twenty-two months without seeing her. Katherine said she'd think about it. Ashley said she needed to know by tomorrow morning.

Katherine went into 109 to call her aunt in Ponchatoula, about forty-five minutes north, and her brother in Houston, to see about staying with them. While Ashley started preparing dinner, Ty and I looked for charcoal. We sat down together in the garage, whispered to one another in the darkness. Ty said there was no way he was leaving, he said he wanted to stay here with me, to help me get the story. I thanked him, though I knew he wanted to stay for the adventure, and to do what good he could here, more than anything. As much as we loved the girls and it was hard to imagine it all without them, now that four had already left us this morning, it seemed a good time for them to exit as well. The two of us could travel lighter. We fantasized going into "stealth mode," creeping through the Quarter, across balconies and rooftops at will, like ninjas. And when they did drag us out of here at the tip of a gun and throw us on a bus out of town, we made a pact that we'd simply get out at the first rest stop, and start walking back. Likely that would be Baton Rouge. We estimated that, at three miles an hour, it would only take about twenty-seven hours.

"But you know, it's not the same with Katherine as it is with Ashley," I said. "You know that. Katherine's a trooper. She might be able to stick this thing out if she sets her mind to it, but it's not the same. These conditions, I don't think they faze Ashley one bit, do they? She digs it."

"I think she feels she needs to get Katherine out of here."

"I hate it, but that'd be the best thing right now. I know that and I hate it and it's selfish of me. You know, I just found out she's been sick."

"Josh, we'll get them out safe. It's best for all of us. Then they can come back whenever the time's right."

"I'm afraid it's going to kill us, Katherine and me, if she stays."

"Was it like this before the storm? Were you all fighting before?"

"Well, I mean, I guess. Yeah, sure, we'd have some arguments. But the next day, none of it mattered. We just, I mean, I love her more than I ever thought it was possible to love someone. I mean that. Arguments, fights, they never weighed on me. I've never looked back at them. Problem is, here, we don't have a chance to pull back to our corners, exhale, and come back together. I don't know. It's just impossible to imagine us not together. I'd like to think these circumstances brought about new problems. So, I'm kind of like dismissing these arguments going on now, and if she decides to stay, any problems we have, it'll have to be because of the storm, not because of us, and time will take care of them. I will just have to deal with them like that. That it's not us, it's *this*."

"They might only get worse that way, if you dismiss them. And *this* might really be you guys."

"You know, this city, our home, I feel like Katherine's crying for it, and me, I'm smiling, trying to smile for it."

"We need both right now."

"And it's like we're standing on these opposite cliffs and we're all pissed and disappointed at each other's reaction to this thing, appalled even, we each think the other's pathetic, and there's New Orleans busted in the abyss between us."

We boiled instant brown rice with Cajun gumbo mix on the grill, threw in some tomatoes, garlic, red curry paste, and the obligatory prosciutto, making a new jambalaya, then grilled the Italian bread Katherine had gotten out of her house, and mixed up a sauce of garlic and canola oil to dip it in. We shared a bottle of Zinfandel and it was a great and calm double date, like that first night TnA had invited us to their apartment, but every word was laced with the uncertainty that this would likely be the last time we'd see the girls for who knows how long. And, after they left, it was possible communication would be cut off.

Dark figures appeared by the gate. We blew out the candles, stayed quiet until they passed. The four of us went to bed earlier than ever before, Ty and Ashley on a foam pool mattress laid out on a chaise longue by the pool—they chose to suffer the greater number of mosquitoes outside for the breeze—and Katherine and I in 217. We lay inches apart, held hands between us, our only sacrifice to the heat.

"Did you talk to your brother?" I asked.

"I just checked my messages. The guy with my purse, he's in Houston but he's coming back in tomorrow to get some of his computers. He said we almost stepped on his face that night after the storm, when we were walking through the Hyatt ballroom.

"Julio? Why didn't he answer us then?"

"Because his name is Jorge," she said. "I don't know how he got permission to get back in, but he said he'll drive over here around nine in the morning."

She leaned over, turned the radio on. Static, soft, layered like the susurrus of a city we once had, flooded the room. "I suppose I haven't had to think about it these last few days, what with everyone living here," she said. "But I wonder how my home is, the one I grew up in. It's right near the 17th Street Canal."

"You just sold it two years ago, right? Before we started going out?"

"We were supposed to split it all up, everything inside. My brothers, they didn't want any of it. It was good, being back here in New Orleans with Mom, in our house, before she died. My husband, I think, did not like me being away so much. He moved on to other things. And then I moved here. Home."

"If you go, I'll understand," I said. "I will understand fully, I'll miss you every single second, but I can't abandon this place now."

"But you'll abandon me?"

"No, of course not. We'd stay in touch every day. Don't say that."

We listened to the static tumble. It seemed to pick up rhythms occasionally, then just as quickly toss them aside.

"None of them called," she said.

"Who?"

"No one. Not my brothers. Not my aunts. No one. This whole time. Not one of them has even left a message for me."

She turned her head from me, blew out the candle, mosquitoes' shadows vanishing. I reached into her back as she curled away from me into the static. My hand fell away from her and I thought about emptiness,

emptiness of the river bottom, the emptiness of sensation down there, the emptiness of her house in Old Metairie, the emptiness of her voice-mails, and I prayed for the emptiness of my bed very soon.

14

Katherine found ripe plantains growing from one of the trees in the courtyard the next morning. They were smooth and sweet as vanilla pudding. Ashley sliced four of them lengthwise, then sautéed them in apple juice and vanilla extract, topped them with pecans, and we ate them between toasted croissants. As I poured us all grapefruit juice the radio said Nagin had issued a forced evacuation this morning, and that the police had caught a sniper and the fire department had managed to put a fire out at their supply house. I turned the radio off and we sat in the sun-freckled shade of the banana tree by the pool and enjoyed the breeze and the quiet in between helicopters and swatted at mosquitoes every once in a while.

"You know, these mosquitoes," said Ashley, finally, "the radio said they've been biting the corpses."

I laughed so hard I got a chuck of pecan stuck up the back of my nose. "You're kidding," I said. "It just gets more and more ridiculous. What would a mosquito want from a corpse? I don't believe that for a second."

"That's what they said," said Ashley. She was not laughing. "They said the blood could be diseased."

"God help us," I said, and let it go.

"I think I'm going to stay," said Katherine.

Ty and I cast fleeting glances at each other. "I'll call Ashley's brother, tell him not to come," he said, then he got up and walked into 109, leaving half his croissant on his plate.

There was a banging at the gate. It was Jorge with Katherine's purse. Now that she had it back in her hands, her entire face lifted. After we cleaned up, I drove Katherine down to Canal Place. The National Guardsmen on duty assured us it would be okay to get her car, and sent another soldier to find the lieutenant to get official approval. Apparently, they'd looted the shopping center pretty bad. Saks was where we'd seen the smoke coming from. The windows were smashed, mannequins torn in half.

Meanwhile, water was literally spraying out of my radiator and I was blocking the street. Katherine said she'd be fine, she was, after all, surrounded by National Guard and Canal Street had become a media camp. So, I kissed her goodbye and roared back into the Quarter. I found TnA cleaning up Bourbon and we swept debris into piles along the sides of the street for an hour or so, dodging as much media as we could, then took a break and walked down to Johnny White's.

The bar had refused to close even for a second and it was fast gaining the grudging acceptance of the various armed forces in town as a simple fact of life. Now there were cots outside, miscellaneous food items like animal crackers and chips piled up beneath the wall-mounted juke box and there were actually cases of bottled water—the Army had delivered it that morning!—in the corner between the two entrances.

Johnny White's was the antithesis of Molly's. Both bars were mostly wood: walls, floor, ceiling, bar, and stools. But, in Molly's, the wood seemed to somehow give off light, whereas Johnny White's soaked it all up, disappeared it into its walls. The whole tiny dive seemed to have been smoked long ago, while Molly's sprawled spacious and hip and clean of dirt and shadow and food and cots and water. This afternoon, inside Johnny White's, was a hodgepodge of sallow-skinned patrons, international media, various off-duty police forces from around the country, and Chester. "It's my birthday!" he shouted at me as I walked in. "I've been here thirty-five years!"

"In this bar?" I asked.

"No, silly billy, in the French Quarter, and for thirty-five years I've gone out at midnight soon as it was my birthday. But I couldn't do that this year because it's martial law."

"How old are you?"

"It's my birthday!"

Chester had a single dollar safety-pinned to his shirt over his heart. This was a New Orleans tradition—everyone would give you a dollar on your birthday until the safety pin couldn't hold anymore. But I had a feeling this one dollar was Chester's and he wasn't likely to get many more. The few people left in town who understood the custom were stuck with whatever cash they'd happened to have in their wallets when they went to bed Sunday, August 28, nine days ago. The only ones with any cash were the media, who didn't understand this tradition, and they had nowhere to spend it but two places: Molly's and Johnny White's. Which made the bartenders the only other ones with disposable income. And, for the rest of us, when we needed it, our drinks wound up on the expense accounts of the world's newspaper and television outlets. It worked out okay for everyone. Even Chester. He simply tapped the woman to his right, who was writing frantically on a note pad, and asked for another.

"Say, how do you stay so clean?" Bartender Bart asked me. He held out his long lanky arms covered in rashes. His skin, like most people's now, had taken on a yellowish tint: the dinge of days without washing, the dinge of the air, the same almost-invisible dinge that the slaves who dug this place into the Earth must have slept with, dinge that had settled over the last three centuries, that was suddenly eight days ago whipped to hell and was now trying to find some resting place all over again, now settling into every wrinkle and pore it could find. "All you guys, Ty and those two girls too, you all are so clean. How?"

I thought how to answer without announcing to all of Johnny White's that we had sovereignty over perhaps the only clean pool left in the Quarter. The phone rang. "That must be the devil calling to negotiate the terms of my fifteen minutes of fame!" said Bartender Bart. He picked it up, listened, sighed, "Yeah, I know, baby. I'm a movie star now."

When he got off the phone I asked how long he'd been working here. "I'm just a local drunk who they made a bartender," said Bartender Bart. "Right now I'm just working for tips. We're still twenty-four hours. If anybody wants to brave the curfew, we let them in because we're still open, you know?"

"What do the cops say?" I asked.

He pointed to one of the two entrances to the bar. "Cops say this is a magic line, don't cross this line. They say there's guys outside who are busting heads. And I'm like, thank God those guys who are busting heads can't cross that magic line."

He sipped on his iceless screwdriver, scratched his patchy nine-day beard with his mottled hands. "If people get tired and want to sleep, we got cardboard for them to sleep there on the floor. We told the owner we'd go to jail to keep this place open. We're helping the community, handing out food, handing out water, doctoring people up."

"It's my birthday!"

Beside Chester were three guys in button-downs and glasses whom I'd never seen before. They were all drinking Coronas. The guy in the middle had bushy short blond hair. He took his glasses off, wiped the sweat from one side of his forehead to the other. I stuck the big tape recorder in his cherubic but serious face. His partners were silent, looking down into the bar.

Where you guys from?

Czechoslovakia. We are two Czechs. He is from Slovakia.

Eastern Europeans, huh?

Czech: We don't like that. We are Central Europeans, actually.

When did you all get here?

Czech: We got here last Sunday, just before the hurricane. We were waiting for it. We stay in the SUV, on the sidewalk, anywhere.

Where's the worst you've seen?

Czech: We went to Waveland, Mississippi, it was the worst. No electricity, mud, people screaming for us to take them out. Black people, you know, very poor. They lost everything, screaming for us to get them out. Like animal.

But for me, personally, it was the whole situation at the airport. It was transport station. I saw the same picture in Africa. I cannot believe that I am in the USA. Because it was the majority of people in the airport were black and they had just some plastic bags with them and I don't know, they had nothing. People are dying on the floor because they had no medical help. I've covered five wars in my journalism and I have never seen something like that. Because every war has its rules. Every war. But this has no rules.

And I was very surprised the American Army didn't use train tracks for transporting people. It's funny for me, you know?

You been to New Orleans before?

Czech: I have been here a few times. And the first time I have been here, it's a long time ago, 1990, I knew it was my favorite spot in the USA. One of my first friends here, he's a horse-car driver. He's very crazy and very poor.

Sounds like everyone else in town now.

Czech: We were doing some shoot on this corner here today and I heard *clop-clop-clop* and there is my friend, he was in the horse car, very drunk with his hat in his hand: "Raaaaaaaa! I'm the first buggy driver in the streets again! All rides are free of charge today!" It was great moment. That is the best experience from this. And the worst was in the airport. I saw that situation the last time during the Rwanda disaster eleven years ago.

More people were piling into the bar, trying to get Bartender Bart's attention while Chester made sure each one knew it was his birthday. I grabbed three Budweisers and squeezed out. Just down the street, the 82nd Airborne was cleaning up the debris in St. Anthony's Garden behind the cathedral. A tarot card reader moaned about his bills. I asked if he'd seen it coming when a group of 82nd Airborne, red berets and all, showed up in a Humvee and started handing out enormous bags of ice. TnA and I grabbed two apiece and bolted, dripping sweet cold water against our chests, down our crotches and legs, all the way back to the Compound. Then we walked across the Quarter, to Burgundy Street, to a brick wall that had fallen out of a building into the street. I'd seen it the day before, blocking the street from emergency vehicles. It was a lot bigger than I'd remembered, about forty feet long, two feet deep, and clear across the street from one sidewalk to another. We hurled the filthy bricks onto either sidewalk with our hands. An NOPD cop car drove up. They didn't get out of their air-conditioned car, but they tossed cold waters, a real delicacy now, into our bleeding hands.

Eventually TnA said it was getting too close to the witching hour for them, and headed back to the Compound. I stayed until I'd gotten a path of bricks down low enough to where a vehicle could make it over them. As sun rose out of Burgundy Street, sure enough, a police SUV turned the corner from Canal, pulled up to the bricks, hesitated for a moment, but then drove over the path I'd finished. Then a couple of Entergy trucks drove through. I stopped the first one. He told me they might have power back on in a week. The second told me it'd be a month. I walked back toward the Compound.

The Quarter had once been a place of smells, step by step shifting from intoxicating to nauseating. Now, even those were gone, consumed by little pockets of quiet on these little streets that seemed littler still without cars parked on them and I realized that, for the first time since the storm, I was by myself, actually alone. I breathed the lull between wind chimes, their reflections dancing in the well of afternoon shadow same as ever falling down Spanish facades into narrow streets, colors only a bit scuffed up now, spray paint on plywood—THANK YOU GOD. NOW SAVE US FROM OURSELVES. KATRINA 2005.—things sweeping up into the air, and others falling, branches, leaves, birds, the white dove amongst pigeons, white parrot escaped to a fallen tree flexing his mohawk, a lime-green dragonfly skittering through shards of light flecked from CDs strung along a balcony down Burgundy Street, all of it alone with me until Greta Van Susteren rounded the corner flanked with armed guards, camera crew in tow, put a microphone in my face, and asked me what I was doing. I was speechless. She was so much hotter in real life.

15

"Less weeping, more sweeping, that's our motto," is the last thing I said to Greta before she led her entourage down the street, around the corner, and again I was alone with the balconied facades lining my path. Unlike homes across the rest of the city, one could never tell what lay within these shuttered French Quarter houses. I knew well enough it could be block-long courtyards like the Compound or invaluable antiques, or it could as easily be a single abandoned slum apartment. There was total separation between what the public saw and what lay inside. It was a gamble that thieves for the most part had not bothered with.

I lost the only's in Jackson Square when a stranger walked by, media clean, nodded, looked at the broom over my shoulder, said, "It's going to take more than a broom."

"Well, it's going to take more than one," I said.

I walked to the river, down the steps where we'd sat and danced and sang that night so long ago with Derek and Petrovski while Ty tai-chi'ed. On one of the pylons coming out of the wooden steps someone had written in black magic marker, NATURAL HABITAT RESTORATION.

The Governor Nicholls Wharf, the closest warehouse to me, just downriver, looked fine, and the two past that seemed to have minimal damage. The next ones lay crumbled, then one was smoldering, then the others past that had ceased to exist.

One of these warehouses here, I was not sure which one, whether it was still standing or not, belonged to the owner of Houmas House. He had had Katherine and me for dinner at the newly restored plantation a week before the storm. He had spent a couple of years and untold sums restoring the house to all its grandeur, and it was the most beautiful plantation we had ever seen. I hoped it was okay.

Two weeks before the storm I had driven down a winding road along this river just south of Vicksburg, Mississippi, until I found the Windsor Ruins, once the country's largest antebellum Greek Revival mansion, got out of the car, and looked up at the charred fluted columns, their iron Corinthian capitals holding up the sky and not a thing else, still crumbling 150 years later. We had a new Old South now, one that would wrestle between abandonment and restoration and renovation, as it shrugged off smoldering ashes yet again.

I walked back up St. Philip Street. They'd finally figured out a way to lock Flanagan's Pub. The sign on the plywood outside said APOCALYPSE 05. I was the last one back in the Compound a few minutes before curfew. I grabbed a plantain off the tree and managed to unearth a bottle of beer from the ice and it burned sweet sweet coldness down my throat, giving me a wonderful stomach cramp. I slouched into a chair beside Ty. We clinked glasses and watched thick summer sun pour up the cottage across the pool like honey and chewed our plantains. "Heard anything on the radio?" I asked.

"People calling in to ask for help. Problem is, no one knows how to get in touch with people here in the city. I'm considering giving this number out live on WWL, the phone that's working in 109, telling them after five o'clock, call me. If it's in this neighborhood I'll do it."

"I'd been thinking about that. I agree. Let's do it. If I go back on NPR I might even give it out on there."

But, when we broached the topic over dinner, Katherine wanted nothing to do with it. She didn't like what we'd be opening ourselves up to. We let it slide for the evening. Then I never brought it up again. Her cheeks had began to sag over her jawbone and the tiniest crease was forming in the center of her brow.

We ate all we could of the Españalaya—well-seasoned Spanish rice with prosciutto—and while we sat around the candlelit table finishing a bottle of Sauvignon Blanc and eating plantains until I felt sick, I took out the recorder and asked Katherine why she still didn't have her car. She found out she wasn't allowed into Canal Place because, as she was told, the FBI was using it. So, she walked through Canal Street talking to media, happily giving interviews to everyone from the Finnish to the French. They were quite excited to have a genuine fifth-generation New Orleanian to interview. Most of the few civilians they'd found still living here had by now become very disinterested with the camera.

Katherine: It was all white media people who had not been through the storm. It's an international media base camp. They truck in in air-conditioned trailers, cell phones, satellite dishes, cappuccino machines, they're editing out of SUVs; and there they are lining up to get food from the Salvation Army and one of them sighed and was like, "Oh, do you have anything else other than hamburgers and hot dogs?"

I walked all the way down Canal Street until you couldn't walk any more, until there was just water, I walked way past the media, down to Basin Street. It was very empty up there. I'll tell you, between Rampart and Basin is where the major looting took place, you could really see it. There's a boat at the portico at the entrance to the Ritz-Carlton. The only person down at that end was a black woman. I don't know what she was doing. She had no water and I watched her sit in the covered seat area of an old bus stop and she just put her head down and closed her eyes.

I met two gentlemen from Los Angeles who are here with Homeland Security. They told me that that they'd been here since Thursday, and they said the delay was on their end, not on New Orleans' end, they couldn't get authorization in time.

What were they doing now that they're here?

Katherine: He said that they were helping to peacekeep and with any kind of relief effort.

How?

Katherine: He didn't get specific. He disappeared for a while and came back with like eight shrimp jambalaya MREs and said, "I figured you'd like this being from New Orleans."

Before I got to your house on Decatur Street, there were some cops, and we were talking about how hot it was and I told them I needed charcoal, so one of them said, "Well, I could really use a haircut," and I smiled and I said, "Well, I can cut hair." I went and got some scissors from your apartment, and I came back, and he had lighter fluid but he couldn't find charcoal. And so, I cut his hair.

Then I roamed around Bourbon Street again, walking slowly, you know, single female, and these police, they rolled up and I asked where they were from and they're from near Lafayette, Cajun cowboy country, and I said, "What I need is a cell-phone charger." And so they took my phone then they just drove off. I hope I see them again.

She did. They picked her phone up the third time she called it and came by around eleven that night. I let the big press-on POLICE decal on the side of their generic silver Crown Victoria run along my fingers as they drove off. Like so many others, they'd rushed down here in whatever they could, too late to do much but recharge cell phones.

16

The night, as always, was a tradeoff between pulling the covers over our heads (turning the bed into a sauna) or trying to stay cool on top of them (getting marauded by mosquitoes). We switched futilely between the two, sleepless until dawn. And then the next thing I knew it was 11:20 and TnA had gone off to find medical supplies.

I called Parker Junior, in Baton Rouge, once again from the landline, trying to get him to smuggle things in for us, the same wishlist I'd given to Neal Conan on NPR after I invited him to my birthday party: mainly ice and purple cocktail umbrellas.

"Are you insane?" he said. "Do you know what's going on over there? Do you know what we're seeing on the TV?"

"C'mon, Parker, you got no balls."

"Actually, I've got three of them."

He was right. I gave up. Katherine and I breakfasted on prosciutto and a pineapple, the last fruit from AJ's. She pulled a *USA Today* out of her backpack. It was dated September 5, yesterday. "What the hell?" I said. "Where did you get that?"

"Someone on Canal had it. One of the media people."

"Holy shit. Let me see a section."

Sure enough, the front page had a picture of our Decadence Parade. And the next section, the one Katherine handed me, had a half-page picture of Bartender Bart sitting behind the bar at Johnny White's. The caption said, "The beer's still flowing at One-Eyed Jacks"—a very different,

and very closed, bar. On the letters to the editor page there was a picture
of a woman trudging through knee-high water and the caption read,
"The flooded French Quarter." Then I read the letter next to it. A woman
from Des Moines expressed her opinion that it was "time to leave the
lights off and close the door on New Orleans."

I folded the paper and set it down beside my plate and took a bit of
the pineapple. There was a coolness inside it somehow. It was the best
pineapple I'd ever had. I cut another slice from it. "I think I'm going to
ration the paper, only read one page a day," I said. "I imagine we're not
getting another one any time soon."

"Okay, honey."

"Soon as we get back up and running and I can catch a plane, I'm
going to Des Moines."

"Iowa?"

"Yeah. There's this woman I need to have a talk with."

"Okay, honey." She walked over, picked the last plantain off the tree.
"You want this?"

"No, I'm cool, thanks."

She peeled it, bit the top off. "This is really pretty good," she said. "Sure
you don't want a bite?"

"I don't want it. I've had enough damn plantains. I'd be happy to
never see one again in my life."

TnA came back and I took Ty in the Sexy Beast to feed his friend's cat
in the Bywater. We came to a screeching halt at the corner of Dauphine
and Kerlerec as a Humvee convoy came roaring through the intersection
in front of me. I guess they didn't know there used to be a stop sign
there. I realized it was going to be a hell of a thing navigating a town with
no traffic lights or stop signs or one-way signs and the only other people
on the road were eighteen-year-old army boys driving massive trucks.
There were three Humvees full of red-beret clad Airborne troops, then
there was a ponytailed guy in nothing but jean shorts guiding a wobbly
woman's Schwinn around small chunks of debris with one hand while
drinking a Corona and trying not to spill it with the other, then, about
three feet behind him, there were another three Humvees with more
82nd Airborne.

We went by what used to be AJ's produce warehouse, now a pile of
bricks, most of them charred black, some still smoldering, some sort of
metal scrap, maybe the coolers, reaching weakly up into the sky along
with wisps of smoke. The only other thing standing was a chimney-
shaped piece of the façade beside the road that read:

3122 Chartres
receiving hours 5:30 thru noon
Monday through Friday
947-3207
LOOTERS WILL BE SHOT!

We got to Ty's friend's place, opened the door, took two steps in, and the smell knocked us on our asses, literally. We sat there on the sidewalk for a bit, letting it waft over us into the street.

"Dude, it's your friend," I said.

Ty stood, took a couple of slow, deep breaths, and bolted back in. Shotgun houses got their name because if you fired a shotgun through the front door it would hit every room in the house and go out the back door. At that moment, Ty himself was just such a shotgun. I watched him fly through the first couple of rooms into the kitchen in the back while I sat there on the sidewalk and listened to my radiator hiss and water splash out onto the street. "You know, I've been thinking, maybe we should change our name," I said. "From Krewe of Nagin. I'm sure Mayor Nagin's doing something, but I don't know what. It might be in our best interest to remain politically neutral, you know?"

"Ahhhhh, God!" said Ty, reeling in the kitchen. Four cats came flying out of the doorway at me and scurried under the house.

"I mean, we haven't even heard one thing from him about what we as his citizens should be doing right now," I said.

There were gagging sounds. Then I saw the back doorway fill with light as he opened it, and Ty's silhouette hunched over, heaving.

"But what should we call ourselves?" I asked.

My radiator was really screaming now. Ty stood up, ran back into the kitchen and started pouring bottled water over the cat dishes on the floor.

"We need an acronym or something. Something catchy."

I heard dishes shattering, cupboards opening and slamming closed, Ty heaving, and finally running toward me. He jumped out of the house, slamming the door shut behind him, and collapsed on the sidewalk beside me. He grunted. My radiator was quieting now. Its water had stopped running into the gutter.

"How about NO END?" he said. "New Orleanians Eliminating Negative Debris."

"Yeah. That's good. Like, 'There's NO END to what we can do!' And Negative Debris can mean so many things too, like attitudes. C'mon let's run it by the women, see what they think."

The women dug it. We got in uniform, grabbed our brooms, and started on Orleans Street. Touchdown Jesus sat still as ever at the far end of the street.

I had always figured the Quarter's trash was indomitable. I just assumed that no matter how long we swept, we'd never be able to get it all. But, because there was no one here to instantly regenerate it, we were actually getting it all. So, I started leaving a few things, maybe a couple of wrappers, plastic cups, a beer can or two, on every block I worked on, just so it would look like home. It was about an hour later that it came to me. "Jesus Swept," I said.

Ty stopped. "Jesus Swept?"

"Like 'Jesus wept,' " I said. "Shortest passage in the Bible."

"I know, I get it," he said. "That's it."

We headed down to Ashley's frame shop halfway between Johnny White's and Jesus and made an enormous sign saying just that. London's Sky News filmed us. They couldn't quite get it together. When they finally got one take right, the interviewer realized he had a beer in his hand the whole time and they had to do it over. Then they followed us down to St. Anthony's Garden. The idea was to hang the sign on Christ's statue and climb up and tape a broom into one of his outstretched hands. We didn't figure this was sacrilege. We figured it was what Jesus would do if he were here—sweep. But the garden was full of 82nd Airborne sawing up the fallen giant oak. So, we settled for hanging the sign on the gate directly in front of Christ, and sticking a broom along the top of it. It took the Sky News team five takes. I noticed Christ was now missing an index finger on his left hand and the pinky finger of his right hand, in addition to the thumb TnA had. An officer from the 82nd Airborne falsely claimed they had all three and were keeping them secure.

Ty and I rolled, one at a time, two pieces of the oak's trunk down the street and into Ashley's frame shop. Each was four feet in diameter, three feet high. I said I'd make a coffee table out of mine, while Ty would call his sculpture "The Eye of the Hurricane." "Art out of disaster," said Ty. "This is what NO END is all about."

Fire trucks, almost a dozen of them, each from a different county in Maryland, rolled by like they were in a parade. We all cheered them. Then came the FDNY, then the NYPD. The crowd went nuts.

Someone stuck a mic in my face and asked what I thought of the NYPD being here. I said it was great and who are you with? They were with a local station in New York City doing a show on how the NYPD is in New Orleans. "These guys here, these are some of the ones that were really involved in 9/11," he told me. "They lost some guys that day."

Possum, the yellow-skinned bartender, refused to let us pay for our drinks because he'd seen us cleaning up the Quarter. Danny, a resident who, like some others in the last few days, had been hanging around Johnny White's enough to find himself working behind the bar from time to time, sat beside me.

How's it been the last couple days?

Danny: Well, okay. The cops tear gassed us last night. About eight last night the state police came in, looked like six or eight squad cars, and told us we had to shut down. Suddenly they walked out and everything was just burning. But we stayed open. Then the Eighth District police stopped by for a beer. They were still on shift. They got out of here soon as some media showed up. Somehow, media's able to ignore curfew.

Excuse me, you're from the media right? Are you allowed to be out after curfew?

Media woman: I don't know. It's kind of hard to enforce with the media. I've driven around after dark and never been pulled over. Are you recording that? Aren't you supposed to ask me first?

V: Hey, look at my ear the Indian sewed up. Healing up pretty good, brah.

What happened to your face?

V: Oh. I fell a couple times, you know. I fell off these kegs over here, brah. I'm trying to help them out here and I just keep falling.

Christ, half your face is open. How's your side, where they hit you with those two by fours? Oh Jesus, that's bad. I'm looking, Christ, I'm looking at black and purple sores and open wounds all down the left side of his body. You from here, V?

V: Nah. I'd only been down here for a couple weeks. I was living on Grand Isle. There is no Grand Isle anymore. I came down here for work and then the hurricane hit. I'm a finisher/carpenter. You got to do something. Until then, I'm just going to be sociable and drink.

You, are you with customs?

Customs guy: Actually, I'm with ICE: Immigration and Custom Enforcement. I don't wear anything that says ICE on it anymore because when I did people started mauling me for ice. Wish I had ice, haven't seen ice in six days.

And who are you?

Dale. I run a tattoo shop on Canal and Rampart. We're holed up at the Dauphine Orleans Hotel now, doing tattoos with a car battery. Just did the first one. It was a dragon, for a cop.

What are your hours?

Dale: Daylight.

Bartender Bart: Hey guys, I got the good shit. Got the good shit! Real SPAM.

How much is it going for?

Bartender Bart: Fifteen an ounce.

How many ounces you got in there?

Bartender Bart: Don't even know. But it's real. It's real SPAM, man. Just fifteen an ounce. I'm hawking it to the 82nd Airborne.

You. Who are you?

Darique: My name's Darique.

You got a life vest on, and—are those boxers? Where have you been?

Darique: I was just up at the zoo, ya. And up at the Audubon golf course.

What were you doing up there?

Darique: I was establishing that as a clothing-optional zone. A little swimming, ya, a little shampooing, a little waving at the helicopters.

Is it pretty deep? The water?

Darique: Ya, it's pretty deep.

See any animals out there?

Darique: Oh, dogs, that's the first thing, I went in and fed the dogs, ya, and geese and ducks a bunch of bread, ya. All the animals are kicking back, ya.

What about animals in the zoo?

Darique: They got generators, ya. They're not evacuating anything.

Oh, the zoo's dry because they're by the levee, is that right? So, did the helicopters enjoy you skinny-dipping?

Darique: Oh, ya. They got these Army guys to grab me and threw me on an Army truck and made me wear this underwear and shipped me down to the convention center. So, I broke down crying. They asked me there, "Do you really want to go?" I said, "Yes, yes, yes, yes!" They said, "Then go! Leave! Right now!" So I ran up here to Johnny White's.

What's Uptown like now?

Darique: Ya, sure. I watched them for like an hour and a half, you know—three helicopters circling around, SWAT teams of twenty men breaking through the windows, getting the animals out, the elderly, it's a total clean sweep out there, Uptown. Mandatory evacuation.

So, now you're down here hanging out because you can't go back up there?

Darique: Na, I'm going back up there! This is just a stop. Just to have a beer.

Bartender Bart: Check it out. This is what you eat SPAM with, this spoon. You don't want to get a fork near it.

Hey, Ty, y'all want to get tattoos tomorrow? Hey, ask that Indian dude if we can borrow his shovels and we'll go finish clearing a path through that brick wall on Burgundy Street.

It was much better with shovels. We could get five or six bricks on the shovel each time. We tore into it silently, just the scrape of shovel through bricks until there came the scraping of shovel against road. An NYPD car rolled up to us. The officers got out, introduced themselves. They kept asking us if we worked for the city. They were both younger than us, about twenty-five or so. Seven hundred of them volunteered to come down three days ago, they said. I mentioned that that was almost the amount of NOPD who supposedly took off, and I remembered how the NOPD officers wouldn't even get out of their car the day before. They told us they were living in some nursing home out in Harahan where there were generators and air-conditioning and running water. They asked if we'd seen the JESUS SWEPT sign behind the Cathedral and wanted to know all about New Orleans, how they could help the most. Ty and I went back to shoveling, trying to keep up a conversation until they drove off. We cleared a clean path through the forty-foot-long wall, wide enough for an ambulance or Humvee or fire truck to speed through—especially vital because it hadn't rained since the hurricane.

On the way back, we passed three guys standing on a porch. "Water's back on!" they all shouted. One picked up his garden hose and started spraying us while we danced a jig in the middle of the street and they cheered. Back at the Compound, the women had a couple of bags loaded with groceries. Running water made them very happy, even though word had already spread that we were not supposed to drink it, not even brush our teeth with it for the time being.

In the Sexy Beast's trunk, beneath an inflatable raft, a bunny costume, a Santa Claus costume, a cow costume, a blue tarp, and a bottle of Amaretto, I found a bag of charcoal. We threw it in the grill, doused it with Skol vodka, and lit it up. "What are we having tonight, Ashley?"

"Skewers of prosciutto, garlic, mango, and pear over a bed of couscous and apricot and almonds and pecans and corn with peanut satay sauce, some grilled carrots, and asparagus with a very nice marinade. On the carrots we sprinkled some teriyaki, sesame, five-spice, black pepper, red pepper, orange juice, canola oil, and red curry paste."

"Asian fusion, huh? So, Katherine, baby, where'd you get the bags from?"

"Well, the officers guarding the A&P let us in there to get some feminine products. I waded through the Odwalla juice on the floor, rotting food everywhere, until we got all we could carry. It's a whole new shopping experience," she said. "On the way home, the NYPD gave us water and said they were sorry about what they're seeing in New Orleans, and they're going to be here indefinitely."

"It's like 9/11 on steroids," Ty said.

"Sure. We made that connection, too," said Katherine. "And they understand, because they've been there and they know. But, I think this is a disaster that is so enormous and so vast, it overwhelmed Mayor Nagin, it overwhelmed the police force, it overwhelmed President Bush. Even though the hurricane was anticipated. There was no preparation for 9/11. It came out of the blue. All of a sudden, that Tuesday morning—"

"And everyone rose to the occasion," I said.

"Yeah."

17

A helicopter chopped into the whine and whistle of mosquitoes spiraling into my ears. After the tearing of the props faded, only the rolling thunder of its engine shaking the mattress, I realized it would not in fact land on me, there they were again, the mosquitoes falling like bombs into my brain. Morning.

I grabbed some toilet paper, walked outside, and was about to squat in my usual spot in the bushes by the parking lot when I remembered we had water. I made my way back into 109, and sat down on a toilet for the first time in almost two weeks. It was about how I remembered it. I flipped through a few of the *Maxim* magazines on the hamper beside me. In one issue, I found instructions on how to properly smash a beer can on one's forehead. The trick was that as you were bringing the can into your forehead you had to put a slight crease in its side with your middle finger to get it started so that when it hit your forehead you were effectively only further crumpling the can. Brilliant.

I realized we had unfettered, by law enforcement and by our own morals, access to everyone else's living conditions. How cool was this to see how total strangers lived, not when they were expecting company, but how they *really* lived. For the time being, it was all ours. We owned everything we could touch.

I took a cold shower and put on deodorant for the first time in twelve days, grabbed my shoulder bag, and went for an early morning walkabout. By the time I made it down to the river, I was sweating more than I ever had since the storm, stinking too, the deodorant like glue on my underarms. River traffic seemed to have returned to its normal levels. Tugboats went back and forth. A bright red cargo ship pushed downriver against the waves, leaned at a thirty-degree angle, and swung its ass out at me as it made the riverbend. Before the storm, New Orleans had been the biggest port in the world measured by gross tonnage. There was no more big black smoke pouring out of the aquarium from the generators. We'd heard almost everything in there had died.

On Decatur Street, shadows slid down façades, sun following them into the well of the street. The only morning traffic was Humvees filled with soldiers. But the ghosts of the French Quarter were still here, home. Those nameless, abandoned shells skulking in shadowed doorways, mumbling, eating out of trash cans, they were indestructible, like the first man we saw outside my door after the hurricane, who wanted to buy a cigarette from us. Now, the ones I knew, as much a part of this place as the streets they walk on, were at last poking their heads out of the shadows. Where their real bodies were, I had always wondered. And I wondered how many people had come here to shed a ghost or two, so they could go back to wherever it was they came from, whether that's dust or the suburbs.

James sat in the shadow of my own entryway, head down, eyes shaking up at me from between knees pulled tight to his chest. From his rare moments of coherence I'd gotten out of him that he'd been a decorated pilot in Vietnam. I believed him. When I worked the graveyard shift at Flanagan's, I would serve him hot coffee in the back. We spent many nights alone like this, me reading and fighting off boredom to the point of depression with cocktails, he watching the fuzzy *Playboy* channel on our small television. He never had a problem with leaving before daylight. The owner said she would fire any of us immediately if he was caught on the premises, Christmas and Thanksgiving included.

The streets were noticeably cleaner. The JESUS SWEPT sign was still hanging in St. Anthony's Garden. Outside the A&P, three cops stood guard, one sitting with his shotgun across his lap, eagerly studying a *Playboy* centerfold's statistics as if they were the morning's stock reports.

TnA and I spent the morning sweeping Dumaine Street before we took a break. "Dale!!!" we stood outside the Dauphine Orleans hotel yelling, as he'd instructed us to. "Yo Dale!" Eventually the tattoo artist popped his head over a fourth-story balcony.

A maintenance engineer named Special Ed let us in. The hotel had let all its staff and their families stay here during the storm. It didn't take long, in the days after, for them to tear the place apart, he told us. "They started breaking things for the sake of breaking things," he said. "Animals."

He took us into Dale's studio, room 405, overlooking Dauphine Street. We handed Dale a six-pack of Busch we'd brought him, just to start out the bartering process. I wanted Katrina written in black cursive on my right pec. Ty wanted just a "K" in the center of a hurricane symbol. And Ashley, the same with wings at the bottom of her spine. Dale donned Special Ed's mother's pink, horned reading glasses, and we each took turns holding a large Maglite so he could see well enough as he tattooed us with a needle hooked up to a car battery.

Dale heavily resembled the serial killer from *Silence of the Lambs*, talked like him too. As he did my tattoo, he told me about protecting his tattoo shop in the middle of the worst looting on Canal Street, how he stood guard between the pulldown metal gate and the glass door entrance with a baseball bat in four feet of water for three days, watching people tear apart the stores around him. "There was this one older guy, he just wouldn't give up. He saw our sign that said 'Jewelry,' you know? We sell body rings. So two days into it, he and some others finally broke through the gate. They were all older dudes. The younger ones just let it go."

"And?" I asked.

"And I started swinging. And they took off."

"With the baseball bat? So, they all were okay?"

"Yeah, they were fine, more or less. There was only one of them that never got back up. On the fourth day, during a lull in the looting, we took all we could into the Quarter and holed up at the hotel here."

While he was dotting the "i" of my Katrina tattoo with the hurricane symbol, the radio informed us Mayor Nagin was requesting twenty-five thousand body bags. I had always been told that a chest tattoo didn't hurt much, but it felt like someone poking my heart with sewing needles.

While he drew Ty's tattoo, I joined Ashley on the balcony. We gazed through the heat at Dauphine Street way below us. "Derek called this morning," she said. "He said, on the way out of town, every time there were cops standing in the road in front of him, he made it a point not to slow down and they always moved out of his way. He dropped Petrovski in Memphis on his way to Indiana where he is now. His expired tags were not an issue: Nobody batted an eye because they're from Louisiana. He could be throwing six packs and whores out of the window for all anyone cares, he said. He applied with the Red Cross, but they won't take him because he doesn't have health insurance."

Dale took twenty dollars and an eighth of an ounce of TnA's weed for all three tattoos. After Special Ed let us back onto the street, I asked how much an eighth of an ounce was worth. "About thirty dollars," said Ty. It was quite a deal.

We'd run out of charcoal, so that night we burned mounds of sticks in the grill until we had a bed of coals hot enough to boil water in the skillet.

"This is the last apple, and life after apples is gonna suck," said Ty, slicing it thin for the cobbler he was preparing after dinner. "I'm really concerned, to be honest with you. Dessert to me is an indication that civilization is still at a pretty high level. So many people don't have dessert. We have a quality of life when we have dessert that people all over the planet are lacking. But, don't worry, we're just gonna have to start getting more creative. I am not going to let us eat a big meal without something sweet to follow it up with."

After dessert, we got Katherine to call WWL, still the one radio station. While the other three of us stood across the pool from her, hunched over the radio turned down low, she explained NO END on air and asked Garland Robinette, New Orleans' most venerated talk show host who had recorded the now-famous interview with Nagin a week ago, "Why are you in Baton Rouge, honey? Why aren't you down here with us?"

<u>18</u>

The next morning, I suddenly remembered that I used to be a writer and a publisher. I hoped that a lot of those who had evacuated were writing about New Orleans, we needed that. And perhaps they were suffering more than us. Because, while they had air-con, we had something they didn't—New Orleans. I thought maybe there was a little of that I could share. By noon, after a bunch of phone calls and deliberation, I agreed to write four articles for Salon.com. Though I usually took my own photos, I set it up so that Katherine would be the photographer, giving us both something to do. I was confused all to hell about what else to do for the time being. So, I went to get my hep and tet shots at the EMS trailer that had set up on Dumaine Street across from TnA's place.

Over the last few days word had it that a new group called Restore the French Quarter had been asking about our clean-up crew. We'd heard their headquarters were down on Esplanade and Decatur, a fake speakeasy place that Harry Anderson, the judge from the old TV show *Night Court*, owned. We found Karen, blond, fortyish, perspiring in a muumuu, coming out of a side entrance. There was a plethora of food stacked up in the carriageway and a long wooden bar piled with liquor at its end. She said there wasn't another meeting until tomorrow morning.

Karen: I run Buffa's Bar. I had prayed so hard, you know, that the parts of this city I loved would still be here. And that's kind of selfish, but you can't pray for everybody all the time, you know?

I understand Nagin can't tell us in the French Quarter we can stay because then we'd be overrun by people we don't want here. But it would be nice if we could be reassured what we're doing is okay. Instead some people are holed up because they're afraid. We don't want much from anybody. We just need to be left alone so we can do what Quarter people do. You know, French Quarter people are so resilient.

I mean, the rebuilding is gonna start here in the Quarter and move outward, you know. We're a little bit of everything here. We're a gumbo.

You can put a gun to my head, I would rather die than not live in the French Quarter.

We headed down Bourbon Street. As always, any flow to conversation was destroyed by the helicopters. We'd heard two collided the other day.

"Hey, man, what kind of helicopter is that?" I asked a soldier standing in the middle of the street. He studied me for second, sweat pouring down his neck into his green fatigues, then looked into the sky.

"That there, that's a Chet Two Prop."

"Chet Two Prop, huh? And what about that one?

"That's a Huey."

"And which are the ones that were dropping those big orange balls of water on the fires?"

"That's Black Hawks. They pick up forty thousand gallons in those balloons."

"Forty thousand? Come on."

"Same ones been dropping fifty-five-thousand-pound bags of sand on the levees and when they ran out of sand they dropped fifty-five thousand pounds of rocks."

"So, how long you been in New Orleans?"

"We've been here since Wednesday. Why we couldn't get here before that, I don't know."

"Why couldn't you?"

"I wanted to. Lord knows I wanted to. But them motherfuckers in D.C., shit. They called my unit down there right after the storm and had us sitting there in D.C., doing shit nothing. Shit nothing! For two days! Getting paperworks and things done. Shit. I wanted to come. I mean what the fuck we doing in Iraq and we can't come down here in time to do nothing?! Huh? Huh?!"

"I don't know."

"Shit—" Another helicopter tore into his last swear. "—motherfucking Bush. I can't understand why we're here two weeks too late. The brass just kept saying, 'Get ready! Get ready!' you know, then 'Wait some more.' Hurry up and wait. That one was a Seahawk by the way."

"Seahawk, huh?"

"Shit."

"Can I record you?"

"Oh no, hell no."

"You're with the National Guard or the army?"

"Guard. Name's Private Washington. Shit. But I like this town. And I heard about that Mardi Gras. I'm a come back down for the Mardi Gras. I don't need all them breasts in my face, I just like the beer. Oh lord, yes, indeed! I love that beer. How late they let you drink beer until?"

"Till you're done," I said.

Katherine went back to my place to make some phone calls. I wandered up Bourbon toward Canal Street. I passed a House of Voodoo, a chain of shops that usually blasted the neighborhood with relentlessly repeating zydeco at ungodly volumes to try to draw in tourists and sell them overpriced hot sauces and beads and boas and other faux-New Orleans stuff. I remembered calling the owner Lenny Motwani while I was working on an article on noise pollution in the Quarter. "Sure, sure, I understand," he told me. "But let me be perfectly honest here: Our neighbors' well-being does *not* come into play."

As the water receded up Canal Street, so did the media. They were still milking it for all it was worth. Then there were police from every Louisiana parish and town, from every state from New York to New Mexico, fire departments and EMS from Sacramento to Cincinnati, Harbor Patrol, Border Patrol, Immigrations, National Guard, Army, Airborne, and hundreds of hired arms strapped to the bone. The men and women within two blocks of me had enough guns to successfully invade half the countries in the world. I realized it had been days since we heard gunshots.

There were barricades outside the Sheraton and dozens of armed men standing guard. I showed one my Sheraton Fitness Center membership card. He had a gold badge hanging down over his bulletproof vest, a 9-mm strapped to each thigh, a small machine gun hanging over one shoulder, a shotgun over the other. He said the fitness center was closed.

There was an amazing amount of single shoes strewn about the steps that lead up to Harrah's Casino. Why leave one shoe? I passed a couple of women wearing yellow t-shirts that said SCIENTOLOGY DISASTER RESPONSE. Another woman walked up to me and asked if I was from New Orleans. She told me her first graders had written letters for us and handed me a college-ruled page with perfect pencil cursive on it. It read,

Dear Citizen of Louisiana,

Hi my name is Jaclyn. I'm sorry of what has happened it must be hard. I hope you are well just as I hope your family is too. Good news, we are having a food drive for you and your family. You are filling all of our hearts with hope. With love . . .

Sincerely,
Jaclyn

It was the kind of thing my own first-grade teacher would have had us do. The dawn of understanding tragedy, and caring about it. It came later for me. I remembered them wheeling a black-and-white television into our classroom the day the space shuttle *Challenger* exploded. Now I was the subject.

She had a stack of them, she said I was the first local she'd found all day. "Are you from there?" asked another woman, pointing into the Quarter. Her red T-shirt said HURRICANE RESPONSE TEAM. "We're from Las Vegas, part of a Baptist ministry. We're here trying to talk people into evacuating." A younger girl walked up wearing an identical shirt. "We've been back that way all day," she said and pointed behind her toward Uptown. "We talked one lady into leaving. We haven't been into the French Quarter yet. We're going over there now."

The younger girl stared down Chartres Street deep into the Quarter, shook her head, moaned. "This is going to be absolutely hopeless," she said.

I wished them luck and walked across Canal back into the Quarter. They didn't follow.

Dr. Brobson Lutz almost knocked me over on his way out of Johnny White's. "Holy shit, Dr. Lutz! You're here."

"Yeeeeeeeeeeeesssss, of course I aim," he replied in his high-pitched twang. He poured half his Corona into a plastic cup, handed it to me. "Heeeeeere. That'll help prevent any gastrointestinal diseeeeeeeeeases!"

Lutz—pronounced Loots—was New Orleans' own unofficial surgeon general, and was actually once the city health director. He got an e-mail whenever a seersucker item appeared on eBay, lived in the house he bought from Tennessee Williams, and before they fired his favorite waiter, his will stated that he should be embalmed with Galatoire's remoulade. It was after Labor Day, so he was, of course, sans seersucker. Instead he wore a tennis shirt with some sort of Medical Services emblem on the chest tucked into slacks, a coroner's badge on his belt, and little circular glasses with thick red rims.

"You the coroner now?" I asked him.

"No, noooooooo. The coroner deputized me one day some years back because he was asked the incubation period of meningococcal meningitis at a press conference. A prisoner had died. He told the reporters that they needed to contact me for that because I was his assistant coroner. He called and appointed me by phone before the TV station had a chance to call me for the answer to the question. And I found this in the bottom of a drawer yesterday."

"When did you get here?"

"I got run out of the city and I just came back today. I was able to slip in through the back roads."

The new manager of Johnny White's, Marci, sat outside on a cot scraping her nails down her mottled calves. Dr. Lutz crouched down in front of her, studied the red spots on her legs. People, mostly those holdouts who clung tightly to Johnny White's around the clock for everything they needed—food, water, drink, bed—gathered around us on the sidewalk.

Now, Dr. Lutz, the radio told us these mosquitoes have been biting corpses.

Dr. Lutz: No, mosquitoes don't bite corpses. They look for warm bodies, for God's sake.

But that's what they told us on the radio!

Dr. Lutz: You heard a lot of myths, people. I heard State Health Department officials say we were gonna be attacked by cholera and salmonella and shield. You don't get gastrointestinal diseases after hurricanes, especially if you drink beer and bottled water. I heard a former head of the Center for Disease Control say that the black mold that will grow in our houses when the flood waters subside will be very dangerous. Well, black mold is more of a plaintiff attorney problem, or a plaintiff attorney bonanza. It's not a human health problem.

The major and predominant infectious disease problem we're gonna have as a result of this hurricane are skin and soft tissue infections just as you see here. Most of them will be trivial and will clear up on their own. I've heard this flooding in New Orleans described as some kind of toxic gumbo, toxic goo, and toxic all kinds of things, but it's probably no more toxic than most Boy Scouts swam in when they were in Lake Pontchartrain forty years ago. There's another rumor, the old rumor that always surfaces with hurricanes, the one minor elected officials like to toss around, that the snakes are gonna come out of the swamps and everybody's gonna be bit by snakes.

Marci: I hate snakes.

Dr. Lutz: Well, I've been in every hurricane in New Orleans since Hurricane Betsy in 1965 and there has never been a documented snake bite after a hurricane in New Orleans or any other city in the world.

What about alligators? Aren't they gonna come up and eat us?

Dr. Lutz: Here's the situation for alligators: Most of them are too small to cause any human harm. Even the larger ones that may end up around humans are not going to cause any problems unless they're cornered. And those poor little pitiful sand sharks that got washed over from Lake Pontchartrain, Lord help anybody who is scared of them.

What about the great whites? I heard there are great whites swimming up Williams Boulevard out in the suburbs.

Dr. Lutz: Uh, it was my understanding that the great whites were swimming out of the suburbs. Listen, usually medical myths and health-related rumors begin locally and spread nationally. Not this time. They've emanated from one of President Bush's highest-most-appointed officials, the Health and Human Services secretary. Misinformation's multiplying faster than our backyard mosquitoes. Least the hurricane winds had blown most mosquitoes away for the first few days.

Were you at your place during the storm?

Dr. Lutz: Yeah. I left that Wednesday. There was no water, and I was a little bit scared of fire, and I'd heard some gunshots the last two nights, and the mayor said you had to get out of town, so I foolishly followed his advice and left. The hurricane was no problem. New Orleans would have survived the hurricane, certainly with some storm damage, but our levees let us down. The Quarter has still been bone dry. The Quarter was bone dry during Hurricane Betsy and the power was turned back on within hours in 80 percent of the Quarter, and I don't understand why it's taking so many days, when we don't even have power lines in the air! No trees fell on our power lines. They're underground. You know, I remember when Johnny White ran for City Council. He would be very proud of you all right now. You all let me know if you need anything and I'll see you all soon. I'll see you, Josh.

Marci, where do you all keep getting stock from?

Marci: Other bars, they're donating their stuff to us.

Were you actually in here during the storm? Did you put plywood up at all or not?

Marci: Just trash bags. We lost two windows and a shutter. I was the only one screaming like an idiot watching out for all the men that are holding the doors shut. Everyone else thought it was funny because I'm the only girl amongst us, you know. I'm like one of the couple girls that are left in the city.

What I love is that this is the dead center of the French Quarter, where you are right here, and you've become the center—you've become the media center of the French Quarter—

Marci: That's why they haven't been able to throw us out yet. But I've been so dead tired that I can't talk to them anymore. It's just—I'll have to go to sleep at some point. I'm trying to stay strong. I've got my breakdown moments, and Paul has taken care of me as far as that goes. He's our clean-up guy. He's gonna hate my guts by the time this is all over with. I live with him, but he's my best friend too. I need his support sometimes and I yell at him for it when he doesn't give it to me. But then he lightens up 'cause I'm like the spokesperson for as far as all this goes. People have seen me all over the world right now. People recognize my voice from the radio, and come introduce themselves to me. They know who I am, and I didn't want any of this. I didn't ask for any of this. But I'm dealing with it the best way that I can. You know, I've got a past I am not proud of. I made some mistakes, I have warrants out, but I'm still brave enough to go on TV every day. So, if that isn't pardoned by all this I don't know what I got to do.

That evening we had Mexican Night. We made burritos for a writer from French *Elle* and her photographer, who both spent the night in the Compound. Their gift to us was an apple, thereby deferring the apple crisis. After dinner, we made a list of the stuff you should have in order to comfortably survive the aftermath of a hurricane. Of course, to stay in the first place, you must meet two conditions: you need to be in a very strong building on high ground that can clearly withstand the storm winds, and stupid but not crazy.

List of what you think you need:
– Water
– Food
– Booze
– Batteries
– Flashlight
– Gun
– Radio

List of what you really need:
– Water (But no need to buy it. Before the storm just fill your bathtub, five-gallon water cooler jugs, milk jugs, Gatorade bottles, whatever you can find. Shove as much of it as you can into your freezer to make ice. When it's all gone, tap the water heaters. This will last you years.)

- ~~Food~~ (Take your neighbor's, you're doing them a favor because it'll go bad anyway. As for the stuff that's nonperishable—well, they'd want you to have it.)
- ~~Booze~~ (Take your neighbors', fuck 'em.)
- Batteries (Your neighbors probably won't have a lot of these but take what they do have and replace later if you can.)
- Flashlight
- ~~Gun~~ (Use firecrackers—they'll scare the hell out of anyone creeping up on you in the night.)
- Radio
- Insect repellent
- Mosquito netting
- Hand sanitizer
- First-aid kit
- Candles
- Lighters
- Charcoal
- Charcoal pit or Hibachi or grill of some sort
- Drugs: If you're too stupid to get off them. (If you are a serious drug user, you will need enough to at least safely wean yourself from them. People looted, died, and killed—themselves and others—as a result of being suddenly without their fix. I myself don't even smoke the wacky weed, but for those who do, stock up on it because it'll be gold when the barter system kicks in and everyone else's supply is totally cut off and the city is ridden with anxiety . . .)

19

An Airborne soldier woke us up the next morning. He just broke right into the Compound and wanted to know what we were doing. We told him exactly what we were doing: living, cleaning up the neighborhood.

He said we were the real heroes. That made us laugh. He was just trying to get old and sick people out of the city. We wouldn't believe the grief he was getting, he said. There was an old couple just down the street and the guy wrapped himself in an American flag, waved the Constitution at him, and started yelling about how he had volunteered in Germany and Japan after World War II and those citizens hadn't had to evacuate, "and it's only been fourteen days, goddammit!"

Dr. Lutz had a sign on his garage gate that said FRENCH QUARTER HEALTH DEPARTMENT IN EXILE. But there was no one there. I popped my head in the EMS trailer down the block, and asked the girl if there was any chance I could plug my computer in for a moment. I mumbled a hundred thank-yous while I tucked it under one of the seats, out of their way. I went back into the heat, introduced myself to their boss.

"Kelly Bumpus," he said. He ran this rogue Bi-County EMS team that had driven down from northern California. "I spend a hundred days here in the Quarter every year. I know the people here and I knew some of them would simply refuse to leave this neighborhood, and they'd need our help. We drove forty-eight hours straight down here. Many of the other EMS teams that volunteered spent three days going through formalities at the state line before they were allowed to enter any of the affected areas. Before they entered they had to take courses in sexual harassment and minority concerns and there was all sorts of bureaucratic steps and permissions we were supposed to obtain. Think how many people could have been saved in those first three days. I finally just said, 'Screw it, people need us.' They continually tried to turn us away because we hadn't got those formal permissions. They still won't recognize us. They refuse to use us for anything official."

One of his crew lit up a cigarette after munching down the last of his muffuletta sandwich, shook his head, and added, "After this thing's over, you'll find out just how much assistance was turned away."

"What do y'all need?" I asked.

"Well, Dr. Lutz got us a whole bunch of syringes, but we're going to need some more. And some NOPD t-shirts would be nice."

I eventually did find some syringes, then I went to the meeting Karen had told us about yesterday. A dozen people were lounging around the courtyard, a good portion of them swilling whiskey and eating hot dogs and spilling red beans on their white T-shirts that read RESTORE THE FRENCH QUARTER VOLUNTEER in black stencil spraypaint. Eventually we filed into the nightclub and a gasman from Entergy took the stage, hardhat and clipboard and all. He looked like Santa Claus if Santa lost a few pounds and got a good tan.

"This is the first gas tragedy that has happened like this anywhere," he told us. He went on to explain what it was exactly that they were dealing with, about 90 percent of which was totally lost on us. But I managed to understand something about how every time a tree or anything had fallen and broken a gas main, even out of the Quarter, water had flooded into the lines and now it needed to be pumped out because our gas lines are low pressure, and before that can happen every single business and residence needed its gas to be turned off because otherwise the lines, and the buildings without their pilot lights on, would be full of gas after they pump the water out. Something like that. And all this needed to happen before they could even consider turning the electricity back on. "And as you know," he finished, "this area is more unique than anywhere in the world as far as where we place the gas meters. They're everywhere."

A man with a jet black toupee sitting up front raised his hand. "There's what—about one hundred people left here in the Quarter? That leaves what—about ten thousand unoccupied houses and apartments you got to break into? And the meters could be hidden anywhere, you're telling us? It'll be years! Years!"

After the meeting I went upstairs and used the bar manager's generator to design fliers to spread the word that Entergy needed access to people's places, then walked down Decatur toward my apartment. V came riding by me on someone's low-rider bicycle. He looked like he'd fallen off the kegs at Johnny White's a couple of more times, but his ear was healing pretty well. He'd even gotten a haircut, his thick, black and gray, close-cropped widow's peak creeping into his wide, bronze face that ended in a cleft chin. "Yo, brah! Molly's is open?" he asked.

"Yup," I said. "Here, take a flier. Entergy needs to turn your gas off!"

"My gas? I ain got gas, brah," he said over his shoulder as he kept on biking. "I ain even got clothes!"

About two minutes later he passed me going in the opposite direction. "Motherfucking bitch cunt wouldn't let me in, told me I had open sores!" he said, pedaling slowly past me.

"You do have open sores, V. Half your face is oozing."

"I got my shirt and shoes on. What more they want? Now they saying I can't have open sores? C'mon, brah."

Another couple of minutes passed and V came back around, headed toward Molly's again. He'd covered 75 percent of his face with dozens of small Band-Aids. His only vantage was through the slit between the bandages over his left eye. "Yo, V," I said, "you look like a mummy."

He had to turn his head halfway around to see me. His bike followed. He slammed into the curb beside me. His bike stayed where it was while V, all 250-plus pounds of him, continued going until a fire hydrant stopped him. I helped him up, got him back on his bike. He looked down at his bleeding elbows and knees. "Were these there before?" he asked me. "Are they fresh ones?"

"You're like one big wound, V."

"Why would you do that to me, brah? Now I got to go back and get more Band-Aids." And he went back toward Johnny White's.

There were a bunch of guys with yellow shirts inside Jackson Square's park chopping up fallen trees, hauling limbs into piles, bagging leaves. They were the first people I'd seen actually inside the square since the storm. The NYPD was standing guard outside the open gate. All the piles of debris we'd made on the corners of the square were gone. I walked along the fence, got the attention of one of the guys in yellow shirts. "Hey, who are you guys?" I asked.

"Navajo Scouts, from Arizona, over by Shiprock. Usually, we deal with forest fires, but the forestry service, they folded us and other organizations into one huge one to come help down here. They did the same thing with the space shuttle recovery, too. So, tell me, is Bourbon Street pretty crazy, huh? Where is that?"

A dozen firefighters from the NYFD stood in a circle outside the fire station on Decatur Street, chuckling and talking animatedly with one another. One of them pointed my beer out—a bottle of Bass I'd grabbed from my place—and they all started laughing their asses off. "Least you're drinking a good beer!" he said. Another guy ran inside, came back with a box of chocolate doughnuts, and offered to trade them for the beer. They all cracked up. I just laughed, thanked them for being here. He tossed me a doughnut. I caught it with my free hand as I left their circle, and then I found myself in another circle of firefighters, this one silent, sitting on folding chairs on the sidewalk, downlooking, avoiding each other's eyes. It said NOFD above the emblems on their T-shirts. One of them looked up at me, the smile still on my face, looked at the doughnut in my hand, the beer, then back to the ground, expressionless.

The perimeter of Harrah's Casino had become Central Command. It was surrounded on all sides with various tents of various organizations, mostly support services for the military and police. I traced the burgers back to the casino's massive front driveway. I got in line behind some DEA guys who were armed to the teeth, smothered my charred black hamburger in enough mustard to make it edible, sat on the sidewalk curb, and watched piles of bags of ice melt across the street. When I was done with the burger, I stacked two massive bags up in my arms, all I could hold, and walked back toward the Compound.

I had to stop and rest my aching and freezing arms every block. I turned off Canal Street at Bourbon, still marveling at all the closed storefronts, strip joints, daiquiri places, not another soul in sight, the only thing missing being tumbleweed. A dragonfly, emerald as the one trapped in Katherine's apartment had been, shot in front of my face, hovered in front of me backwards, facing me, pacing me perfectly. It shot up high into the air, then straight down at me and picked a mosquito I had not noticed off my left shoulder. It alighted on the ice, inches from my face, its bulbous spherical eyes gazing into my own, rubbing its legs together as it ate the other insect. When the giant shade of the Krystal Burger joint rose beside me, the dragonfly stopped chewing, dropped the half-eaten mosquito on the ice, then disappeared. I watched its silhouette blend into the blue sky and realized something was very, very wrong.

I had walked between Krystal Burger and what seemed to be at least a hundred industrial-sized garbage bags to my left on the curb. The smell hurt, like someone had stuck a knife up my nostrils into my brain. I had no idea how I'd gotten so far into the line of garbage bags without noticing, but I had about forty feet to go in either direction before I was in the clear. In a second I was in a black cloud of flies, all of them trying to get into my face, but they were the least of my concerns. It was the smell that got me. I dropped the ice, sunk to my knees, steadied myself. I waved weakly at the flies, tried to get them out of my ears, my nose, one got stuck in my eye. I felt for the tips of the bags of ice, grabbed hold, dragged them, trudged forward through flies thick as syrup. The smell got so bad it was no longer a smell. It was psychosis. I hit the ground again. My neurons ceased where they were. I became a pathetic, moaning slob. The ice burned cold beneath me as it melted on the warm ground. I remembered again (this was the one thought that came into my mind) how I used to describe the Quarter as a place of smells, every ten feet another olfactory sensation—crawfish, cigars, puke, piss, gumbo, perfume, étouffée, puke, piss—and here I'd thought they had all vanished since the storm. But every one of those smells had been bundled into these garbage bags here beside me and rotted in the heat for two weeks. It occurred to me that the flies were all over me because they too were stuck here, they hoped I was some sort of vehicle they could ride to safety on. I managed to get back onto my feet. I reached for the ice but only found more flies. I crumpled to the ground again. This was it. Bourbon Street really would kill me.

Then the flies began pushing me. I was sure of it. They got me onto my knees and I dragged the bags of ice through the last ten feet. It was ice or death. When I was out the flies shot skyward in a black cloud and there was only the putrid rancid smell of garbage for a while, until it finally descended into the stink of any normal corner on Bourbon, until that too went away and I was just me in the heat and emptiness. I dropped the ice, picked a dead fly out of my ear and one from the beard I was growing. There was a cluster of pigeons in the middle of the street, just looking at me, clucking, laughing, picking at some cracker crumbs, no doubt from an MRE. They knew better than to go any further.

It took another half hour, resting every block or so for half a mile, freezing water dripping down my legs and aching arms, half the ice still frozen, before I walked proudly up to our coolers. Their tops were off because there was so much ice already in them it was overflowing. I heard a door open and close above me. Some guy I'd never seen before walked out onto the balcony above me, looked down at me. "Hey, I got you all some ice," he said.

"Yeah," I said, and dumped my bags out into the bushes in front of me. I pulled a chair over and stuck my feet in the sun, wiggled my fingers until I could move them enough to pull a Corona out of the cooler closest to me. "Yeah."

"My name's David," he said, looking down at me against the blue sky, a thin guy with real short hair, freckles, and a small goatee.

"Yeah."

"So you guys live here?" he asked. "Never seen you before. I'm right here, in 216. Which unit are you in?"

"All of them," I said.

"Oh."

"Thanks for the ice."

"No problem. I'm here working for a few hotels, to get them back up and running, so I have access to all that stuff. Katherine will be back in a few minutes. We were thinking about trying to get up on the interstate, to see down into the flooded areas. You can come along. Why are there flies in your beard?"

I sipped the Corona while my hands went from blue to purple to red and finally back to skin. When Katherine came back we got into David's Saturn and followed a fleet of firetrucks the wrong way up an off ramp onto the highway. We parked in the emergency lane and looked down into the city's oldest cemetery, in the Tremé. Centuries ago, the dead had been buried underground, and coffins and bodies would drift through the city after floods. Now the sun-bleached aboveground tombs poked up out of a few feet of brown water.

New Orleans was stretched out flat before us north to the horizon, filled with sky's dirty reflection, pierced only with whatever poked out of the flooding: cars at first, then only a few trucks, then only houses and lampposts, and I realized that we had been in Flanagan's sucking on Budweisers blocks away while there was a man, many of them probably, women and children, too, who had seen this water coming up under their front door and waded out to this sidewalk, realized it was getting worse, and taken a right toward this overpass, figuring the interstate was built on high ground, instead of turning left toward the Quarter. I wondered how many noses went under about the time we were telling the bartender how to make Elle in Augusts, where the bodies had washed to, how many had been found, what would be here a year from now?

"They say eighty percent of the city was covered in water," said David.

"Eighty percent water," said Katherine. "Like the heart."

"Well, whatever percent it is now, smells like it's still got a hundred percent of the crap in it," I said. Judging from the waterlines, the flooding had receded considerably, concentrating any contamination that had been further diluted before. Clouds of black and brown and gray swirled in and out of one another and I wondered where it would go.

At dinner, Ashley announced that she got a job bartending at Molly's. I grabbed two bottles of wine, headed over to the EMS trailer on Dumaine, the first time I'd been out after curfew since we'd been in the Compound. I snuck into the empty trailer, unplugged my computer, and turned it on to make sure it had fully charged. The desktop image was Katherine, a picture that had simply become everyday background for the last year, her lying on my futon looking at the river the morning after Hurricane Ivan passed us last year and we were waiting for the rest of the city to return, her cheeks glowing red from my stubble, her pink tank top mussed up above her belly button, her naked hips slanting out of the photograph. I left the bottles of wine on the counter and walked back to the Compound, crept into the darkness, candlelit and fluttering with static, beside Katherine on the bed in 217, and lay very still.

"Do you know what deciduous means?" she asked me.

"Sure," I said.

"What?"

"I don't know."

"In autumn, the rays of the sun fall," she said. "They don't come straight down overhead on the trees like in the summer. Deciduous trees respond with hormonal changes, changes that take nourishment away from their leaves to keep what little there is stored in the roots. The leaves turn colors as they starve, and eventually they fall. The tree becomes naked and gray."

"Like the ones coming up out of the water we saw today."

"I was thinking of Maine," she said. "Are the trees dying in Maine now?"

"The leaves? Maybe in a few weeks."

"I would like to see them slowly dying. That's the thing I miss about back east most. Down here everything was always so alive."

We woke, as usual, about two in the morning, gasping for air while satiated mosquitoes rained upon us. I took a cold shower, sprayed myself with repellent from head to toe again, and lay down. With the first sliver of dream came a mosquito into my ear—*nnnneow!* The heat was such that the energy it took to swat it sent sweat flooding out of every pore from my scalp to the bottoms of my feet and I was back where I started. I lay still, still as the bottom of the river I tried to hear in the radio's static, trying to bring my heart rate back down, trying to breathe in the heat, stifling despite the windows I'd opened, until sleep again whispered, and again a mosquito into my ear.

Even if I didn't swat at it, some muscle somewhere on my body would tighten in reaction, maybe just my cheek, and this exertion would send sweat flooding over me again, sweat that had nowhere to go in the tight wet air but heat up with my body until I thought I'd drown because I was already suffocating.

I walked out to the balcony, the night twitching gently with breeze. I grabbed a couple of blankets and pillows and took Katherine by the hand. We lay down side by side there and pulled a sheet over our heads. It was cool and wonderful. There was the silence we had so long blocked out with radio static, silence empty of the susurrus of a city. We could hear only the mosquitoes inches from our faces, frustrated by the protective sheet. Even with the hardness of the wood beneath us, dreams came again.

Then vanished as Katherine shifted beside me. We were shoulder to shoulder, the width of the slim balcony. I settled back into sleep. Then, a slight tug at the covers, and it was starting all over again. I went inside, got another couple of blankets and lay down on another part of the balcony, below her, so that we were feet to feet. When sleep came again, she shifted, her toes hit mine, and I was awake. I inched further away from her. As I was about to fall asleep, I convinced myself that she might at any moment stretch her feet out and they would hit mine again. I lay there frozen in fear. I could not take being torn from another dream. And then her feet touched mine. I moved two feet further away, far enough away that there was no threat of her feet touching mine. The next thing I knew it was almost ten in the morning.

Trees shimmered in breeze through the shade above. For the first time since the storm, I had woken not because I couldn't take the heat and mosquitoes anymore, but because I was ready to wake. When I sat up I saw Katherine sleeping soundly, unmoving, the sheet tucked under her toes, still pulled up over her face.

On this day four years ago, I had been working all morning in my home office, and it was about this time, not until 10:34 A.M., that I finally turned my phone on, checked my messages, then ran downstairs to the nearest bar where I stayed all day and night watching television with an old friend from New York and when we couldn't keep our heads up anymore she and I went back to my place. Today, on Canal Street, here amidst the millennium's second American Tragedy, this one still unfolding, the NYPD and FD were holding a memorial for their co-workers who fell four years earlier. I supposed our generation, one that grew up in a lull of history, would have to start building its own vocabulary for disaster, as those before us had.

I went down to see Ashley at Molly's and there was Ken Wells from the *Wall Street Journal.* "Jesus," he said, giving me a hug. "Look at you. You've gone native." Ken was used to seeing me in a suit at literary festivals and now I was in a USMC T-shirt with the sleeves cut off and a bathing suit, my blond hair shooting out at every angle, mosquito-bitten arms, a survival knife tied around my waist.

"Welcome to billfree, taxfree America," I said.

He was down here doing a cover story for the *Wall Street Journal* on St. Bernard Parish. He said five out of 27,000 homes were still inhabitable. "Must have been like five thousand dogs roaming, swimming in oil slicks, trying to get into the boat and we couldn't do anything for them. How's Katherine? You realize I'm in love with her, right? I mean, not as much as my wife, but you know."

I shrugged. "She's here, you know."

Ken laughed, said, "If you guys can make it through this, you can make it through anything."

20

Between charging my computer in the EMS trailer for a couple of hours, writing a story every day, and trying to get an Internet connection through a phone line that lasted long enough to send it by five o'clock, I was left with little time to experience the world, or lack of one, around me before curfew. And so my days shrank while writing for Salon.

The first night an article was due, the Internet connection was not working in the Compound and Katherine had yet to send her photos to Salon. We needed to go to my place. It was well after curfew, about ten. It had been a week since we'd heard gunshots and we'd seen a media SUV rolling past last night so we figured we'd give it a go. I threw two gallons of water into the radiator and drove the Sexy Beast real slow down the six blocks to my apartment. I'd barely turned off the ignition when a car screeched around the corner, its spotlight drowning our vision.

"We have our guns drawn! We are going to shoot you if you move! Put your hands in the air!"

We poked our hands out the windows.

"Hands in the air! We're going to shoot!"

We poked them out further.

I watched the rear view mirror as a cop approached each side of the car, crouching slightly, Glocks pointed at us.

"Get out of the vehicle with your hands up!"

We did.

"Put your goddamned hands on the vehicle!"

I did. Katherine hesitated, tried to shield her eyes for a second.

"Put your fucking hands on the fucking vehicle or we'll shoot!" one yelled at her.

She did.

They patted us down, then told us to slide our hands down to the trunk.

"Do you have any drugs or firearms?" asked one officer, who looked like a mustachioed umpire in his black bulletproof vest and cap.

"No sir," I said. "You can search it if you want."

"Oh, I *am* going to search this car!" he responded. "It's martial law! We don't need a warrant!"

With that he began tearing through the books, magazines, empty bottles, and other trash piled neck-deep in my back seat. Meanwhile the other cop, who looked like a real pissed-off Curly from the Three Stooges, handcuffed Katherine and me together and had us sit on the curb. He was not at all interested when I tried to show him my driver's license hanging from the lanyard around my neck, proving that I lived upstairs, thus decreasing the likelihood that I was robbing the place. When the first officer had finished rearranging my backseat he fumbled through my keys trying to get in the trunk. "It's the small oval one," I told him.

Beneath my Santa, bunny, and cow costumes, he unearthed things I'd long forgotten about—a bucket with my old running shoes inside, spray paint, acrylic paint, paint brushes, boxers, a portable shower for camping, two license plates, three frisbees, a biography of Max Perkins, a pair of dress shoes I'd been looking for for two years, and then a couple of boxes of *SCAT* magazine. He yanked out an issue and held it up to my face. "What's this? How'd you get this?!" he asked.

"I'm the associate editor."

"Who's the publisher? Who's the publisher?!"

"Elena."

He tossed the magazine back in my trunk and said, "You're okay! They're okay! Mario's my best friend in the world!"

The NOPD. Some things even Katrina can't change.

He shut the trunk. "You know Mario, her cousin, right?" he asked.

"Oh, yeah, I know Mario," said Katherine, elated, still handcuffed to me. "Oh my God, how is he? Where is he? Is he okay?"

"Oh yeah, he's great, took off to Hammond before the storm . . ." He gave us a detailed report of Mario's ongoings in the last couple weeks. Eventually I interrupted to ask if someone might unlock the handcuffs at some point. Officer Curly took care of that, and handed me my keys. After another few minutes of Katherine and the cop exchanging Mario gossip, they said they'd give us an escort back up St. Peter. I was about to drive when the mustachioed cop came running back up to Katherine's window.

"Oh, my God," he said. "Did you hear that they pushed the wedding back to last Saturday?!"

"Oh, no, really, I was wondering what they were going to do because of the storm and all that," said Katherine.

"They told me it was beautiful," he beamed.

"Well, you give him a big hug from Katherine and Josh," she said.

"Katherine and Josh. Got it! All right, you all be safe." With that, he went back to his car and escorted us across Jackson Square and up St. Peter Street.

"Don't know any of Elena's cousins, myself," I said.

"Neither do I," said Katherine.

I wrote about that in my second article for Salon. The police officer who handcuffed us read the article a few days later and wrote a letter that Salon wanted to post. The officer called it "fictional poop" and "BULL-SHIT" attributed to my being under "a rather potent mind-altering hallucinogen" during my "rusty, one taillight, no-blinker, venture," and also warned in the actual letter, "If I see you again, please don't expect that I will show you the mercy and patience that I showed that night."

I didn't think his letter needed any response. I thought it illustrated my point better than the actual article did. But the editor asked me to write one. I restated the facts of that night, all of them true, corrected two small discrepancies, and then wrote about the general frustration and anger left in Katrina's wake, how the storm has irrevocably destroyed so much of our city, but we must not let it take our spirit.

But neither it nor the officer's letter made it onto the site. Months later, when I actually had time to read my articles, I was disheartened to find Salon had simply slapped a G-rating on the piece and toned it way down under pressure from the NOPD.

21

Canal was no longer flooded with media campers, no chance of Greta lingering around the corner, only stringers and others left behind to provide updates, just in case another Big Thing happened.

The day after our encounter with the NOPD, John Barry, author of the seminal *Rising Tide*, about the Mississippi River flood of 1927, who also happened to own one of the apartments in the Compound, called me from his other home in D.C. Not that he could enjoy it, he said, but he'd been on every major network by now at least once talking about the flooding of New Orleans. He finally gets to the point: "My wife, she'd really appreciate it if you could water our plants." The irony was beyond words. I watered his plants.

That evening I pushed a shopping cart loaded with bottled water down Bourbon Street while Black Hawks swam in the nectarine of setting sun. We found Royce Bumpkin, a local painter and handyman, sitting on his stoop, handing out free cold beer to anyone who walked by, wearing his red beret and a poncho with Bourbon Street signs on it. He just kept handing me Abita Ambers until I insisted he stop. A Humvee rolled by real slow, came to a stop about forty feet past us. A soldier got out of the passenger seat, looked up and down the street, then walked up to us. Bumpkin reached into his house behind him and pulled out a fifth of Wild Turkey. "What you ordered, right?" he said. "Just don't get caught back at base with it, okay?"

"We're army," said the soldier. "This ain gonna make it back to base."

Bumpkin: I'm protecting my shit.

Have you moved all day?

Bumpkin: Yeah, I moved to restock my ice chest. You know, my girl-friend, she took the hurricane, the looters, the mosquitoes, but when Nagin started his stuff about physically taking people out of their homes, she couldn't take it anymore. So she left. She went down to the convention center and they said they was flying her to Vegas to meet her mom, but they flew her to North Carolina. She called me from there, and she was crying. Then some church people gave her one hun-dred thirty dollars and she got on the bus to Vegas.

When Nagin started that shit about taking people out their house, I was scared. So, I locked myself up, and I would look out the shutters like a criminal. I saw some soldiers, you know, talking about ripping peo-ple off to make it worth their while for coming down here. They were right where you were standing, the guys with the red berets, six of them. They said, "Well, we'll do it the last night before we leave." So, I'm just here to protect my home. The best way I know how. Here, take some more beers.

We walked a block over to Royal Street and shouted up to Jackie. Jackie's was the first of many bleeding faces we saw after the storm, a casu-alty of falling down stairs in the dark. For a week now he'd been offering me the use of his generator and landline if I needed it—electricity and Internet at the same time! As always, he wore white rubber boots and a kind face, tanned almost to leather. The sound of the generator in the courtyard was tremendous. He took us onto his balcony where he'd hung enough plants along the railing to shield his television and the light up there from the street. I downloaded my e-mails for the first time since the storm, while he rolled a joint and Katherine ate a couple of his apples and they watched the news out of Baton Rouge beside me.

I had over four hundred e-mails, nonspam. Many had come the day of my birthday from NPR listeners, thanking me and wishing me happy birthday. I almost cried. I'd had the smallest birthday party ever, and yet I felt as though I had shared it with the whole world. Katherine said we should get back, it was dark now, way past curfew. I pasted the same response into each e-mail—that we were okay—and fired off a few dozen, then we pushed the shopping cart back toward the Compound.

"Why did you abandon me?" she asked. "You just left me there with that guy while you were checking e-mails."

"With Jackie? I was sitting right there next to you. I'm right here. I didn't even answer most of my e-mails from people wondering if I'm alive."

"I don't even see you anymore in the days. And then at night you can't even touch me."

"Katherine, we're all just trying to get sleep here. We've been together for two-and-a-half weeks now. What the hell do you mean abandoning you?"

"We have not been together."

"Because you won't join us. You insist on going off and doing your own thing, wandering around and taking photos, while we're sweeping the streets and stuff. Shit, you abandon us. We just look at this neighborhood different, I guess."

"I grew up here. I've been going to the Quarter since before you were born."

"I don't care how many Sundays you strolled through the square with your parents when you were little, you've never lived here, you don't know it the same way. And if you did, you'd care more. You'd be out with us."

We didn't speak for the rest of the night, and ate dinner without eye contact while doing our best to talk with TnA and David; then I lit a citronella candle between us and lay down on the cushions I'd brought out to the balcony, pulled the bedsheet up over my face and slept without dreams until late the next morning. I stepped around Katherine shifting restlessly beneath the sheet pulled high over her head, grabbed my computer, and headed to the EMS station. A media van pulled up alongside me, screeched to a halt soon as I exited the gate. A petite blonde poked her head out and asked if I were a resident. She told me President Bush had just accepted responsibility for the mismanagement of the hurricane response and would I care to respond to him?

"Sure, you got him in the back seat?"

An ABC News camera crew rolled out of the van and clustered around me. They seemed terribly excited to have found a live body at this point. I mumbled something about how much the outside world might be able to get done in those regions not as fortunate as this neighborhood if they stopped pointing fingers and started helping, let the anger roll later, the buck stops with each of us right now, you and me. They were wholly unimpressed.

That evening down at Molly's, after I sent off my third article, Ty informed me that he and Ashley would start living in their own place again. I asked if it were Katherine and me, our tension. Ashley said she just wanted to get into her own bed.

Without TnA there, the silence between Katherine and me grew louder. We each took turns conversing with David to cover it up. He didn't seem to mind, so long as we were talking with him. He told us it was frightening being there alone, without us.

That night, she begged me to at least turn around so our heads could be closer together, so maybe we could talk for a while, or just hold hands until we slept, maybe while we slept, maybe anything.

"Can we just sleep?" I said. I didn't turn around. There would be plenty of time for that someday in the future.

22

The next afternoon I ran into the mayor and chief of police finishing a press conference on Jackson Square. The mayor, wearing a white tennis shirt, wiping the beads of sweat breaking over his massive, glistening, bald head with a handkerchief, strode off into an SUV with tinted windows soon as he was done. I walked up to the police chief, Eddie Compass, and stood next to a reporter asking him questions. Compass grabbed his crotch, seemingly without knowing it, when he wanted to emphasize something, which was quite a lot.

Compass: Just imagine it—no food, no water, no vehicles, waist-deep water, no restroom facilities, nowhere to sleep, fighting a very well-armed opponent who had total disregard for human life.

Reporter: I've never seen anything like it. Now you've been quoted as saying, "We've faced the greatest challenge any city has faced in the history of mankind." You stand firm with that?

Compass: I still stand by that. Just imagine the circumstances. With thirty thousand people at the Superdome that we had to protect. We had thirty thousand people at the convention center. We had the entire city to police. Our vehicles were down; our communication systems were down. Like I said, no ammunition, no food, no water, no rest. The water was polluted. Officers were getting infections in their legs and hands from cuts. I don't know any police department or any army that has ever faced such insurmountable odds.

I decided against asking if he'd ever taken a history course, much less heard of places like Leningrad. I walked back to the Compound, and asked Katherine if she wanted to do some exercises with me by the pool. We were doing sit-ups when TnA walked into the Compound and told us to come have a look at what they bought this morning. There was an ambulance parked on the curb. "You're kidding," I said.

They assured me they were not, showed me the paperwork.

"How much?"

"A dollar, officially. But they wouldn't even take the dollar," said Ty, climbing into the back of the ambulance behind us. "We told the EMS guys we don't have a car because some of our friends got a little worried about the situation and we gave them our car. And they just handed me the keys to one of their ambulances. We signed the paperwork this morning."

"Do you realize the possibilities?" I said.

"What next?" asked Ty. "You know what I'm saying? What friggin next?"

They drove me the couple of blocks over to the EMS station where I plugged in and read all the e-mails I had downloaded into my mail manager. The last message informed me that my regional distributor's warehouse had flooded and most of my last printing of *French Quarter Fiction: The Newest Stories of America's Oldest Bohemia*—my publishing company's first book—was now totally uninsured mush. I folded the computer and left it there under the trailer to charge and walked down to Perkins Petucci's place to get a tree out of his house.

He emerged from the side gate in nothing but slippers and a blue towel tied around his waist, his glasses on, hair coiffed, hauling a tree branch four times the length of him across the street. I asked what exactly in hell he thought he was doing. He looked at me, squinting into the sun with those kind eyes that seemed accustomed to another time, one not so useless to him as the twenty-first century. I followed him through his gate, and into his back garden. The tree had been uprooted and fallen into the back of his house. I picked up his little hand saw, climbed the ladder, and started going at it. Petucci asked if I wouldn't mind if he sat down, he felt the vertigo coming on. He rested below me in a lawn chair. After about an hour his phone rang inside. He walked in with his cane, got it on the tenth ring. "Hello . . . ? Oh my goodness, well hello . . . Yes . . . Yes. Well, I'm doing fine . . . Do I still think about you? I'm looking at your picture right now . . . The one with those beautiful legs . . . The legs that used to be wrapped around me . . ."

He laughed and laughed. A branch fell on my face. I spat sawdust, then started working on the last limb until there was nothing left but the trunk. I descended the ladder as Petucci came back out with a small framed picture. "My goodness. That was my first true love. She called all the way from England. She read my name in a paper over there. I hadn't spoken to her in fifty-four years." He looked down at the picture in his lap upon his blue towel. It was the size of his palm.

"Yes. My goodness. That was me," said Petucci, running his fingertip over the young man in the photograph, then the young woman beside him. "And there she is." She was facing into the wind, smiling at Petucci, who was smiling into the camera, her mop of light curled hair shooting behind her. They were sitting on a sea wall somewhere far away from here, a gray ocean stretching to the horizon between their faces. Petucci's wavy hair was combed perfectly, parted to the side, a little rise up front, just as it was now, only black instead of white.

Inside his home were shelves and shelves of antiques and his walls were covered with old oil paintings—dim smoky landscapes burning with autumn and once-golden skies that filled you with deep dark nostalgia, a longing to stand in these places impossible as touching a memory. He handed me a bottle of Korbel champagne. "For you," he said. "That's what I miss. Listening to my records and cold champagne."

"It'll come back before we're ready," I said.

"Yes, well, when it does, won't you please come over for dinner?"

As I walked out the door, I noticed for the first time that in front of each house the military had spraypainted the number of people still living inside. Zeros stretched far as I could see in both directions, except for the 1 right in front of me. "Wish they hadn't put that there," said Petucci, standing in his doorway behind me. "I didn't think it was a good idea to let the bad guys know that an eighty-one-year-old man is the only one protecting this entire street."

"See ya later," I said.

"That's the only way now, babe," he said.

When I got back to the EMS station Dr. Lutz was standing out front, making sure, as usual, that they had everything they needed. Despite the fact that many people were still afraid to bathe in the tap water, I'd heard that he started drinking it three days ago. And I hadn't seen him in three days, so I'd feared the worst. "Dr. Lutz, is it true you've been drinking the water?"

"Yeeeeeees. I have."

"Are you okay?"

"No! I'm constipated."

"From the water?"

"No, no. The water's fine."

"So, it's okay for us to drink it, then?"

"Well, I'm not telling people to drink it. I'm telling them *I'm* drinking it."

So, I started drinking the water. It tasted a little funky, put hair on my teeth, and strangely never quite seemed to quench my thirst, no matter how many glasses of it I chugged. But there was a certain pride in being one of only two people that I knew of in the entire city drinking the water.

That evening, Katherine walked into the Compound leading a pit bull by a thick dirty rope tied around its neck. "Meet Mad Max. It's going to be David's dog."

"He just walked up to Johnny White's," said David. "No tag, nothing."

"Look how thin he is though," she said. "Look at his ribs."

"Look at his coat," I said. "All glinting in the candlelight. It's beautiful. Like a tiger or something."

We played with Max, fed him a meatloaf MRE, fed ourselves, too, and took turns talking to David until he took the dog into his apartment. We sat in silence until I told Katherine I wanted to show her something.

I led her into the garage, out into another small parking lot inside the Compound, then up a set of dark winding stairs. These led to other condos, ones we did not have access to. "K.K. showed me this once," I said.

"How much higher are we going?"

"Just a couple more flights. C'mon, there—watch it here, just stay close. Keep holding my hand. There. There. Okay I think we're here."

"Wait, where are you?"

"Here. Oop, sorry babe. I'm trying to find—here just hold my hand. Here."

"Why didn't we just bring a flashlight?"

"That would have made too much sense."

"I'm going to go back down and get a flashlight, I don't like this."

"No. Wait. Dammit. There. I think. Got it."

I yanked hard on the chain and a window of stars opened over our heads. I climbed up the ladder on the wall in front of us, about fifteen feet high, pulled myself up onto the roof. Katherine followed behind me. It was a wide, flat roof. We walked to the edge, holding hands, two helicopters clipping away any chance at silence, dancing their spotlights over the buildings below us.

"It never ceases to amaze me, huh?" I said. "How low the Quarter is. We're only—what?—six stories up? And yet we can see over the whole damn thing because most of the buildings are like three stories. I love it."

"My God," she said. "The business district. They've got their lights back."

"Whoa. Wow. A few of the buildings, yeah, you're right. Think they're using generators?"

"Look at the Quarter, all the different pointy facades and roofs pointing silver back up at the sky, into the moonlight. The cathedral's the only thing that seems whole, that seems itself, all crazy white like that needling the night."

"And the black river."

"Dark like space. But space doesn't seem as dark tonight. Doesn't seem there's as many stars."

"Where do you think they went?"

"They're in our feet, remember?"

"Not mine. I had a good look down into my feet this morning. They've pretty much cracked open from the chlorine in the pool."

"Sky's split in two."

"I know. I've never seen that. Half stars, half lavender haze from those downtown buildings with their lights on. It'll be here in the Quarter first, I guess. Electricity. We'll live in my place. Together."

"God, you think we can do that?"

"We're going to have to try it sometime," I said. "We can't spend the rest of our lives in separate apartments."

"The Superdome."

"The Hyatt."

"We walked that far that first night? In our sandals? Seems a universe away from here."

"Andromeda like peanut brittle."

"Huh? Peanut brittle?"

"That's how it tasted. I wanted to make love to you out there, on Poydras Street, right in the middle of it, but then a cop car rolled by and so I swallowed the Andromeda Nebula instead. I know that sounds fucking stupid, but that's what it was like. And it's gone now. Gone in that dirty lavender."

"In your belly, huh? In our feet."

I put my hands on her shoulders. Her cell phone rang for the first time since the storm.

"No," I said. "Please don't."

But she answered it. It was a friend from back east. I got up on the ledge, walked around the roof. It was attached to the roof of the Maison Dupuy Hotel next door. I walked across that roof as well. As far from Katherine as I could get. I lay down, my belly on the roof, only my head off it, looking into the streets below, flashing red and blues gliding along the buildings of Dumaine Street like UFOs, the white strings of helicopter spotlights dancing through it all, and I waited and hoped for Katherine to come lie beside me, to hear her footsteps approaching. I finally gave up, walked back to the Compound roof. She wasn't there. I left the emergency door open and descended into the darkness of the building, walked back to the courtyard. No one was there. I went into 109 and checked the messages on my cell phone.

The first was from Babysitter, who was now in the Montgomery, Alabama, Hooters. He was staying with our friend Patty, whose girlfriend Joelle worked at the Hooters. He put her on the phone and said she was thinking about us down in New Orleans and if I wanted to get out we should come up there. I tried real hard, but could not remember ever meeting her. Babysitter was getting sick of buffalo shrimp and buffalo chicken and buffalo wings and his kid had gotten into the 3-Mile Island sauce and had diarrhea, and none of the waitresses thought it was so cool to hold him anymore and he'd lost all interest in boobies and his mother was having serious trouble getting him to breastfeed. "Tittie fatigue," Babysitter cried into my voicemail. "Oh, this refugee life—Can I have another Bud Light?—But Joelle's got some great boobies. I keep hanging around the bathroom in the morning in case one falls out of her bathrobe . . ." I hit delete. The second message was to please, please let him know if I'd died yet, because if I had he was going to come down here and kick my ass for staying. The third message was to tell me that last night Joelle was sitting alone in a bar having a drink after work at Hooters, about one, waiting for Patty to pick her up and a girl walked into the bar and ordered a shot of Jaegermeister and the bartender refused to serve this other girl, said she was too drunk and so the girl walked out, got into her '98 Mustang, and drove it into the bar, killing one person. Joelle.

There had been a security camera outside the bar's front entrance and the footage had been all over the nightly news there. I hung the phone up, sat for a while in that dark, and swallowed it until it made me sick to my stomach.

What was one death? Just one. We had thousands here. And what would be the difference between 1000 and 1001 people being killed? Everything.

Here I was surrounded by single deaths, but I was a part of that machinery. And it was way too in my face to feel sick about it. They stayed, as I had stayed, and they died. And if I let that get to me, I was done.

I knew the deaths around me were a horrible thing, and I wished it all had never happened. I prayed and prayed for it before and afterward not to happen. And I knew that, had I the chance, I would probably give my own life to save those lost—I say *probably* because I cannot be sure about such things. I felt mentally anguished about it. But I had not yet felt physically, emotionally sick, really truly sick to my stomach, about it. (Did you? Do you?)

I did not know Joelle, at least I could not remember her. These bodies around me in my city, I did not know them either. But no doubt I was somehow connected to them, everyone in this village of New Orleans was connected, even if I'd just passed them on the street. But without knowing *how* we were connected, there was nothing there, no sick-to-my-stomach anguish, and that emptiness, that failing of emotion, is what burned me, not the lifeless bodies decomposing blocks from me, but my failing of emotion for them.

So, I sat there in that dark room, anguished over the emptiness inside me, but not the life gone out of those around me. I did not see how I could possibly be more selfish, more self-absorbed. And when I realized that, how selfish this all was, another wave of anguish consumed me. This, of course, was even more selfish of me. And so an even deeper wave of anguish spread over me. And so it went, a downward spiral of self-absorption and anguish until I realized the whole damn thing was pointless and if I didn't feel emotionally sick about the deaths, I could at least fake it through physical expression, which was what I'd been doing, and would continue doing. I thought instead about Joelle. For now, for a little while, that sickness in my gut over her filled the burning emptiness I had for those in my own city, and in a horrible way, it satisfied me.

I grabbed a flashlight and climbed back up onto the roof. The breeze was beautiful. If not for the sun in the morning and the helicopters in the night I would have made it bed. And there was Katherine, curled into a ball in the far corner, beside the ledge, sleeping. "Fuck it," I said. "Stay there." She opened her eyes, confused, as I descended the fire hatch.

That night I dreamt of the Ripley's kids hanging me from chains in place of their sign. I woke with a start, thinking I'd forgotten to check to see if my windows were locked, realized where I was. Even in my wildest dreams I tick-tocked away the routines. I squashed a mosquito in my ear, flicked one out of the corner of my eye, pulled the bedsheet back over my face, and woke hours later to someone calling through the daylight, "Hello! Hello!" through the gate.

It was Brett the pool guy. An archangel shoulder tattoo spanned out of his sleeveless shirt that said FALLEN ANGEL POOL SERVICE. I'd met him the day before, a thinner, better-looking Mr. Clean, and he'd promised to stop by this morning with some stuff for the pool. He dumped some white calcium hypochlorite powder into each corner of the pool and I stirred it around with the net while he told me about tearing down I-10 on his motorcycle last night after he left Johnny White's. "When else you gonna go 140 in third gear in either direction on any side of the highway you want? Nothing like a good tequila and Red Bull buzz to get you doing that."

"After curfew and everything? You don't get stopped?"

"White boy on a Harley? They love that shit. Even if I wanted to loot, where the hell would I put any of it? Last night a bunch of 82nd Airborne guys stopped me just so they could get a picture with me. Now, just keep stirring this stuff in for about ten more minutes, should clear it up a bit."

That afternoon, as I was finishing the last Salon article in my apartment on Decatur Street, the massive picture of the two-headed cow above the Ripley's entrance across the street was suddenly framed with lime-green fluorescent light. I walked out onto my balcony. All of Jax Brewery had electricity, but there was still nothing on this side of the street.

I walked back inside, finished the article. My battery died an instant before I could push "Send." I saw a CNN van parked across the street, in the parking lot along the river, so I took my computer down there, explained to the two producers out front that I desperately need to e-mail my family to let them know I was okay and could I possibly please just charge my computer up for a couple minutes? No problem, they said.

Other media campers rolled in around me. Ten minutes later, I unplugged my computer and walked back toward my apartment. A couple of buck-toothed pimply-faced 82nd Airborne soldiers asked if they could help me. I told them I was just going back to my place right there across the street. They told me the president was speaking in Jackson Square in an hour, and it would be another three before I could return. "Who's your commanding officer?" I asked.

They sent another soldier off to find their lieutenant while they asked me about Bourbon Street and all the boobs there. They said they wanted to come back for Mardi Gras, but they'd have to wait another two years until they were old enough to drink. They were headed to Iraq next. They wanted to get over there as soon as possible.

Eventually, I spoke with officer after officer and then I tried sneaking back to my building from various angles. Impossible. If only I'd known, I would have stayed in my damn apartment and watched the president from my balcony. Instead I was forced to wander the Quarter carrying my laptop outside the three-block radius of security around Jackson Square. I called the editor at Salon, said I'd have the piece to him in a couple of hours.

He asked if I'd seen his e-mails. No, of course not, I said, I haven't even seen my articles online, I never had enough battery power for all that. Apparently, even though there'd been some positive responses, my articles had pissed enough people off, caused enough controversy, that Salon thought they should nip it in the bud, keep it down to just those first three and not risk any further backlash from a fourth and final piece. Apparently, some of their readers were unhappy about the positive slant I put on how people were getting along in the French Quarter, they felt it selfish after they'd heard such "accurate" reporting of the horrors from other news networks. (Later, when I could actually read the pieces online, I learned this was partly due to Salon's renaming my column "Partying at the End of the World," unbeknownst to me, using a beer photo as its thumbnail, and excerpting only a small part about wine on the bottom of the Compound pool for nonsubscribers to see.) He said I could read their letters online and respond if I wanted.

I told him I had no time or electricity to read their responses, nor did I wish to engage desktop critics around the country while they sat in their air-conditioning glancing at CNN every once in while, feeling sorry for us, firing off letters over their broadband, believing they have any sense of what it was like right here. Maybe CNN did show them something I didn't know. Maybe I too was ignorant about the situation, maybe even more ignorant than they were. But the fact was that I was here. I shared what I knew, what I could see and touch and smell and hear and taste and that was it. No one could doubt me in that. That's all my shitty pieces had ever done and that's all this fourth one did and it built upon and concluded the three others and I was going to send it anyway and I really, really wished they'd take a look at it because I spent the afternoon writing it and mouthed off to the 82nd Airborne and Secret Service trying to get the damn thing to him.

He said okay. I walked back to Bourbon, told Anderson Cooper to "Keep it real, man"—which made him giggle right before he went live. Johnny White's was of course only two blocks from the square, but not even the president could shut that place down. It was packed. I dodged between two patrols and someone bought me a double screwdriver, and we listened to Bush speak a couple of blocks away on the radio. It's fair to say that pretty much everyone there hated the president—as did the vocal majority of Quarterites even in normal times—but it was the first speech I'd heard with real details, a real plan for recovery. It gave us hope. Yet it was still only words, words like, "There is no way to imagine America without New Orleans." Of course, New Orleans had not had to imagine itself without America these last few weeks. It had been without it. And a year and a half later, when many of these plans had yet to come to fruition, neither the words "Katrina" nor "New Orleans" would be heard in his state of the union address.

When Bush was done, I took the long way around, crept through what seemed like a thousand 82nd Airborne troops and Humvees, and slid back into my entryway to send the article. I waited ten minutes, then called the editor. He said they'd run it, said it put a lot of things into perspective.

When I left, there were still police cars blocking off Jackson Square. I made sure my lanyard and ID were showing, pulled out my tape recorder, and started walking toward them.

Okay, don't make eye contact, just keep on talking, talking into this thing like it's something official, oh yeah, no eye contact, walking right between the police cars and made it onto Jackson Square right now and I am official, you bet your ass I am. Looks like they only let a couple camera crews in to film, maybe just White House cameras. So where's Bush at? Man, he disappears fast. Okey-dokey, just going to play with these cords here like these other tech people. That's right. They got their IDs around their necks just like me. . . . Here we go. . . . Walking into the park now. First time since the storm the gate's been open. Those Navajo guys really did a bang-up job in here. Wow. Huge blinding spotlight lighting up the cathedral just white as can be, like it's just a paper façade against such a black night. Here's my silhouette against General Jackson's horse. Huh. Electric cords all around. Red duct tape on the walkway around the statue, like marking a little path. Oh, this is where Bush must have stepped, okay. Gotcha. Wow. I guess he stood right in front here by those low bushes. Spotlights are blinding. So this is where he gave his speech a few minutes ago. All I can see is these little green glowing things on the ground by my feet. Must have marked his place. Glow sticks? Bush's glow sticks? Holy shit, they kept Bush from falling into the bush. Okay, sticking them into my pocket. Everything's cool. Oh yeah. Okay. Oops. My drink is spilling fucking everywhere because I got one of those little ten-ounce fucking cups, man. Anyway, walking through the rest of the park. Will I be let out this way? Probably not. Although it looks like the gate might be open. Is it? Could not be. . . . Oh my God, I think I'm actually going to get out. Well, maybe Katherine won't totally fucking hate me tonight. Okay, all right. No eye contact, just keep on walking, yup, that's right, just keep walking through the soldiers, through the Humvees, funny they're stopping people from walking in, and here I go out. Cathedral's clock still at six thirty-seven. Wonder if that was in the shot, wonder if the rest of the country know's time's stopped here now.

I walked up to the EMS station. Ty and I and a couple of the EMS guys started dancing with Bush's glow sticks in the middle of Dumaine street. Me and the chain-smoking muffuletta-eating EMS guy were really getting into it when a media van pulled up. The driver leaned her head out and said, "From the looks of it, you guys are gay, huh?"

"Say what?"

"You're not?"

"Sorry."

"Dammit!" she said. "We're from QTV."

"Ummmm . . ."

"Queer Television. We've been looking everywhere for gay people. Didn't there used to be a lot of them here? Where the hell did they all go?!"

23

A tall guy, at least half a foot taller than me, went flying past me on his bike. He missed me by about an inch, then skidded to a stop, put his bike down, and hugged me. "Dude, I've been biking all over the Quarter looking for you," said Parker Junior.

"How the fuck did you get into town?" I asked.

We spent the afternoon catching up by the pool, then biked uptown to Junior's house, and tore the plywood off his door. Inside, everything was just as it should be, his television where I'd last seen the commercials, my plate, Junior and the Professor's plates too, all empty but for the corn cob on each, now small and dry and brown. I realized it had been a week or so since I'd heard from the Professor about his pod. Junior poured us two healthy shots of hot Ezra Brooks that burned like hell. We put bandanas over our noses and he swung the freezer open. It wasn't that bad. The maggots seemed to have taken care of almost everything. They were still crawling around green glass shards, what was left of the Heineken I'd stuck in there and forgotten about. It had frozen, exploded, thawed, and now become this puddle of little white maggots. "Sorry, man," I said.

Junior put on some rubber gloves and tried scooping the glass into a shopping bag. The maggots writhed over his gloves, onto his bare wrists. He started jumping up and down, screaming that they were burrowing into his skin. He ran outside, still screaming, tore off his gloves, plunged his hands into a puddle in the street. I came outside, offered him some Ezra Brooks. He poured it over the maggots now crawling up his arms, still burrowing. "AHHHHHHHHHHH GOD!" he cried. "Get them off! Get them off!"

I couldn't stop laughing. Until he came at me with his maggot arms, stretched out in front of him like a zombie. He chased me two blocks until he found a dry patch of grass to roll around in.

We hustled back through downtown as twilight and curfew approached, the turquoise sky stabbed with fluorescent pink clouds around office buildings. Dr. Lutz showed up for dinner with some reporters from the *Wall Street Journal* who were staying in his home. Someone brought tiki torches, set them up around the pool. Heidi and John, TnA's friends who'd moved in with them, had gotten Katrina tattoos from Dale shortly after us. They had never met one another before the storm, but rescued each other from flooding and fallen in love along the way and already had an offer to make a TV movie out of their ordeal, but they figured that'd really mess their relationship up and so declined.

After dinner it rained and everyone scurried away after curfew except for Katherine, David, Junior, and Brett, the Harley-driving, Red-Bull-and-tequila-drinking poolman. We sat on David's balcony watching the first rain since Katrina fall into the tiki torches, dismissing them one by one. Brett told us about Wal-Mart right after the storm.

Brett: I live right near there. I see out of my back window people with shopping carts. The parking lot was packed like it was opening day! I'm thinking, "Oh my God, Wal-Mart is open. Fantastic! I need some shit." Well, when I get there, I see people by the door, they're smacking each other, stealing things from each other's shopping carts and I said, "Oh, wait a minute. This is not shopping."

The first people to the guns, did they start shooting people?

Brett: No. Back door, side doors, everything was open at that point so they just left. But there were only six NOPD out front, and there were at least twenty-five hundred people at this point, so they were saying, "We're just here to supervise the looting." But the NOPD was fucking lame anyway, you know. I mean, these guys were just as bad as the dregs looting.

Junior: I saw them talking about the convention center the other day, and Ted Koppel was saying, "You have two hundred well-trained policemen going in there," and the Police Chief kept saying, "Thirty thousand people, Ted." He's like, "Do you even know the odds of two hundred to thirty thousand?" He was like, "Every time we walked in, they were getting shot at," and they couldn't return fire, because they were getting shot at from a civilian population. Of course, he also told Oprah little babies were getting raped in the Superdome.

David: It's like, had we gotten these people food and water, they would have been controllable. Anyone will start looting if you have no food, no water, and you're sitting in that heat or whatever. You have nothing left to lose. There's no consequence.

Brett: Where do you get supplies at? Nobody thought of the river. There's a wharf right behind them. The river never stops.

David: If something happens on the other side of the world, and we can drop food and water within twenty-four hours, and it took four days to get food and water to them . . .

Junior: And we had two days warning before the thing.

Brett: Put shit on barges from Baton Rouge.

David: I was there for a little while, the majority of them were not crazy. They were mothers, they were old people, they were like, "We need food. We need water. We need someone to tell us what's going on."

Junior: Did you see the pictures of the people giving their babies away to people? There were like three hundred in line, and they were giving their infants away to people who were closer in line, "Please, just get them out of here."

Brett: In our microview, we didn't see it. We didn't see a lot.

David: And some news crew guy walks into the middle of all this—

Brett: He's gonna get mugged!

David: No he's not! The majority of them are like old people sitting in wheelchairs, and mothers and their kids and stuff and—shit. When did the rain stop?

You ever been up to the roof of those units over there? Come on.

As ever, a helicopter dangled its spotlight over moonlit rooftops. And then we saw the lights. Streetlights lined the way toward us from downtown, three blocks into the Quarter, just three blocks from us now. The stars wiped clean to Conti Street. No one spoke. We had had no idea. We finally broke the silence by trying to name all the skyscapers downtown, but couldn't name a single one, and realized we didn't recognize our city anymore.

A helicopter turned and came in our direction. "Quick. YMCA!" Junior cried.

We got in a line beside him and made the YMCA formation with our arms. The Black Hawk put us in its blinding spotlight. We closed our eyes, held the formation. "Hold it!" cried Junior. "Hold it!" It got louder and louder and louder, then began to fade, and when the backs of my eyelids stopped glowing it was gone toward the river.

We walked down to Johnny White's with Katherine, oblivious to curfew. There was a smattering of media there and a few 82nd Airborne officers "gathering intelligence." Reid, who had owned the tattoo shop Dale worked in, but who couldn't tattoo anymore because he had Hep C, was bartending.

"Yall want some tequila?" asked the media guy beside us. Shots of tequila, six ounces each, arrived in front of us. Brett was going on about how a couple of days after the storm he was on a boat with some people and they saw a dead woman floating and he tried to push her with a pole to get her out of the way. "The press people on board starting puking up all over the place when they saw that pole go through her arm," said Brett. "Just went right through." Another round of tequila shots came, this time filled to the brim of the ten-ounce cups.

Next thing I knew, I was on top of Touchdown Jesus.

"I'm just consoling him about his missing fingers!" I said to Katherine, who was pleading with me to get down. I wasn't quite sure how I'd gotten up there. I was on the base of the statue, about ten feet up, well above David, who was standing below me. And all the trees that had fallen were gone by now. The only thing near this height was Parker Junior, who was looking through the bushes, calling, "Here, kitty, kitty. Here, kitty."

I turned back to Christ. We stood nose to nose, His blank and pure eyes soaking in moonlight. "It'll be okay, man. It'll all be okay." I caressed the waves of His hair, His softly curving chin. "We'll get through this together. We will. Don't worry. We'll put you back together."

He didn't say anything. He was about my height, only His head was a bit bigger than mine, a bit nobler, a face as white as the whiteness of memory. I got on my tip-toes, kissed Him on His forehead, then tried to figure out how I was going to get down. I grabbed ahold of one of his outstretched arms, the one with the missing thumb that TnA had, shimmied up it till I was dangling from his wrist. My feet were probably about ten feet above the grass. Katherine was standing below me. "I love you, baby," I said. "And I think you better move because I'm going to let go." And I did.

Everything went black real quick. Then there were seven stars, big ones I tried to grab in front of my face, which felt like it had just married a sledgehammer. That was nothing compared to how my wrists felt. I was lying on the concrete pathway that led from the entrance of the garden up to Touchdown Jesus. What I hadn't planned was for David trying to catch me. He had succeeded in grabbing hold of my feet on the way down—one of which he was still holding—but not the rest of me, spinning me headfirst into the ground. There was a dime-sized spot of blood where my nose had hit the concrete. It seemed I'd just barely broken my fall with my hands, giving me a hurt nose and shot wrists but not a cracked skull. I felt warm blood trickling down the side of my nose and looked up to see Katherine walking out of the garden alone. "He'll be fine," she said. "He's indestructible."

24

The next morning, radio told us they were going to phase people back into the city zip code by zip code later this week. Also that tropical storm Rita could become a hurricane later today and it might possibly hit the Gulf Coast several days from now.

I took Junior with me to check on Señor Petucci. He was sitting on his step, tank top and slacks, coiffed white hair, sunspots spread across his small sagging chest, with five grocery bags of food around him. The pile of limbs and branches I'd chopped off the tree in his roof had sunk and withered to the size of a car across the street.

"What is that?" he asked us, gesturing to the bags around him. "Jackie Clarkson, our councilwoman, she had some man come bring me all this stuff this morning."

"Let's see, you got a couple bags of Tostitos."

"I don't want that. Take it."

"A box of Honey Nut Cheerios and some corn flakes."

"Take it!"

"Señor Petucci, this is food, you can eat it."

"I don't eat that stuff!"

"And there's some taco shells here and some chili and some refried beans."

"I don't want it!"

"But you can have Mexican night!"

"I don't want to have Mexican night!"

"Well, you know how all these Mexicans and Hondurans and Guatemalans are moving into town now? To come work and help get the hotels back up and running and stuff? This way you can entertain them."

"I don't want to entertain Guatemalans! Take it!"

"Okay, we'll take a bag, but you use the rest, okay?"

"No!"

Junior took one bag—I couldn't lift anything because of my wrists—and we walked down to Johnny White's. There was a terrible amount of junk food—Chocolate Teddy Grahams, Zapp's Cajun Crawfish potato chips, Oreos, cheese puffs—heaped chest-high in the corner. People were sneaking back into town, thinking that we needed this stuff to keep from starving to death. V was healing nicely and pouring warm Corona over ice out of his own cooler in the corner of the cramped bar, which was hidden somewhere under all the junk food. He tried to hand me one, but my wrist gave out and I dropped it.

Members of the Chicago Fire Department asked me to take their picture outside the bar. They held their beers high and said cheese. While we walked to the EMS station I saw two kids pushing themselves down Dauphine Street on scooters, their mother walking behind them. It seemed impossible. Children. I hadn't seen a child in weeks. And on scooters?

An EMS guy found their last Ace bandage, cut it in two, wrapped each half real tight around my wrists which stabilized them enough to cut the pain a bit. It was all they had. The radio was on beside us. They were trying to figure out what to do with a city of rotting refrigerators. The broadcaster advocated burying it in your yard, letting the things in the ground eat it up, saving the city from having to take care of the disposal, and buying a new one. Some guy with a thick Cajun accent called in, asked what would happen if he just waited until the electricity came back on and everything refroze, *then* he cleaned it out. There was silence on the air for some time. No one had thought of that.

Junior wanted to see the University of New Orleans, where he taught English Composition. It was about six miles away, up on the lakefront. As with so many parts of the city, we'd heard the worst—that the students, hundreds of them, their campus surrounded by water, had looted a nearby supermarket and thrown outrageous barbecue parties on the quad the first days after the storm, then, when food and water started running out, they ransacked the school buildings taking anything they could find, and, after another couple of days, started shooting each other.

Katherine and I biked with him. A couple of blocks out of the Quarter, up Esplanade Avenue, we passed a man raking fallen branches from his yard, the first person we saw. He stopped, looked at us, and asked Katherine if we were just out for a Sunday jaunt. Katherine, a bit bewildered, smiled and replied, "Sure."

"Well, fuck you very much!" the man responded, veins inflating in his forehead. "That's a nice fucking attitude to have!"

It wasn't until about fifty feet later that we realized he could possibly have been serious. I turned to see him still glaring at us, a thin, pale man with glasses, holding his rake up like a spear, like he was going to throw it at me. We kept going.

Esplanade had been one of the most beautiful avenues in the world. And now it was just dead, leaves and branches from the trees that had once canopied the avenue were strewn about the road, X's spraypainted on every single house indicating who had searched it, on what date, and, in the bottom portion of the X, how many dead bodies were still inside. Only two homes had numbers other than zero. A retirement home had 7 DB there. It was all dry now, but the further we got from the Quarter, the more it all seemed uninhabitable for the foreseeable future.

We veered off Esplanade to the Fairgrounds horse racing track. This was a place where normally I was either weaving through sunburnt hordes at Jazz Fest, or watching horses race while pulling the collar of my pea coat against the humid chill that pinches your bones here in winter, as the five-story clubhouse loomed behind me. Now, the roof was crushed and crinkled like tin foil into the glass walls overlooking the track and the emptiness of the massive white asphalt parking lot was like desert. Only with a boat in middle of it. Inside the motor boat, which was lying on its side, we found three plastic chairs and two MREs. "Sloppy Joe," I said. "Haven't had that yet."

As always, there was a world inside every MRE package. Each food item—entrée, sides, and dessert—was sealed in thick brown foil. Then there was a clear package of assorted and inappropriate condiments like blackberry jam and a miniature bottle of Tabasco to complement the food along with salt, gum, a moist towelette, iced tea or coffee mix, matches "designed especially for damp climates," and a dozen pieces of toilet paper.

Junior mixed Tabasco into the mashed potatoes. They were practically steaming from having been in the sun. He chucked the empty miniature Tabasco bottle into the parking lot. I walked over, picked it up.

"I know it's stupid," I said, "but we can't do that anymore. This entire city has become America's biggest garbage dump and someday, somehow, it's going to have to be cleaned up, and when that happens I don't want anyone having the extra burden of this miniature Tabasco bottle. We worked too hard to clean up the Quarter to throw trash into another section of the city." I looked down at the little Tabasco bottle in my hand. "The rain."

"Rain?" asked Junior.

"Remember? On that éclair? In the Children's Museum?"

"Our noodle," said Katherine.

We biked up the long straight drive to the New Orleans Museum of Art, lined with oaks, most of them still standing but badly torn. Geese floated lazily as ever along the lagoons to either side. A few army soldiers gazed at us with indifference in the silence and sun, sitting in front of the museum, a columned monolith that rose out of three dozen steps in the center of a circular road. One soldier sat in a beach chair in a tiny patch of shade beneath a myrtle tree, his rifle across his lap, feeding an enormous white duck pieces of the toasted pastry from his MRE. A plainclothed man walked up to us, held his hand out for us to stop there in front of the museum.

He eyed us silently one by one. A soldier came around the circle on a kid's Huffy Dirt Bike, his M-16 swung around behind him, dodged around us, then went back around the museum.

"We're just biking around," said Katherine. "We haven't been up here since the storm, and just wanted to see if the museum was okay. We're locals."

"Name's Doogle," he said. "Billy Doogle. Detective with the New York Police Department. Got me here in charge of guarding the museum." We each shook hands with him, introduced ourselves. "Everything's fine in there. We're just here to guard the art now."

"I suppose if you were a serious art thief it'd be pretty smart to strike immediately after a disaster like this," I said.

"Yeah, we were lucky," said Doogle. "You know, the museum, they got these warehouses in the city where they keep some of their stuff. Some of the warehouses, they were right in the middle of the worst looting these animals were doing. Anyone coulda taken millions of dollars of art. But what would they do with it? Monets and Pissarros and everything? Give it to their grandmother? What, she'd put it up in her attic?"

"Have you been here before?" asked Katherine.

"You know, I've never been here before, to New Orleans. But I'm recognizing a lot of faces here. It's the same ones from all around the country who responded to 9/11, we all seen each other before. But 9/11, that was four by four blocks, ya know? This here, shit, it's two hundred by two hundred miles. We could go back to our homes, sleep in our beds at night after 9/11."

Doogle leaned in real close to the three of us. "You know what they tell me," he whispered, "I got this on real good authority—they tell me they dropped a Navy SEAL team in here that first night when all hell broke loose in the city to take out any bad guys they could find, then got out before dawn."

He turned around and gazed at the museum that loomed at the top of the steps above us. "You know what the greatest thing is? I play the piano. I play right in there, in the atrium, that big center hall they got in there. I have the grand piano all to myself at night. I go in there, the moon and stars coming down through those big skylights they got on the roof, and play for hours. It's a gift."

We wished him well and biked along City Park toward the lake. America's second largest urban park was gray and orange and drowned in a few inches of water, sometimes a few feet, still.

It looked like an earthquake had hit the lake's shore. Benches and concrete were torn and there were enormous sink holes all along it.

We found the army a couple of miles east, on the University of New Orleans campus. There was a unit of MP's getting ready for dinner. Junior and I hid around the corner while Katherine sweet-talked her way in, then we meekly followed.

Apparently, the campus had served as a drop point before people were evacuated after the flooding. No one there knew anything about any violence breaking out after the storm between students. After dinner, we grabbed a pack of Juicy Fruit, the last thing left in a looted vending machine, and wandered the halls of the English department, most of it unharmed, including Junior's office.

Curfew neared and we were eight miles from home. Elysian Fields, the quickest route back, was still flooded and rancid. The waterlines on the buildings were about ten feet up. A lone brown dog walked along the ash-gray neutral ground and the sun raged a hot pink hole above the silver horizon, but its light couldn't make it to us. We were in a black-and-white movie, ourselves fleeting shocks of color as we finally navigated down Paris Avenue. The cars were covered in gray crap, some on the sidewalk, but everything else was where it should be, simply another shade of gray, the light dying with the day, not a living soul, not even a ghost, anywhere. It was not a place I knew. Little restaurants, KJ's, Rock's Lock and Key, the Circle Grocery, and all of them without light. The landscape was so dead it killed the sky, too. The only other life we saw was one police car that pulled up alongside us to inform us we would be arrested if we were out after six and that was in five minutes. Where do we go? I thought. We're headed there. Home. And here, home after home after home after

home after home after home after home after home after home after
home after home after block after block after block after mile after mile
after mile. . . . All with their spray paint crosses signifying when and how
and who had checked them for bodies, parts of the city that I had never
discovered, would never be able to, "the end" crying silently to be written.

That night, Parker Junior sleeping on the couch in 109 below us, I
stepped over the citronella candle burning between Katherine and me,
lay beside her sleeping, ran my hand across her back, down the muscles
there, hard and tight currents tumbling over themselves with her every
finger's twitch in sleep, only thinner now, thin clothing over bones, my
finger down along her ribs defined and smooth as the waved sand of
Nova Scotia when it was still below the last water, until it settled on the
last of them, the extra rib, and I felt breeze over us a last time before
pulling the sheet over our heads against the mosquitoes and went to
sleep, my hand resting upon that rib which did not move with her
breath, firm as the white sand when the water had gone away.

25

*Well, it's Monday now. About 9 A.M. Guess it's exactly three weeks after
the storm. Sunny, cloudless blue sky. Woke up to a blue jay screaming
in the tree branch just over our heads. The birds—they come right up
close to you. It's as if we've been taken down a notch, knocked closer
to the animals without our electricity and everything. It's like somehow
they know that and there's less of us here and we're sleeping outside
with them and all the rest.*

*Parker Junior went back to Baton Rouge this morning. A couple min-
utes ago, Katherine got a call from the* Wall Street Journal *to go take
pictures of three levee breaches today. We don't know exactly where
they are, I'm not even sure where the canals are.*

*Cleaned the pool already, of course, dropped off my computer with the
EMS guys, and Katherine and I are going to do a little workout here*

shortly. This normalcy returning to our lives, it aches. The new things have stopped coming at us, or maybe they're just old now.

[tape breaks]

We're here in Katherine's car, almost 1:00, driving up to Lakeview to find the 17th Street Canal levee breach and the mayor's on the radio. He's suspending all reentry back into New Orleans because of Hurricane Rita.

[tape breaks]

What is this black—is that mud? Big black rocks of mud? Looking at a car that's up on about a forty-five degree angle, propped up against a tree. There's a home that is just completely collapsed. The roof is just like coming up out of the street around a tree, and we're now along the 17th Street Canal. It's just to the left of us, we're driving up towards the lake. These are big nice houses. This is the most devastation we've seen. Cars that have floated up onto trees and basically the water came down and they came down on the trees, and they're up on their sides and stood up on their backs, just destroyed. This home did that too, look at the whole front of this home. Right, the whole house floated and shifted and that's what happened, it came down around a tree and broke in half. Here we have brown mud, as opposed to the gray ash we saw yesterday. It's a Corvette upside down sandwiched between what appears to be, what was a big fence, a big metal fence, a tree and a fire hydrant. The fire hydrant is leaking. Just mangled. And it's on top of another picket fence. When will these people see their homes?

[tape breaks]

Walking now, couldn't drive any further, too much in the street. It's getting worse and worse, I think we're coming up on the breach here. The force of water. Piles of rubble, bricks, mud, sticks, oyster shells, massive trees uprooted, concrete all over, piping, telephone poles. Still seeing a big pool of water on this side of the levee. Army Corps of Engineers guy just told us a barge, the storm drove a barge into the lock where this canal enters the lake, destroying that, and the lake water kept flooding in, flooding in, flooding in, and then this levee burst that evening. The earth here slopes up about ten feet tall to form the levee, and a two-foot-thick concrete wall runs through that and goes about eight feet up above the top of the earth. Canal's about one hundred feet across. Some of the houses nearest where the levee broke look just like a big monster came and took a chomp out of them. Mud-caked socks hanging from trees.

[tape breaks]

. . . force to mangle these trees I'm seeing. The telephone poles mangled up in them and then bed sheets and stuff, more socks hanging from trees. Standing on a little patch of what used to be a driveway, no the foundation of a home here, house cleanly swept away. Massive pipes, tree roots everywhere, water putrid, smells disgusting. School bus picked up and put on top of what looks like a pine tree, the leaves now dying. Air burns like ammonia, then after a while it starts prickling your lungs, like little needles in my lungs now, and your stomach gets nauseous like motion sickness. A can of Coca-Cola, paper plates, a sock hanging. Can of Coca-Cola. I picked up a piece of rock from the place here, the foundation to the home, all that's left, that and this muddy sock. The next plot doesn't appear to have even its foundation there, there's nothing, and then the next one right . . . here . . . walking up to it now . . . where the levee broke, there's just a pool of water and mud in front of me where the house was. How such a small break in such a small levee can totally erase someone's home.

[tape breaks]

Note to self: Stop saying as a greeting "How you doing?" or "What's up?" and just "Hi" from now on.

When I turned Katherine was gone. She'd been keeping pace a couple of houses behind me, just out of earshot, enough distance between us to absorb it in our own ways. We had free rein of the destruction, one tractor the only official-looking thing anywhere around.

Ahead was an oak, perfectly uprooted, lying on its side. A bed sheet, lavender and muddy, was caught in its roots, hanging to the ground. Its was wrapped around something beneath the roots. It shifted. It wasn't until I was about ten feet away, the mud around my toes hard and sandy, that I saw Katherine's thin ankles and pink Aqua Socks sticking out of the bottom, realized she was clenching the sheet around her. I had no idea what to do, but stood there, looking at her, scared to death.

I turned and walked away, over to the small two-lane bridge that ran over the canal, connecting Orleans and Jefferson parishes. I stood there on the Orleans side and looked across the bridge into the area of town known as Old Metairie, not even two hundred feet away, where Katherine had grown up, untouched. I could see her house. There were a couple of small trees piled up on the sidewalk, but that was it.

There were two men standing beside me, both of them white, upper thirties, wearing glasses, one in Bermuda shorts and a madras button-down shirt, the other in knee-high rubber boots and soiled jeans.

"Hi," I said. They looked at me, nodded. "You guys, are you from over here?"

"His house is right there," said the one in the shorts, pointing to a row of town houses, the water above their doorways.

"And what about you?" I asked.

"I'm over there," he said, pointing across the bridge into Old Metairie, near Katherine's parents' house. "Place is fine. Had a couple of feet of water in the street after the storm, but it was fine."

"You guys been back for a while?"

"I've been back about a week. John here just got back in today. You know, you really shouldn't be wearing open shoes out here."

We looked down at my flip-flops. Even here, where the ground was relatively dry, the soles were sunk into the dirt up to my scratched, cracked, sediment-speckled feet.

The man with the boots and Oilers baseball cap looked at me with this baffled expression, as though he'd just asked me some question, the answer to which would solve some serious problem. We stood there for a little bit, the three of us, me still trying to take it all in, them no doubt wondering what the hell I was doing, the tape recorder tucked under my arm the last thing they needed to deal with. Finally, the man in Bermuda shorts turned to the other one. "So, your wife have any breakdowns yet?" he said, smiling out of the corner of his mouth, rolling his eyes. "She had her emotional breakdown yet?" The man in boots said nothing.

"You know, I envy your attitude," I said and had no idea if I was joking or not. I never ever wanted to be such a man, whose world could be so separate from his partner that he could look down upon her this way, could so dismiss her problems and not struggle with them as his own. It depressed me that people everywhere had these relationships, how many of them. And yet, had I seen Katherine this way, it would have saved us so much.

The man in boots glanced over my shoulder and he finally seemed to resume control of his face. "Katherine Mae Dufrene?" he said.

"Yeah?" It was Katherine, she had walked up behind me. "Oh my God? John?"

"I guess yall know each other?" I said.

"Yeah, John and I went to St. Martin's together," she said. "Oh my God." She walked up to him and gave him a big hug and kiss. He actually smiled. "You live here?" she asked. "Which one was your house?"

"Well, it's down there." He looked at the ground, pointed down the row of town houses that shot off perpendicular to the street, then shook his head, smiled. "Kathy Mae. Wow. Kathy Mae."

I looked at Katherine. She was blushing. A razor-thin line of red ringed her eyes.

John's was the middle house in the row of town houses, a neck-high khaki waterline stretching across them all. The door was open. He stood at the beginning of his walkway, told us to go up and have a look. Katherine told me to go ahead. As I approached the front door, it seemed strange that the house should be so quiet. And I wondered why we hadn't stopped the day before with Parker Junior, anywhere along the way, to peer inside the miles of homes we had passed. It was not simply out of respect, not the fear of being caught by the police. It just hadn't been an option. Maybe because once you opened the inside, it all became so real. Why open a corpse? Open up the walls that keep body and spirit, house and home, all wrapped up in one? Viscera can reduce life to such a messy thing.

Here I was looking into it, past the buckled front door that had been forced open. You could taste it, like a mouthful of milk that had gone bad but was fine just the day before. The smell was like wrapping your face in a mildewed T-shirt that was left wet in your trunk for several hot months.

While I stood there, Katherine and John caught up. New Orleans is a village and its true natives seem to always return. Since Katherine had returned two years ago, she'd run into about five of the other fifteen people in her graduating class, and I supposed it was only a matter of time until she found the other ten. Eventually the man in Bermuda shorts offered to show Katherine around the other side of the bridge, around Old Metairie, her childhood home, and they walked over the bridge.

John and I walked back out to the road. He found a small banana in the backseat of his rented Ford Explorer. "I'm sorry," he said. "I haven't eaten since I left Houston."

He peeled the banana like he was scared to see what was beneath the skin.

"Yeah, that's fine, man," I said. "Would you mind if I recorded this?"

He shook his head. "Long as there's no photos. Would you like half?" he asked me, holding the peeled banana out by its end.

"No, no, I'm fine. Thank you though."

I turned the tape recorder on. The banana broke from its end and fell out of its peel into the dirt between us. We both stared at it, his boots, my toes smudged with sediment, nothing but the soft whir of the tape rolling around us for almost a minute . . .

John: Huh.

Do you have another one? Do you have anything else?

John: No.

You know, I have some parts of an MRE in Katherine's car. Like some bread and a toasted pastry and a cookie or something.

John: No, I'm not even hungry.

Really.

John: Really. I don't want to eat.

Okay. Okay . . . So you drove in from Houston, is that right? You heard about this before you drove in? What it was like? First-hand accounts?

John: I'm sorry . . .

That's okay.

John: My neighbor was here. He told me . . . Let me sit down.

Sure . . . You've got what? A few inches of caked mud in there, don't you?

John: It looks sorta like in Hawaii, where the lava has dried up.

How did you get in?

John: I came here and they wouldn't let me . . . I went to Veteran's Highway and there was a line, and I knew a way to come around it. I went down side streets.

You got a family here?

John: Two little girls.

And you think your . . .

John: I'm sorry . . .

. . . home is going to be destroyed?

John: Yes. I think it will be. I mean, downstairs everything is buckled. The doors don't fit. The molding's popped. When I walked in there was a soup bowl placed right in the middle of the staircase, five or six steps up. Upright. Like someone had just placed it there. I mean it came from a cabinet in the kitchen, which is in the back of the house, nowhere near the stairs.

How much did you manage to get out and take with you when you went to Texas?

John: We left Sunday night. I mean Sunday morning. My days are all screwed up. I brought a pair of blue jeans and a pair of shorts. We went to Dallas. I gotta tell you, everyone's been super nice in Texas.

What's the most—what's the thing that kills you the most, that you've lost in the house here?

John: Pictures. Everything on the first floor is pretty much destroyed. But then upstairs, you could spend the night.

You didn't move much upstairs, did you? You didn't think you had to.

John: No. I told my wife, "If we'd have moved it upstairs, the roof would have come off." The only thing . . . I laughed when we left town. Nobody was packed to leave. No U-Hauls. Everybody was just going for the weekend. And I left Sunday thinking I wouldn't—I kinda like hurricanes. Sitting though them, you know?

You've been through other hurricanes here?

John: Yeah. This has never really flooded. Like this—Look at this house here, been here probably forty years. He probably does not have flood insurance.

Were you and your neighbors aware of your vulnerability?

John: Everybody in New Orleans is aware that it can happen. I just never expected it would.

You're going to continue working here? You're gonna come back and work?

John: Would I come back here? Yeah, for the right opportunity. The problem here is—I think a lot of people are going to have to go elsewhere for work . . . Sorry I'm not the best interview. I'm just honestly wiped. Honestly, it's not . . . I mean, it's not the end of the world. It's just a hassle.

Was there a car in your garage?

John: Yeah.

What was it?

John: A BMW.

Was there anything else you wanted to add?

John: I don't think everybody should be blaming . . . Did FEMA screw up? Yeah, they screwed up. But nobody expected all this. Everybody left not knowing the . . .

Thank you, John.

I left him sitting there on the curb. Katherine was just across the canal, on the Jefferson Parish side, talking to a man wearing a construction hat.

"Yo, Katherine!" I yelled. I didn't feel like walking up to the bridge to cross over.

She didn't respond, just kept listening to the guy in the hard hat, and behind her, it was as though none of it had ever happened. A woman wearing gardening gloves walked out of the house beside Katherine's old one, kneeled down in her front lawn, and began tearing weeds out.

"Yo! Katherine!"

Nothing. She just kept talking to the man.

"*Katherine! Goddammit!*"

The woman kneeling in her lawn stood, shielded the sun from her eyes with a fistful of weeds, and looked at me. But Katherine would not. I walked back to the car and waited.

[Radio] . . . the first deputy was fired for desertion during the hurricane. Now he's been charged with looting. Another suspect was also picked up. The sheriff says among the looted items: seven weapons. The Army Corps of Engineers report that 85 percent of the city has been drained . . .

We're driving toward—There's a yacht just on its side, just over here at the entrance to West End park. What was that it fell on top of? A restaurant, a house on the dock?

Katherine: Remember when we went there, baby? Acme Oyster House?

Of course.

Katherine: And we were arm wrestling and we ended up on the floor?

Oh my god, all those masts from the yachts are sticking up and they . . .

Katherine: Yeah. We went there after—

They've been put up on top of the docks, and they're just heaped on top of each other.

Katherine: —your apartment-warming party.

Wow. The yacht club's just a charred black skeleton. Don't know what happened there.

Katherine: We were still getting to know each other.

(Radio) Nagin: . . . prepare yourself to evacuate on Wednesday or even earlier. Our pumping stations are still not at full capacity. I am urging and encouraging everyone who knows of someone who may be in a home somewhere in Orleans Parish to call them and encourage them to leave the city. Any type of storm that heads this way will put Orleans Parish in very significant harm's way.

[tape breaks]

We just went by the Orleans Street Canal, saw where it overtopped. Now we're here at the London Street Canal. It runs between the University of New Orleans and the neighborhood of Lakeview.

A black Labrador slid by us like shadow, down the levee, and simply merged into the destroyed landscape. We were losing light. Colors were falling into gray tones, gray like that moment a mind seizes on something and carries it down out of consciousness into sleep.

There was one media trailer, parked just off the levee, the only other vehicle there besides Katherine's Maxima. Sean Caleb from CNN was sipping a bottle of water, leaning against the trailer, talking with an assistant. While Katherine took pictures of the levee and the neighborhood below, I followed the thick cords that ran out of the CNN trailer, up the levee and along its flat top lined with loose gravel the width of a car. The cords ran the length of a city block until they came to a camera, all by itself, chest-high on a tripod, pointing at a slant into the neighborhood below. And a man. He was halfway down the levee, holding a Tupperware container, trying to balance on the rocks they used to reinforce the dirt with which they filled the breach. He was facing down the slope into mounds of earth the size of houses, where there once were homes.

"Ma' honey!" he called. He contemplated which rock to step on next. They were the size of full grocery bags. He tested one, it moved, then another before shifting his weight to it, stumbling a bit, water sloshing out of the Tupperware container, darkening his gray T-shirt. His back and underarms were already dark with sweat. "Yo ma' honey," he called.

"Whatcha doing, man?" I asked.

He turned, twisted at the waist as much as he could to look at me. "I'm okay," he said. He was black and had a radio on his belt.

"You with CNN?" I asked. "What do you do?

"Camera." He lifted his right foot but then the rock under his left tilted and he put it back. The coming night gave no sounds, no insects or birds, no hint of time.

"Ma' honey," he called to the darkness below. "Where are you, ma' honey?"

"So, what are you doing now?" I asked.

"Look, man, I'm okay, I'm just trying to find ma' honey."

"Who's your honey?"

"Ma' honey, not my honey."

"Your honey?"

"Ma-ho-neeeeeee. Mahoney. He's a dog."

"Mahoney? You brought a dog here with you and now you lost him?"

"No, I didn't lose him. I found him. He was here. He's been here every day since we've been filming, a week now. We've been feeding him, making sure he has water."

He lost his balance and dropped the Tupperware. "Damn," he said. He stuck his hands out carefully, started to bend down but the rocks twisted under his ankles. He steadied himself, then stood back up. The water from the Tupperware spread over the dirt on the rock in front of him, made it dark as the air, invisible. "Damn."

"You want me to come down there?"

"I'm fine, man."

"How do you know he's Mahoney?"

"Because that's his name."

"His tag said that?"

"Tag only had a phone number that doesn't work no more. C'mon, Mahoney! Where are you goddammit?!"

"Let me come down and help you," I said.

His arms were out, teetering, his waist bent, legs bent at the knees, trying to keep from falling. "I'm fine," he said. "Just need to find Mahoney. Mahoney!"

Not a thing moved among the piles of wood and metal and concrete and dirt, twice as high as the man, below him. I stood beside the camera, looked down the other side of the levee, the canal now shielded with a corrugated metal wall, the soft footsteps on gravel behind me, light failing so fast I could see it flickering out. Katherine stood on top of the repaired breach with me, looked down over the metal wall, into the water, only barely dimmer than the rest of the world now. The acrid, ammoniac taste that hung in the homes below lingered within the thick summer dark, stripped of all sound but "Ma' honey . . . ma' honey . . . my honey . . ."

This was the third and final levee failure on this side of the Industrial Canal. Two days ago I could not have even found these canals on a map, I had not even heard of them. Now that I saw them, I realized I had jogged along each before, several times, and driven by them many, many times. Now I understood it. The lake levees had held, but the surge pushed lake water into these three drainage canals until it overtopped or breached their levees. Water arced through the northern portion of the city, from the Jefferson Parish line at the 17th Street Canal to the walls of the Orleans Street Canal, to this London Street Canal, to the western levee of the Industrial Canal, and south toward us, to the Hyatt, a couple inches of it into the Quarter.

David had left us a note back at the Compound. He was going to start spending nights at the Christopher Inn, one of the hotels he was helping get started back up. We could come stay at the hotel if we wanted. I decided against it, said spending a night or two in air-conditioning would ruin us, make us miserable all over again when we returned to this. So, we spent the night on the balcony. I flipped my cushions around so that our heads were facing one another, blew the citronella candle out between us. We pulled our sheets over our heads and stuck our arms out, holding hands in the space between us. I woke some hours later to find my empty hand burning with mosquito bites. I pulled it under the sheet with the rest of me, clawed at the bites for over an hour until they bled and cooled and woke in sunlight to the blue jay screaming again in the tree above us.

26

The next morning we went down to Central Command and found an abandoned crate of ravioli-sauce cans. We traded these with some relief agency from Alabama for twelve bags of ice, eight of which we then traded to another organization from Texas for a crate of smoked salmon and Oreos. We traded the Oreos for tuna and Pringles from some cook from Michigan, and traded half of the smoked salmon and all the Pringles with an Arkansas cop for thirty-six MREs and two more bags of ice.

After a late lunch, we biked into the Upper 9th Ward, just to see it. There was a checkpoint a few blocks out of the Quarter at Elysian Fields and St. Claude. We pleaded with the soldiers, part of a battalion from Oregon, about how badly we needed to check on our property and it was just a few blocks up and we wouldn't be long at all. Please?

"All right, I'll let you guys on through," said the commanding officer quietly, looking both ways down the street to be sure no one saw, but there was no one to see. "You guys ready to evac, before Rita hits?" he asked.

"Oh, yeah," I said. "First thing in the morning. We just need to check on this property."

He looked back and forth between us. "Listen, come here," he said. "You need to know, you got to understand . . . we're leaving tonight or tomorrow," he said. "Not just us. Most of the divisions are. We're evac'ing. You understand what I'm saying?"

"Oh," I said.

"Yeah. Exactly."

"The NOPD . . . So it'll be just them and us again."

"We don't want to come back and be scraping up dead civilians, you know. We don't like that. I can't force you to get out of here, but I'm advising you."

We thanked him and biked up St. Claude Avenue which we had not seen since it was covered with water and refugees. The doors to Robért's supermarket were shut, and did not appear broken. Along three houses in a row, in man-sized letters was spray-painted HELP HELP HELP. The X's were on every door, the bottom portion signifying how many bodies were still inside—again, zeros as far as I could see. The neutral ground, about wide enough for three lanes of traffic, was piled with garbage and trees and other debris. The homes lay there battered, a few corner stores, one St. Roch's Grocery—a Vietnamese-owned place where I had my first half fried oyster, half fried shrimp po'boy and ate it opposite a friend from New York who just stared aghast and said he "can't eat that stuff this early in the day," had clearly been broken into and ravaged. Across the street from that was the tiny used furniture store from which I bought the coffee table my television still rests on, the box springs and mattress I still sleep on. Next to that was a house with an "8" in the bottom portion of its X.

There were several mounds of trash on the corner of Desire and St. Claude that were simply too composed to have just been thrown there. The top half of a silver mannequin, upright, crowned the pile. Across the street a bunch of white, tattooed, long-haired kids were sitting on a balcony. They said they were changing the debris every day and posting new pictures of it online. It was their Toxic Art exhibit.

We biked through the streets north of St. Claude, where we had seen the first real flooding while walking back to Tayl's place with our bottle of wine the day after the storm. Waterlines, about waist-high, ringed every home. This was where the water had settled, not where it was at its highest. The streets were crusted gray, the air burning and nauseous, thin like ammonia.

There were more barricades at the St. Claude Bridge. A soldier put his hand out for us to stop. "Restricted access," he said.

"Hey," I said. "We're just going to check on my aunt's place. It's just over the bridge. We're going to leave tomorrow and this is our last chance to see it."

"Where is it?"

I thought of the man trying to sell me the bottles of sparkling wine out of his garbage bag outside Molly's three weeks ago. "Egania," I said. "Y'all from Oregon, too?"

"Yup," he said. "You talked to the guys back there?"

"Yeah, of course," I said. "How do you like it down here?"

"Well, it's pretty great not having to speak broken Iraqi to you, tell you that. That's the best thing."

"They sending you guys back?"

"Nah, we're headed over to Afghanistan in a month. This whole battalion that's here, there's about fifteen hundred of us."

We walked our bikes up the small four-lane drawbridge to the top, where we'd heard the Coast Guard had dropped people after the waters came, the beginning of the Industrial Canal a calm shadow below us, and looked back at the soldiers who were watching us. They went up on their tiptoes as the bridge's crest rose between us, like they were trying to get one last look at us. The lieutenant waved. His hand was the last thing to disappear beneath the crest. We got on our bikes, coasted over the canal, the grating, the Lower 9th Ward, quiet as a grave, opening before us as we descended into it.

There were no art installations made from debris here. Shotgun homes and small businesses—Head Hunters Hair Stylist, Family Discount Food Store, Popeye's, Light City Human Services, Mickie Bees Lounge, No LOITERING still painted red all over a long-abandoned building—stretched along the avenue, each ringed with a waterline just above our heads. Everything below the waterlines was pale gray. Here, all was in its proper place. To our right, it looked that way for the five blocks between us and the river. To the left, just a few blocks away, things were crumbled—windows, doors, signs, cars, fences gone, buildings shifted. Past that it became something unrecognizable, something that could not possibly be real.

Katherine stopped. There was the silence again, that same silence we had tasted sitting with T and Tayl in the middle of Chartres Street as he was siphoning gasoline, the silence you expected at any moment to be filled with the bird's call, the insect. But it was no longer unnerving. It was the only thing imaginable here. A cricket would have shot every nerve inside us, and our breath nearly shattered the place. I could feel, hear, my heart, slow, the blood sliding through my veins and that too was too much for this. I swallowed it, the stench.

"So?" I whispered. We were on the corner of Jourdan, one street off the canal. The breach was obviously to our left, away from the river. As with yesterday, we would only need to follow the destruction to find it. But this did not look like yesterday. I could see no end to it all. The debris simply became impenetrable in the distance.

"So," said Katherine, "why are we here? This isn't where we'd been meaning to come."

"No."

"So, let's go back."

"No. Let's just go to the river. Just for a bit."

I biked into the neighborhood to our right, the part where things were in their proper place. She followed. The streets that ran between St. Claude and the river, parallel to both, had the same names as those on the other side of the Industrial Canal, those in the Bywater and French Quarter. We passed Burgundy, and Dauphine was ahead, the same two streets Tayl lived between, and like Tayl's house, we were only one block off the canal. But here, several hundred feet from his house, the street was cracked into a trillion pieces the size of bottle caps, and cars were on the sidewalks and flood lines slanted down century-old clapboard homes toward the river and I wondered if the smell of our barbecues those first nights had wafted over here, maybe our music, T gyrating in the middle of the street, Katherine hiding, crying for her purse in Tayl's dark living room.

"This is some alternate universe," said Katherine, looking up into the top of a tree lit with sun like fire against the blue sky, sun that would not fall here, a few brown wrinkled leaves dripping toward the cracked sidewalk. "Some place like our own, where all the physical things remain, but rotted without life, like reality shifted in a dream. You know the place, it is recognizable, culled from your subconscious, the things are there, and yet it's totally foreign, frustrating because it's not quite as it should be."

"And, eventually, you see enough of it, and you realize it's all a dream."

"Yes."

"You know, I think it's maybe the opposite, the opposite of a dream. Everything's in its proper place, unlike a dream, the doorknobs are all there, but nothing is culled from memory, no symbols slapped together to represent something in a dream's landscape, there is no memory of this."

We reached the river levee, pushed our bikes up through grass taller than it had ever been, swaying in breeze, waves of it washing green around our shins, the falling copper sun casting our shadows long ahead of us as we rose up the levee into another world entirely, green, green, green, and I tried to resist the temptation to look back, and could not. There was no high ground back there. When the levee breached, the levees would have been the only safe place.

There was a gravel path along the top, a couple of benches. "I used to jog this," I said. "I'd run across the bridge, along the Industrial Canal, until it joined the river there, then along the river on top the levee here until I couldn't go any further."

"I had no idea," said Katherine, gazing upriver. "You can see the whole city here. My God. What we think of as the city anyway."

She meant our half of the city. This side of the Industrial Canal, from here to the lake, the Lower 9th to New Orleans East, was the ghost of *our* city, one that the rest of New Orleans would only catch a glint of if they shot over it on the interstate, or if they were a naïve newcomer simply looking for a safe, nearby jogging route. Our New Orleans only went from the suburbs in the west (where we shopped at malls and went to movies) until it dead-ended at the Bywater in the east (where we danced to Kermit Ruffins and ate barbecue). This was not necessarily a white-black thing. On our side at least, there were plenty of races mixed. It's just that we simply didn't cross the Industrial Canal. I suppose we felt there was nothing there for us. Now there was just nothing there.

We biked downriver, through the loading docks of two warehouses, storage yards, then back onto the levee, until it came to a low wall above Jackson Barracks, normally occupied by the Lousiana National Guard. Past that, the levee became a tangle of trees and bushes. There was a small bench there, just big enough for us.

"This is where I'd turn around," I said. "No one seemed to know this was here, this path along the top of the levee. I'd see plenty of people down in the neighborhood, playing, talking, doing whatever, but they never came up here. And I also never saw a single white person on this side of the canal."

"I just had no idea," said Katherine. "The whole skyline laid out like that. Look at that."

"Look at that. And you know another thing, there's—what?—maybe one or two apartment complexes along the entire river, all the way to uptown? I've never seen anything like this in the world. All this waterfront property that no one lives on. You suppose they're scared of it? Of the river? People here?"

A cricket tore into the quiet for a second. We both flinched.

"I suppose they have reason," she said.

"But we're sitting on the safest spot in the entire Lower 9th Ward. The closer to the river, the higher you are. The further, the lower. That's all that matters with water. It doesn't matter how far you are from it."

"That's not how people think. Out of sight, out of mind; that's how they think."

I took out two MREs. A mutt, long orange matted hair clinging tight to a gaunt body, stood at the bottom of the levee, opened its mouth, craned its neck, and made a barking motion, but nothing came out. I filled my bottle cap with water and held it out. The dog walked up the levee cautiously. He drank ten capfuls until he quit, tongue dripping, eyes darting back and forth between us and the neighborhood below. I broke open an MRE bread package. The bread was the shape of a big flattened piece of toast and tasted like a dense, chewy, slightly sweet cracker. The dog took the whole thing in its mouth, ran down the levee, and disappeared underneath a house.

"That was my bread," said Katherine.

"Here, we'll split mine," I said. I opened my package, broke the bread, gave half to her. The downtown buildings became indistinguishable, simply different-sized rectangles of blue silver, same color as the clouds above them, against a pale sky. We just sat there eating and watching the water until the sun burned a crimson hole above the skyline and threw that light like blood around our shadows slanting down into the river.

"Back when I was jogging this, when I saw a barge coming I'd sprint the whole rest of the way, try to get over the Industrial Canal before they raised the bridge," I said. "I always made it. Sometimes I'd feel like I was going to faint, but I always made it, just barely. And while I was running toward the bridge, chasing the barge, the skyline there in front of me like that, I'd say to myself, even out loud, 'There's my city.' And I would laugh because it sounded so stupid. I thought maybe one day it would become my city. But still, I never dreamed I would be here this long. Since school, I'd never lived in one place for more than a few months. I thought I'd just be here for a summer. Because it had always been the road ahead for me. I always wanted to be like Neal Cassady, you know, burning for the next something more. Motion, the American virtue, I guess. But, you know, the more you change, the more you stay the same. So, I decided I wouldn't change places, and maybe I'd change instead. You know, I guess it's like you can change places, but only when you stay somewhere can the place change you."

"Now your place has changed on you."

The cricket began again, then cut off abruptly. The sun had fallen behind the slyline. We biked back along the levee. Above their floodlines, the houses had fallen blue like the rest of the city now. Below the floodlines they were gray, stone, and below that the streets were flooding low with shadow like fog, rising almost perceptibly. Dogs came out. They just appeared when I looked down into the neighborhood, one by one. They were not in feral packs as we had heard. They would stare at us, no barking, no wagging tail, legs disappearing into that rising shadow.

The smell rose up out of the place. It must have been the smell of death. There is no other way to describe it. Death simply could not possibly smell any different. We got back onto the bridge, and the smell, the shadow, sank back into the hollow, the now-dry valley, the bottom behind us.

That evening, Katherine and I, alone again, ate Beef Steak MREs while the radio told us Rita was expected to become a Category 3 hurricane tomorrow, Wednesday, and it was projected to make landfall Friday near Houston. "The irony never stops, huh?" I said, laughing. "There's a hundred fifty thousand refugees from New Orleans in Houston now."

Katherine's eyes came alive, open and deeper than I'd seen them in weeks, and candlelight weaved and grew in twin reflections as they filled with pity until the first tear fell. "Did you think about what was behind us today?" she asked. "Right there behind our backs while we ate? How it came over all those people and it was there coming up at us and you just sitting there talking about . . ."

[Radio] New Orleans Mayor Ray Nagin held a press conference a little bit ago. Lt. General Russel Honoré stepped in and literally took over. Here's what he had to say:

Honoré: We're talking here about getting people to buses outside the convention center. Let's not get stuck on the last storm. You're asking last storm questions for people who are concerned about the future storm, Rita. Don't get stuck on stupid, reporters. We are moving forward.

Male reporter: General, if we could just understand a little bit more about why that's happening this time, though, and did not happen last time . . .

Honoré: You are stuck on stupid! I'm not going to answer that question! We are going to deal with Rita! Let's talk about the future! Rita is happening.

"Don't think you're the only one this pains for this city," I said, "the only one who can love this place because you're the one from here."

"It's me. It's me who's crying, Josh. Not the city."

"Let's just get through this thing, this whole damn thing no matter how many hurricanes they throw at us," I said. "You know what Ken said to me down at Molly's, he said if we can make it through this we can make it through anything. And I know we can and we will."

"Silent and dry," she said. "That's how I feel. Like the city." Tears fell to the corners of her wide lips, curled into their curling ends, and it looked like she might even smile until she looked down into her lap. "Christ, my fingers."

"You cut yourself?"

"They're just all wrinkled, like I was in the pool too long. But I haven't been in. Have I?" she asked. "Hydrating our hearts, what happened to that?"

I spooned the last of my beef steak into my mouth, swallowed it with red wine, stood, walked into the pool's deep end, and closed my eyes. As I hit bottom, I heard her fall into the water above me, felt her hands over me, taking my swim trunks off, hands on my shoulders, legs around my waist, and my eyes opened.

My bubbles went white with helicoper's spotlight in them, then dark again, hers too now up into moon on the surface, her holding us down on the bottom, and no more bubbles and me gaping at the shrinking moon and drinking her bubbles until it burned and I started twitching, stars over her face, her face going away, coming, going, and up, coughing up water as she dragged me to the edge of the pool. I held myself there and coughed for a while, then pulled myself out, lay my head on the brick and heaved until it subsided into breath. She was standing over me in a new moon, looking down at me, and I was seeing her for first time since the storm. Naked and pale. This person.

We had each lost some weight. But Katherine never had much to lose. I pulled her down to me. New water with all the old currents. The pool water evaporated, and the sweat came, and, with the sweat, mosquitoes. We scurried upstairs, hid beneath my bed sheet. Aching sweat mingled with tears into the balcony's planks until we lay still, still tangled into each other, listening to our blood heaving through our heads, chests, arms, legs, and sleep . . . And then—

A car door had slammed, I was sure of that. An engine starting. I pulled the sheet off my face, sat up. I walked to the end of the balcony where it looked over St. Peter Street in time to see her taillights round the corner.

27

I took a long, cold shower, covered my arms and legs in calamine lotion, then bug repellent, and laid back down, pulled the sheet over my face, and tried to pound back into sleep, trying to remember the wonderful uncertainty of a hurricane coming in the dark, until gray leaked through the sheet and I gave up.

There was no blue jay screaming this morning. There were only flies. I walked downstairs, swatting at them, to fix myself a bowl of cereal, but we were out of powdered milk, so I had some Johnnie Walker Red Label instead, took the radio into 109, shut the flies out, and let the heat build.

[Radio] Rita's expected to reach Category 4 by tomorrow evening with winds at least a hundred thirty-one miles an hour. The storm is still on track to make landfall in Texas by the end of the week, but a slight turn to the right is still possible. And engineers warn that as little as three inches of rain could swamp New Orleans' levees.

Over the last week or so, I'd made the living room into my publishing office. I felt like it was all a big mess, all dependent on these torn scraps of paper that connected me to pieces strewn about the country that I could never seem to fit into a whole and too many different things that might or might not happen and I could not set my head around any of it. So, I did what little I could with my hour and forty-seven minutes of battery power, trying to get books reprinted—proceeds from which would go to the KARES writers relief fund which I had set up the week before (I still had no idea exactly where the money would go, only that people would need it when they returned, if they ever did)—began work on an op-ed, sent most of the e-mails I needed to, then dropped the laptop off at the EMS trailer to recharge it.

The winds came an hour behind the flies, and the flies found refuge, like the rest of us, in Johnny White's. Some were clinging to the wounds on V's face. "What the hell is Rita doing throwing flies at us?" he cried. "I mean c'mon, brah! What the hell is this?"

"She's skirting the coast right now," said the guy beside me as I took the last seat at the bar. Like the others, he had his hand over his cocktail to keep the flies out of it. "We're going to see the worst of her long before she makes landfall."

Possum got me a Budweiser while he talked to a CNN crew who were crammed in with the rest of us. The guy next to me said, "You're the dude made my hand famous."

"I what?"

"This hand," he said. "I was holding a beer while I was getting my haircut outside Big Daddy's and your girl took a photo of me, and they zoomed in on my hand and my beer and used it as the thumbnail for your article online."

"Oh, that's great, no wonder," I said.

"So, how you been making it?"

"Been making it okay."

"Me, too. You know, never even occurred to me that the government would come and help us. All the government's ever done for me is taken away all my goddamn profits every April fifteenth. I suppose they build roads and do shit like that, but the idea that they'd rescue me—or shit, give me some bottled water when I was thirsty?—would never have occurred to me in a million friggin years. We stayed here, flooded and not, rich and poor, against the law, and we thrived, while them people who did what the government told them and went to the Superdome slept in shit and piss and went hungry. It's just a different way of thinking those people have. I don't know who's fault it is. It's all ours I suppose. And I'm not sure anything's ever going to be done about it. We give them just enough to keep them in their place, just enough to keep them down, but not pissed enough to start a revolution. You're not recording this are you?"

"Thing I remember most," I say, "was watching the palm trees on top of Jax Brewery getting hit with wind. It bent them over clean to the ground, but then suddenly, when it was at its worst, they were standing straight up like there wasn't even the slightest breeze, like there was so much wind they had no idea what to do, had no way to react. And then, next time I looked, they were all gone."

"Saw them snap one by one and fly into the river," he said.

"No shit?"

"Yeah, it was that and them pigeons all over Jackson Square which got me the most. All shook up, feathers missing, wild-eyed and bloody. Fucking bloody pigeons."

"Here's to bloody pigeons," I said.

"That's not funny. Those poor things were scared shitless."

"No, they were shitting themselves all over the place. I saw it."

"Then to pigeons shitting themselves!"

"To shitty pigeons!"

Possum smashed a bunch of flies on the bar in front of me. Over the last weeks, I'd watched his face shift from sallow yellow to gray like so many others, all the more apparent now that CNN had a light on it. "Made sixteen hundred dollars yesterday's shift," he said, while the cameraman moved around me to get another shot of him in action.

"Fuck you," I said.

"Really. These media dudes, you should see the tips they throw at me," he said. He flashed a wad of cash, two inches thick, from his pocket, then shoved it back in before anyone else saw. "Still got nowhere else to spend their expense accounts."

"He's the richest man in the poorest city in the world," said the guy beside me. "Too bad you can't spend it anywhere."

"Hey! Who's media?" I asked.

"I am!"

"Buy me a goddamn drink."

"What are you having?"

"A bloody goddamn pigeon!"

"Get us a couple bloody goddamn pigeons, please, goddammit," said the media man.

"What's in it?" asked Possum.

"Shit. I don't know, make something up," I said. "Just make it bloody. And make it taste like a goddamn pigeon."

He poured bloody Mary mix, beer, gin, and lots of Tabasco over ice in a couple of pint cups.

The media man took one sip. "Now, that's dead pigeon!" he declared. The CNN crew left and he started an interview with Possum. The bar's phone rang. It was a radio station from Ireland. Possum ignored the man at the bar and started doing the phone interview instead.

I stepped outside the bar to call Katherine but there was no answer. It must have been ninety degrees outside, but the wind whipped hell out of the heat, threw it around long enough for it not to stick. The pressure was thinning already. There was that feeling, at least a hint of it, of something coming, that same terrifying electric aloneness we'd felt the evening before Katrina.

The pay phone across the street started ringing. I finally walked over and picked it up. "Hello?"

"Hello. Yes, I would like to speak with Dagmar. Dagmar is there?"

I looked down Bourbon Street, both ways, from Esplanade to Canal, not a soul in sight. "What does he look like?"

"She has brown hair, and she is almost two meters tall. Very thin waist."

"Sounds great."

"Please, she is there? Please?"

"Ma'am, I think you got the wrong number."

"This is not 1-504-523-9487?"

"Yeah, that's it. Where do you think you are calling?"

"I am calling New Orleans, USA, yes?"

"Yes. You got it. Dead center bull's-eye."

"They are tourists. She is with a group of four Denmark tourists. I am looking for the tourists."

"Ma'am, you ask me, that might be the only good thing about this whole hurricane, it blew away the tourists. Haven't seen one in over three weeks."

"Oh. I suppose that is a funny."

"No, I'm serious."

"I am glad you make a funny that the tourists blow away. But my daughter was there and I do not hear from my daughter since August twenty-eight, one morning before the storm."

"Ma'am, how did you get this number?"

"The Denmark consulate in Miami, they received a phone call from here just before the storm. It is only number that works inside New Orleans they know." She was crying. There was a man's voice in the background, and then an old woman's.

"Ma'am, where was she?"

The old woman began screaming.

"Ma'am, please, tell me where she was."

"She was in Holiday Inn."

"Well, I don't think she's there now. I will tell you this, please, listen. Please. Are you there? Listen, it's not as bad as what you may have seen. If she was here in the Quarter or on Canal Street she has not been shot, she has not drowned. There is very little chance that that has happened to your daughter. There are many people who were taken to Houston and other places, and she may not have had a way to get in touch with you."

"But it has been too long. She has calling card."

"I wish I could do something, could tell you something else. If she was here, and wandering the streets, I would have seen her by now."

"You should have seen her by now?"

"Ma'am, please, please, I tell you she's probably okay, she's probably just fine. Stop crying. Please stop it. Please. Please. Fuck." I hung the phone up, and went back into the bar.

28

The next morning I woke to no mosquitoes, no blue jay, and no flies. The air was full of water instead. Not heavy and close and thick with water as after a summer rainstorm, but thin with it, like dust-sized shards prickling my skin, my eyes, leaving a dew on everything. The sky burned with clouds as the pressure dropped further. Rita had grown to Category 5, the most intense storm ever in the Gulf and one of the largest storms ever recorded, with maximum sustained winds of 175 mph, and she was whispering at us.

I moved the leftovers and coolers and food into unit 109, locked and bungeed the shutters and doors. Molly's and Johnny White's were open but empty. The Carnival Cruise ships, docked by the Aquarium for the last week to house aid workers, were gone.

In the late afternoon, Rita's first outer rainbands fell as I walked through the deserted Quarter until I found Touché, a small, cozy bar attached to the Omni Royal Hotel, had opened its tall French doors. It was close enough to Canal Street that the lights were on. I took a seat beside the lone patron at the far end of the bar facing the street as the sun failed and the Quarter turned blue and we listened to the radio. I ordered a can of Bud from the bartender. She had bangs that came to her eyebrows and long curly blond hair, a black crown where her roots had grown out over the last three weeks, fingernails bitten into nubs with chips of pink still clinging to them, and she wore enough makeup that you could tell she'd always lived about one Greyhound stop away from any city. She told me she was from Chalmette and had lost everything. She and her family were living in a shelter in Baton Rouge now, but the hotel let her stay here during the week. The man beside me was sixtyish, short, squat, wearing a USS *Iwo Jima* baseball cap, and no ID tags. I asked if he was in the service. He looked stunned, like I'd just slapped him. "Your hat," I said.

"Oh. No. Just got it on a tour of the ship."

"So, what brings you here, then?"

He shrugged his shoulders, looked around the empty bar, at the bartender, waited until she turned away, then leaned into me, whispered, "I work with FEMA."

"No kidding," I said. "So y'all are real?"

He shied his glance down at his can of Bud.

"I didn't mean that as a joke," I said. "Really. It's just that you're the first one I've actually met, that's all."

He got up, left his mostly full beer on the bar without a tip, and walked out into the light rain. Garland Robinette was on the radio, the same broadcaster Katherine and the mayor had spoken to. A man named Conrad called in. He was wandering the streets of Baton Rouge with his wife and daughter, trying to find a shelter. After he broke down, Conrad handed the phone to his wife, so she could talk to Robinette. Then, eventually, Conrad took the phone back from her. Robinette suggested he try the River Center shelter. The bartender told me that was where her family was, in the River Center.

Conrad: No, sir. We left there. They had three children, they got raped in there, and one guy pulled a gun because he couldn't take a shower, and that's the reason why we left. And I'm not taking my daughter back in there. I just want a place where I can put my kids. I can go back to work and put my kids in school, that's all I want to do. I can't go back home and . . . There's nothing left . . . I've got seventy dollars in my pocket, if I could go find a motel, but they tell me it's a hundred dollars.

Robinette: All right. Conrad. Well, hopefully, someone's gonna call and help you . . .

They gave Conrad's phone number on air. Eventually, another man, Jack, called in.

Jack: Listen, I can't reach him, but if that guy Conrad can get himself to a hotel room, just get himself to any hotel and have him call me, I will pay for it with my credit card. Okay, and I'll give you my number off the air here and you can contact me and I'll take care of it.

Robinette: Jack, thank you a million times over. Now, Conrad, if you're listening, you need to give us a call back here.

We waited and waited, and the announcers continued, in between other calls, to plead with Conrad to call them back. He never did. I left a dollar tip, and she turned the lights off and closed the doors behind me as the radio reported that there were only 500 civilians left in New Orleans.

And one percent of them were in Johnny White's. As I walked in, two black kids shot out the door around me and vomited red stuff in unison on the sidewalk in front of the bar. A crazed fish-eyed man stood behind the bar watching them with a devil's grin spread over half his face bearing his one black tooth. He was so happy it seemed the slightest movement might pop his eyes the rest of the way out of his head. He pointed those eyeballs at me like I was a young boy he wanted to molest. "Who the hell are you?" I asked.

"Banjo!"

"Banjo, I'm Josh and—shit!" I tripped on something and hit the floor. It was a dog, just lying in the middle of the floor, the biggest Rottweiler I'd ever seen. It did not even open its eyes.

"He is not dead," said a guy standing in the doorway, one I hadn't noticed as I'd passed him which was odd seeing as how he was built like a Rottweiler himself, like the Hulk only shorter and flesh-colored, even handsome, shirtless, wearing only Umbro soccer shorts and combat boots. "He's got the invisible spirit," he said, leaning down to pet the dog.

He had a voice deep as God, so heavy in fact that he seemed incapable of lifting it out of his gut. "As soon as you die, you lose weight."

"Yeah, I know," I said. "The body loses twenty-one grams, that's what they say."

"That's the invisible spirit."

"You one of those Jesus dudes?"

"I believe in the invisible spirit."

"I believe I'll have a drink." I sat at the bar, the only one there now.

"What kind?!" said Banjo. He was very excited.

"The visible kind. A visible spirit. Something bloody. Like a pigeon."

"People been drinking that shit all day, man. Some of them been leaving it out there on the sidewalk too."

The kids finished retching outside, came back in, tripped over the Invisible Spirit, then sat next to me and started sipping their bloody pigeons. Two more kids came in, one a thickset Hispanic with a shaved head and a thin mustache wearing a loose white T-shirt and jeans and the other a white kid wearing a Detroit Lions baseball cap askew and jeans with the crotch down to his knees.

"Couple Heineys, yo," said the white kid.

"Where you from?" I asked.

"Rapid City, up in the plains."

"So, how'd you get down here?"

"Aw, shit, yo, I was workin up there in the Chili's, know what I'm sayin?"

"I guess."

"And my friend, he was like hooked up with this catering service, yo, and they got a contract to come down here and cook and shit for the police and shit. Man, they payin me sixteen dollars and fifty cents an hour down here, know what I'm sayin? Shit, I walked right outta that Chili's. Shit."

"Who are you cooking for? I didn't think anyone was left in town. Aren't y'all supposed to be evacuated?"

"Yeah, yo. All that, shit."

"Huh?"

I turned toward the Hispanic. "What about you?" I asked. "Y'all work together?"

"Naw, homes. We both catering for the police but we with different folks. I'm with a ministry out of Compton L.A. But I'm from the I.E. I'm Al."

"Inland Empire?!" said Banjo. "I used to live in San Bernardino!"

"Yeah, esé, that's where I'm from," said Al. He flicked his chin up at me. "So what's the murder rate like here? How many people y'all got getting killed here every day? Where I come from, we got like five people getting killed every day."

"Oh yeah sure," said Banjo, opening a couple of Heinekens for the two quiet black kids at the end of the bar. "All them Chicano gangs out there. We never had no problem with the Mexicans, though. You all were cool. It was the niggers we all hated. That's six dollars."

"You ever kill anyone?" I asked.

"Naw, homes. I got out." He pulled up his shirt, pointed to three different spots of tangled red flesh. "Got stabbed here and here, shot right here," he said, pointing to the scar on his right rib cage. "But God opened a door for me. I moved down to Compton and the ministry's taking care of me. I know sometime soon I gotta go back home, though. They ain gonna understand all this shit I'm into now, Jesus and stuff, know what I'm saying? My gang is like eighty-five deep. Thirty of them I really grew up with, and I can talk to them about it, they'll let me slide. But that leaves about fifty other fools to deal with when I get back. They ain down with my new thing, I'll get stabbed, I'll take that. I just don't wanna be shot again. But, Jesus, man. He don't need us. We need Him, you know? You know Jesus?"

"Sure, he's right down the street."

"Jesus?"

"Yeah. Come see." I walked outside and pointed Touchdown Jesus out to Al. He flickered white off and on with the stars as clouds poured over the city like smoke. But the rain had stopped.

"Yeah, there he is," said Al. "Judgment Day is coming. They say time will cease forever and everyone, dead or alive, small or big, will appear before the Lord God on His Judgment Seat. Hey homes, you do the cocaine?"

"Nope."

"Yeah, I like the rock myself, you know."

"No, not really."

"You know where I can find some rock?"

"No."

"What the hell's that dead damn dog doing in my bar?" It was V.

"It's the invisible spirit," said the guy in Umbros and combat boots. Despite the strength with which his chest heaved them, his words barely made it past his lips, then they sort of fell to the floor, along with V.

V got up, frowned at his scabs, which had started bleeding again, ran his thick bronze fingers through his graying hair. "What? Are you talking American, brah?"

"They still let you in this place?" I asked.

"Hell, best thing about the hurricane. I ain been 86'd in twenty-six days!" He pointed a fat finger at Banjo. "But I been 172'd by you because I done pissed you off two times today already!"

"Don't test me, V," said Banjo. "I ain been laid in twenty-six days and I've had it with taking any shit."

"Dude, you're lying," said V. "It's been a year and twenty-six days."

"What I wouldn't give for a woman," said Banjo. "Just to even talk to one for a while."

"I assure you," I said, "the only thing worse than not having a woman around for twenty-six days without electricity, is having one around for twenty-six days without electricity."

"You betcha ass, brah," said V. "I ain doing that thing. It's too damn hot at night. I told my old woman, I love you, but don't touch me, baby. I need to be getting supplies. I mean how's my dog supposed to eat and drink water in the morning after I fuck your ass? C'mon, brah, how the hell is that supposed to happen?"

The Invisible Spirit guy tapped me on the shoulder. "What does he mean fuck the ass?"

"Speak American, please," V said to him.

"Dude, it's just an expression," I said.

"He fucks the ass?"

"What are you—Slovakian?" said V.

"No he doesn't fuck the ass, that's the point," I said. "He's not fucking anything because that would prevent his dog from eating and drinking. Can't you understand?"

"Must be a Slovak," said V.

A guy wearing a Domino's Pizza polo and baseball cap walked in, downtrodden. Banjo gave him a beer because they'd been here giving away free pizzas. He sat beside me, said they were trying to give away one hundred thousand free pizzas in New Orleans. "We've only given sixteen thousand so far, mostly to military and media. Television says there's less than five hundred residents left in the city now. So, I did the math. We just need to find them and get them to eat at least one hundred sixty-eight pizzas apiece in the next four days. A hundred sixty-eight. Think you can do that for us?"

"Take them to the Lower 9th Ward," I said. "I was there the other day. There's no people, but there's hungry dogs."

"The levees! Drop them on the levees!" said Banjo.

"Domino's, rebuilding New Orleans in thirty minutes or less," said V.

A couple came running in the door. "Woo-hoo!" screamed the girl, waving her Michelob Ultra in the air. Her stubby fingernails were painted scarlet red with sparkles and she wore her freshly dyed blond hair back in a ponytail. "We are happy to be home!"

"Did you all just get in? How on earth did you do that?" I asked. "Welcome home."

"We got back this morning. We snuck in along river road."

"Where do you live? Your place okay?"

"Wait a minute, you guys are refugees?" asked V. "Oh look, oh my God, we've got some re-fu-gees here! Quick get them some water!" But Banjo had disappeared into the back.

"But we're back, now!"

"Oh, excuse me," said V. "If I had known you were outta town I would have watered your plants for you."

"We're just glad to be back."

"What? You've decided to come back now and help us rebuild? Thanks, sister, but we'll take care of it from here. Go back to wherever it is and we'll send you a text message when we're done."

"Hey!" It was the Domino's guy. "Put it right here!" He cupped his hands together, like he was holding them out to scoop water. "Put it right here! Okay? Is it here?" he asked. He threw the air in his hands out the door. "It's all gone. See?"

You could see V's mind working over it. "Brah, you want me to unload my troubles into your little goddamn hand? C'mon, brah, god-damn Superdome couldn't hold my troubles."

"Couldn't hold very many others', either," I said.

"The invisible spirit will hold your troubles."

"No, esé, Jesus can hold them."

"Jesus better get some fingers back before he holds anything," I said. "Give me another bloody pigeon, please, Banjo," I called into the back.

"What's a bloody pigeon?" asked the girl. "I want to try a bloody pigeon too."

"No! Don't give her bloody pigeon," said V. "She doesn't get bloody pigeon. She's not from here."

"Look, don't tell me I'm not from here. I was born and raised here. I've lived here thirty-seven years." Her boyfriend stood frozen by the bar, a nervous smile on his face. "Don't tell me I don't live here!"

"Sister, you better get back uptown and water your plants, 'cause no one else is."

She slugged him in the neck.

"In the neck?" cried V, bent over laughing. "Who hits someone in the neck?!"

"I was trying to hit you in the goddamn face." She had another go at it but V moved out of the way, and she hit empty air. He was surprisingly fast for someone who's always falling down. "What the fuck have you done for New Orleans?!" she screamed.

Banjo came out of the back, totally confused about what was happening. She was rearing up again when he came running around the bar and stood between them.

"Hey, V, why don't you leave the tourists alone?" said Banjo.

He was being serious. I spat my beer out onto the boyfriend to save it from shooting out of my nose. The girl threw the rest of her beer at Banjo then stormed out. The boyfriend just stood there, his crotch dark with my mouthful of beer, not knowing what to do. I couldn't stop laughing long enough to apologize. V looked like he might go postal. The guy bolted. V sat down beside me, and told Banjo that was a good one between raspy laughs.

"What? What did I say?" asked Banjo, wiping his shirt with a bar towel. "Why did she pour beer on me?"

The kids ordered another round of Jameson and one for Banjo. He filled quite a bit of those eight-ounce cups. They all threw them back. They put their empty cups down, looked at each other. "You know the drill," said Banjo, tossing their cups into the garbage. "Just go outside."

They puked on top of their first vomit, then Banjo, still standing, bent over, laid his head down on the bar, and started snoring with those fish-eyes wide open looking down at the Rottweiler who had still not moved a muscle. I couldn't even see the dog breathe.

V leaned over, whispered in my ear, "Hey brah, what if I told you I knew where they got a bar with air-conditioning? What would you say?"

I backslapped the Domino's guy, hunched over his bloody pigeon mumbling something about one hundred thousand, and told him to come with us. The three of us walked beneath the clouds and emptiness and remaining darkness of Bourbon Street into the streetlamps stretched out from Conti Street to Canal. Signs to most places were lit, and sure enough one was actually open.

We followed V into Déjà Vu. Our nipples shriveled to peas. A bouncer walked up, told us we needed to put our shirts on. A woman on stage was taking her shirt off. V, his T-shirt sticking to his wounds, walked over to the bar, came back with a bucket filled with ice and four Heinekens, and we sat at a table in the corner, our backs to the stage. The place was way too bright for a strip club. Besides us, there were a half-dozen guys wearing police caps backwards and T-shirts, looking like they'd just finished football practice, sprawled out in chairs around the center stage, and the only dancer was clad in the obligatory flesh-colored G-string, shaking her dimpled thighs and bottom and the small oval pudge over her stomach, her small but fake breasts like little water balloons. The police really thought this was something, slouched like kings, sucking on beers like frat boys, smacking each other on the shoulders and howling with laughter just because they could, oozing with authority. *Take me down to the Paradise City where the grass is green and the girls are pretty . . .*

When the song ended, the dancer walked through the policemen and over to us. She sat on V's lap while she put her top on. V whispered to her as the Domino's guy rocked back and forth repeating to himself, "Eighty-four thousand . . . eighty-four thousand . . ." Then the girl got up and went into the back, returned a minute later, handed V a wad of twenties without a word, and walked off. V called the waiter over, got us another round of Heinekens.

"Is she the only dancer?" I asked.

"They smuggled her in from Texas, brah."

There seemed to be a functioning ATM by the rest rooms. "Someday, we're gonna need money again," I said.

"Money?" asked V. "How much you want?" He held out a few twenties toward me.

"Nah, I don't want money. That's the point."

"Eighty-four thousand . . ." moaned the Domino's man. "Eighty-four thousand . . ."

"Here, brah," said V, holding the money out to the Domino's man now. "Can you get me some pizzas? How many pizzas can this get me?"

"You can't buy the pizzas! We're trying to give them away! Oh, it just gets worse . . ."

In the mirror on the wall in front of us the dancer was shaking her dimples again. I left as the next song kicked into gear . . . *I wanna fuck you like an animal. I wanna feel you from the inside* . . . The place fell away and I had Bourbon Street, warm and all alone, lit with every gaudy fluorescent as though it were any regular night, only no one had decided to go out. It was frightening. And it was only when the lights cut off as I crossed Conti Street that I heard the soft whistling from the Gulf.

Johnny White's was empty now, the doors open, the darkness inside naked but for a single candle, wind whipping its light around like the place was burning, Banjo's sleeping shadow moving against the bottles behind the bar. His eyes were still open, looking out at me, moving in and out of their sockets with every snore, even as a gust knocked two bottles onto the floor beside him, shattering them. The trees behind the cathedral were rattling their leafless branches against one another as wind howled through them, through my apartment too, a whisper of that banshee wail twenty-six days earlier, still trying to find its way back outside, my hands finding the last bottle of wine from Robért's, then a hammer and nail, smashing the cork in—Merlot, shit—wrestling the whisper and finding my way downstairs, outside again, realizing I'd just locked myself out, a news crew huddled in an SUV across the street the only people anywhere, watching trash and debris fly, watching me pour wine down my throat, wink at them, the remaining leaves on remaining limbs of remaining trees shivering, to the levee, down the steps to the river, sitting on the last step, legs hanging off into the water, all my own and waves like ocean.

This was not the water one hundred days ago dripping from ice caps in Montana, cold as it should be. It was warm. I had never felt the river warm. Until the storm I had never felt it at all. The waves knocked against my knees, splashed into my chest, and I toasted the torn-up warm goddamn river and howled right back at it. It took my left sandal so I gave it my right. It soaked into the bandages on my wrists, so I unwrapped them, dangled them over the waves until one took them, hit me in the chest, warm water soaking into my shirt turning cool under the wind. So I gave it that too, then my bathing suit, and I got goose bumps. I slid down off the step into the water, chest deep, rocks under foot, waves slamming my chest, howling, drinking, not worrying anymore if water got into the bottle when it crashed over my head until water and wine were indistinguishable and drank whatever came into my mouth when I opened it and let it beat me back against the steps, pin me there, opened my arms to it and laughed and laughed and *laughed* until I was coughing water again, sediment souring the back of my throat, and laughing and laughing, sediment pumping through veins and arteries, heart and liver and lungs, twenty-one grams each breath between the waves, and the bottle was full again and I drank until I choked it back up what was me what was water and what was wine and Katherine? Where.

I pulled myself onto the bottom step, lay there on my back, on the wood, lay very still. The river came over me in blankets, drained through the wood back into itself. Between the waves I opened my eyes, watched clouds scrape through downtown's glow.

I walked naked to Decatur Street. The news van was gone. Gusts swept month-old trash past my ankles. I caught a beer can rolling down the street, tore it in half, flattened it, used it to jimmy the entryway door. I opened my window all the way and the wind found its way out and the whistling died. I shoved my futon to the window and lay with my legs open to Rita. At times the wind came in spasms over me, but it wouldn't come in far enough for long enough to cool me. And yet she was too violent to sleep within, on the balcony. So, I lay inside just out of her reach, hot as ever but no mosquitoes, sleep slipping into the minutes between furious howling gusts that made me worry about microbursts, the shards of a thousand unfinished dreams cutting into ash daybreak, then breaking, reforming into something still gray but whole, rain stroking the day, slanting it into my window, and that last wine bottle no doubt lost on its way into rolling sediment two hundred feet down, bottom of dreams.

My hand searched for water, found a bottle of eighteen-year-old Macallan. Derek. My birthday. God. I filled my mouth with it, swished it around, swallowed, wandered how Conrad had slept last night, if he, and his family, were still walking Baton Rouge, hoping that all this hadn't hit that far inland. I turned the radio on. Water from the Industrial Canal had overtopped its levee just north of Claiborne Avenue, flooding the Lower 9th Ward all over again.

29

Through billowing sheets of rain I watched the sole remaining chain that once held the Ripley's sign lash against its façade. My landline began ringing in my kitchen. My computer lay charged on the coffee table, and beside it, that miniature boom box still tuned to 1460 AM. I found a pair of old swim trunks, old sandals, and a Foot Action baseball cap I'd bought from the store on Canal Street long before they burned it. I closed my shoulder bag tightly, the phone still ringing, and descended my stairs, got on the bike and pedaled into the rain, down Decatur Street, through the Marigny, into the Bywater, legs burning against driving headwind and rain like nails into my bowed face, the cap barely keeping it out of my eyes. There was yelling. I realized an army truck was alongside me, the driver shouting at me. I watched his mouth work through the rain bitter against my tongue. I must have been quite a silly sight, some half-naked guy biking into it all. "*Are you okay?!*"

"Just another day at the beach!" I said, realizing how stupid it was.

"*WHAT ABOUT THE BREACH?!*"

I smiled, gave him thumbs up. He nodded, drove ahead of me, the soldiers huddled up in the covered back glaring at me, machine guns between their knees, as I pedaled behind until I had to look down at my front tire lest the rain knock my eyes out. When I looked back up they were gone. I wound through the Upper 9th Ward for another mile as gusts bullied me, relented, bullied again, creeping up to the Claiborne Avenue Bridge. It was over half a mile long, considerably wider and longer than the St. Claude Bridge, high enough for most ships to pass underneath.

About a dozen media trailers were parked along the railing on the way up, most of them full with rain-coated bodies huddled together. As I neared the crest, three middle-aged Airborne officers came into view, eyeing me with clenched, chiseled jaws, their red berets holding tight in the wind and rain lashing in spasms. I nodded, pushed by them. It was a vertical lift bridge and the center span was raised up parallel to the rest of it several stories above me between two towers. I'd never seen it up before, had no idea it could even be raised. There were a dozen or so reporters up ahead, each of them in a heavy hooded raincoat and thigh-high rubber boots. The two who were doing "live" broadcasts were overly compensating for the wind, bent over, leaning into it like it was Katrina. A cameraman told one to hold on as I passed behind him. The reporter relaxed, stood back upright, waited until the kid wearing nothing but surf shorts and sandals got out of the shot. The rain lightened to a sprinkle and I rested my bike against the side of the bridge, hopped over a barricade, walked to the edge and looked down and thought that the little things would never matter again.

The canal was a choppy, milky gray brown a hundred feet below. A few blocks to the north, water bowed over its levee half a block wide, falling effortlessly down into the Lower 9th like from an endless bucket being dumped out. Once it crashed to the bottom, into the lower level of water already there, white water roiled out, frothing until it all fell calm, flat as glass, pouring sky into the entire Lower 9th Ward splayed out below me.

The homes within two blocks of the opening had disappeared. Past that, houses were only betrayed by a roof or frame or unidentifiable viscera sticking up out of the water. Then, further out, the houses were heaped upon one another in great pieces and, past that, they were crumpled and askew and not quite where they should have been, and finally there were the others further away that still sat in grids, along streets as they always had, water up well over their raised porches, up to their door knobs, as though they'd just sunken into this strange new foundation of roiling mercury sky, patches of sediment like clouds curling in upon one another until they touched the real thing on the horizon.

The houses made no reflection in the water around them. They lay like textured, unparented shadows falling, lost from light and source alike, into this ghost of a sky. It was Katrina's ghost, too, a residual spirit, an impression of the original without the human lives, no one on rooftops now, no one awaiting evacuation, it was only there to see. But unloading with the same violence. And those few of us up there stood and watched, as though it would stop at some point.

"Are you from here?" I turned around. Two Indian guys were hunched together in raincoats. One had a small microphone held out to me, a digital recorder in his hand.

"No," I said.

I peered back down into the roiling canal, about a hundred feet across. A few summers ago, at the end of an eight-mile run, a friend and I swam across it, right here near this bridge. We thought it would be a good way to cool off. It almost killed us. A ship came down when we were halfway across, bobbing heads in the oil-slicked, wreaking, syrupy black water. We caught the crew's attention finally and the ship slowed enough for us to make it across.

A man walked up beside me in a raincoat, stood with arms crossed, watching the Lower 9th. I recognized him as a local reporter but didn't know his name. "So, that's the exact spot it breached before?" I asked.

"Think so," he said. He did not look at me.

"Looks like it's just overtopped this time, not breached, maybe eroded the top of whatever they dropped on there to repair the breach."

He shrugged his shoulders, inches from mine, said, "Well, it already got flooded. This doesn't make much of a difference."

I gave this man that same confused glare I'd seen on all the dogs down there a couple of days before. I thought about how much longer it would be now until these people could return to their homes, see what was left of them. How much further the little things that make up life would be from where these people had left them. An engagement ring, a favorite doll, how many photo albums might have been salvageable after Katrina's waters had receded. How much deeper their feet would sink into sediment searching for these things. I thought about the dog I'd given Katherine's piece of wheat bread to. He turned without seeing me, walked back to his cameraman. I pulled out my phone, dialed.

"Where are you?" she asked.

"I'm here. I'm on the Claiborne Bridge, looking down at it. You should come. You should see. I think you can sneak up here and Katherine? Katherine? Hello?" A gust of wind nearly took the phone out of my hand. I turned my back to it. My phone was blinking on and off. Then it went dark. Water ran around the keys, out of the little microphone hole in the bottom. Rain came screaming straight up from the ground, from the canal below. My hat was gone. I clutched my bag to my chest, sat on my heels, hunched to the ground, arms around my head as all was erased in a tornado of gray. I clenched every muscle against it, trying to hold myself to the ground. And then I just let go, stood up, eyes closed, and relaxed into it. The wind beat every side of me, propped me straight up. I felt for my bike with my feet. It was shaking. I lifted it, walked down the slope of the bridge, feeling the gray, light then dark then light again through my eyelids, bitter rain like pennies against my tongue, and wished it were more, wished I had been here twenty-seven days ago. Wished I had felt that.

<u>30</u>

When I felt the tornado go, only breeze and mist on my cheeks and chest, I opened my eyes. A sheet of water glistening like thin ice rolled down from the top of the bridge, where I'd been, over my sandal, disappearing into a tension gap the width of my pinky. I got on my bike, coasted back into the world.

The wind picked up again a few minutes later, and I found shelter in an abandoned city bus on the corner of Desire and Burgundy. The door was open, water draining down the steps into the street. The emergency door was off the roof, framing birds against white sky. They were in a V formation, facing into the wind, gliding against it to survive it, the whole V swaying back and forth, but otherwise unmoving as though they were hanging from strings. When the rain stopped, I grabbed the top of the emergency exit and pulled myself onto the roof. There were thirty of them, not birds, but bats, the gray skin of their large ∧-shaped wings translucent against the blinding white sky, bones and bodies dark.

The wind at my back now, I coasted the rest of the way into the Quarter. By the time I got to Molly's, it had calmed considerably, but I was soaked to the bone, panting. Ty was outside showing off his ambulance. "Where'd you come from?" he asked.

Before I could answer someone shouted, "Hey Ty! You all need to paint RED RUM over the grille!"

They all cracked up. I didn't really get it. And when they stopped laughing they started discussing how the gurney hooks could be used for kayaks. I walked into the bar. Ashley was working. I spooned myself three bowls of jambalaya from the steaming pot by the door. There were more new faces now. Eventually Katherine walked in wearing a white tank-top undershirt of mine and shiny orange Adidas sweatpants.

"Where were you?" I asked.

"I was up there, on the bridge."

"You went there? I didn't even think you'd heard me. I left. The wind and rain and stuff just got ridiculous."

"It was calm when I got there."

Everyone I knew who had bartended at Johnny White's since the storm, about a dozen of them, rolled into the bar, and whatever argument Katherine and I were about to have was lost in the shots of Jameson that came our way. Then we all barhopped over to Stella's which had just opened a block away. There was air-conditioning and you could order hamburgers. They must have had some kind of generator in the back. It was the first time any of us had ordered food in almost a month. Dr. Lutz rolled in and the bartender bought him a martini before I had a chance. I asked him how the French Quarter Health Department in Exile was going.

"I put that banner up after hearing so much bad health information from poorly briefed public officials, and a few days ago a military patrol came by," he said, grabbing a handful of the jellybeans the bartender had laid out in a dish. "I saw them writing down something and a few minutes later some sort of major of some sort with a bunch of stars on his uniform came by. Turned out he was the chief psychiatrist for the 82nd Airborne. They asked me to attend a meeting on the USS *Iwo Jima* to talk to some of their troops about how to deal with people suffering from post-traumatic stress. They were concerned with these dazed folks who wander around the French Quarter all day."

He waved a hand over the entire bar.

"Well, I told them to leave those guys alone," he said. "They're survivors. They may be crazy, but they survived this thing. They coped. Take them out of their environment, and they'll develop more acute problems. You cannot transplant a weed and expect it to thrive. The primary psychiatric care in this city's being provided by the bartenders at Johnny White's and Molly's."

The bartenders from Johnny White's let out a cheer. Katherine and I relaxed into each other as the hours passed. She told me where she had been living: in the Warehouse District, with electricity and air-conditioning, in the condo of a friend who worked for the local NBC affiliate. The day was fading when Ken Wells, my friend from the *Wall Street Journal*, walked into Stella's. He was thrilled to find out Katherine had been taking photos for the paper. We told him about the Claiborne Bridge, then the three of us piled into his SUV and we took him up there.

The flooding had almost leveled off now. The canal was considerably calmer. It was still flowing into the Lower 9th but there were no more whitecaps. When the Airborne guys were looking the other way, I ran up the first flight of stairs in the bridge tower. The steps were grating, only a few inches deep, and a couple of feet wide. I held tight to the thin railing and hiked up the next flight, bracing myself each time a gust rattled the tower. I made it to the fourth-story platform before I couldn't go any further.

The world below me was flat to any horizon, as it was in this latitude from Florida to Texas, more or less. To the north was the lake. To the northwest were the three drainage canals we had visited. To the west, the bridge dropped down into Claiborne Avenue through the Upper 9th Ward, until the I-10 overpass hid Claiborne, the same overpass that many had sought shelter on, from which David and Katherine and I had looked down onto the city. The interstate shot into downtown and past the Superdome. Below it, to the south, St. Louis Cathedral's peaks poked through the Quarter, the river past that curling toward me, then away. I could make out Tayl's street seven blocks straight south. The bridge was still speckled with a few media campers at the bottom, a dozen people standing at the top directly below me, and then it fell off, the canal hundreds of feet below me. On the other side was a very different picture. It was no longer city. It was sky.

And the sky shook the bridge with wind, almost sending me over. I held fast to the little waist-high railing, looked below me, at the reporters milling about, the Airborne soldiers, and Ken and Katherine looking out at the breach. If it was not for the orange sweatpants I would not have recognized her. I wanted to call to her, to show her where I was, to share it. Then she turned, looked at the sky somewhere above me, and her eyes fell down the machinery of the bridge, to me. She tapped Ken, pointed up. He laughed, shook his head. She waited until the Airborne soldiers were looking the other way, then dashed to the stairs. I watched her through the grille of the steps below me climbing up.

She said nothing when she got to my platform, but looked at it all as I had, the only things higher than us in the entire city being those three or four downtown buildings that had once cut out our stars, left their windows in our feet. She took pictures from every angle, then climbed the next flight of stairs and took a picture of me against the part of the city that was now dry. I climbed up to her, took the camera from her hand, climbed to the next platform and took a picture of her. Behind her lay the entire Lower 9th Ward, then Arabi into Chalmette, St. Bernard Parish. From this breach in the levee below, only half a block wide, water had spread past that horizon. It was as though every street, every bit of earth, had simply been cut out of the world and what lay below, after all, was sky like the earth's silver heart.

A gust came. We held fast to our separate places, staring at each other, the air clear between us, as the bridge trembled beneath our feet, in our palms. I inched down toward her, clasping the railing. She reached a hand out. I pulled her into me. She let go, curled her arms into my chest. I quickly handed her the camera and grabbed the railing behind her, to either side of her, and held her there, between me and the railing, the camera between us, my mouth by her ear, eyes in her hair beating around my face. Her scalp smelled of sweat. I always liked that. As the wind died, some of it still stuck in my beard, I saw for the first time that her roots were gray. And I thought maybe this is what she meant when she sometimes used to tell me, until Katrina, that she'd fallen in love with me all over again.

She stayed there, her arms curled between our chests, and mine around her, the way I used to hold her, used to try to pull her into my ribs, her face into my neck until it felt as though she was inside me. Now so much smaller, her arms, the veins and muscles still there, no longer fighting her olive skin, her lying down small below her flesh now.

We said nothing when she drove me and my bike back to the Compound. Not even when she got out of the car to give me a hug. In the courtyard hung the sound of her car pulling away again, and the new debris, the roof slating under my feet, tree limbs, branches, leaves that I would clean tomorrow.

31

"Fire, bombs, they ain nothin. Put one hole in a dam you destroy a place. Water. Thas the great destroyer. Water's the death of us. We crawled outta it long ago, and we gonna do everythin we can not to get back in it. Hell, you know well as I do most the people from the neighborhood never even learned swimmin."

"What you talkin bout water? Water what make this place. This city's heart is water. Water shape our land and animals. Man, you drinkin water right now. Hell, sevendy percent a body's water. Lose that, you ashes. You dust."

"That what I'm talkin bout ashes. Don tell me ashes. Thas whas lefta our neighborhood, ashes. Thas what it done."

"Fire woulda smote em to the ground."

"Fire woulda stopped. How you gonna put water out? God himself caint put no water out. Water'll go where even light caint and it won stop till it levels off with all the oceans they got in the world. It *will* consume everythin in its path, *includin* fire. And water ain kind nuff to leave just some little ol pile a ashes. It leave the ashes standin straight up! It take the home away, but leave the house. It leave your home in zactly the same size you left it, but ain nothin but an unhabitable shadow of what it was, shadow so mean you can touch it. Hell ain fire, hell water."

"Man, then why you here? Huh? Why you down here in the bottom of the United States of America livin in a city thas surrounded by water? And specially why you here now that you ain even sposed to be here now? Now that water's left your city in all these mean ashes you talkin bout?"

"Cause I ain lovin any other place."

"You lovin it? Oh you lovin all this? Whas there to love bout all this, man? You lovin this because of *what*?"

"You cain be lovin somethin *because*—cause a this and cause a that. Thas nice, but that ain love. You love *despite*. When you love it *despite* the way it is, thas when you know you lovin somethin."

The other one shoved a handful of the lemon-yellow rice cereal in his mouth, crunched it slowly with his mouth open until it was like pollen all around his lips and tongue while he watched me. "Heard that, man."

"Shit. Gimme some a that snap crackle pop. How ya doing, dude?" They nodded at me. They sat alone in the shadow of the New Orleans World Trade Center, on the curb beside brown boxes labeled CRISPED RICE CEREAL stacked up to my chest, the only evidence Central Command had ever existed here. The sky was bright and clear, as though yesterday had never happened

I broke a box open, stuck a couple of bags in my basket, and continued biking down Convention Center Boulevard until the convention center ran between me and the river. It stretched almost three quarters of a mile long, the side facing the street mostly glass. There were no bullet holes, no broken glass I could see anywhere. There was not a single person in sight, not a car or anything. I put my face up to the glass. Inside, it was as though Judgment Day had come and gone, everyone vanished. And no one had touched a thing since.

A can of concentrated milk, cans of Pepsi, bottles of Diet Coke, hundreds of unopened bottles of water, a full bottle of wine, an unmarked plastic bottle of brown liquid, a carton of Tropicana, Cocoa Puffs, M&Ms, Lay's potato chips, unopened MREs, unopened Cowboy menthol cigarettes, new Reeboks, Nikes, Adidas, empty shoeboxes, a Banana Republic bag full of dirty clothes, quilts, bed sheets, pillows, pillows used as mattresses, actual mattresses, thousands of folding chairs, and a wheelbarrow, all of it covered in flies, millions of them flitting about lazily between the food items that had actually been opened. But nearly everything in there was unopened. What could have caused so many people to leave behind so much? Even whole packs of cigarettes.

Hallway after hallway, it was the same thing. This is where the people from those Lower 9th Ward homes had come to. And all the little things they couldn't take with them, these last temporary possessions they had after losing everything else, lay where they left them, in a city, for now, no longer threatened by poverty or crime or wind or water.

Two torn pages were pressed up against the window with a pillow, like someone wanted any passersby to read them. They were from the Bible, The Book of Lamentations:

> How lonely sits the city
>   that was once full of people!
> How like a widow has she become,
> · she who was great among the nations!
> She who was a princess among the provinces
>   has become a slave.
>
> She weeps bitterly in the night,
>   with tears on her cheeks;
> among all her lovers
>   she has none to comfort her;
> all her friends have dealt treacherously with her;
>   they have become her enemies.
>
> Give yourself no rest,
>   your eyes no respite!
> Arise, cry out in the night,
>   pour out your heart like water . . .

The streets further uptown had largely been cleared. Many houses had minimal damage, but there were seemingly random blocks of erratic destruction. On Chestnut and Josephine Streets all that remained of one house was the frame, charred to a crisp. Yet the house next door was just fine. The next one was a pile of black bricks. And the next was fine, but the car in front of it looked like it had exploded and melted into the ground.

On Tchoupitoulas Street chairs and mattresses and new electronics were piled two stories high in a vacant lot. I suppose quite a few people had chosen to depart with their new electronics rather than remain in the city. I biked up Felicity toward Magazine Street, avoiding the fallen electrical lines draped through large puddles, buzzing loudly like wet flies.

On Magazine Street I ran into an old woman wearing a large pearl necklace and gold earrings, a black silk top, black slacks, and high heels. She was probably about five feet tall, but so hunched over, half from a curved back and half from a limp, that her eyes came to my belly button. She was grasping the iron bars over a store's display window, clinging to them as though she were bracing herself against a violent wind. She seemed perfectly resigned to her struggle. "Ma'am, can I help you?" I asked. "Where you headed?"

She stopped, craned her neck to look up at me. "The store," she said.

"Store? Ma'am, what store?"

"I just thought I would head down to the store."

"Ma'am, there are no stores open."

She smiled, then bowed her head, keeping it in line with her curved back. "Why is the store not open?" she asked, her eyes on the sidewalk.

"Ma'am, why don't you let me know what you need and I'll see if I can find it for you."

She put both hands on the iron bars and began to slowly shift her body around, back in the direction she'd come from.

"I'm Joshua. What's your name?"

She finished turning around, shuffled one foot slightly in front of the other, and stopped. "Joshua. He asked the Lord to make the sun stay up all night so he could go on killing those Amorites," she said. "Only time the Lord ever heeded the voice of a man and the only thing science can't explain away in the Bible."

"And what's your name?"

"Leona."

"Leona, if you tell me what you need, I'll get it for you."

"No, I don't need anything."

"Leona, is there anyone with you? Anyone living with you now?"

She shuffled the other foot forward, still clinging to the same two bars.

"Leona, please tell me where you live. I'll have some real nice EMS guys come by. They will not make you leave, I promise."

I followed her along, about five feet in five minutes, until she told me her address on Philip Street. I sat on the curb, ate some crisped rice cereal, and kept watch over her. A guy came walking down the middle of the street covered in red paint, hands crusted with dirt, wearing torn shorts and shoes, an open short-sleeved shirt, and askew glasses with only one lens. "Hey," I said, "you're that dude who was wearing underwear and a life vest in Johnny White's a couple weeks back after you went skinny-dipping in Audubon Park, aren't you?"

"Yah. Darique. Hey, how you doing?" I still couldn't place his accent, maybe Italian. He told me he'd spent the last week breaking into places and rescuing animals with some organization called MuttShack. We stood there in the middle of the street and I took out my tape recorder as the old woman held fast to the gate over a restaurant entrance.

How'd you split your thumb open?

Darique: I was helping rescue some animals and I cut myself on some glass. I stopped by the convention center to get patched up yesterday. The National Guard has a medical tent behind there. They stitched it up and the police were nice enough to actually let them finish the procedure before they arrested me for trespassing and disturbing the peace.

They took you to jail?

It's at the Greyhound bus station. There's a big sign above the station: "We're taking back New Orleans." They have fenced enclosures, on the concrete, where the buses were dripping oil and stuff. And it's funny because there's actually, there's police dogs in cages in the same enclosures. But the amazing thing is during the night, the city jail population was seven people. By noon, it was only two of us. We were the only two—

Says here in your paperwork, "Section C of the Court of New Orleans at 727 South Broad Street on the 28th day of September." What?! That shit ain't gonna be open. That's just a few days.

Yah, yah. I guess they're gonna be opening it up.

You kidding? Here, are you hungry? It's all I got, this yellow cereal stuff, but here take a bag. God, I hope that old lady's okay. Look at her. Just standing there holding onto that building. She won't let me help her. Anyway, so you lost one lens of your glasses, but you still got them on. What happened there?

Oh, when I was sleeping on the concrete up there in the jail, I rolled over on my glasses. It was when this black guy was yelling and screaming, being really obnoxious. It was night, dark, everybody was like, you know, either asleep or something, and he just starts screaming crazy. So, they just put a shotgun through the cyclone fencing and pulled the trigger. They blasted him. It was a loud boom. The guy dropped to the ground.

No way.

Yah. With a shotgun. Yah, I saw this. And then he starts moaning. Dude, everybody thought he was dead, but then he got up again, and he goes "uuuuuunngggggghhhhh." And they shot him again. Yah. Then he gets up again and starts yelling crazy this time, so they stuck the shotgun through the fencing and blasted him again.

Shit.

He started moaning again, and got to his feet. This cereal is good, man.

Was he bleeding all over?

They shot him again and then I looked down, and I saw this.

Oh, shit. These are little sandbag things they use instead of bullets. It's like a little yellow sock that's tied up on both ends.

That's sand?

That's what they fill it with. I've seen this on TV. And this is what they were shooting him with?

Yah. The next day he was up and laughing. He was like, "Yeah, that was me! I got shot!"

This red paint all over you, is that also from the enclosures?

Oh, no, no, no. What happened is I walked into this restroom, it was real dark, and picked up what I thought was room freshener, deodorizer, because I was smelling horrible, but it was red spray paint, dude.

Where you headed to now?

I was helping this dude clean up up here, this one place, it's his boarding house.

Two large white SUVs have just pulled up. Says K-9 on their sides. About a dozen huge police guys with bulletproof vests and shotguns are getting out with a couple German shepherds and they're—Okay, I guess they're coming up to us. Hey—

What are you doing here? Turn that off.

Darique: I just got out of jail!

You know, you might want to check on that old lady there.

They ignored the old woman. After questioning our motives for a while, they got back in their SUVs and drove off. When I looked back, she was gone.

32

David and I sat in the lobby of the St. Christopher Hotel, waiting for Katherine, while his pit bull Mad Max tried to make love to me. David was living here now. He and a dozen Hondurans were getting the place ready for an insurance group to stay in for a couple of months. Most of downtown, alone, had power now.

In the lobby hung vast watercolor paintings of Jackson Square scenes. A clown bending over to hand a child a balloon. A band outside the A&P. Another one in front of the cathedral. An artist painting the portrait of a little girl. A tarot-card reader telling a young couple their fortune. A mime. Like the trees of Jackson Square, the tourists watching them in the paintings were just backdrop, strokes of bright colors on the landscape. This had been the landscape of my everydayness, something I'd seen long ago, a movie, totally unreal.

Katherine eventually showed up. She'd gone out with some cops to the suburbs to run errands. They told her people were still looting in Lakeview, that they drove U-Haul trucks around at night and robbed houses at will because there was no military presence there now. One of the cops also told her there were three prostitutes working Bourbon Street the night before and the ugliest one showed him the $1000 she had made.

With great effort, I pried Mad Max off my kneecap, which he had been rolling around with his crotch, and the three of us walked fifteen stories up to the roof of the hotel. Rita was still plowing lavender-bellied clouds through the sky after sunset, pink and violet and violent. She had made landfall this morning on the Texas-Louisiana border as a Category 3 and decimated the small communities of Cameron Parish, but we'd heard of no reported deaths. The Sheraton across Magazine Street rose easily twice as high as us, full with power like the Marriott across Canal Street. Both hotels' signs were missing half their letters.

"It's mostly media in there, in the Sheraton," said Katherine. "I hear Chris Rose is staying in there."

"He's in town?" I asked.

"He's been here off and on for a while. He's been writing on nola.com, all the *Times-Picayune* articles have appeared there. Supposedly they're getting something like thirty million hits a day."

"Hope he goes back to stalking Britney Spears and Kate Hudson," said David. "His column was the only reason I read the paper."

"It's the reason half the people in this city read the paper," I said.

"I remember when none of this was here," said Katherine.

"What, these hotels?" I asked. "Really? How old are they?"

"Marriot, I think, went up in the seventies, the Sheraton sometime in the eighties."

"Huh. What about the others? Like One Shell Square, that's the tallest, right?"

"Yeah, that was in the seventies too, I think."

"No. What was here when you were little, then?"

"Only the Hibernia building, right there, and when it was built in the twenties it was the tallest building in the South." She pointed to the domed top of the Hibernia building, twenty-three stories high, glowing white against the raging sky.

"Had no idea it was all so new."

"It's not anymore," she said, then, "You know, Josh, I never asked to stay."

"Excuse me?"

"I never asked to stay that morning before the storm, when we woke at your place and realized it was a Category 5 and everyone had left messages for me telling me to leave. You never even asked me if I wanted to stay."

"Yeah, okay, I'll be downstairs," said David, and he walked back down into the emergency exit.

"I'm sorry," I said. "It never occurred to me. I didn't really choose it. I couldn't. I just needed to stay here."

"I couldn't choose either," she said. "Because you were going to stay. And I couldn't leave you."

We were turning violet in the dying light. She stepped toward me, rose on her toes, and kept her eyes open. We kissed like we had under Mars on Mimi's balcony, like I had wanted to beside that lost lamppost in front of the Windsor Court twenty-three months ago. "I love you," she said, then stuck her tongue out, licked the tear that had rolled down to her lip, into her mouth, and swallowed. "I love you so much that all I ever want is for you to be happy, no matter what becomes of me. Please, please know that."

33

Katherine and I agreed to meet at Molly's the next evening and she went back to her friend's condo. I biked back into the Quarter. Ever since I'd read the police officer's response to my Salon article, replete with thinly veiled threat, I'd been trying to keep on the beaten, and, if possible, well lit, track at nighttime. So, I went down Bourbon Street, both curbs of which were lined with empty cop cars far as I could see. Still, no one was on the street. I passed Conti Street, the last working street light, and dark enveloped me. I'd hardly gone a block when I heard, "Josh Clark!"

A large silhouetted figure was charging at me out of a side street. "Josh Clark!" He lunged with his arms out at me. I put my own arms out in weak defense, closed my eyes, braced myself.

He started hugging me. "Josh!"

I felt beard stubble against my face. I opened my eyes, reared back in his embrace. It was Chris Rose. "You scared fuck out of me, dude," I said. "Now quit hugging me."

"It's just so great to see someone I know. Jesus, man. What are you doing?"

"What am I doing? What the hell are you doing? I hear you're up at the Sheraton."

"Yeah, on a couch in a room with about six other reporters," he said. "Jesus Christ, what are we all going to do, man? What do we do?"

"We go to a strip club," I said. "Relax. It's just for the air-conditioning."

And so, we walked back into the lights on Bourbon toward Déjà Vu. Chris had evacuated for the storm, spent time in Maryland where his family was, and then come and gone and come again since. He had one of those rare faces that always gave you the impression he was doing something fun that you wanted to be a part of. For New Orleanians, it defied cogent physical description because we were so used to it. It was there at least twice a week on top of his front page column in the *Times-Picayune*'s Living section. His head was simply a landmark of the city. But, if pressed, I'd say it's something about halfway between George Clooney and Crusty the Clown. I'd used his work in the first book I edited, *French Quarter Fiction*, and we saw each other around town a bit, but the last time I could remember he actually called me was to see if I knew where Kate Hudson was working out while she was filming here the year before. That was his beat. But I sensed that'd all changed now. As had his face. The skin seemed no longer tied to bone. It simply hung from his skull.

I left my bike beside the entrance, ice from the Christopher Inn melting around the Ziplocs of yellow cereal, and we walked into the blasting air-conditioning. The same girl as before was dancing center stage. We sat at the bar and ordered a bucket of Budweisers.

Once again, we were the only ones in there without a badge. This accounted for all the empty police cars lining the street. Bourbon Street strip clubs were usually full of middle-American conventioneers who'd escaped their wives for the weekend shoulder-to-shoulder with wasted underage frat boys. And that was bad enough. But this was like someone had given those same people badges and guns and set them loose on one of the only girls left in town who also happened to be naked and shaking her butt cheeks to Guns n' Roses.

More trickled in every couple of minutes and every time they did others would stand up and hug them and smack them on the back. The music drowned their shouts and left only their mouths working away at each other while they sucked on Bud Lights and tried to grope the dancer.

Chris wrote *diaspora* on a cocktail napkin. "How do you say that word?" he asked me.

"I don't."

"You know, I tried to say that word on CNN the other day, talking about what's happened to the city's residents. It was my one chance on CNN and I didn't want to fuck it up, so I said, 'spread out.' You have a cigarette? Did you know I stopped drinking and smoking for three months before Katrina?"

"No and no." I asked the guy beside me for one, handed it to Chris. He grabbed some matches off the bar, lit it, and blew smoke into the dim, blue-neon lighting. They'd turned the lights down considerably since I was first here with V, so now it actually looked like a strip club.

"You know, people will use any excuse to get off the wagon," I said. "Tough day at work, car broke down, got a parking ticket, got in a fight with their girlfriend, you name it. But this, well, I figure it's a pretty good one."

"Sure."

"Buck up, man. Christ, look at your posture. Get your back straight, pull your head up. You look like a dying weed."

"Take your hands off me. Not in here."

"There. See now don't you feel better when you sit up straight?"

"Shit."

"I tell you, man, maybe it's worse for you. You get to go see your wife and kids up in Maryland and all that, you get to get out of all this, but, I don't know, having that time to exhale, maybe that makes it all worse. You know, there's something about being here this whole time. We don't have time to get depressed about it all, and mope around. Even those who lost almost everything, even if the kid who mowed your lawn every Thursday was floating out in front of your house, even if you dragged a dead body to a church on your way to Molly's, we're all too busy just trying to make sure we got food and water. There's no chance to let our guard down, to really sit back and exhale. Your guard goes down, you break down."

"Should we order another bucket?"

"Of course," I said. "This smile you see, it's just here to quiet the frustration."

"Over?"

"Over the fact that there wasn't more we did, wasn't more we felt we could do because we didn't have any real information about who needed saving and how we could save them. Someday that'll hit me, that'll burn me right up, you know? But not now. Now, there's not enough room to step back and look at all that. Just like there's not room for all this anger and sadness and fingerpointing we hear about people doing all over this country. Suppose all that needs to happen at some point, but now we gotta get through this, and start thinking about how we're going to fix it."

"And how's that?"

"How in fuck should I know? Now quit sulking and smile, motherfucker."

"What time is it?" he asked. "Is it midnight?"

"Eight-thirty."

"You kidding?"

"I know. It's this whole no electricity thing. Our bodies start to shut down when the sun goes."

There was some porn mag lying on the bar in front of us. I flipped through it lazily while Chris peeled at the label on his beer. In the middle of it was a four-page spread of mutilated people. A guy's head after he'd blown it open with a shotgun. What was left of someone after they were hit with a semi. "What the fuck is this?!" I cried. "Who the fuck wants to look at this *shit*?!"

Chris shrugged his shoulders, sunk back into a slump.

"Shit!" I kept flipping back and forth through the pages, scanning the photographs over and over to make sure they revulsed me no matter how long I looked at them, and when they stopped doing that I hurled the magazine five feet into a trash can behind the bar. "Shit!"

<u>34</u>

"Man, I'll tell you, this hurricane's messed up more relationships than herpes," said the kid. His was one of the familiar faces I'd seen over the last month, but never spoken to. His scalp was freshly razor shaven and cut up around a mohawk. "And the evacuees, man, they're out there in their dee-ass-per-a, dee-ass-per-izing the shit out of their own relationships all over America."

I plugged my computer into an external socket on the EMS trailer and laid it on the ground underneath.

"You the one used to ride around with that girl," he said. "Tall skinny blond one with the tight body?"

"Well, we're not broken up quite yet," I said. "I'm not going to let any hurricane break us up. I'm just not going to let the weather have that much control over my life. We're just taking a break, kind of."

"Fucking right, man. Maybe, dude, maybe your love just wants to break out of the course you set for it, you know? Maybe it needs to deviate, flood a bit, you know, get rid of this sediment y'all have piled up, and maybe it'll come back together okay, fall back into its groove, just like the river used to do from time to time back when people let it, before the levees. Course, maybe it'll just spread out thin forever, you never know. But you ain got much of a choice. Levees are a short-term fix, dude. You gotta let it flow its own course. You know?"

"Pass me one of those waters, will you? Thanks." I drank half the bottle, until the cold cramped my stomach, then poured the rest down the back of my neck as alarms went off all around us. We ignored them. We'd become numb to new sights and sounds flying at us. "River levees held—"

"What?!" he said.

"I said the river levees held, though! Through all this, it wasn't the river. The river never touched us."

"It touched them people down in Plaquemines Parish where it made landfall! It wiped that place off the face of the Earth! So I hear. I've never been there."

"I've only been to Plaquemines once. I just remember all the satsuma groves stretching between the road and the river and everything was raging green and . . . Oh shit."

"What?! What is it?!"

"Well, that's that," I said. I unplugged my laptop, folded it up. "That's the end."

The kid looked all around him, then it dawned on him too. These alarms, buzzing and ringing and whining and jingling, were coming from inside homes. Electricity. He shook his head, disbelieving it.

"Them motherfuckers come back they're going have to get their own provisions now, man," he said. "There's gonna be two kinds of people in town: Those who stayed and lived like animals, and then the rest of them who come back and say, 'Oh, wow, we made it.' " He sneered mockingly.

Sirens drew near. Suddenly there were firemen all around us, a Japanese television crew running behind them toward the corner.

"I'll see you!" I said to the kid.

"I'm not so sure, dude!" he said. "Good luck!"

I walked up to the corner. It smelled like burnt toast. There were about half a dozen fire trucks now. Smoke poured out of the second-floor dormer window of the St. Pierre Hotel, a small B&B. A couple of firemen ripped the side off the hydrant beside me, screwed a hose onto it. A couple of others climbed up a ladder and onto the low slanting roof around the dormer window and smashed the window with an ax. They shot water inside and smoke poured out. The truck in front of me, the first one that had pulled up, was from New York City. *The Spirit of Louisiana* was written on its side.

"Why's a New York fire truck say, 'The Spirit of Louisiana'?" I asked the firefighter standing beside me. He had NYFD on the breast of his shirt.

"They donated it to us after 9/11, and we drove it back down here to help out after the storm. Got your camera, Danny?"

He stood with his fellow firemen beside the fire truck, in front of the burning building, its address over his shoulder. It was 911 Burgundy Street. The alarms stopped.

David and Mad Max were leaving the Compound as I walked in, both gleaming a smile cheek to cheek. He was just taking Max for a walk and couldn't wait to get back in his aircon. "Never been camping in my life and I don't want to try it again," he said. When I informed him they'd just turned it all back off, he cursed me.

The radio told me they were shutting off all electricity in Orleans Parish at one o'clock, and that there were already over a thousand confirmed deaths from Katrina with body recovery still ensuing, zero from Rita, and one from a tornado in Mississippi.

35

I spent the rest of the afternoon biking up St. Charles. LOOTERS SHOT was spraypainted on a few banks. Next to Emeril's Delmonico was a store that sold Oriental rugs. Starting at the top of its façade, huge handpainted letters read:

DON'T TRY. I AM SLEEPING INSIDE WITH A BIG DOG,
AN UGLY WOMAN, 2 SHOTGUNS, AND A CLAW HAMMER.

9-4-05.
STILL HERE, WOMAN LEFT FRIDAY,
COOKING A POT OF DOG GUMBO.

9-11-05
YOU KNOW WHAT IT MEANS TO MISS NEW ORLEANS.
Y'ALL COME BACK FOR CARNIVAL. I HAVE MY PARADE SPOT.
HEY, THROW ME SOMETHING MISTER.

9-24
WELCOME BACK, Y'ALL. GRIN AND BEAR IT.

The only humans I found were two old guys reading in beach chairs in front of the Circle Bar in the shade of downtown's skyscrapers, fragments of MREs in a neat pile between them. Across the street, General Lee loomed above his traffic circle atop his 100-foot column, defiantly facing North. I biked up to them but they paid me no attention whatsoever. The one right in front of me had on a white dress shirt with the sleeves rolled up above his elbows, a blue baseball cap, headphones draped around his neck, huge round glasses thick as a finger, and a sandy moustache that seemed to consist of about a dozen thick hairs. He spat something out of his mouth onto the ground between my feet. It looked like a tooth. He leaned over, picked it up, examined it, then flicked it over my shoulder toward Lee Circle, and went back to his book.

I crouched down beside him. Far as I could tell he had only two giant teeth, both black, one hanging down, one coming up, touching perfectly in the dead center of his mouth. I cleared my throat. He looked at me, then turned the page in his book and went on reading. "Hello?" I said.

He nodded, spat another white thing onto the sidewalk.

"Is that a tooth?" I asked.

He picked it up, studied it. It was a piece of cracker, probably from the giant saltinelike ones that came in MREs. Again, he flicked it into Lee Circle.

"I wondered if I could talk to y'all for a little bit."

He nodded.

"And record it? Is that okay?"

He closed his book on his finger. "All right."

So, where do you live?

In that apartment building there.

The retirement home?

It's an apartment building.

Did you have any storm damage?

Yes.

What happened?

I thought I was stronger than I was. It was damage to my ego.

And people have been bringing you food, or you get food?

Oh, a combination. The kindness of strangers.

You sit outside here most days?

Yeah, we change places according to the sun. I guess the canopy of trees that used to be here was swept away by Katrina. It's been a most quiet place. But thanks to the Army and the patrols and the police there's been no looting. Oh they did originally when it first started—the filling stations there across the street were both crackered pretty good.

So, otherwise it's been pretty chill, huh?

Well, no, not as far as sympathetic vibratory patterns—you cry for those who are still living after having everything taken away from them, like jobs, livelihood, mementos, memorabilia, anything. There are lots of good stories. But the good stories are put away by the horror.

No one has come over here and tried to get you guys out of here?

The building manager told us "The water's coming up, it's gonna be up to the second floor! We've got to evacuate!" To where? I asked. His answer was, "Walk toward the Superdome." Fie that. Totally ridiculous. And there was no central place to get the true information. No unity and thought and direction and purpose. It's the ghost of evacuation, is what happened. In other words, you grabbity grab a ghost, you get a handful of sheet. The zoo run by the animals, everybody seeking power, which is a level of being the devil.

What's the worst thing you've seen in your time here in the last four weeks?

Well, one of the little old ladies who lives in our building was walking around the corner and got mugged and the police passed her up while she was laying in the street bleeding.

And you're the only two left in your whole building?

Everybody abandoned it, with fear and loathing. That's the one thing that permeated the whole atmosphere was fear.

Were there any deaths in the building?

Not at the time, no. I'm sure that there are many since they've evacuated. God knows how they're gonna push a little old lady on crutches, and who has had a stroke, and wherever they sent all of them I don't know. You know, not too many people have stuck together. They all ran their separate ways. Like the rats who leave the ship, and it didn't sink. And Nagin saying we should leave, and I wanted a seat on the airplane that his wife took. And when Mr. Bush was flying around, I wonder what he ate that night. But this is making the best of what is here. It's been an experience. I'm a witness. Why I have to witness I don't know, but I'm here. It's not the best, but I think I can do it. I'd rather be a number of places. I used to visit the Twin Towers. There was a great fine restaurant there—not the best food . . . but it had a great view. Just delightful. And that was one of the places—because I lived there, on Long Island—everybody wanted to go there. Not to the top of the Empire State.

Do you guys pretty much spend all your time out here reading, until the curfew?

I do other things, too. I write and I paint and I draw and plan. You know, it used to be that we made friends with a lot of the people who walked by. It's very quiet now.

What are you reading right now, can I ask?

Yes, I'm reading *All I Need to Know I Learned in Kindergarten* by Robert Fulghum. Listen to this: "I believe that the imagination is stronger than knowledge, that myth is more potent than history, that dreams are more powerful than facts, that hope always triumphs over experience, that laughter is the only cure for grief, and I believe that love is stronger than death."

Do y'all need anything? Water or anything?

We want two things. Tell him what they are, Jimmy.

Dancing girls! And bourbon!

36

The same bald police officer who'd pulled Katherine and me over that night after curfew, the one that resembled Curly from *The Three Stooges,* drove into my bike. Fortunately I was not on it, and he was in a golf cart. He reversed, went around the bike, jumped the curb, and barreled down the sidewalk straight at me. I jumped out of the way barely in time. He paid me no attention, but turned on a little flashing light on the top of the cart. I realized he had about twenty bags of ice in the back. "Ice delivery!" someone shouted.

Everyone cheered. "Hey, we've got to have priorities!"

People started helping him unload the ice. There was a healthy little crowd at Molly's. I struck up a conversation with Jim Doogan, a guy about my age who'd just returned this afternoon.

Doogan: It's a circus here. I used to work in a circus, actually. I dropped out of college and ran away and joined the circus and was a fire eater for a couple of years. There was about 110 of us.

About what we've got in the Quarter now.

Doogan: Yes, it's the same people over and over again. It's intimate and incestuous. You live off generators together.

What were your first impressions coming back?

Drunk Man: You're recording this.

Doogan: Yes, he is.

Drunk Man: You're getting this for prosperity.

And uh, yeah. Now returning to the question: What were your first impressions coming back into the—

Drunk Man: The little button is pressed down!

You're double-fisting here, man, you got a couple drinks, don't you?

Drunk Man: I'm a native.

Good. Where you live at?

Drunk Man: Tremé.

And how have you been making out?

Drunk Man: Hot.

Hot?

Drunk Man: With the mosquitoes and everything, it's crazy.

Did you ever leave?

Drunk Man: No . . . I want looters.

You want looters?

Drunk Man: I don't want no looters.

Did people try to loot your place?

Drunk Man: I got a 25 gauge . . . I got a shotgun!

Did you have to use it?

Drunk Man: No. I'll shoot off firecrackers, instead. I got firecrackers.

Did you see any looting in your street?

Drunk Man: No. No. People in my area are copasetic.

Good. That's good. Now, just let me finish asking Jim here a question, okay? So what were your first impressions coming back?

My first impression started at Jackson, Mississippi, and there's wind damage up there, two hundred miles inland there was damage. Then, all the way home, as things got more and more familiar, it got harder and harder emotionally. The best thing, the only good thing, is these people who stayed through it all. I was not here. I've heard some stories. The people who just rode it out, I mean, it sounds really cliché to say that they're inspirational or anything like that, but they do set an example and they, you know, they're doing it right, and they're being what this city's all about.

Katherine was supposed to have shown half an hour earler. I thought I'd avoid an encounter with Curly. So I walked into the river. I stumbled over loose rocks in the shallow until I was waist deep, dunked my head in the cold dark water, scrubbed my underarms, crouched down in it up to my neck. The sky shone milky on the surface, smooth as skin, swirling shadows through it with my every finger's twitch like little colliding currents. Something nudged my back. A piece of driftwood, striations flowing in and out of each other until they ended in splinters. But the river had not shaped it. It was a piece of a two-by-four, spotless canary yellow paint still clinging to one side.

When I got back to Molly's, Katherine's car was parked out front. She was starting her engine. I ran around, got into the passenger seat. "Where ya been?" she asked.

"I just went down to the river for a bit. How are you?"

"You just left me here."

"Left you where? What the fuck? Will you stop this? Will you?" I asked her. "You fucking left me, remember?"

"Where do you want to go?" she asked.

"I don't know. Fuck."

She took a right on St. Philip—one-way signs had long since ceased to matter—and drove further into the Quarter. "Penelope, the girl I'm staying with, she's meeting a bunch of people after work at Touché for a couple drinks."

"A couple drinks sucks," I said.

"I think they're having a special or something. Anyway, all the people at the station are going to start meeting over there at six every day."

"Are we having happy hours already? Christ. Spend our lives working eight hours, then throwing back a couple drinks, eat some dinner, watch some TV, go to sleep, do the whole thing over again. Maybe hit the gym in the morning or at lunch, then clean the car and do the laundry on Sunday. Goddamn. Shit. Get in the grave."

"Well, what do you prefer to do?"

"Stop here. I want to see how Señor Petucci's doing."

Perkins Petucci was on his stoop, his cane across his lap, his coiffed hair longer now, like all of ours, watching the orange sun crawl away up the houses across Orleans Street from him. His eyes shifted onto us, once again refocusing on the twenty-first century. He said his vertigo was getting better. I introduced him to Katherine.

A white van pulled up across the street. A skinny, short guy, maybe forty, with a baseball cap and thick black-rimmed glasses resting on chipmunk cheeks got out, walked up to us, and asked if we knew if Bob and Evelyn had returned to their house across the street yet.

"Which house is that?" asked Petucci.

"The one there," said the guy, pointing to a peach creole cottage with closed pale blue shutters.

"No, no. I'm the only one on this street now. Bob and Evelyn?"

"Yeah."

"That house is owned by Dale and Richard."

"Oh, well, maybe it's another one."

"I don't think so. Let's see, Bob and Evelyn. I know everyone on this street. Are you sure it's this street?"

"I may be wrong. Okay, thanks."

The guy walked back to his van and got in the front seat. He sat there for a while, staring straight ahead, finally put the key in the ignition, started it, sat there for another minute or so, then turned it off, got out, and walked back over to us. "Excuse me," he said, standing in the middle of the street. "I'm sorry, look, I'm just going to be honest, I'm just looking for someone to talk to."

"Someone to talk to?" said Petucci.

"I'm just real lonely. I've been back for almost a week, been all by myself at my place uptown."

"Well, come on, come sit with us, man," I said.

"Yeah. Okay. Thank you. And, I just want you all to know that I'm gay."

"Okay," I said. "I'm Josh."

"Richard."

We talked until the sun left the buildings across the street and Richard let me turn the recorder on.

Richard: I met this girl in Florida when I evacuated and she had the hots for me and took me to the Comfort Inn. But I can't do girls anymore. And I didn't have enough money to stay there on my own so I went to this Baptist Resort in Marianna, Florida, by myself, and adopted a five-month-old black Labrador. So I'm staying there and basically I'm like, you know, incognito, not telling anyone I'm gay. But then the Chalmations and the St. Bernardians—I shouldn't say ignorant white people because who I am to judge?—started feuding and fighting. All of ems talking crap about each other—this one's accusing that one of sleeping with another one, all that stuff. So, they started hitting each other with two-by-fours and they had blood on the street and Pastor Jeff had to call Florida State Highway Patrol to the resort. That was when I decided I had to leave.

Petucci: But why don't you give girls a try? It's so much fun.

Richard: Hey, I done it and I can still do it, but, it's like, it's not there. I was in the closet since I was fourteen. I mean, I'm a big old closet case. I got to do this. And y'all are the first ones I'm telling this to. You know, I was ninety days sober the 19th of this month, September.

You haven't been drinking in ninety days, but you got a beer in your hand?

Richard: I'm gonna be able to handle it.

Katherine: You want to stay in New Orleans now?

Richard: Yeah, because tomorrow they're supposed to open up Algiers, the CBD, and the French Quarter, from what I've heard on the radio, and then like Uptown where I live—

Petucci: I've heard so many different things. I've heard that the Quarter's the last that's supposed to be opened. How about that fifteen minutes of power we had this morning? I began sorting my laundry.

Richard: So, to continue the story—

Petucci: Listen. Pardon me for interrupting. You don't have to hold up a sign that you're gay. No one cares.

Katherine: In this city, it just doesn't matter as much. You know, I'm embarrassed to be straight here. And I've said that on record.

Petucci: It would be a waste if you were not.

Richard: This hurricane, you know, I believe you close one door, and you open another one.

So, Petucci, how you making it? You going to get bored once life gets normal again?

Petucci: No, I occupy myself very, very well. Opera, symphony, art galleries, and museums, things of that nature. Right now, my phone works but my record player does not. That's a problem. Because sometimes, when I'm in a reverie, listening to Chopin, Beethoven, whoever, and enjoying a glass of sherry, I do not hear the phone. That is a good thing. But now—

Richard, what are you doing?

Richard: I couldn't find any bug repellent.

WD-40? For real? Are you kidding me? You're spraying WD-40 on your legs? What if someone lights a candle near you, or matches? You'll go up in flames.

Richard: Yeah, I gotta watch for that.

So, anyway, Petucci, you were saying now you can hear the phone . . .

Petucci: Yes, the phone rings and I hear it. Last night, my sister called me, she said, "Why won't you leave?! I suppose you didn't leave because of all of your treasures." Meaning, I'm a collector. I said, "Susie, I am not open for lectures, you have three sons to lecture. I've been on my own since I was twenty and I've managed quite well without any lectures. If I want to hear a lecture, I'll go to church. Now, I will say goodnight, and I love you." And I hung up. See, she's eighty-five and I'm eighty-one. So, I'm still her kid brother. And I don't need it. I'm under enough pressure as it is. The other day, the doctors over there by the convention center, they wanted to put me in the hospital.

Okay. I can't take it anymore. Give me some WD-40. Watch out y'all.

Katherine: Was it because of the vertigo, Señor Petucci, that they tried to put you in the hospital?

You know, this actually smells better than bug repellent.

Petucci: Well, the vertigo, and being under stress, amongst other things. I said, "Of course I'm under stress. Who isn't?" Now, if you don't mind, I don't want to keep you all here talking to an old man. I think it's best if I go lay down for the night.

He walked inside, leaving the three of us alone with the "1" spray-painted on the street in front of his home.

Half a block down, V was standing in the middle of Bourbon street, pissing off some reporter. After she walked off, throwing him the finger over her shoulder, he managed to talk Katherine into driving a bunch of us to Déjà Vu.

Opal, a girl with large Egyptian eyes and raven-black hair and porce-lain-white skin blossoming with tattoos, who had come down from New York City to do relief work, and quickly given it up to become a full-time member of Johnny White's scallywag crew, hopped into Katherine's car with Possum, who said he was trying to avoid the news crews. Richard barely squeezed in after V and promptly and proudly informed all those in the backseat that he was gay. Bourbon's sidewalks were again lined with police cars. The only open space was directly in front of the entrance to Déjà Vu.

We opened the door and got hammered with Metallica and air-conditioning. Apparently word had spread: The place was wall-to-wall with camo fatigues and black police gear drinking Bud Light, speckled with the odd media person hunched over a cocktail. Opal and Katherine were the only women in there besides the dancer. We took the last table, tucked away just to the right of the entrance, farthest from the stage, beside two National Guardsmen gazing spellbound at the the muti-lated people in the porn mag I'd thrown into the trash the other day. Richard went up to the bar and hauled back six buckets of Abita Amber. He said it was cheaper that way. Opal went to sucking on Possum's gray neck while he told me about being a Navy Seal in Mogadishu, how he got court-martialed because he'd "compromised his men" by saving an old woman who was getting her head kicked in for a gallon of milk. He stared stone cold into me, fighting tears, turning paler as Opal sucked on him, telling me how the crying children tried to swat flies out of that woman's bleeding head until Opal started licking the dirt off his face and I said that Bartender Bart told me yesterday that he used to be in the Delta Force and it was really awesome that Johnny White's was so full of Special Ops now, and Possum pushed her head away, leaned into me, whispered how the media tried to really make a story out of him when they found out who he was and I was about to ask what he was talking about when Opal hopped onto his lap between us and started biting his lips and I suppose those of us who emerge from this unscathed will be tempted to create our own scars—we had been through something, sure, but it had not been through us—and there was certainly no one here to doubt it now and why not pluck an emotion or two while the rest of us tried to relax in the only air-conditioning in town and Opal grinding into him biting his lips till they bled while Possum did his damnedest to ignore her wiping blood off his chin staring at the pig-faced dancer with breasts like tightly rolled sweat socks swinging her cottage cheese stomach upside down around a pole amidst police boys slouched like kings working their hands and mouths away at each other soundlessly beneath guitar bass drums Metallica and the National Guardsmen unable to take their eyes off that same page of mutilated people ignoring Katherine as she hit V in the face a good solid haymaker knocking him and his chair over onto the floor at their feet and Richard grabbed her and started jitterbugging to *tuck you in, warm within, keep you free from sin* his hands everywhere they shouldn't be seeing as how he can't do girls anymore, smiling ear to ear eyes rolling loose in glaze *sleep with one eye open, gripping your pillow tight* and V up again and saying he's seen a lot of people turn gay when they got drunk but he'd never seen a gay dude drink himself straight before, and Katherine cocked her fist again and V out the door and never came back *exit light, enter night, off to neverneverland* now Possum telling me how to single-handedly kill a unit of Serbs in the night with only my teeth and I was sure he was going to cry at any moment while Opal was dry humping him *dreams of war, dreams of liars, dreams of dragon's fire* both their belts undone and blood rolling down his neck and Richard falling over them into his bucket of beer empty now anyway on the floor with him and the knocked-over table and V's knocked-over chair and Richard humping the carpet like he was having a fit and Katherine and I doing some wretched lambada bastardization over him the only ones dancing in the whole place *something's wrong, shut the light, heavy thoughts tonight* and the girls' clawing hands disappeared beneath clothes now while Possum screamed at me about Iraqis making him drink crude oil which gave him the runs for four days while they tortured him in Kuwait and how he still tastes it in the middle of the night no matter his silver star and a policeman jumping up bulging his black uniform shouting pointing in the face of a soldier and Katherine and I on and on with clothes on and Possum moaning that Opal tasted like oil and milk and blood scraping the back of his throat until Katherine dragged me away through police shoving camouflage waving fingers and mouths shouting without words grunts growls semen and Katherine dragging me into the ladies a good thirty minutes before the stripper walked in and said Ummmm I'm gonna leave now and if one of you is not a woman, they need to leave too . . . and another half hour later we split ourselves into each of two people again and came back out and everyone we knew was gone only the National Guardsmen fighting over the porn mag now ripped in half and new black shoving new camo and the rest in each other's faces and the rest trying to break it up and we push through their spit into my face cold on my lips my tongue like sour orange juice when we got outside to Katherine's car.

She drove me to the Compound. I kissed her goodnight. She went back to the Warehouse District and I dropped into the pool.

I got out the other end, sat by the table and coolers, listened to myself drip dry and watched clouds break apart constellations. I could not find the moon. There was no sign of David. I turned the radio on, and mixed myself a piña colada. Nagin said he wanted 250,000 people back in the city by Friday, tomorrow. They would begin letting them in zip code by zip code, the radio said. As I finished my drink, a car pulled up onto the sidewalk outside the gate. I turned the radio off. Brake lights and headlights vanished, a door closed, a key in the gate, footsteps through the scant leaves I had missed after Rita.

She stood there, across the pool, facing me, and sighed. Then she turned and walked up the steps to the balcony, where we used to sleep, wood beneath her sandals creaking. Her steps did not falter until they stopped. I took the last sip of my piña colada. She walked back down to the patio again, directly across the pool from me, not twenty feet away. I had missed the second-to-bottom button on her blouse.

"Joshua?" she whispered, "Joshua . . ." like coming into consciousness beneath my mother's lips in mornings long ago, and I would not answer, would pretend I was asleep not because I was afraid, but because I wanted to hear it again. I would whisper it to myself in the dark for nights and years afterward, the eeriness of speaking my own name softly to myself, giving myself the illusion that someone else was there though it was only me. I wanted to hear it again, hear that it was not only me now.

She walked to the table nearest her, groping the night until her hand hit Tayl's old throne, the beads clacking, then she found the table, fumbled through the candles, cans of insect repellent, a small Maglite. She turned it on, swung it over the patio quickly, its white scar arcing across my retina. "Joshua?"

"Here," I said.

She swung the light through the pool, the unmoving water between us. "*Where* is here?" Then the light stung my eyes. She covered the bulb with her hand, letting just enough light dribble out for her to walk around the pool without hitting anything. She walked up to me, her fingers glowing apricot between us.

"Hey," she said.

"Hey."

"You're naked."

"What's going on?" I asked.

She turned the light off and we vanished.

"Scared hell out of me, baby," she said.

"What's going on?"

"I lost my key."

"Shit."

Her shape began separating from the darkness, just out of arm's reach, above me. I wanted to tell her that she needed to rebutton her blouse, but thought it might sound indecent.

"Penelope's not answering her phone," she said. "I don't know where she is."

"Isn't there an access code to that place, on the gate or something?"

"It wouldn't work. I tried it for fifteen minutes and it wouldn't work. Then I went back to the strip club, retraced all our steps, and it wasn't there and I even looked outside Señor Petucci's."

"Christ, baby."

"I know."

"So."

"Yeah."

"You want to sleep here?"

"Yeah."

"Yeah."

"Is that okay?" she asked.

"Sure. Of course."

"Our blankets, the pillows aren't up there on the balcony any more."

"I've been sleeping in 111. It's the only unit the mosquitoes haven't gotten into. It's hot, but I've found the heat's okay if you stay still in it. We'll lie down, just be still, sleep. Come on."

I closed my eyes and led her back around the pool, through the two garages, and felt for the door just inside the Toulouse Street gate, unlocked it, pushed it in, a heavier dark scented with mildew, still and close. We pushed through it, through the living room into the bedroom hardly larger than the queen-size bed. I had remade it every morning for the past couple of days, never knowing when someone might return. I tossed all the pillows off but two and lay on the comforter. She turned the flashlight on, walked into the bathroom, shut the door. The sound of water running was enough to start me sweating. These last nights, alone here, I had made a peace with the heat. I would not move it more than was necessary to get to the bed, I would hardly even breathe it, and, in return, it would let me be.

She came out, a flash of white, naked and skeletal, before she turned the flashlight out and found the bed. I stayed still as she crept over me, onto the empty side of the bed, and settled. I lay on my side, letting the sweat dry down my spine. The darkness took shape around her. It was a long time, filled only with breathing, before she said, "My rib. Do you want to see my rib? I would like it if you saw it."

"I can't. Can barely see you."

"I mean, I guess I meant, touch it." She was lying on her side facing me. "It's here. I want you to touch."

I worked fingers through the dark like fine sand between us. Heat shivered from the point of contact. I felt my forehead warming, pores opening, pooling, and withdrew my finger.

"We need to be still," I said. "That's the only way it works in here."

"Please," she said.

A cop car slid down Toulouse Street, lights spun across the room, breaking her into blue and red and white. I reached out again. It was her hip, the crescent bone there slanting, ending in her waist draped like cloth, up again into the thirteenth rib, the tiny extra rib on her left side. Muscles flickered, squeezed the bone beneath my touch, then let it go. "See?" she said. "Still as the bottom of the river."

I could feel her body rise and fall around the rib as it took on light, bent it to its shape, my finger like shadow upon it. The rest of her grew slow from the rib. As she got warmer, my fingers sunk into the skin, looser now that she was smaller. "We'll be still," I said.

My fingers reached into her until I could feel the bottom side of her rib. I pushed further, curling her skin beneath the rib, until I felt the inside of it, and held it, and the night over it turning pale as the sand on Nova Scotia when the water ran out. "Hold us there," she said. "Where the currents stop bullying you."

"Still," I said. "Sleep, baby."

"Do you see now how much my eyes have to look at, see why they open so wide?"

"Still. Please, still. Please, please, please, please, please . . ."

"Please tell me you see why."

"I do."

Her body tightened around the rib. "I will leave."

"No," I said, trying to hold on, not wanting to hurt her. "Please. Just stop. Just please stop. Please."

"You used to care."

I let go, let her have it back, sweat cascading down my spine, down my scalp, forehead, my eyes. It was far too hot to evaporate. I turned on my back, let it pool on the silk sheets.

I had no idea if she was awake or asleep. Her every breath chipped away at the balance I had achieved here in this room these nights. It kept me hot and sweating and the sweating made me angry that she was here, making it this way. And the anger only made me sweat more until the sweat tinged with hate, salty, like my mouth filling with salt water. But it made it easier, and it was thinking of salt water, the ocean, the taste, the way water should be, that calmed me finally, finally as gray spread into the living room, through the open bedroom door.

Then, suddenly, day.

A small crash, soft and strange as the tick of a clock. Something closing. The front door. She was gone. I had been asleep. The clock said 6:37. I reached across the bed into her wet body print, still hot, then grabbed the glass of water on the bedside table, two days old, sipped, put it back, this tap water that only makes me thirstier, puts hair on my teeth, tongue like sand, her print cooling, me pushing into it, burying myself in it, tasting the salt in it, all that remains, cooler now, cold now, cold and heavy thundering into a womb two hundred feet deep, burying myself in sleep, holding tight to it fighting the fright of hours of dark and heavy space and me alone in it fighting it to stay in it out of daylight rushing over it and get back to the start, colder, calmer as I beat upriver, river thinning, stream light through fingers and toes like spilling sun a drip drop from a mountain top then a snowflake separate from any other, me just me, no weight of hand or land or river but sky and a smile before I realize electricity is about to come back for good.

I open my eyes. Air-conditioning falls into them. I taste it thin and dry. See the overhead fan begin to turn. I blink, squint into this absurd yellow light spilling from the open closet, and America returns whispering this time.

CITY OF NEW ORLEANS
MAYORS OFFICE OF COMMUNICATIONS
1300 PERDIDO STREET, SUITE 2E04
NEW ORLEANS, LOUISIANA 70112
504-658-4940

C. Ray Nagin
MAYOR

HURRICANE KATRINA SAFETY AND SECURITY RE-ENTRY INFORMATION

On behalf of Mayor C. Ray Nagin and the City of New Orleans, Welcome Home! We are putting back our City and need your cooperation. Please be advised that although we are slowly returning our City back to normal operations, there are some precautionary measures you need to know about to follow. **PLEASE READ THE FOLLOWING INFORMATION CAREFULLY!**

1. You are entering at your own risk. The City of New Orleans remains a hazardous site, and ongoing health and safety issues are being assessed. The City of New Orleans is still undergoing testing and recommends that you take great caution before entering the city and your premises, whether business or residential.

2. THERE IS A CURFEW IN PLACE FROM 6 PM to 8 AM EVERY NIGHT that will be strictly enforced until further notice. This means you may not be outside between 6 pm and 8 am, by vehicle or on foot. Keep personal identification with you at all times.

3. Police and fire services are limited. The 911 system is not fully functional at this time.

4. The traffic lights are out throughout the city. You are required to observe a city-wide speed limit of 35 mph, regardless of the posted limit, and treat all intersections as four-way stops. Follow all street directions. Some roads may be blocked. Proceed with extreme caution, especially around downed power lines.

5. You are not permitted to go beyond your designated zip code area. Travel in your zip code only when absolutely necessary.

6. There is very little access to medical services at this time. We are not prepared to handle critical care patients. You should have tetanus shots before you enter the City.

7. YOUR HOME OR BUSINESS MAY NOT BE STRUCTURALLY SOUND; ENTER AT YOUR OWN RISK. Use extra caution when navigating upper floors and attic space.

8. The sewage system has been compromised. With the exception of Algiers, you are advised not to drink, bathe or wash your hands in water from your tap. You may flush toilets.

9. Standing water and soil may be seriously contaminated; avoid contact. If you come in contact with dirt or water you should wash with antibacterial soap and bottled water as soon as possible. Federal authorities suggest you limit your exposure to airborne mold and wear gloves, masks and other protective materials to protect yourself. You must supply your own protective equipment.

10. Food and water will not be provided to you. Bring sufficient food, water and any medical supplies required to sustain you and your family, keeping in mind curfew times and store inventories may limit access to these supplies. You must bring sufficient fuel with you before you enter the city. Gas stations are not fully operational.

11. AVOID CARBON MONOXIDE POISONING. Do not use fuel-burning devices indoors (e.g., gasoline or diesel generators or equipment, grills, etc.). Opening doors and windows or using fans will not prevent Carbon Monoxide build-up. Do not connect electrical generators to the electrical panel or an outlet in your business or home.

12. No temporary housing is currently available within the city for returning evacuees. Such temporary housing may not be available within the city for six months. Returning residents whose homes are not habitable must leave the city by 6 p.m. each day.

37

Just back at my place now. Monday, September 26, MSNBC was on when I got here, showing images of the damage, raving about Katrina just as it was when it went off a month ago. Little ants crawling all over my floor; horrible stink coming up from the café below me. The alarm was horribly screeching so I unscrewed the whole thing and then bashed it with a hammer until it stopped, and now there's just every other alarm in the building and city screaming through my ceiling and floor and walls and open windows which I won't close. Four weeks ago, almost to the hour, I suppose I was sitting here in candlelight listening to the storm scream.

Let's see, I cleaned up 111 a bit after the electricity came on, cookies dipped in chicken soup for breakfast, left a note, took the cookies. I gathered up as much as I could from the courtyard and put it in boxes and bags and the old baskets from AJ's produce and piled it into the Sexy Beast, only the battery was dead. Walked over to the EMS station, picked up my computer, told them I might have to start working again, ha ha ha, blah blah blah. I asked Ty if he could give me a jump with the ambulance later on.

So, I'm walking back here and it seemed like every block I ran into someone else getting back into town. They all want to know what it was like, and I got no idea how to answer, and so I tell them it was interesting and they smile and think I'm being condescending. I mean, I have no fucking idea how to talk to these people.

All business owners are supposedly allowed back in Uptown, CBD, and French Quarter. I don't exactly understand that myself, the traffic lights don't even work, much less potable water and shit. Shit! And then she fucking just leaves me.

[tape breaks]

So, Ross tells me that Elena is folding SCAT magazine so I suppose I'm not the associate editor of that anymore, and then I see Bill from the

Ogden Museum and he's telling me how the museum let seventy per-cent of its staff go before they even came back to town and how it would be impossible to do the big scavenger-hunt fundraiser in Novem-ber, we'd spent the summer planning it, and my friend Jake asks how the Mississippi writers book is going and it's not, of course, and he says it looks like I lost some weight, and I told him I've been working out without a gym and oh shit, the fitness book I was going to publish and is there even a Mississippi Delta to write about anymore for the LA Times *and shit, fuck it, I'm back here at my place, and I'm not closing these fucking windows. Lights are on, goddamn refrigerator's on and everything. Shit. I guess I could have microwaved this MRE. It's Santa Fe chicken and I dumped the fucking minestrone soup on top of it and I'm fucking eating it with silverware and damn is it good and our coun-cilwoman who left all that food for Petucci is on* Fox News. *Looks like she's on the other side of the river, the West Bank.*

Jacquelyn Clarkson: . . . in fact, Algiers is the second-oldest part of the city, second only to the French Quarter. We were blessed, spared, through Hurricane Katrina, and have gotten our act together very fast so we could lead the rebuilding. We have medical clinics here in Algiers, and food distribution and major grocery stores and drugstores open, small ones, too. But the most important thing, we have The Old Point Bar open with jazz music. What more could you want than that?

Shepard Smith: Hey, I tell you what, love to hear that, and I know the good people of New Orleans East, and the western part of St. Bernard Parish and the rest would love to hear it too. But, you know, they're gone. Their neighborhoods are under mud and sewage, and politicians talk about rebuilding and repopulating that area. Is that realistic, or is that just a pipe dream?

Clarkson: No, it's very realistic. We will do it progressively. Algiers was first. Downtown, the business district, and French Quarter being next up, which are the heart of our commerce in the city, as well as our port and our river. And, then, we'll go to neighborhoods downriver and upriver, uptown and downtown, as they were dry, they will be the next ones in line, and by the time we get to the eastern part of our city, and St. Bernard is a different parish—that's not New Orleans, so I really can't speak for them, but . . .

Smith: Miss Clarkson, Miss Clarkson. I've been in New Orleans East today, the eastern side of the city of New Orleans. Ma'am, those houses have been flooded to the roofs. Where do people who come there work? Where do their kids go to school? I mean, it's great to talk about rebuilding, I mean, not in your heart of hearts, but in your mind, is that really realistic?

Clarkson: Yes, sir, and let me finish and you'll understand. Because I'm talking about progressively. I'm talking ninety days to have downtown ready, I'm talking six months to have the rest of the city ready, and these are just my timetables. So, by the time we get to the East, the rest of the city is ready to help. And, yes sir, we will make it work.

Smith: Well, now wait. Now wait. I know, nobody loves the can-do spirit more than I do, but every house, every house for miles, every one of them, thousands and thousands and thousands have to be bulldozed. And then you have to get people in here in space suits to decontaminate the ground. And that's before you put in a single sewer or put in a single light pole. I mean, this is not a small thing. This is not a few miles. This would take billions and billions and billions of dollars, and many months or years, wouldn't it?

Clarkson: No one has proven yet that anything has to be bulldozed, nor have we proven that anything has to be decontaminated. I can tell you right now we are planning on repopulating the eastern part of our city without a doubt, and we will do it very prudently, we will do it when the rest of the city is ready to help do it. And if that's too candid a message for you, I apologize. But it's real—

Smith: There's no question—

Clarkson: They told me I couldn't open Algiers and look—

Smith: I'm over my time, I wish I had more time, I wish I had more time, but I'm totally out of it. Ten seconds left to go. Here's the thing. We wish you well; we hope it happens. Reality's a tough thing sometimes, and it—

You fucking shithead!

Smith: . . . here's hoping.

38

"My mom, she used to say hope is survival. She said she raised me to be a survivor," he says, some face I don't recognize, jumping into the seat beside me at a table in Molly's. "I put her in a retirement home yesterday, where I hope she begins dying."

The place is full of light like old times, glowing the polished wood, sparkling the beer signs and memorabilia cluttered on the walls and ceiling. I'm drinking a white Anheuser-Busch can of water. They donated a whole lot of them to the city.

"I have this black Lab," he says. "Armstrong. Spent eight years raising him up, then six years ago I have my son and turns out he's allergic so I give him to Mom. The dog, not my son. Though it was a tough choice, loved that dog like nothing before. Holy shit, give me some cheap bourbon on the rocks, please. So Mom, she takes water the day after the storm, seven feet in Gentilly. So she tells Freddie our neighbor that she's going to evacuate if a helicopter comes by and she asks him to shoot Armstrong after she leaves!

"Now, don't get me wrong, being trapped in your attic or on your roof exposed to the sun or clinging to a telephone pole or being out of food or having children or elderly or handicap or sick people with you was one thing—you should evacuate as soon as possible—but this was another. She could have grabbed a few books, lied there on her bed upstairs with Armstrong and relaxed for a week or so. Don't people know eventually the water will go down? And it's not friggin lava for God's sake.

"She told me she looked at the drawing my son Will made for her last Christmas and realized how worthless she'd be to all of us—my sisters and me and our kids—if we found Armstrong standing guard over her dead body. Now, that one made no sense whatsoever. Why would she expire before the fucking dog? She had food and enough water for weeks. Anyway, so Freddie her neighbor's like, 'What? Are you joking? Dogs can survive just fine.' And he offers to throw food over to Armstrong after she's gone and she just starts crying all over the place. He told me all about that part.

"So, she gets in a rescue boat the next day and the Coast Guard guy asks if she's taking the dog with her and she just starts falling apart all over him, says it's no use, he's got to put Armstrong out of his suffering. He refuses, so she just starts sobbing some more all over this Wildlife and Fisheries woman who's also in the boat, begging her to put him out of his misery, and finally the Wildlife woman agrees to come back the next day and do it. So, Mom gets dropped off on an interstate overpass where she's left starving and dehydrated for three days waiting to get evacuated, almost dies. And I just spent this morning burying Armstrong's rotting corpse, his brains blown all to hell.

"I mean, she gave up a ton of food on the dry second story of her house where she could have lived just fine, in order to kill our dog and nearly die herself. Have human beings been deconditioned into total fucking self-defeating pussies?"

"Dogs'll survive just fine on their own," says the guy to my left. I've never seen him before either.

"Sure they would," says the first.

"I been keeping most of them out in Marigny alive these four weeks," says the other. "First few days I only had little nuggets of cat food, so I'd press them into stale bread so the dogs would eat it. Finally, got the National Guard to escort me up to Robért's and got these huge bags of cat food and dog food and I'd just leave whole open bags out every day for them at different places around the neighborhood. Then, all these damn animal rescue organizations start coming in and breaking into these homes and taking away the pets I was feeding just fine and now they're gonna end up God knows where and get euthanized."

"People should have taken their animals with them," I say.

"A lot of people couldn't afford to take their pets or couldn't afford to leave," he says. "Then, they were forced to evacuate to the Superdome."

"Okay, sure," I say. "But, as for the rest, I mean, most people who can afford to take care of a pet could have gotten them out. Way I see it, if you decide to own an animal, you are responsible for it, like a child. If you leave town because a hurricane might hit and your house might get flooded, don't leave motherfucking Lassie locked in the kitchen with a bowl of water and some chow and some newspaper to pee on. Lots of folks say they only expected to be away for a couple of days, only packed a couple of shorts and T-shirts. Well, that's understandable, but pack Lassie, too, goddammit. If you leave at all, you're doing so because you believe there's a chance, however small, your life could be in danger; and if that's the case, what the fuck are you doing leaving your dog locked up in your kitchen? *If* she makes it through the hurricane, Lassie doesn't have directions to the Superdome, and she can't flag a boat down—especially if she's locked up."

"You know, I had five cats, older cats, had them forever," says another man, sitting at the corner of the bar, facing us. "I got five feet of water and tried to hold out and I did for a few days, but then I knew I had to swim out of there, had to get to the Superdome, and I was about to run out of medicine for the cats, and they needed that medicine. So, I put them up on the kitchen counter one by one and shot them with my .38."

"Love makes you do some things," says the first guy.

I turn around and there's Officer Curly, the golf-cart-driving ice-delivering policeman, standing face to face with me. "You never should have written that article," he says. "And if I ever see that piece of shit rusted, no taillight car again I am not going to have the mercy on you I did last time."

His words sound very familiar. But that letter, the one to the editor at Salon, had been written by the other police officer who had handcuffed Katherine and me.

"Did you read the article, man?" I asked.

He looks at me for a while, his face like stone, heavy with the furious snarl of a Mayan god. "No, but someone near me in the station did." And he walks off.

The others sit there looking snowed. "Did that just happen?" one of them says.

I make my way to the bar. The place is packed with homecoming. I look down and realize there's a guy standing beside me, his shining bald head at my elbow, holding his space there, his chin barely higher than the bar. He's got shoulder-length hair around the back and sides and a long mustache that winds around his mouth down to his chin. He's wearing a military ID clipped to his shirt pocket. I ask who he's with. He just looks at me for a while.

"No one," he says. He flips the ID over and under "NAVY" there's a picture, him, only a long time ago. "I was in Vietnam. Been wearing this thing down to Central Command every day to get my meals."

I ask him his name. He won't tell me, says he doesn't want to get in trouble with the authorities. I tell him I'm not going to get anyone in trouble, I live here, I've been here eight years.

"Yeah, well I've been here *fifty*-eight years." He tells me Katrina tore half his roof off and he hunkered down there with an eighty-year-old woman during Rita. "When all these people who are coming back now ask me why I stayed, I don't answer them. I don't say a thing," he says. "If you have to ask that fucking question, than you'll never fucking understand, and that's all there is to it."

That night, I lie on top of my covers staring into the ceiling, watching the cold empty dark fill with the lavender haze seeping into my bedroom. I fall asleep, then wake at 2 A.M. with my bladder burning. I pee for longer than I have in a month because I haven't been sweating it out. Then, the itching starts. For the next few hours, every time I'm about to fall asleep another part starts itching. Everything's dry. And when a dream finally starts knocking at me, I wake myself up. I make sure the door is locked and it is already. I go to turn the ringer off on my office phone and it's already off and so is my cell phone and the intercom is off the hook and the fan is on in the bedroom even though I had not heard it. I walk into the living room to close the windows and I see they're already closed, and I check the locks and they're already locked. I take two packets of Tylenol PM and flip the light switch in my room off and on wondering how light can be silent and off and on and off and on until the city in my room becomes dark again and I lie there and I finally fall asleep for an hour until dawn.

I flip on the television and I cannot find a single channel that doesn't make some sort of reference to Katrina within ten minutes. I go to the computer, my DSL connection working for the first time in a month, and it is the same thing with all news sites, we are the headlines, and I'm sweating and my underarms are cold and they smell.

39

I'm eating a hamburger on the bar at Stella! when a man walks in, orders one for himself, and we start up a conversation about the only thing that really matters this time of year in New Orleans—the Saints. What's not to love about a team that transforms every game into a Greek tragedy? When they're down a touchdown with seconds left, they'll return a kick ninety yards for six points, then miss the extra point to lose with no time on the clock. We reminisce about this and other great Saints moments. The pepper hairs shooting out of his shoulders around his tank top shake with his laughter. His name's Hank. With his high-pitched and kind voice his fervor only adds to his teddy-bear demeanor. The Saints are playing in Baton Rouge this weekend, and no one knows when they'll return to the Superdome. I tell him I heard that ESPN set up a satellite dish and generator during their last game, last Monday night, at the Maple Leaf bar uptown, one of the most popular music clubs in the city, and broadcast the gathering.

Hank: Yeah, that's right. Well, I own the Maple Leaf.

No shit?

And ESPN crapped out on us. The day of the game they said they couldn't get a signal. But really, they wanted some big bouncy bubbly crowd, and we just didn't have that, so they went out to some big sports pub in the suburbs, in Metairie, instead.

I'd think it would've been a better story to do it at your place.

You know, it really would have been something nice to see that game. They really had us looking forward to something. And yeah, I agree it would've been a better story. We're the people who sat out there with guns against looters.

How soon did that start?

They started looting Tuesday, the day after the storm. You see, everybody in Pigeontown, which is a neighborhood up near us, near Carrollton, they knew that no cops were gonna be able to get to them, every street was blocked completely with trees and powerlines and stuff.

There were these guys all wearing these bandanas driving big pickup trucks through Oak Street. They all had AK-47s, you know, and I had a chair in front of the place, and I was sitting on that chair a lot, and next to me was Mr. Rossi. Mr. Rossi is my .38 police special. Me and Rossi, he's my good friend, we've been through the worst. But, it's like, I've got a revolver. I shoot once, and then you know . . . proommm proommm proommm proommm proommm proommm proommm . . . they blow a thousand holes in me. But the gunplay never started.

They preferred easy targets, huh?

Sure, and I think my association with the Rebirth Brass Band had to give us some protection. They played at my club for fifteen years, and a lot of them grew up in Pigeontown. And some of them came by and they said, "Listen, the word is out—don't hit the Maple Leaf." Oh, and plus I was helping the Ninja Restaurant cook meals, and we gave out four hundred meals to everybody, looters included. After a while, some of them were trying to give stuff to us like all these batteries they'd stolen from the Ace Hardware store.

They kept looting till they ran out of sizes. You'd see grandmomma, and then the daughter and grandchildren all doing it together. It was a family outing. My god, we saw a big fat lady with two little kids, she'd walk them store to store, one on each hand, and send them in. If they came out with the wrong thing she'd smack them up against the head and send them back in.

Did it quiet down after a while?

Yeah, because, no matter what they say, they were forcibly evacuating people at some point. I saw how Pigeontown emptied and those people had no way to get out of there, most of them were from generations of utter poverty, but every day there'd be fewer people walking down Oak Street, until it got empty. Anyway, we'll be open this Friday, actually. We don't care if we have electricity. You should come by.

You know, now you have to look at the city like it's been through a war, and when is the last time that's happened? World War II. You gotta look at the destruction that was done there, and how did they rebuild? That's gotta be our model.

That night, Jim Doogan lends me some gas and I tear over the Mississippi River for the first time in a month, two hours after curfew, in search of sleeping pills. I drive twenty miles through closed storefronts into Westwego, until at the end of the line there's a jam-packed In 'n' Out with Vietnamese kids behind the counter running the register like stenographers. I take all eleven individual packets of Tylenol PM they have and twenty minutes later, with my radiator hissing and shooting like a geyser, I pull up to the checkpoint on the bridge back into Orleans Parish, show the female officer my business card, tell her I just desperately needed tampons and water and she laughs and waves me through. I head to my outdoor parking lot across the street from my apartment. I'm thanking God I've made it back into the Quarter okay when a tiny woman security guard starts shouting at me that I can't park there as I'm driving through the broken gate ignoring her. She follows me in and starts yelling at me as I'm getting out of my car, telling me this entirely empty lot, half a mile long, is reserved for a certain news network. I just ignore her completely while she writes down my license plate number and tells me she's going to tell them I stole all the lights that disappeared last night. "Where are you from?" I ask.

"Across the river, Westwego."

"We're neighbors, and you treat me like this? We need to be helping each other out. Who made you like this?"

"Those lights that got stolen last night are on you," she says, and walks back to her little folding chair by the parking lot entrance.

I head down to Molly's where Coco Robicheaux's sitting on a little stool in the back by the pay phone tearing up new wasted faces, first live music in the city since the storm, and I don't have anybody to talk to until the EMS guys show up, so I buy them a round and they ask me how many people in there are locals and I realize we all are but them. Shit.

I walk back to my place below a starless sky, empty, lonely clubs throwing open their doors. Halfway down Decatur, a kid who couldn't be older than seven holds up a HUGE ASS BEER sign while he's talking on his cell phone. The security guard's sitting cattycorner from my door, watching me. I grab an MRE and some water from my apartment and walk back across the street. A red dot appears on my chest. She's holding a taser, little blue sparks running across its end—*eeeeee eeeeee eeeeeee e-e-e-e-e-e-e-e.*

I stop in the middle of the street. "Hi," I say.

More blue sparks.

"Listen, I brought you an MRE here, it's Shrimp and Ham Jambalaya. It's my favorite. And some water."

The sparks don't stop. I walk toward her. I can't tell if she's looking at me. Her eyes have sunken into the shadows of her brows. I set the MRE and the water down on the curb about ten feet from her, that little red dot into my eye now, and turn around and walk back toward my place. It's when I'm about halfway across the empty street that she says, "You ever get to the point where you're so hungry you can't eat?"

Her voice has a Cajun lilt not usually heard in the city. I turn, tell her I've felt that before.

"You don't understand the people I'm working for," she says.

"That's no excuse."

I stand there in the middle of the street. Her child-size clothes consume her. "Please don't tell them I took their lights," I say. "I don't need that right now."

She looks at the MRE on the curb. "Maybe my son wanna eat it. He tears into those things."

"Why are you hungry?"

"They not even letting me use the bathroom. I go to ask for the keys to the port-a-let they had over there and the woman I'm working for wants to know who's gonna watch the lights now? Then, they took it away two days ago."

"When you get a break why don't you come up to my place? I live right there, that's my door. I've got an extra key I can give you if you want. I've got plenty to eat and you can use the bathroom there whenever you want. Seriously. I'm not a creep and you're the one with the taser."

"She don't let me get up to eat."

"So don't they give you meals then?"

"They have a barbecue every once in a while there in the parking lot. I can only go up if she asks me to, and then they give me dirty looks like I don't belong there. But I don't like to eat in front of people cause I gotta take my teeth out."

"You need to eat. You have to eat. Will you eat that?"

She stands up, walks over to the MRE between us, picks it up. "Shrimp and Ham Jambalaya," she says.

"I have others too. Hold on. I'll be right back."

I return two minutes later with a box of them and a gallon of water. She's still standing there on the curb, Taser in one hand, MRE in the other. I put the box down by her chair. "I got all this stuff here left over and I want you to have it, okay? You got to start eating."

She looks up into me towering over her, little eyes quiet as dim stars in the caves of their sockets.

"I'm sorry," I say. "The way I talked to you before, I'm ashamed of it."

"I won't tell them you took the lights," she says.

"I'm Josh." I reach my hand out and her little one flutters into it, out of it.

"Priscilla."

"That's a pretty big gun you got on your belt there, Priscilla."

She lifts the gun out of its holster, cradles it in bent knuckles and fingers like wishbones ready to snap beneath the weight of the shiny revolver. "Three fifty-seven magnum," she says, making sure it's pointed at the ground, the hard black thing rubbing loose flesh over the tiny bones, fingers caressing it, then lowering it back into her holster.

"Take a look at my Taser," she says. "Peak open circuit arcing voltage of fifty thousand volts. Penetrates two inches of animal hide from thirty-five feet out."

While I flip the thing around in my hands, she goes through the box of MREs. "Cheese omelet with hash browns and bacon?" she says. "I know what I'm gonna have for breakfast."

"I want you to eat one of those now, even just the toasted pastry or something, anything you think you can eat. Please."

"I told you, I don't like to take my teeth out in front of folks."

"Well, in that case, seeing as how it's past my bedtime anyway, I'm going upstairs. I'll be seeing you." I hand back the taser.

"I'll be here. I'll probably be here when you get up. I'm working twelve-hour shifts. Get off at eight in the morning, get home just after my husband's left for his work. He's on the river. He gets home about seven in the evening. Sometimes I see him for a minute before I go to work. I take care of the kid in the morning for a bit until I get too tired, and he does it in the evening before he goes to bed. It would be special to get to sit down with them and have a meal sometime soon, real special." She sits in the foldout chair with the Shrimp and Ham Jambalaya MRE in her lap.

"Y'all get a day off together anytime?"

"Not the same days."

"Well, I really hope you can set it up so that you do. You have a good night."

"You know, I work casino boats mostly, did before the storm. They have some big fellas that come after me in there. I don't care. I go right to the nut."

I turn back around, walk back over to the curb, sit down against the broken lamppost there. "Is that right?" I say.

She tells me about every casino she ever worked, the heat, the lights, cargo ships sliding down the river behind us, and next thing I know I wake up and the MRE wrapper is empty beside her, and she's putting her teeth back in.

40

When I finally tire of trying to sleep in my bed, I walk toward the river, stand inside my window, and laugh out loud at it convulsing within its levees. It looks like a child throwing a temper tantrum, screaming with energy, just as stupid as all those alarms two days ago.

Here, now, New Orleans, still quiet. Sun slanting over Jax Brewery into me. The river, then Ripley's, no sign, my panorama. On the corner, a man loads a news camera into the back of an SUV marked TV. He gets into the truck, backs it onto the curb, right up to the lamppost I slept against last night. Priscilla is no longer there, nor is anyone else.

The man gets out, pulls the tailgate down so that it's almost touching the lamppost, then casually looks both ways down empty Decatur Street. He climbs onto the tailgate, quickly pulls a screwdriver out of his pocket, gets up on his toes, and holds the ST. PETER sign with the fingers of one outstretched hand while he works at the screws with the other. I think of the little girl walking by with her family on my birthday, checking for loose plywood or unlocked doors right there behind him, my disgust and pity and heartbreak. Here, now, there is only disgust. I do nothing. He works at the screws, frantic. They fall to the street one at a time and the sign comes free in his hand. He tosses it into the truck, then hops down. He scans the street one last time, only this time he looks up, all the way up to my balcony, catches my eyes. Then laughs, shakes his head, gets into the truck, and drives off. I wonder if he shows people that sign now, if it's hanging in his kitchen, if he's so used to seeing it he no longer notices it, or if it's in the bottom of a drawer forgotten somewhere. Two years later, it will still not be replaced.

And in the window, me. Naked. I suppose I'd laugh too. Mottled arms and legs scarred with mosquito bites, bearded face, a barely healed tattoo on my chest, a bandaged wrist that I can't imagine will ever stop hurting. The darkness beside me, between the two windows, in which Katherine once sat, tiny, alone now.

I pick up the T-shirts around my place, the towels, throw them in the washing machine, my bathing suit, my sandals, my bandage, take a shower with the little water pressure I have, then clean my apartment, my refrigerator, my office, and put all the things now strewn on the floor back up where they belong, put things back on the floor that I'd put up because I'd expected my windows to break and water to pour in.

There's only one message today. The Professor telling me his pod is okay but his house took six feet of water and he'll be back in a couple of weeks and wants me to help him move in in return for the barbecue he threw before the storm. By midnight, I have caught up on e-mails, told friends I am still alive, told authors and my distributor that I have no idea when I can get back to those books, catalogued and copied the tapes I've made so far, and partially designed the website www.NewOrleansLiterary Institute.com, which in addition to containing information about the KARES relief fund is becoming a home base for displaced New Orleans writers. Then, I walk downstairs to the bottom of my entryway and piss all over the Ripley's *Believe It or Not!* sign.

For a year, I have watched it hang above those unfortunate kids across the street, battling the river for my panorama. And the kids are no doubt on their way back now, along with all the usual securities and certainties. Certainty will be the last to return, and, when it does, I'm gone, maybe I'll take a little vacation, spend the extra $14.99 on insurance for a rental car and teeter it off small desert cliffs. But, for now, I'll just try to sleep in air-conditioning.

41

"No one knows what it's like just to be fucking people!" Possum leans over the bar in Johnny White's, raised fist clenched around his dog leash, screaming his gray face through all the new faces ignoring him, including the bartender who's just returned to claim his old job. "No one knows what it's like to be a person! But it's all over now. The fucking bourgeois are coming back!"

And there's some fluorescent-T-shirt-tucked-into-jean-shorts-wearing contractors from out of town with big-hair wives telling each other that their screwdrivers taste like shit, standing beside me. A couple lazy-eyed locals singing along to Patsy Cline. And the black dude in the bar simple as a shadow sitting in the dead center of it all, crossed legs so skinny you don't realize there's two of them, a little graying beard, a face I'd seen but never noticed a thousand times since I'd been in New Orleans, and now media crowding in the bar around him, and him just sipping on his Budweiser can through it all, as he has these last four weeks because that's all there is to it.

"Gimme a damn Budweiser," says Possum. "King of beers!"

The bartender tells him he has to pay for his last one first. "I was the richest man in the city," says Possum.

"Get out of my bar," says the bartender.

Possum stands, takes a hundred-dollar bill out of his pocket, puts it on the bar in front of him, says, "My last cent," and walks out. When the rope around his neck grows taut, the German shepherd rises and follows. It's an old gutter-punk trick: Dogs deter arrest, since the police would have to call a K-9 unit and then place the dog. Possum leads the dog through the pickup trucks with ladders strapped on top that line the curbs outside, and past a man huddled in an alcove of the hotel across the street, one of our resident abandoned ghosts who offers a simple smile which Possum ignores, clutching his rope leash to his heart, wearing his scowl like a medal of honor. He rounds the corner, out of view, and I realize I never noticed him before the storm.

When I walk back to my place the lights are on in the A&P, a couple of brooms leaning against the entrance, and the manager comes outside, tells me, "Goddamn looters tore it up." I laugh and tell him it was the cops. "Guess that explains why the liquor's still here," he says.

Next morning, Andy, bartender and owner of Flanagan's, is hauling a dripping garbage bag out into the street. "Maggots and meat juice," he says, as he pulls his bandana down delicately with his rubber gloves, then tells me to come in for the first beer they serve after having been closed for the first time, ever.

"Watch your step," he says. "Last time I saw you, morning after the storm, you and that girl were telling me how to make some cocktail, something in Augusts."

"And you were trying to sleep on the pool table in an air mattress."

"So, where'd you go to?"

"We didn't. We still haven't."

He looks at me funny, twists the top off my Budweiser, sets it down on the tiled bar.

"So, where'd you find a lock for the front door, anyway?" I ask. "When I worked here we always prided ourselves on the fact that we didn't have one."

Andy: We didn't. We screwed the doors shut with two-by-fours from the inside like *Night of the Living Dead*, then went out the back.

You weren't taking any customers before then?

If someone came by and wanted something, we just gave it to them. We kept people comfortable. Our evacuation plan was always go to the French Quarter, high ground, and that's what we did. We housed thirty people for four days with no electricity and water and the place was pretty trashed. So, Wednesday, we loaded everyone and their pets into two vans, and we drove cross-country dropping everybody with their families and friends. We didn't drop one person at a shelter. Eventually, last week, all the boys met in Champaign, Illinois, and then we all got down here today.

We were worried. We'd heard so many horror stories like this family I knew that drove for three days just to get here and then waited in traffic for two days, and then were turned around.

What was the worst thing about being away?

All the misinformation. Even from people who were here. You got one person telling you, "It's a nightmare, it smells like shit, and I'm dodging bullets." Then you've got another person going, "What the hell are you doing in Illinois? It's a booming metropolis! You could have lines out the door if you were open right now!" And I don't think I have to touch on the media. They're fucking useless. You got a guy who says, "I'm here on Bourbon Street," when he's in fucking Chalmette. And everyday you got a message from the mayor that conflicts with the day before.

The thing is, about what people here were telling you, Andy, it's all true. Parts of the town are toxic, and parts of the town have lines out the door. And yeah, I'd get calls from people watching CNN telling me there was am armed gang in the Quarter and I never saw anything like that.

Andy points to the tape recorder, then draws a finger across his throat. I turn it off. He pulls a photo out from under the bar. It's him and twelve others, bare chests covered in tattoos, faces covered up with bandanas, posing outside the bar with enough revolvers, automatics, and shotguns to invade Canada. One of the women is kneeling on the curb in front of them, eyes peering out of thick black eyeliner over a bandana which disappears into her white and black hair, wearing brass knuckles, holding a baseball bat in one hand and a hatchet in the other. Above her, the guy in the center, towering over them all, wears a hockey mask and raises a thick piece of lead piping over his head. "Just some of the guys and girls who work here. My wife took this just for fun. A CNN helicopter passed overhead a couple times as we were posing for this."

This morning, for the first time, doors gape open to the sidewalk. I walk straight into the apartments and houses and clubs of old friends. The people themselves, just returned this morning, huddle inside their dank rooms, plywood still shutting light out of windows, peering out of their darkness at me, aghast with gray eyes wondering what do we do now?, afraid to close the door, turn on the light. Their skin has sallowed and every one of them is either fatter or skinnier than when they left. I have no answers.

The Compound pool is circulating. The stone angel beside it is spraying water into the deep end. Two caretakers are cleaning the patio. I
scrape the last of the candle wax off the bricks with a spatula. "You
want these beads?" one asks, pointing to a trash bag full of what once
adorned Tayl's throne.

I take the beads down to Señor Petucci's house, sit beside him in his
bed, and we talk for an hour. His air-conditioning hums, and end of
summer light falls muted through his curtains, glowing his oil paintings,
landscapes burning with golden skies, filling us with longing to stand in
these impossible places. On his bedside table sits the tiny framed photograph he showed me, the ocean between him and his first true love. He
lies dressed as ever in his tank top undershirt and slacks, white hair
perfect. There is no Chopin, no reverie, only vertigo now. As I leave he
asks me to take a box of MREs down to Johnny White's. He doesn't want
them.

I swallow a plate of beans and chili from the Salvation Army on
Canal Street, and bike up St. Charles six miles until it ends. Halfway there,
a Hispanic kid stops me with the traffic in order for his crew to chop a
branch off a power line. We speak in Spanish. He is from Atlanta, and
before that, Belize. His wife is coming next week. He thinks this is going
to be home. Within two minutes traffic is stopped behind me for three
blocks, only a few Humvees, no media, among all the cars.

Just before the avenue ends is Cooter Brown's, open. I eat a chicken
sandwich at the bar, beside a man built like an NFL lineman. He's sipping Heineken, wearing a black T-shirt that says "I PROTECTED, I
DEFENDED, I SACRIFICED. I STAYED THROUGH IT ALL. I AM N.O.P.D."

"Watch out, the next five days, it's going to be insane," he's telling a
couple. "People are going to get back, despair's going to set in, they're not
going to have anything they would normally have, the looting's going to
start. Every day I have a gun pointed at me." Behind us there's a woman
proudly sticking her FEMA money into the video poker machines.

I walk outside, where St. Charles meets Carrollton, corner of the
streetcar line, the Riverbend, and cross the street, the train tracks, over
the levee through a gate to the river, unlocked for the first time. I have no
idea what the gate is there for, to keep people away from the river here,
I suppose. Necessity—our need for food and water and other things to
survive—pried out the toughest nail, busted locks, climbed fences,
clipped wire around neighbors' shutters, forced open French doors, and
gates like this were left open because there was simply no one here to
shut them again. For four weeks, nothing was seen from a distance.

The slur of traffic crests the levee. A fish jumps. Seashells under my feet, flies, breeze, and I'm sweaty again and me again. I walk out of the gate, along the base of the levee, a thick batture of trees between me and the river, wade through thigh-high grass normally mowed for children and dogs and picnics. Here, now, the levee is a simple barrier between nature and incoming cars, dragonfly wings clattering, monarch butterfly fluttering between tiny blue flowers I will never learn the name of, and a bumblebee lands on my belly and the goddamn phone.

I turn the ringer off, see that I missed three other calls from Katherine, and turn the phone off. A single biker, sweating hard in spandex and helmet, shoulders low, butt in the air over his racing bike, shoots along the top of the levee above me, does not see me wave. Silence in his wake. Then, it all comes alive again. Shy calls of insects and birds, knocking of a woodpecker. A light rain falls in the sunshine, a common phenomenon here, our summertime rainshine. I lie against the levee's slope, warmth of cement underneath me, and stare into the thick sliver of trees between levee and river until I can see how many are broken, their snapped branches and limbs tangled into each other, into the few trees that are still standing, and eventually the birds fall away from the leaves.

When dusk falls, I walk the bike the couple of blocks to Oak Street. Still without electricity like most of the city, Oak is just as torn up as Hank described it a few days earlier. The looters broke open the front of the Super 10—where nothing's over ten dollars—but left most of the boutiques and antiques stores alone. Hank's sitting on a bench outside the Maple Leaf, no. 38 special today, only a small congregation of employees, musicians, and devotees, making plans for the next time around.

"Fort Leaf, we're going to call it," he says. "Look at this building, it isn't coming down. I'm redoing the attic so we can put people up. I'm getting a thirty-kilowatt generator. We'll run it off natural gas. We'll tie into the city gas supply and it will kick on automatically. I'm going to make up uniforms for us to wear. We'll have gunner posts there and there and there. And I'll keep enough steaks in the freezer for months."

While he gets the barbecue pit ready for red beans and sausage, they toss around evacuation stories. Greg wins. He and a buddy were in his apartment on the first floor in the American Can Company, an old warehouse converted to condos near City Park. His unit was surrounded by glass overlooking the pool area. Daylight hits, the storm is peaking, and only then does it occur to him that they need to get the hell out of there. So they run into his car against 100-plus mph winds, as the eye is about to hit just east in Slidell. And they drive east toward Slidell. They go fifteen miles per hour with no visibility down the interstate into the storm. They make it over the twinspan bridge, then it collapses behind them. "So, you evac'd *during* the hurricane, *into* the hurricane?!" someone asks.

The beer arrives, the beans start cooking and the crowd grows with familiar faces. Like many, Larissa's just gotten back to her Uptown house today. "I saw a guy dumpster diving in the Bywater, wearing a sheet that he had turned into a loincloth," she says. "Animals become feral fairly quickly, and so do humans. New Orleans has an abysmal mental-health record. And I think a lot of the people who had some serious mental-health challenges, who either didn't or couldn't get evacuated, have hit the streets in a primitive way. And speaking of feral, my dear friend and neighbor, she works at the zoo, and apparently part of her work involves bringing home some of the smaller animals when they die, which she freezes in her refrigerators until she can hang them in the garden to desiccate to be studied. Yeah, I didn't know this when I figured I'd do her a big favor and clean her fridge before she got back."

Evening sets, the generators crank up, and Walter "Wolfman" Washington careens into a bluesy version of "When the Levee Breaks" while the *Today* show films. It doesn't matter that it's over a hundred degrees inside the club and Wolfman has traded his funky polyester bell-bottoms for little shorts and his skinny knees are knocking over navy blue socks. A quadriplegic would get up and dance to him.

I step outside to breathe and almost get run over by a Bronco pulling onto the sidewalk. "Boom!" Big Shot T-Nasty leaps out of the driver's seat. He's designed his own press passes to get into town, since his zip code's apparently still not allowed back. He has laminated press credentials with his photo like a mugshot between the words TIME and MEDIA in large letters and enough mumbo-jumbo in smaller letters to look official. He's got them on his dashboard, his rearview mirror, one clipped to his jeans, one on his shirt, one safety-pinned to the front of his leopard-spotted beanie and one around his neck the size of an actual magazine cover. "Henry Luce is turning in his goddamn grave," I say.

"Who that? Yo, grab some Busch, people! C'mon people!" T tosses people cans out of the cooler in the back. My phone rings. "Where's Katherine?" he asks.

"I'm about to find out," I say.

"Where are you?" she asks.

"The Maple Leaf. Where are you?"

"Here."

"You don't sound good."

"I've not really been sleeping."

"We have electricity too now, you know," I say.

"I heard."

"Why haven't you slept well?"

"It's—I don't really have a bed."

"I thought you were in some guest room."

"Josh, I'm in a laundry room. On the floor. I have a phone book for a pillow."

"Why didn't you tell me that? Why did you choose that? What about your place?"

"My place? There won't be electricity up there forever. And the broken windows, and no one in the neighborhood, is that what you think is a good idea?"

I suddenly realize how far from the club I've walked. There's someone leaning against a telephone poll not ten feet from me, a silhouette against the Maple Leaf's generator-driven lights, watching the people, the *Today* show cameras, all of it at the other end of the block. I must have walked right by him. "You could stay at my place," I say. "You could use my futon if you wanted."

"Well, let me, I've got all my stuff here. I'm kind of settled," she says. "I'll call you next week."

The silhouette is gone when I turn. As I'm walking back to the club I hear footsteps behind me. I swing around.

"Plaquemines," the shadow says.

"Plaquemines Parish?"

"Have you been there yet?"

"No," I say. "You?"

"No."

"How do we get down there?"

"We need a truck and press passes," he says. "I can make the press passes."

"C'mon," I say, walking up to the Bronco. "Yo T, can we go to Plaquemines tomorrow?"

"Sure, yeah, sure. Boom! Wet down there I hear!"

"T, this is—What the hell's your name anyway?" I ask the Indian, the same one who sewed V's ear up. I can see now he's holding a video-camera carrying case. I've seen him shooting his documentary around the Quarter for a couple of weeks now.

"Ride."

42

Down here in Louisiana we blame a whole lot on our unique Napoleonic Code, which is the technical name many assign to our legal system. No one I've ever met, lawyers included, has been able to explain it in comprehensible terms. Nevertheless, people blame all sorts of eccentricities on it, such as the police being able to arrest you for pretty much anything they like (some of the charges I've heard from prisoners include "leaning with the intent to fall" and "molestation of a hamburger"). Though technically we've never had any such thing called the Napoleonic Code, the Louisiana Civil Code was indeed influenced far more by the Code Napoléon than it was by English common law, which gave rise to the legal systems of the other forty-nine states.

In earlier times, the Louisiana Civil Code required forced heirship, creating an equal division of land between sons in a family. So, younger sons tended to stay put rather than move in search of new land and, to this day, Louisiana leads the nation in native residents. The mud they first learn to walk in is the mud they'll rest in for eternity, and somewhere in between they learn to love it like nothing else.

Another residual from our French governance is that we refused to call our counties "counties," instead calling them "parishes." And because so many families remain in their home parish, generation after generation, each parish has developed a distinct culture and pride. And arguably none so much as Plaquemines—pronounced *plak-a-mins*—the only parish in the state that is not on the way to anything but itself. The enigmatic, secluded, forgotten parish. Now more than ever.

Despite the fact that Katrina made landfall there, little news is coming out of Plaquemines. There's supposedly all sorts of checkpoints and you need all sorts of passes even to get in. What we do know is there's still water, a lot of it. And, therefore, we need a truck to drive on the levees if we have to. But there are no trucks. T gets stuck helping a friend demolish his place for a couple of weeks, so I scour the town, call every friend I know with a truck but they're all being used or out of town and contractors have snatched every single one from every rental agency within a fifty-mile radius. I find a Ferrari, no problem, but not a truck.

So, the intrigue over Plaquemines builds while I spend the next few days working in my office, nursing my wrist which still hurts to bend, and taking breaks walking the sidewalks littered with duct-taped refrigerators, itching to get back into the fray. We would have to wait for Plaquemines to dry enough to make it by car. In the meantime, Ride and I decide that if we can't see the first place Katrina made landfall, we'll see the final. The Mississippi Gulf Coast.

So, Thursday noon, we fill my radiator, put another fifteen gallons of water in the back seat, and we're about to take off from Molly's when Ride's friend Kimberly shows up with a brand-new white Mercedes and says she's not doing anything for the next couple of days and would like to see her brother on the Coast anyway. She used to live with him there. Ride asks where the Benz came from. "It's George Bush's," she explains.

A minute later we're doing 102 mph down the interstate with the new Nine-Inch Nails blasting—*Don't you know what you are?!!!!*—AC on max, all windows down, sunroof open, and everyone's hair flying— mine practically white now, Kimberley's dirty blond, and Ride's long straight and black shooting into the backseat at me. I suggest putting the windows up since the air-con's on. The third time I shout it she catches my drift.

"Who cares?! It's not my car! It's the president's!"

"So, what's Ride short for?!"

He hands me his driver's license. It says, "RideofTwo Fires Hamilton." "It was too long for the space they had for the first name so they split it up like that! It was always too long for every space, so I've just been Ride everywhere I go that doesn't have enough spaces!"

"Where you from?!"

"All over!"

"Okay, man. Will you tell me where you were born?!"

"You won't know it!"

"Jesus, man, where?!"

"Valentine, Nebraska!"

"Bullshit! I know Valentine, Nebraska. I was there this time last year!"

He closes his eyes, leans back. "I don't know anything about it," he says, then slumps over.

"Ride?"

"He's sleeping!" said Kimblerly. "He gets tired in the days now! He hasn't slept in like a month!"

"Were you here?!" I asked. "For the storm?!"

"I was here for the storm, but then I went to Texas! That's how come I got George Bush's Mercedes!"

"So, you and your brother, you had a house out here on the coast?!"

"Yeah, in Waveland! I haven't seen it since the storm! I'd like to go see it tomorrow, if that's okay! Jimmy said he'll be around then! I tried to visit him right after the storm but I lost my car!"

I reached into the front seat and turned the volume down. "Lost it?"

"It was a Saturn. I drove from Uptown to check on my apartment in the Quarter the night after the storm. I was going down off the Claiborne overpass and I went right into the water coming in. It swept the car. There was a heavy, heavy current. The water was up over my door handles and I couldn't get the doors open. I broke the windshield with the key. I smashed it out and got out. It was tit-high water. But the current was too strong to stand, to walk, you had to swim. There was a lot of things in the water. You couldn't see, it was too dark, the only thing you could see were some car lights shining underwater still, but you could feel, it was dead bodies hitting you and sharp objects. I couldn't walk until I made it to Poydras Street, by the Superdome. The National Guard made me enter the Superdome at point-blank range. As soon as I got in there I was trying to get out."

"What was it like?"

"Screaming and . . . Just screaming and you couldn't see a hand in front of your face. Screaming from pain, terror, stuff like that. There was gunk on the ground, shit and stuff. I saw people face down in it. There's parts I still don't like to talk about. Somebody grabbed me. I kicked him. Then I went through the garages."

"Grabbed you? Do you know what he wanted?"

"Yeah."

"He was trying to rape you?"

She nods. "We struggled for a while. But, yeah, I kicked him. Then he kicked me in the back. I landed on my chin in the gunk and got seven broken teeth. See? This one here's been redone. I got out after that."

"How?"

"I went through the Superdome's parking garages. A National Guard stopped me in the parking garage. I said go ahead and shoot me, it's not safe me being in there. My face was all bloody. And so he said, 'Go, just be careful.' And I just kept going. I kept walking down Poydras, took a left on Baronne, and a cop stopped me and he said, 'Get in,' and he brought me home. On the way home he stopped at Foot Locker and got the looters out and took some shoes for his kids. When I finally got to my apartment in the Quarter and took my clothes off you could see a handprint bruise on my torso. The only thing that hit me in the torso was when I was swimming in the water."

"What time was this?"

"Have no idea of time. It was dark. I don't know how long I was in the Superdome for. When I finally got to civilization when I got evacuated there was glass in my mouth and I had to go through surgery to get all that repaired, because it was badly, badly infected."

"What did you see in the Superdome?"

"There was babies thrown. They were throwing them because they were crying. This is from the top levels of the Superdome. You could hear them. You could hear their bodies slapping the ground."

"Did you see babies actually hit the ground?"

"No. I could see them flying through the air. And it wasn't just babies, it was people too. You could hear that. I need to keep telling it until the nightmares go away."

"You know, I was there that night, just outside the Superdome," I say. "In my pajamas." But she's turned the stereo back up, lighting a cigarette, doesn't hear me.

We get off on Highway 11, just before the Mississippi border, and find a Salvation Army trailer. We each grab some Styrofoam containers of red beans and rice and six bags of peanuts. As usual, no one looks funny at RideofTwoFires, despite the fact that he's wearing thick leather motorcycle pants, a silver studded belt, and a spike though his right eyebrow. We put the beans in the trunk for later, letting them slop around back there. I sit in the back seat eating peanuts. Kimberly says just to toss the shells on the floor, let the president clean them up. Ride tells me he's filming a Katrina documentary. I finally convince him to do an interview.

How soon did you start getting supplies?

Instantly. You just go in with your shopping cart and come out with food and you'd see some people with ten electric clocks, and five microwaves, and two freezers and a fifty-inch TV. I took nothing but food, water, medical stuff. And I did that for about three days, until the police finally took it over and made it a command post. You know, you just try to keep it calm, keep the peace. You say good morning to everyone, you help people out. I helped a man walk out with a workout machine, like a huge-ass weight machine that he fit on a big dolly, and I held the doors open for him. I went with Bart, one of the bartenders—

Bartender Bart.

Yeah, he was drunk off his ass. He went in and came out with two shopping carts of stuff I had to throw away. He said he was in Delta Force and knew how to get survival gear. But every time I sent him in to get something, he just got a bunch of trash like twenty CDs and the ex-wife of Brad Pitt whatever magazine that she was on. And he actually got into a couple fights in there.

Actual fistfights?

The first one, he got knocked on the ground by a woman. They were fighting over a pillow. You know, before that he tried to break into the antique gun store, and it's like watching *The Three Stooges—*

The antique gun store in the Quarter?!

I'm like, "You know it's across from the police station, maybe we shouldn't do this." So, he gets out and was trying to pull off these hunks of plywood for five minutes, and kept falling on his ass. I asked him where he was going to find gun powder and antique bullets for his antique gun. I could just see him loading up his musket as someone points an AK at him.

So at Wal-Mart, would some cops let you in?

You just try and find the officers that aren't gonna kick you out. It was kinda tough getting into Wal-Mart because at first they were only letting black people in, to be honest with you. And so we had to wait around until the police left. And then, after that, it wasn't much of a problem, I mean there were a lot of threats. They said, "If you go in there, I'll shoot you." And then they'd come at the end of the day and say, "Okay, we're closing it down. Everyone get out!" and they'd have machine guns. There were people in every aisle. It smelled so bad in there, because so many chemicals and things had been spilled. Your eyes would water, you would slip everywhere, you know. And you would just grasp for anything, like a can of soda became gold. I had people in the neighborhood to take care of for two months. That was my plan, to get it for the neighborhood. I mean, the Gatorades we're drinking were from Walgreens.

Wal-Mart.

Walgreens and Wal-Mart.

So, did you make up the Red Cross symbol—the one you did on magic marker on a piece of typing paper—and put it on your windshield immediately?

No. That was a couple days later. Just to get through roadblocks and keep the car safe I put on an EMT uniform, and then people thought I was the only medic, so people would actually come up to me asking for help, and I couldn't really tell them no. I was already taking care of cuts and stuff so I thought, hell, I'm the one with all the medical supplies and I'm sober, I don't drink at all, I want to help people, and I might as well make it semiofficial. And that's when I put on the Red Cross thing. And I had the only working car, so after EMS guys started showing up after a week or so I began running people to get medication and shots and evacuated.

I noticed you had those little gasoline tanks on top.

I gave someone from the press a bunch of MREs and they gave me a bunch of gas. You know, I got a flat tire during the first two days of the hurricane, and I had to drive around on a complete flat until we came across a small fire station and they helped put a doughnut tire on it. As we were putting the doughnut on, a police officer came by and told them to get out of there because there was a seventeen-foot wall of water coming. Note that the police officer did not care to warn civilians. I just happened to overhear it. For over two weeks I drove around on a doughnut tire.

One day, I was loading up with hygiene and medical stuff at the Walgreens near Canal Street. I found the back door. It was like El Dorado. There were cases and cases of bottled water and Gatorade. The liquid literally glinted in the few rays of light from a window. After a half hour, I had the station wagon half-way stocked. So, this boy comes strutting down the alley, two girls at his side, wearing a white muscle T-shirt. He grabbed the keys on my belt and pushed me out of the way and got in the driver's seat. I told him if he took the car, he would be hurting a lot of people. He thought about it and looked at the girls. He got out, still proud, still the showoff. He knew he could have stolen the car if he wanted.

What were you proudest of?

Probably V's ear. Every time I took him to a real doctor, they were surprised I wasn't a medic. You know, I knew how thick that skin was and how hard it was to get a sewing needle through that cartilage because I'd pierced my own ears.

How many times?

Thirty-one. People would come back weeks later and show me their wounds and they would say, "You were the only medical treatment I could find. I don't have an infection. I'm fine now." Made me feel good. I would give people baths, and these are people that you normally would not even touch or talk to.

You do that in front of Johnny White's? Out on the street?

Yeah, I would put on gloves and hydrogen peroxide and things that kill germs, water and soap and stuff, you know. And maybe that was the only bath they got for a couple weeks. If they wanted privacy, I would take them into my apartment which is next to Johnny White's.

You know, a couple days after the storm, about two-thirty in the morning I walked into Johnny White's to pass out some food and supplies one last time before I went to sleep and a middle-aged woman with reddish hair was sitting there with her leg propped up on a stool, everyone surrounding her. She told me that she swam from her house, and a metal fence that was underwater punctured the side of her leg. She said she swam and then walked miles to get to Johnny White's, because she heard it was the only place still open on the radio. I put a flashlight on her. The wound was about three-quarters of an inch long and the same deep, with this green pus oozing from it. It glowed slimy green. Up close, it smelled. Bart, the bartender, correctly identified it as gangrene, and panicked.

I knew there was nothing I could do, besides try to treat it and keep it from spreading in the next few days. I washed the area, removed all the pus possible with Q-tips, poured disinfectants on it until the wound stopped bubbling, and carefully bandaged it up. Bart quickly took me outside in the dark, alone. He was like, "You know we have to amputate her leg." He told me, "I don't want to, but we have to. I'll drug her tonight, and you just have to hold her leg." I said, "Why don't we wait a few days, see how bad it gets. Besides, we don't have any drugs or a saw." But he was just adamant, "I can drug her. I have drugs!" You know, like that solves everything. He went on and on, "No one's coming for us. I used to be a medic in the Delta Force. I don't want to do this, but I have to. I had to do this once before in the field in Afghanistan. And the guy died on me."

I thought a couple things: This Afghan war amputation thing really haunted him, real or not, and I sure as hell never want to be treated by this guy in a battle. He literally wanted to hack off a perfectly good leg, because of a three-quarter-inch wound on her thigh. I kept wondering if the other people around would let him do it. What scared me is, I think most would have. They believed that he was a medic. The last thing Bart said was, "It's gonna get worse, it's gonna spread. That leg's going to have to come off to save her." I pleaded with him not to do it, then went home and laid on my bed and had just fallen asleep when I heard an explosion so loud I thought half the Quarter was blowing up.

The warehouses. That was my birthday. Did he cut the leg off?

No. Thank God. I treated the woman until I could evacuate her, and many others. This off-duty National Guardsman showed up in a stolen Cadillac Escalade, and started evacuating a carload of people at a time. I arranged so that the woman went with him. I also got him to take V—this was a couple days after I sewed up his ear. But the National Guardsman returned fifteen minutes later and told V to get out of the car.

So, did it ever occur to you to leave?

No, never. No. And I got mad every time someone broke down, to be honest with you, because I knew in the French Quarter, we were all gonna be fine. But it would demoralize me. Of course, it affects me if people living with me are crying all the time, and it drains on you emotionally.

I mean, in no way did I suffer, and I'm glad for that. I would hate to be a person that was trapped in their attic or broke their neck. And I can sympathize with them. I have seen a lot. I can't say I've been through a lot. I haven't been through anywhere near one one-thousandth of what anyone that had to swim through water went through.

But, at the same time, being here and going through it, basic survival for a month, without power, now that everyone's back, it's kind of alienating, you know. People are breaking down and they haven't been through it. You only have a handful of people you can relate to and those are the people that stayed.

And now the Quarter's filled with people who just came from nowhere, you know, these contractors that are looking for Bourbon Street, these strange people getting drunk every night, you know, I couldn't even get out my door last night because a contractor was blocking it getting a blow job, right on the sidewalk, and he refused to move until he was finished.

It's the same thing as when the Red Cross first came in—not the blow jobs, but the rest. I mean, I was doing first aid for a week. I'm like, "Where the fuck is the Red Cross?" And, all of a sudden, they parade in, swagger in, they're clean, they've got haircuts, they're shaved, they have new clothes, and all they're doing is taking photographs in front of Johnny White's. They're the professional good-deed-doers, like a butterfly, go everywhere after the fact, and of course they help people, but to just swagger in with this attitude like they're everyone's savior. . . .

[tape breaks]

Okay, we're here in the town of Bay St. Louis, finally getting out of the car, all alone out here on the bay. So, Kimberly—you used to live out near here—these houses, they were just being built, I guess? They'd only laid these foundations before the storm came? A few pilings?

Kimberly: No. These were houses. They were enormous, old mansions. They'd been through many hurricanes.

But, then—where did the pieces go?

[tape breaks]

Just nothing. No toys, bedsheets, appliances, details, nothing. All that's on some of these lots is a single piece of broken plywood with their address spraypainted on, I guess to let insurance people know where they used to be. This was water. Wind could not do this. Yet there's no levee here. It's not like some levee broke and simply let the water in. That bay there, it would have had to have risen thirty feet to do this. This little bay I could probably swim to the other side of, flat as glass, rose up and fucked hell out of every manmade thing near it, and then fell back down. It sits there now looking so welcoming. Does the land take its revenge on the water?

[tape breaks]

A truck in a ditch, one side totally caved in. Tattered American flag hanging over the windshield, huge flag, all that's left is pieces of blue-and-white stars, shreds of the red-and-white stripes. Says on the side in black spray paint, "Please don't loot. It's all we have left. God bless."

Spraypaint on plywood says, "Job 1:21." Biblical passages and American flags. What they've come back and left in place of everything they had. God and Country. God came at them with water, and their government forsook them. And still this. This is immaculate.

While he was still speaking, yet another messenger came and said, "Your sons and daughters were feasting and drinking wine at the oldest brother's house, when suddenly a mighty wind swept in from the desert and struck the four corners of the house. It collapsed on them and they are dead, and I am the only one who has escaped to tell you!"

At this, Job got up and tore his robe and shaved his head. Then he fell to the ground in worship and said: "Naked I came from my mother's womb, and naked I will depart. The Lord gave and the Lord has taken away; may the name of the Lord be praised."

43

The maître d' at T.G.I. Friday's in Gulfport, Mississippi, scribbles my name down. "It'll be about two hours."

"What?"

"More like five, really."

"I guess we'll come back for breakfast," says Ride.

"Why don't you just grab a drink in the bar and we'll call you before you know it?"

We wedge ourselves into the bar area, which is five deep on all sides with people ordering jumbo virgin daiquiris and frozen coconut rum fruit drinks in glasses large enough to stick your head into. And all I want is a goddamn beer. This is supposed to be the only place open anywhere near Biloxi. We're here to meet Babysitter, who eventually walks in, and we leave. He came back to town today to find out he had no roof, so he's staying with a friend. They tell him it may be over a year before Hooters opens again. He's thinking about moving. His kid has started breast-feeding again. He says we can sleep in his place. He leaves us there in his bedroom on a couple of mattresses looking up at the stars.

The next day, we drive the few miles further east into Biloxi to meet up with Bumm Steer. Like Babysitter, Bumm Steer is a founder of the Gulfport Hash House Harriers—a group of elite ex-military athletes who like to have a beer or two after grueling ten-plus-mile Sunday runs, otherwise known as a drinking club with a serious running problem. They only earn nicknames after clocking in three hundred miles with the group. I'd drive the hour and a half east to join them for a few runs every year, and it always turned into a punishing but memorable weekend, the easiest escape from the excesses of New Orleans.

Bumm's house is about a quarter mile from the coast. Like all those on his street, it has a flood line up to my chest. On the other side of the street, the Gulf side, is a deep ditch. That is what left these houses standing at all. Bumm eventually drives up in his red Jeep Wrangler, its own floodline matching perfectly against his house's as he parks in front of his garage. He's got a white pick sticking up out of his Afro.

Yeah, I'm here with Bumm Steer. His two big TVs are out in the—They don't look so big now that they're out on the front lawn.

Bumm: Yeah.

So that ditch right there saved your house? I mean, at least it's where you left it.

That ditch cut off about twenty-five feet of the surge.

And when you came back here after the storm?

When I came in, that garage door was still on, buckled. When I looked underneath, the Jeep I'm driving now was pushed through the kitchen wall. It was in the kitchen.

Is that a fence from a golf course? That says 8 for Hole 8? Where's the golf course?

About a mile and a half that way.

Jesus, that's an ice-cream vending machine.

This church woman called me, she's like, "There's this church group, they're wanting to come pick up your debris. Do you want them to?" I said, "Ummmmm, is that a trick question?" So, the next day I'm trying to watch football over at Twinkle's, but then I've got to come over here for a bit because the church people want to see me, so I come over at halftime, and they've put everything from my front lawn and backyard into these big piles and the woman says, "We sorted your things out as best as we could. Do you want to keep any of this stuff?" I go, "There's nothing here that's mine. I mean, why would I keep a boat in the backyard?" There's tables, there's an espresso machine, there's shoes, a lot of kids' gear, I have bicycle helmets, no bicycles, but bicycle helmets, cleaning utensils, there's anything you can think of, computer monitors, out there. But they're all from other people's houses. So, I watched them clean up for about five more minutes, and then . . . it was hot. It was too hot. I went back and watched football.

Kimberly: Why is your name Bumm Steer?

Ride: Can we go inside?

Bumm: Come on.

Wow. What just knocks me out is your cabinets here, which are what— four feet up?—look untouched, your ceiling, untouched. But then, basically from chest level down, you have no house. You've really cleaned it out, gutted it, huh? Why is there a rake in your house?

There was leaves and trees and stuff in here, all sorts of stuff, like this—"Creighton Jr. High School, Lakewood, Colorado Student Identification. 1982." That's my neighbor Bill. My neighbor, he's got so much money and yet he hadn't really paid anything on his house, so he's just gonna let them have it. He's like, "What are they gonna do? Put it on my credit?" He has a Viper.

Look, your protein bars are still here. Do you mind if I eat them? So, you're going to rebuild this? This was your first house, huh?

It was about $44,000 without appliances.

Now are you in deep shit because you started working on this before the insurance company came?

In deep shit how? The insurance company never owes anything.

You didn't have flood insurance?

We're not in a flood zone—

Kimberly: But flood insurance doesn't cover storm surge anyway.

Bumm: Yeah, I understand that, now. They tell you that you don't need it, like this elevation right here, it's twenty-three and a half feet, which isn't even close to the flood plain, so they tell you you don't need flood insurance, because it would never—even if it just rained forever and ever and ever—it would never flood. It would only flood in a surge from a hurricane. And you think that you're covered from hurricanes because you get wind and hail insurance, which is basically hurricane insurance. But that doesn't cover tidal surge, nobody really knew that. The only thing that saves you is if you have a tree fall though your roof.

We could saw that tree in your yard and push it this way.

With my luck it'll just go into my neighbor Bill's house, and then he'll get all the money so he can buy himself another Viper. What happened to your wrist?

I fell from Christ.

You fell from Christ?

So, you were working at the Biloxi VA Hospital during the storm and when did you come back here?

I couldn't get here for five days.

Was it the authorities, or was it a physical impossibility or both?

Impossibility. I couldn't get here because of downed trees, and then, after people looted, they put up a police barricade, but no police. You know, go figure.

Where's your water bed?

The water bed actually floated. That's what saved one of the TVs out there. I put that TV on top of the water bed. When I came back the water bed was way over in the corner; everything I put on top of the water bed was dry.

You're just skipping around from different people's houses now, staying with them, basically?

Till they get tired of me. I'm kinda staying as close to work as possible because I don't know when the Jeep's going to stop working.

So you had no interruption at work?

Uh-uh.

You were working at the VA Hospital during the hurricane?

Well, it was seven o'clock in the morning, and I was working since two in the afternoon the day before. So, I went to sleep about seven-thirty or so. You have to realize when you stay on the VA property, it's like living in your own little city. You have like massive generators outside that flip on automatically, so you don't know, it doesn't seem that bad.

Were you getting news reports of what was happening up here, though?

No. The only radio station that we did finally end up getting was one out of New Orleans.

WWL. When did it start dawning on you: "My property might be fucked"?

Immediately. Most of the cars in the VA parking lot had tree limbs in them. But I didn't know how bad it was until I walked in here.

When you got here, and you saw your place, did you just laugh? Cry? What?

Went back to work.

Immediately, huh?

I mean, it's just money. That I don't have.

So, yeah, let's go in the backyard. Hey, at least your fence is up.

That's not mine. I don't know where mine is.

Is that a golf-cart seat?

You know, I had timber, massive timber from some of the bigger houses that just washed up. You'd think it would knock the house over. I wish it had knocked the roof off. That would have been great. There was this picnic table sitting perfectly upright in the backyard when I got here after the storm, a whole case of Miller Lite underneath it.

So, what'd you do with the beer?

I gave it away. I like Bud Light. You want me to get that?

I pull my phone out of my bag. It's Katherine. I stay in the yard while Ride takes Bumm back inside his house for an interview.

"It's been a week," she says. "I said I'd call."

"How are you? Where are you?"

"Shreveport? Where are you?"

"Biloxi. Shreveport?"

"Biloxi?"

"What the hell are you doing in Shreveport?"

"What are you doing in Biloxi?"

"Biloxi's not six hours away!"

"There's a film coming here. I might work on it. I don't know. Isn't it time to get back into a routine? Don't you have a job, Josh?"

"There's more important stuff right now."

"Like hanging out with that fucking Indian. I heard."

"And anyway, I'm sorry, are you spending money? Are you even paying rent? Are you even paying for your cell phone bill this month? I'm not."

"Do you have any idea what those windows are going to cost in my place?"

"The landlord will take care of the windows."

"Can you imagine what this is like for me? You can hardly move around in there and there's no lights to see anything and I trip over all my stuff and the pages of those books are all stuck together. I loved those books. You gave me some of those books."

"Don't you ever forget, you chose this."

"Oh, fuck you, Josh Clark. What did you think this whole time? You'd be able to flip some switch like Entergy and it would all go back to the way it was? And you thought we'd be able to live together."

Bumm opens his back door. "Can you keep it down, please?" he asks. "There's holes in this house."

"Who was that?"

"Bumm."

"Oh, my God, how is he? Jesus. I need to go. I need to get inside. I just called, I don't know."

"We have so much left in New Orleans, Katherine."

"I need to go."

"Bye." But she has already hung up. I walk inside.

"That was Katherine. She says hi."

"Why didn't you bring her?" asks Bumm. "That time when you brought her over here, we all liked her a lot better than you. It's just too bad she's not black. Tell her to come without you next time."

The three of us stand there in the empty gutted house. Kimberly's in the front lawn, talking to her brother on the phone. We're out of questions. This is the time when I shut up and, if there is anything left to say, the interviewee says it. And while we wait, I can't help but smile, this place forever now imbued only with sweet memories for me, even some of Katherine, totally absent of routine.

"I guess, it just depends on the person, you know," says Bumm. "I've had nothing before, so this, it's not hardly a big deal for me. There's different levels of shock, I guess. See, I have places to sleep, I have all the comforts now, and too much food. Most people are still living in tents, and they don't have anything at all, and no jobs either. The majority of my friends that live here, I haven't even seen them because they don't have jobs now. Most of them worked at the casinos. They're just floating around here, homeless and penniless."

44

Bumm takes us a few blocks down to the coast to see those casinos. We turn onto Highway 90, hug the Gulf of Mexico to our right. All that's left of a putt-putt course to our left is a Humpty-Dumpty statue sitting on top of a chunk of brick wall holding an American flag flapping in the wind.

"I was just here," I say. "Like less than two months ago. Didn't Mark live somewhere around here?"

Mark's condo complex looks the way bombed-out buildings look on television. The entire outer wall is missing and the insides of all the rooms have been exposed and torn to scraps, completely unrecognizable. Bumm points a thumb out his window without looking. "That was his place right there," he says. "See? Where that thing is hanging down?" It's supposed to be funny. That's all there is: things hanging down.

When I was last here, this road was a nonstop twenty-mile stretch of strip malls and casinos speckled with the obligatory Waffle House every mile. A few of the buildings are left in piles. The rest is gone. Trees, once hidden from sight, now stand leafless and alone, charred black skeletal hands groping for sky. I'd spent eight years with Bumm and Babysitter sticking little memories into these places, building this coast into something I cared about. Now this is not a place I know.

"Is that . . . ?" I ask.

"That's the Grand Casino."

"No way. The surge moved that thing out of the water and across the highway? It's the size of a shopping mall. How the hell are they going to get rid of that?"

"Blow it up," says Bumm. "The President Casino's also on that side of the road now. Landed on top of the Holiday Inn."

The Treasure Bay casino, built to resemble an enormous pirate ship, now resembles an enormous shipwreck. Empty billboard frames bow to the ground, a ladder dangling in the air from one by a nail. We're driving along at twenty miles per hour while Ride hangs out the passenger window filming. It's not long before the Indiana State Police stop us, twice. No one, not press, not residents, no one but construction crews are allowed along this stretch of coast. While he's telling us just how lucky we are that he's not a Mississippi cop, I realize there's a ten-story-high guitar beside me. It's perfectly upright, only missing a couple of strings. The Hard Rock Casino was supposed to open the day after Katrina. On the other side of the road, the old mansions that survived Betsy and Camille have disappeared but for one. It seems suspended in midair, its first story mostly vanished, only a few pilings left, its second unscathed.

We pull away from the coast. Bumm goes back to work. We head back west to Waveland, the modest neighbor of Bay St. Louis, to meet Kimberly's brother. I remember the Czech reporter in Johnny White's weeks ago telling me it was the worst he had seen. For as far as we can see, trucks with empty twenty-foot-high trailers for debris removal are parked on the side of the road into Waveland. The parts of the houses that are still intact are all moved off their foundations and closer to the bay, where the receding tidal surge dragged them.

Jimmy James is flipping through a Japanese porn magazine, sitting in a beach chair where his front porch used to be, once Kimberly's front porch, too, until last year when she moved to New Orleans. His dog is curled up on the mud-caked concrete slab of his foundation, raising an eyebrow at us, a slight lift of the tail. His house is more or less in one piece, but it's a good forty feet from its foundation and askew like an empty cardboard box that's almost totally flattened, so that the roof is just a few feet above and parallel to the ground while all the walls are slanting at nearly horizontal angles. A massive oak stands in the center of it all, unmoved, limbs spidering out, other trees and limbs tangled into it, a tricycle and a bicycle with training wheels up in its branches. A single white picket fencepost is the only man-made thing still standing upright. It says No Trespassing.

Jimmy's tall and thin like Ride and I, wears work boots and cargo shorts, a white Baltimore Ravens T-shirt with the sleeves cut off, exposing a fleur-de-lis on his left shoulder. There's a roughened hardness to his movements that belies his age; the thin beard that traces his jawline gives an edge to an otherwise soft face. Then he takes his sunglasses off, exposing ice blue eyes like a Siberian Husky, eyes that slap us all around for a while, eyes that'd put butterflies in any woman's belly.

I sit on an overturned, cracked tub, its rim submerged in the six-inch-deep dried mud. He tosses the Japanese porn mag into a pile of others in the dirt beside him.

Jimmy: My cousin's in the Marines and he's been sending these magazines to me from Okinawa since I was a kid. I had a collection, a nice-size stack, that was pretty cool. You turn the pages from the other side, the pages that aren't stuck together now from the water. I got a thing about hairy bush. No one's got it anymore. Only in these Japanese magazines.

Where were you for the storm?

Ponchatoula, about an hour north of New Orleans. Some friends came got me at the last second. I was planning on staying in that tub you're sitting on there. Got back here a couple days later, in a lot better shape than that tub. I told all my friends I was gonna stay, so they came looking for me and they went digging through the rubble and couldn't find me, so they tried to find me at the morgue. My buddy found his grandparents there instead.

You know, I was most worried about that tree falling into the house. Funny, because my house fell into the tree. Chevy's the only thing didn't move much. It's not scratched. It was like that before the storm. But without the boat on top of it.

It had that crack in the window?

Oh, no, that was me and a beer bottle.

Just getting pissed at stuff and throwing things around?

I've been doing that a lot lately.

Did people here understand the danger of where they were, being close to the water and all the rest?

These houses been here for a hundred years. That house that was right there was almost two hundred. Betsy, Camille, everything else, it's just—I mean we took direct hits with those storms. What are you doing with a Mercedes, Kim?

Kimberly: I got it from FEMA. I was in Houston, it was the last car they had at the rental agency so they had to give it to me.

You're staying with friends right now?

Trying to get a FEMA trailer, but it's awfully hard because I don't have anything left that says I live here.

So, this bike sticking up here out of the dirt—

That's like *Easy Rider* right there, '69 Triumph. Handlebars came from a guy who was in the Hell's Angels. A biker buddy of mine used to steal bikes. He would just pick em up and throw em in the back of the truck and take off. He's the one lent me this hammer I found, this big old fucking big framing hammer. He gave it to me one day, said, "Bring this back tomorrow." He died that night. And I still got the hammer, that's the only thing I pulled out the house. I'll give it to somebody. I don't want none of this shit no more.

What's the thing that you lost in there that sucks the most?

I don't really think about shit like that.

But little things like photos, letters, anything like that?

I miss my CDs, I miss my music. I was stuck over at my sister's house, and she listens to fucking Madonna and shit. Tori Amos. My dog, Stains, there, she's curled up right where her favorite couch used to be.

Ride: Do you think any politicians are to blame?

I know nothing about that.

Ride: Have they been taking care of you?

I've been working, and I've been making pretty good money at work. You know, there's other people that probably need the money more than me. I got a place to stay and I got a few friends, so, you know, I'll get by. Cause they got a lot of older people that don't have anything left, you know. It'd be cool to have some money to rebuild, but . . .

What did you do before all this?

Everything. Fixed motors, houses, pretty much anything. I mean, before the storm, if I couldn't take the trash out, my neighbors would come and take the trash out for me. And the guy who owns the gas station on my street, he would just let me in, even if they were closed, and just give me stuff. You know, I had some girl sleeping over here who wanted French toast in the morning, so I went down there—

Kimberly: Jo Anne?

Yeah, it was Jo Anne. Every morning she wants some French toast. He was like, "Yeah, come on in." And I had money—I tried to give him some money—he wouldn't even take it, just gave me a box of French toast.

His store got wiped out?

Yeah, I'll probably never see him again.

Are you pissed at what happened, pissed at the storm? Pissed at your luck for living here, or what?

No, none of that really. Just—I don't know, I just feel like I'm in a shitty—you know, I just feel like I'm imposing on people, staying with them and, you know, I got my buddy Wade, and him and his girlfriend doing my laundry for me and all that, and I don't really like that. I mean, they tell me that it's not a problem, they're happy for me to be there and everything, but I just like—I like my little routine. I wouldn't open that fridge, Kim. There's a dead cat in there.

Kimberly: What's Stains eating?

I don't know. Probably dog doo-doo. I felt pretty good in that tub you're sitting on. And my buddy Wade's got this little regular tub, you know, just like a regular little house tub, and I don't fit too good in that. The third window right there was my bathroom window.

That crackling in the background, that's trees being cut down?

Yeah. They're cleaning the bay up first. They're not worried about this place. C'mon, let's go drive along the bay.

[tape breaks]

Driving in Jimmy's pickup truck now down a narrow road to St. Louis Bay where we were yesterday. Going by all the places, fucking wheelchairs sitting in the road, bathtubs, everything imaginable that everyone owned, debris all pushed to the side enough for a single car or truck to get through. These pieces of wood, I can't even tell what was trees and what was a house. Note to self: Go to Payless Shoes and get the black Champion shoes that Kimberly has, preferably by Oakwood

Mall if it hasn't burned down, as WWL reported. There is so much fuck-ing debris on the other side of me, yet it's all lit up with this gold dying light, my silhouette, sitting in the back of the pickup truck, gliding right though it all.

[tape breaks]

Jimmy: I love to come drive down here, they always have the pelicans sitting on those pilings. The pelicans used to keep a smile on my drunk face.

Kimberly: They still do.

[tape breaks]

Facing the bay, the final place Katrina made landfall, Beach Boulevard, near where we were yesterday, but at the end of the road. Behind me, of course, the land's just cleansed of everything man put on it. Except this cement staircase I'm standing on, all alone. Sound of those bugs in the background filling the spaces where there were once rooms, where people ate, where they drank, slept, where they made love, fell in love, grew up, grew sick, grew bored, now this desert of cracked white mud. Deep footprints here, sunken three inches into the earth. My feet aren't sinking in.

Earth and wind and water and fire. Fire's the only thing missing. Only fire in the sky. These sunsets. I guess we always think about water being shaped by the object that holds it, but it is the Earth that is actu-ally shaped by its water, created by it, whether that's oceans dividing continents, or the river creating land from its sediment. It just did it all a bit faster than usual with a violence like this.

Bay is holding the sunset's last pink in it, distances obscured, colors in the sky raging. No colors left down here. Ride trying to film it all. I'm keeping it for myself.

[tape breaks]

Jimmy: Look there. You see that? It's a house. See it? On the shore all the way across the bay? Big white fucking house sitting there whole, all by itself in the forest there. No one knows where it came from, wasn't there before the storm. Just appeared soon as the rains stopped.

We watch the house turn blue in twilight, while the water between it and us breaks the sky apart until there is nothing left of it. Jimmy leaves us at the Mercedes in front of his house, drives to Diamondhead to pick up some cash from his boss, and says he'll be back in an hour with some beer and charcoal and steaks to grill. Kimberly keeps Stains, and we go looking for dog food. We wind through the dark streets, the majority of them still blocked off. Finally, we see lights up ahead. Two trailers are parked on the foundation of a home, three rows of Christmas lights strung up between them over foldout tables with a couple of coolers on each. Kimberly gets out and starts walking across the lawn. A man, middle-aged, thin, glasses, balding, comes out in sweat shorts. "Who are you?" he asks.

"Hey. I'm Kimberly, I'm your neighbor and I was just maybe hoping, I need some dog food."

"Who are you?"

"I'm your neighbor. I had a house right down there. I don't have any more dog food and I was just wondering if you did."

"Who are you?"

She stops three feet from him.

"Don't be coming out here," he says.

"Okay. All right." She turns, walks back toward the car.

"Take off," he says.

She climbs back into the car.

"You come back, you might get shot," he says.

I stick my head out the window. "Sir, did you just threaten to kill her?"

"Just drive," says Kimberly, tears in her voice. "That guy's a fucking asshole. Just, please just drive."

Ride starts to back out. A woman comes out of the trailer carrying something like a small purse. The man is slowly walking toward us, his wife following. It's a holster. I can see the handle of an automatic pistol sticking out. "They're from Texas, David!" she screams, chasing our reversing license plate.

"What are you doing?!" I shout. "Do *not* point that gun in our direction! Point it at the fucking ground!"

She points it at the ground, but leans down, still trying to chase us and read the license plate. "They're from Texas, David! Texas!"

"What made you people this way?" I ask as Ride shifts into drive.

Two police cars show up at Jimmy's house within five minutes, responding to a call about a gang of looters from Texas driving a white Mercedes. We tell them that those people are fucking crazy.

"Yeah, people are kinda crazy now," says the officer sitting in the first car. He's wearing a bulletproof vest. "You know, I still get a gun pointed at me almost every single night."

"You know, we all need to be helping each other out," says Kimberly, voice still quavering between anger and tears.

"If more people thought that way we wouldn't have these problems," he says. The other police car drives off. The officer in front of us lights a Newport light. There's a flash of gold among his teeth. "Listen, you can get dog food down at the police station, you know where that is?"

"Yes," says Kimberly. "Could I please have a cigarette?"

"Sure. You know, my dad's in New Orleans. Good luck, and stay safe, y'all."

Jimmy shows up about twenty minutes later. He got the last seven beers, two bottles of warm white zinfandel and a fifth of Canadian Mist whiskey from the only gas station he could find, seconds before it closed. Nothing else was open.

Ride sleeps in the Mercedes while Kimberly, Jimmy, and I drink the beers, then I pound the corks into the wine with a stick and a rock. We hang from downed power lines, watch the little red lights of planes move through the Milky Way, lost now in New Orleans, found here, stretching clean and white from horizon to horizon. Jimmy turns the truck's headlights on, illuminating the space where his house used to be. He finishes the first bottle of wine, hurls it after all the other beer bottles at his house. We've smashed the windows in pretty well, dented the roof more than Jimmy had been able to do alone the last weeks. I take the first sip from the second bottle, hand it to him. "This'd be so cool," he says, "if we could just go inside and chill out on my couch."

Kimberly and I split the whiskey with Jimmy and Ride drives us back to New Orleans. Halfway home, somewhere just off Highway 11, we get lost trying to find Louisiana, the interstate, anything. There are no street lights, signs are down, cars have thinned out. We assume this is because of curfew. Then they disappear altogether. The road, whatever road it is, has been cleared of debris, so we figure it must be a thoroughfare. Kimberly asks to stop. We pull off into the parking lot of an abandoned gas station. She shuffles off to pee behind an overturned car while I get out and stretch.

The headlights go deep into the front of the Kwik Mart, its entrance and glass front and pieces of the walls blown out. There's a can of Hormel chili sitting upright just inside. I walk over, pick it up. It's been torn open, as though it were made of cardboard. Inside is nothing but rust. A cat meows. Again. A kitten. There's only jagged shadows, the mess between them made blinding by the headlights. *Meooowww.* I step inside, make a kissing sound, the universal cat call. A shadow flinches in my periphery. I crouch down, crawl toward it into the tangle of shelves, displays, coolers, tables, benches, chairs. And wait. Something falls. *Meooowww.* It is within arm's reach. I slide forward until I can't get my shoulders in any further. *Meooowww.* I reach my hand into my shadow, touch fur. It runs its tiny spine along my finger. I grab its tail, start to pull it gently toward me. It hisses, sinks teeth into my hand. I do not let go. It withdraws, slides its tail between my fingers soundlessly until it's gone. I make the kissing sound again, over and over. But nothing. I can't reach any further. Something is cutting into my knee, but I can't move my leg back. I can't even turn my head. It takes a long time to slither out backwards, and we go back the way we came, the dark roads, the day's reflections yet to be cast, the sediment yet to dry and cake, as the gristle of the universe creaks on around us, goes through its own ancient movements across Kimberly's sunroof for this little while longer.

45

Seven years ago, because it was Sunday and I had nothing else to do, I drove dead straight south out of New Orleans until there was nothing left in my headlights and came to a screeching halt. I stepped out onto the tattered dock, sat on its edge beside the front end of my car, and watched shrimp's eyes glow like stars below my toes. This is how I found Lafitte, Louisiana.

Now, tangled green jungle swallows the dribble of suburban subdivisions and RideofTwoFires, Kimberly, and I have Highway 45 to ourselves. It is two days after we returned from Mississippi. We left the Quarter twenty minutes ago, stopping on the West Bank for a long police-escorted motorcade to pass—we've heard Bush is in town—and in twenty minutes more we'll be in Lafitte. We've heard nothing about it in the news.

Lafitte is a forgotten Cajun relic sandwiched between the swamp and the Gulf, almost as old as New Orleans itself. After the pirate Jean Lafitte and his privateers double-crossed the British to help Andrew Jackson win the Battle of New Orleans in 1815 (no one told them the War of 1812 was already over), they were granted land alongside the French, Germans, and Spanish already here, and so the town got its name. But that first evening seven years ago, I didn't really care about all that. I caught a stingray with this guy named Wacko who lived in a trailer beside the dock and, after we pulled his crab traps up, some guy materialized out of the woods and grilled it up for us. I didn't see the heron beside us until it twitched its wings, feathers brushing against its body light as a shrimp boat's wave stroking the rocks beneath us, swamp's sweet stink heavy with cicadas, owls, a shrill Parula warbler, other rhythms and animals I did not yet know, and now Kimberly descends the bridge into Lafitte, and there are no sounds. No egrets, no herons by the side of the road. But man-made things, at least this far north in town, look fine, more or less.

Just after the town's only traffic light, which blinks yellow, we pass the Piggly Wiggly, Lafitte's largest business, a few letters missing from its sign but otherwise all right. I once walked in there asking if there was a Hibernia Bank in town. When they got finished laughing, someone explained that they once had a First National Bank. Shrimpers started walking in with plastic bags full of hundred-dollar bills. The IRS had a field day.

Over the last few years, as their shrimp lose value and their land gains it, residents have been selling their property, and big empty houses are rising up between the single shotguns and trailers. Lafitte stretches along one two-lane road which runs parallel to Bayou Barataria. It's not until we cross the small bridge beside a marina halfway into town that the smell hits us. The sediment. It smells a little different everywhere I go. Here, it leaves an acidic taste in my mouth. Vehicles are covered in it above their roofs, trees ripped up, water in pools where their roots were, trailers and huge fishing camps torn up all the same, front yards caved in and caked with dried mud like parched cracked skin. I tell Kimberly to take a right at the sign that says VOLEO'S RESTAURANT.

There's a trailer out front, and there's Rooster on the concrete porch in front of the restaurant sitting with his rubber boots up on a table. Voleo's mother sits beside him, watching me get out of the car. "You the insurance man?" she asks.

Rooster laughs. "You try getting any damn insurance man to show up round here," he says, shaking my hand. "No, this is Josh, he won the oyster-eating contest couple years back. Been coming down to Fuzzy's bar for a few years now."

She looks up at me, as if he might not be telling the truth. "I've been waiting one week right here for the insurance man," she says.

"Yall hungry at all?" asks Kimberly. "We brought down a whole bunch of Salvation Army meals."

In return, Rooster tosses Kimberly and me Bud Lights while Ride opens his fifth Gatorade bottle of the day. He's Rooster because he raises and conditions fighting cocks. I've never seen him in anything but a T-shirt, blue jeans tucked into white rubber shrimping boots, and the obligatory baseball cap—any baseball cap—that all shrimpers wear, with his large bronze fingers, scarred and creased with seemingly bottomless furrows around a can of Bud Light, and an easy smile below his white mustache. "How y'all making it?" I ask.

"Well, we was doing terrible, but we gettin by now," she says.

"Katrina got you pretty bad, huh?"

"It was Rita got us."

"Rita?"

"Rita gave us the water. Katrina gave us the wind. Tore the roof off here, and the roof off my motor home, but that's not so bad. No flooding at all. It was Rita. They said it was a hundred eighty miles away from New Orleans. They kept saying it was going up into Texas. We wasn't expecting no surge. But it pushed the water up, six foot of water back here. And it left that black silt and the smell is so bad. We been shoveling three or four inches of that mud out the restaurant. This trailer's the only place we have to stay."

"Y'all had flooding like this ever before?"

"Juan hit us about twenty years ago. It was like a big tidal wave, but here, the water came in, the water run right back out. And, in about a week's time, we were cleaned up and everything, but this time all that flood . . . all that flood. And then, you know, we give whatever we can. We never turn nobody away when they're hungry, you know? But they broke in and stole all our beer and cigarettes. You know, I mean it's bad enough you lose everything, then somebody go ahead and steal. I mean, it's terrible. And they know who did it."

"We ain't gonna call the parish sheriff we catch looters," says Rooster.

"We take care of our own," she says.

"You killed any?" I ask.

"We don't talk about them things," she says.

"That . . . that'd be against the law," says Rooster. "C'mon, yall need to see this nutria drink beer."

We follow him about a hundred feet over to the bayou, where Barbara, a waitress at Voleo's, is staying since her home flooded. Nutria are basically giant swamp rats. The most many people ever glimpse of one, those who've glimpsed them at all, is a sliver of a tail as it scurries under brush or water. But, there it is, just larger than an adult cat, sitting on the porch. Rooster goes charging at it with a fresh beer. It perks up, comes to the edge of the porch, and sniffs the air between us. Barbara bursts out of the house, finger pointing at Rooster.

Barbara: You stay away from my baby with dat!

Rooster: How many nutrias yall saw like that?

No way.

Barbara: You keep that beer away from Baby! He all hung over from last night.

Can you actually pet him?

Barbara: Sure. You gotta raise em from babies.

Can I—Can I hold him. Really? Awwww. He is so soft.

Barbara: They like a cat. They constantly groom.

And he eats these vegetables here?

Barbara: Baby's strictly vegetarian, and he likes cat food. Baby eats side by side with the cat.

Rooster: Look what I got, Baby.

What's his name?

Barbara: Baby.

You want some beer, Baby? Huh, Baby? Here let me put him down.

Barbara: Don't you give him too much. He's a lush.

Oh yeah, he's . . . he's grabbing it between his front paws. Oh, wow. He just figured which side is up. Holy shit, he's swilling it!

Barbara: He had a buzz last night. He needs something to take the edge off.

So, how did he deal with the flooding?

Rooster: Just like the rest of us—got drunk.

Barbara: He was freaky. He was like, "Why can I swim in my house?"

So, are y'all looking to move elsewhere now?

Barbara: Hell no I'm not going anywhere. This is home. Once every twenty years a flood's no big deal. We can rebuild.

Rooster volunteers to be our tour guide for the day. He gets into George Bush's Mercedes with us, in the back seat with me, but won't let Ride film him. Kimberly drives while Ride leans out the passenger window with his camera. As we cruise through his town, smiles flicker involuntarlily across Rooster's face, true smiles with the corners of his eyes, while at the same time those eyes well up with tears, like how it rains when it's sunny here, summertime rainshine.

"No rabbits down here in Lafitte since Katrina," he says, and he bursts into another smile, his eyes scrunching up, this time squeezing the tears down his cheeks, and then his face falls flat again and he tells Kimberly to take a left here. We park in front of his house. He takes us inside, rests his hands on a window sill and looks out at what was once a green lawn, smiles again, those tears drying, unwiped, new ones building.

Rooster: I was standing right here when the water come up like a heart-beat. Water was high enough outside that the boat was level up with the window, and it was just rising. My car, *hah*—up to the roof already. Water's up over the window sill and all I had was this metal window to jump out of and try to get to the boat. Snakes everywhere you shine your light, moccasins everywhere. The air-conditioner unit was plugged in here; it was smoking. All I could grab was this metal. I knew I was gonna get electrocuted. The fuses up top was still on and the circuit breaker was smoking, too. But I got out, jumped right out.

Where were you for Katrina?

Rooster: Katrina got me over in Mississippi, over in Waveland. But I come over here for Rita. I come in early from offshore. Our company lost four rigs.

Jesus, man, you were in the worst possible place during both storms?

Kimberly: I had a house on Leonard.

Rooster directs us through the little streets that run off the main road. We see a man walking along wearing a baseball cap, about my age. His skin is the brown of the bayou dulled by low sun.

Rooster: That's Popcorn's son! Get him! Start shooting!

I know Popcorn.

Rooster: Now he won't drink no beer, but he'll watch us drink beer. Get him! Get him!

How you doing? I remember y'all were building a shrimp boat called My Four Sons, *right? I'm Josh. I've known Popcorn for a few years now.*

Popcorn Junior: We sold that one and we built a twenty-nine-foot one. I gotta get a crane truck to pick it back up.

How'd you make it through the storm?

Popcorn Junior: His trailer broke, lost everything inside. Stayin by a neighbor. It's all you can do.

You been down here through Katrina and Rita?

Popcorn Junior: Yeah. Katrina wasn't too bad, messed up the roof on our trailer and the next door neighbor's roof went through our trailer, busted a hole in it. Not too bad. I was stayin on my brother-in-law's boat. But this one, Rita, that's when we got the water. We lost everything. It's Mother Nature.

What are your plans right now? Are you going anywhere?

Popcorn Junior: No, we ain't goin nowhere. This is God's country. I'm not leaving God's country.

Eventually, we find Peggy Sue, who helps run her father, Fuzzy's, bar. She's pulling up all her carpets when I poke my head in the front door. Her husband, Pal, drives up, and we lean against the hood of his truck, looking across the street into swamp. He's already working again. Both of them are looking clean, tan, and refreshed.

This is Ride, by the way.

Peggy Sue: Oh, no, tell him get that camera off me. I've been running away from camera people all day.

How about a little audiotape?

Yeah, do that, that'd be best. You have to leave that camera off.

Y'all got electricity?

We just turned our main on. We don't have the hot water, no electric.

How's the bar doing?

Oh Lord, they ain't even started digging the mud out of there.

Well, give me a call when they start, and I'll come down and help.

They had a band come Saturday before the storm, I mean, this was a band that played Lynyrd Skynyrd and stuff like that, not all that Cajun shit. We was goin wild. Had about thirty people, you know.

I hear they hit it up, looted the bar.

That was for Katrina. Same old people. We see them in the store every day. They got proof, they got different people saying they saw them coming out the door. The day we came back from Katrina, one of them had the nerve to go on my daddy Big Fuzz's porch and ask him for a beer. They walking the streets like nothin ever happened. Every time they wave at me I shoot em the bird and start cursing at em. Don't frickin wave to me no more. I don't want nothin to do with you. I'm gonna kill em. They won't confess to me, I'll kill em. Your friend Rod loves to put me on that video. I tell him to take it off of me.

So has FEMA declared this a disaster zone?

Nope. They not declaring it. I can't get nothing. The ones that left here, and went to Texas, and all like that, they got all their money. They got Red Cross, they got FEMA, the motels were giving them free rooms. The ones that stayed here, and tried to save what they had, we get almost nothing. A church gave my friend money to come back home with. For gas and stuff. Next time, I'm gonna find me a preacher. [laughing]

There's a picture on my refrigerator of my girlfriend swinging on these swings here at the Fourth of July. We had so much fun . . . God, it breaks my heart seeing this.

Ain't nobody gonna sit on those swings no more. The pool when I come home was black. That's when I cried. I didn't give a shit about my roof, or nothin, till I seen my black pool I cried. But this Rita, this was the worst it's ever been, even from Betsy.

Pal: You can look behind in between them two trails there and see the woods. I mean, the woods are just gutted out. Look that way. All the trees are . . . They're turning green again already, but you can see, from six feet down, everything looks dead. I tell you, right after Rita, you could see two hundred yards into that swamp.

Peggy Sue: Two-thirty that morning they come in the army trucks. Betty calls me up, my mama, hollerin and screamin, "The water's comin over the levee! Hurry up, get up, get up!" I'm like, "I am up!" I looked in my yard, I had a little bit of water over there by that tree. "Betty, I ain't got no damn water in my yard. Come over here," I said. She said, "No, the water's comin over the levee, the police is outside wantin me to get in this Army truck. Don't want to let me take my dogs." I said, "Well, bring your dogs over here. I don't have water." By the time they got here, I had about ten inches of water in my yard. I mean, that's five minutes right there. Well, I hurried up. We started throwing stuff in the truck. Within another five minutes, it's coming up like three inches at a time. When we got outta here, they had about a foot-and-a-half wave behind the truck where we was pushing so much water. I was the last one goin up the road. Nobody was behind me. It was pitch dark. Nobody could make it. If we'd a had to stop, we'd a been done. We barely floated down to the other side of the bridge, like a boat. Then they wouldn't let nobody down here till three days after the storm. The only way you could get down here was if you had a boat. That's all. You shoulda seen when we went down to Fuzzy's in the pirogue. Shrimp and fish were jumping in the pirogue.

That your dog?

This's Miracle. Big Fuzz named him Miracle because him and Tutu found him tied up, trapped under a boat trailer that was under a shed. He was under all that seven days before they found him. You know Nigger?

Yeah, I met him a couple times at the bar.

Kimberly: What?

That's his nickname. Everyone has a nickname.

Peggy Sue: We call him Nig sometimes. That's his trailer there. It's completely flipped upside down and smashed. What happened to your wrist?

I had a fall from Christ.

You fell from Jesus? Why? You like hurting yourself, don't you? I remember you swimming around in that water with a bleeding foot, right by the dock where we had that big alligator.

So, would you consider moving?

I was born here and I got my feet in this sloppy mud, and they ain't gonna go nowhere. Nothin like Lafitte mud.

Peggy Sue looks over her front yard, then back into the swamp across the street. Where once Spanish moss wept down from the tallest branches to the ground, only gray tufts remain clinging to the few unbroken branches, slowly turning copper in the golden hour. The spaces between trees hold dying sun like tarnished brass, like the impossible glow inside Señor Petucci's landscape paintings, and make things seem all right.

We drive to the marina, scraps of boat-shed roofs hanging like drapes over half-sunk boats, then cruise through the town. Again, Ride films out the window while Kimberly drives.

Rooster: There's Britney! Get her on film.

Ride: Here's Britney, running away . . .

Rooster: Get her! Get her! Ya daddy here? Get her on film before she runs in!

Britney: Just my gramma.

Rooster: Oh, just your gramma? Ya daddy ain't here? Get her!

Kimberly: You want to be interviewed?

Britney: For what?

Kimberly: They're just recording people, their stories. You want to do it? You should. It's easier once you let it out. Trust me.

Rooster: [whispering in car] You oughtta see her sister. Oh, she is so fine.

[whispering] *She's older?*

Rooster: [whispering] She's almost legal.

Britney: No, I ain got my eye shadow on right.

Kimberly: All right, baby.

Rooster: [whispering] She's got a fake ID. [yelling out window] Hey Britney, have a good night, all right?! Don't let the mosquitoes bite your ass up! [whispering] Nah. Her sister danced in a few clubs. She is extra fine.

Dancing clubs upfront?

Rooster: Yeah, I took her several times. She promised me free lap dances. I never had a lap dance in my life. She was so fine, her sister. Uh. Yeah, oh, she is nice, oh, God. She got a little weight on her, she's extrafine. Oh, back up! Back up! I'll show you where—let me see. Make a left right here. Left right here. Does your freezer work?

We have electricity in the French Quarter, yeah.

Rooster: Do you love shrimp?

Are you kidding me?

Rooster: Can you take like one hundred, two hundred pounds?

What? Where the hell would I put that?

Rooster: I mean, they nice. They nice. You get em off the boat.

Kimberly: You gonna tell me where to go?

Rooster: Straight. Go across the bridge.

Who's this guy walking up to the car? He looks interesting.

Ride: You want to be interviewed?

Rooster: No! No. Go. Let's go.

Ride: I think he wants to be interviewed. Do you want to be interviewed?

Rooster: No! Go, go, go!

Kimberly: Why couldn't Ride interview him?

Rooster: That's illegal. That's a Mexican!

You have Mexicans down here?

Rooster: They illegal working on shrimp boats. Yeah, take a right.

How do Mexicans know how to work on a shrimp boat?

Rooster: They work, they learn. Oh, man! Raul and his wife Rose! Take a left up here. See that white truck? All them people on that porch. Start filming them. Now! Don't let em leave. Get em!

Here. Let's get out here. How you doing? I'm Josh.

Raul.

You down here for Rita?

Raul: I tell ya, we was stuck here four days, couldn't get out. All because, when the flooding started, about two in the morning, we had a couple inches and a neighbor came and woke me up so I went and brushed my teeth, combed my hair, washed my face, all that. By the time I walked out, I mean, no more than five minutes, they had a foot of water already. Then it just kept coming faster and faster. So, cause I brushed my teeth, I got stuck here four days. We had boats going up and down the street.

Rose: Yeah, we even rowed in this pirogue here. Five of us. It was nothin nice.

Raul: Here, let's go inside.

You stripped the carpet off here, huh?

Raul: Yeah, it was black mud, over the whole entire house. After we took pictures for our insurance, we put holes in the floor for the water to go, then hosed it down, swept it out, scraped it, cleaned it, painted, everything.

It looks really good.

Raul: I could have just declared this a total loss. But if I did that, where I be at? We'd be in other people's houses. So, I worked hard. You see now, it's livable.

Rose: We just glad to be alive. Still here on our Lafitte mud.

Raul: I haven't caught my breath yet.

Rose: It wasn't nothing nice, going through there in the pirogue and seeing all those graveyards floating. They actually had one where the body came out of it. It was a lady, yeah, it was a lady, because she had a dress on. She had been dead for a long time. Scary. You could probably walk back there and still see it.

Ride: It's just back this way? Could you show us?

Rose: Yeah. Right there, just down the street. Show him the graveyard, babe. That's a sight to see. I done seen enough of that.

[tape breaks]

The coffin just popped right out of its grave. Another one, cement and everything, just popped up. And then one is just completely missing.

Raul: That one opened up and there ain't no telling if the body's down in there or not. These here, they got picked up and moved over. Another one is popping up right there. It's movin.

Are the families of these people still around?

Raul: Yeah, this is for people around here. That's the one with the skeleton right there.

Oh my God.

New guy: What you all doing? You filming this stuff?! You filming our cemetery?

Rooster: He's doing just a documentary.

Kimberly: Yeah, reality. But reality as in—reality TV isn't reality.

Rooster: No, it's all edited. If it wasn't, it'd be a boring show.

Kimberly: Not when this is your reality. Today reality it is.

New guy: What? Okay, what's going on here? So you filming our ceme-tery? You filming these graves?

Ride: I was. Is that not okay?

New guy: You wanna see her hip replacement?

Is that it? Where's the hip replacement?

New guy: See this bone over here?

Oh, that's the hip replacement.

New guy: It's gotta be. What else can it be? See? It look like a ball on the trailer.

So, this is Mrs. Florence A. Cooper.

Rooster: No, her name is under there.

Oh, that's the wrong gravestone.

New guy: The gravestone's upside down.

Rooster: I don't think it's got her name on there, either.

Do you know her family? Is her family around still?

New guy: Yeah. They're not back yet, though.

Kimberly: Look, there's the date. This grave's a hundred years old.

Well, did they have hip replacements like that a hundred years ago?

Rooster: I think they just cut your leg off.

Kimberly: I wonder if my grandfather is still where he was.

Your grandfather's in Lafitte?

Kimberly: No. Lakelawn, on Metairie Road.

Rooster: I think they're okay. Depending how long ago he died.

Kimberly: Um, I don't know. I was ten, so it was about twenty years ago.

Rooster: I mean, they just started putting them in the metal boxes where they wouldn't float up.

Kimberly: It wasn't metal. It was wood.

Rooster: If they flooded, it's a good possibility that grave came up.

Kimberly: I need to find my grandfather. Hey, when we get back to New Orleans tonight, I gotta go to Lakelawn and look for my Pappy, okay?

These mosquitoes—son of a bitch!

Rooster: Oh yeah, once it gets dark, you gotta go inside.

Some tombs still hold their coffins, others are rectangular stone holes full of black water. The coffins that lifted out of them are lying thirty feet away upon the roots of a massive oak, upright, on their sides, upside down, overturned, two smashed into the trunk. The shadow of the oak has grown into the red, then purple light on the ground until the shadow is all there is now. Now is the time the French call *le temps entre chien et loup*—the time between dog and wolf, when the piece of earth you stand in falls into early shadow, and what is familiar becomes uncertain. Things lose their color, and all that is white in day glows pale blue, like the tiny skull by itself, size of my fist, at my feet, wrapped in a white veil caught in an eye socket, the long veil torn but clean, shooting off to the side as if frozen in breeze, the white dress tangled through disconnected bones like driftwood.

A dog stands beside the tree. It is covered in mud, almost invisible against it. It finally stops barking as I approach, nuzzles the wet ground, lifts something in its mouth. It is the splintered end of a plank, one side of it still painted a gray that makes it too almost invisible in this light. It places the piece of wood in my open palm. I hurl the wood back toward Raul's house and the dog flies after it, kicking mud up at me. He's only got one front leg. Insects lift into the air, the high hum of evening pulses. Wisps of clouds streak the sky, catching some last purple. Ride comes up beside me, replaying his footage of the graves. "Not enough light," he says.

We walk the mud between the graves and the car, me in my flip-flops and shorts, my legs freckling with mosquitoes. As always, Ride wears a long-sleeve button-down silk shirt that hides the tribal tattoo on his left arm, biker boots, and his dirt-caked thick black leather motorcycle pants: dressed for a night club, yet impenetrable by earth or sun or mosquitoes. While the rest of us drown in perspiration, not once have I seen a single bead of sweat roll off his pierced eyebrows. Ride's perfect posture, shoulders back, tall, lean body, long straight black hair, slightly round face, and thick chapped lips grant him just enough femininity to be sexy, to make women like Kimberly willing to drive him just about anywhere. One would think he'd stand way out in a crowd. But he has a skill: He is quiet. So quiet he becomes, at times, invisible. You simply forget he is there. The people we interview do. The looters in Wal-Mart did. The police did. And, unless he was sewing someone's ear back on or bathing them for the first time in a month, the whole Quarter did. And now he was vanishing beside me.

"Suppose it's easier seeing them without the flesh on them," I say. "This whole time, you ever see a dead body in New Orleans?"

"No. Not once. Everyone's always talking about dead bodies all over the place everywhere, but I've never seen one. Have you?"

"No. I knew where some were, though. That's probably why I never looked."

Just ahead, we can hear the dog panting beneath these insects, the other three talking softly somewhere ahead of us. I reach out to touch Ride's shoulder, make sure he's there. "How'd you get to New Orleans in the first place?" I ask.

"I ran away from the reservation in Nebraska when I was ten, came to live with my father's French relatives there," he says.

"So how you liking it now that our urban wilderness is eroding?"

"I liked it the old way."

"You know something I was thinking about today, the people here in Lafitte, I've never seen any that seem lonely. Why is it people get so much more lonely living in a city surrounded by people everywhere they go, as opposed to people out here in small places like this? Do you suppose the reason they're not lonely down here is because they're more alone?"

"I don't know," he says. "Could you imagine really truly being totally alone?"

"It just might be the furthest thing from being lonely imaginable. No need to be loved."

"I don't know, but it is, it's getting lonely up there in the city now, you know? Now that they've started coming back."

"I know," I say. "I'd rather be alone."

"But we weren't. The city was with us."

That evening I'm lying on top of my covers, specks of mud and blood from mosquitoes dried on my legs, pretending to fall asleep, when Ride calls to tell me my "buddy" has been on all the news stations and right now he's on MSNBC. I flip on the television and there he is, Officer Curly, bending a man backwards over the hood of a car on Bourbon Street. He's grabbing him by the scruff of the neck, yelling at him as the man appears to be holding up a press pass. He shoves the man into the car some more, shaking him, still yelling, spit flying out of his mouth, points a finger in his face, then jabs him in the stomach. They show the tape again and again. It turns out the man is an Associated Press producer and his cameraman was trying to film an arrest across the street during which four white NOPD officers appear to be beating a black man on the ground. "Maybe that guy wrote an article about him too," says Ride.

"How do you even know about that?"

"I was there, at Molly's. I saw him threaten you."

"They just don't give a flying fuck, do they?"

46

Strange, what's strong, what's weak in a time of wind and water. Water rises, ravages, then collapses right back into sleep. We do not know when it will rise again, cast confidence aside, and show us only what still stands.

In the Lower 9th Ward, now that the second flood, Rita's water, is gone, homes are again washed clean of color, trees leafless and the roads cracked ash. Everything else is just slightly out of place: cars askew on curbs, their doors spraypainted with X's like the houses, electric cables tangled on the ground like snakes around the things that should be inside homes: mattresses, toys, dishes, furniture. I stop. Not a sound, not anywhere. Then, birds. Two of them, caught in call and response, over and over, like a record that skips.

Half an hour ago, the guards at the St. Claude Bridge wouldn't let me in no matter what. So, I parked the car, snuck on foot through the Bywater around them, and literally climbed up onto the bridge past the checkpoint when their heads were turned.

I keep walking along Dauphine Street, parallel to the river three blocks to my right, toward my friend's house. She called me this morning from Utah, frantic, asked if I would go. It is two miles away, toward the bird calls, a little louder with every block, never changing. The smell is the deepest corners of my grandmother's attic, with all the things that once made up lives coated in dust, mildewed with nostalgia. An advertisement still stapled to a telephone poll, "4 BEDROOM SECTION 8, 277-3298." Another, "CALL ME, BERT'S BAIL BOND'S, LOWER 9TH WARD. SEVEN DAYS A WEEK BECAUSE WE CARE."

Many houses have four X's spraypainted on them—purple over orange over yellow over red. A couple after Katrina, a couple after Rita. The ones from before Rita look ancient. Doors have been pried open and shut as carefully as possible, but no longer fit quite right in their broken frames. The sound is not birds, I realize that now. It is too constant, monotonous to be alive.

A chain-link fence around a high-school baseball diamond became a net for passing debris—sticks, styrofoam, wood planks, two lawn chairs—until it too was swept into the road. An oak made into a weeping willow, limbs and branches snapped, falling like water toward the ground, hanging by threads, gray and dead as stone, leaves gone. Power lines drooping, swaying lazily in breeze. A Monte Carlo, '86, same year as mine, perfectly intact, standing on its front end, its tail seven feet up a tree. A Ford Escort slammed into the side of a new Jaguar. How things are left when weight returns to them. My nostrils pull weakly at shadowless gray light, lungs now burning, stomach nauseated, this sediment air I wish I could puke out. I'm on Flood Street.

And those noises, louder now, somewhere on this block, whining, then moaning, higher in pitch with every step. Finally it rings true from between two houses. I walk over the fallen chain link fence, into a driveway, around a long bench five feet up in the air, half hanging out of the side of the house. It is a small, once-white clapboard house with unchipped, once-green shutters. Cement steps lead up to the back door, which is creaking open and closed. A door? Christ. Opening now, closing now in breeze. It's the coolest day we've had since last spring. I walk up the steps, put my hand out, grab the doorknob when it is almost shut. But the creaking continues. It is inside. I let go of the door. It sways inward.

"Hello?" I call inside. Nothing. Just the noise, high-pitched, a rising and falling, inhaling, exhaling, over and over again. "Yo, anyone there?"

I move up one step. Something moves inside and I flinch. The door swings out toward me, then opens again, and there it is, just darkness moving back and forth, creaking, pieces of it I cannot make out. How frightened I was that night before Katrina came, how I went to bed like a child hiding in a closet, then peering out the keyhole of my top shutter at the monster coming. Now, I am outside and it is the inside that is no longer certain, secure. It is what's not in there. And I know it is the same for every house once a home for miles in any direction. I leave it be.

By the time I get to my friend's place, I'm sick to my stomach, shallow of breath, head aching. Everything looks so ugly on the sidewalk out front, a green plastic comb, an empty bag of Fritos, a pair of blue headphones, a beach chair, and dragonflies everywhere, only pushing it all into stark relief against their impossible color.

It is only a block off the levee. The floodline is just below the front step about three feet up and the front of the house is fine, only the door askew since it was pried open, purple spray paint overlapping fluorescent yellow. I walk along the side of the house, one window frame broken, otherwise okay, and into the yard. An oak tree has fallen from her neighbor's yard through a fence into the back of my friend's house, collapsing the entire roof beneath it.

On my way back, I no longer think about every breath, trying to keep them as shallow as possible. I breathe deep and easy. Seven black Suburbans with tinted windows, flashing lights, zoom by me out of nowhere, swarm around a house ahead. I catch up, ask what's going on. A U.S. Marshal tells me a helicopter spotted someone crawling out of a window in back of that house five minutes ago. I walk on. Two blocks later the Suburbans surround me, and the U.S. Marshal asks if I was crawling out of a window in back of that house five minutes ago.

A female marshal examines my hands and arms for cuts from the broken glass windows, asks how I got into the neighborhood. They run my information as a lanky kid cop from Arizona stands silently watching me. Another marshal tells me his own home was destroyed in Lakeview. The woman searches my bag and has a good laugh at my giant RadioShack tape recorder. I ask her for a ride back to the other side of the Industrial Canal, since I'm not even supposed to be over here. She chuckles, waves goodbye, and I walk the last mile back myself while the sky collapses and stars unfold and dogs emerge for a last taste of day, much fewer now since Rita.

There's cars strewn about the bottom of the Industrial Canal's levee, upside down, squashed. No doubt they were parked on the levee to avoid flooding, then wind tumbled them into the water. I walk up the levee, through knee-deep grass, fluorescent green here, little white butterflies, moths maybe, exploding out from my steps like petals blown around me, a white wake through the last of the blue hour. The darkness, everything that's no longer there, rises behind me as it did before, with Katherine. This is not an aloneness that I want. This is not a part of the city I want to myself. There should be people here.

There are police waiting by my car. They tell me I'm not allowed out here past six, not to do this again. The radio tells me they are opening the Lower 9th Ward for the first time tomorrow morning at nine for residents. They must be out by curfew. The mayor calls it a chance to "look and leave."

When I get to Molly's, it's too much like civilization, which, as the Professor once said, has always been crowded with too many people I don't know. So, I stand outside and watch two guys yell at each other over some girl while I lean against the BBC World Radio van. They asked two days ago to do two live interviews with me on the street here, to discuss the KARES relief fund. I call Katherine, ask her if she'd like to come down and do the interview with me. She comes over and before I know it she's on the air talking about the Rebirth Brass Band out of nowhere and then our time is up. The reporter tells his audience to listen to the live jazz in the background, then holds the mic up to the jukebox. I say nothing to Katherine. I walk around the corner, stand by the Ursuline Convent, and call my friend whose home I checked on today in the Lower 9th to tell her about the oak in her house, hoping she won't pick up, but she does.

47

In the middle of Flood Street, all six of them are bowed in a circle, their heads touching. Three wear bright-red Salvation Army T-shirts and blue jeans. The other three look as though they are about to perform surgery. They wear scrubs, masks, plastic gloves, head and shoe covers. There is only one male. He is young, in one of the red T-shirts, talking about the Lord God opening new doors and closing old ones. The other two in red shirts say, "Amen." The other three, the residents, are silent as they stand upright, open their eyes. They are holding brooms like weapons, like some strange science-fiction warriors in a landscape dead as the moon. The Salvation Army workers shoot me a glance, but the others pay no attention.

Ride stays by the car at the end of the block. This he will not film. They just opened the Lower 9th Ward to residents twenty minutes ago. These were the first ones in. I stand across the street from them, do not stare. The middle woman says, "I realize it's just material stuff, as long as you walk away with your life." The others all stand in the street as she alone walks through the gate into her garden. "I just want my mama's picture off the wall," she says, ascending the stairs to her porch. "She's dead and gone, but I want my mama's picture."

She stops on her porch, looks back at the other two women, maybe her daughter and her sister, meets only vacant stares above their masks, the Salvation Army volunteers behind them holding their shoulders. She turns, puts her hand on the doorknob, then jumps back like it's full of electricity. "Oh my God!" she screams. "It's open. The door is open!"

As the door drifts inward away from her, she backs up. She gets down to the second stair before she falls to her knees, then onto her side. The younger women begin to cry too, loud enough now to make it onto my tape. They move toward her, but stop at the open gate, go no further, hold each other there. "I grew up here," cries the woman on the steps. "Fifty-eight years . . . I've been here since a baby. I'm fifty-eight years old now. Fifty-eight years . . ."

I walk back to the end of the block in my khaki shorts, my Radio-Shack tape recorder tucked under my arm, get back into the car. Most of the few residents who heard the news that the Lower 9th would be open today were probably too far away to be here yet. These first ones back will have to cushion it for their neighbors. They're only allowed into about half of the neighborhood today, the part that fared the best, the part where homes still stand on their foundations. The army has made a rectangle out of this area, bounded by the Industrial Canal to our west, the river to the south. To the east they have heaped dozens of destroyed cars upon each other, forming a barricade along the St. Bernard Parish line, to prevent people from using this as an opportunity to sneak into that parish to see their homes. And to the north are barricades all along Claiborne Avenue, the road which I stared down two weeks ago during

Rita as it filled with silver sky to the horizon. Army soldiers stand there at every intersection. No one is getting above Claiborne, not media, and certainly not residents. This is where the levee breached. The streets have yet to be cleared. They're still doing body recovery, they tell us.

On Egania Street we find Cassandra and Curtis on their porch. Family photos are scattered around their feet. All are ringed with iridescent water stains. Among them, Cassandra's Social Security card, driver's license, and some bills are laid out to dry. These will be used to prove their identity to the government, insurance, whoever. They wear surgical masks around their necks, plastic gloves, and shoe covers. Cassandra sits on the top step above her photos arching her back with the dignity and slender fierce beauty of a lioness protecting her cubs. Curtis stands beside her, shining gold teeth, a thick build, and a mane of thick dreadlocks that would only make it up to his wife's shoulders if she stood beside him.

Cassandra: Nothing! Everybody say she had been on TV all that week, but I didn't hear nothing about that Katrina!

Was everyone here in the Lower 9th aware of their vulnerability to flooding?

Cassandra: You should go ask them bout how they broke the levee!

Yeah, I saw the broken levee during Rita.

Curtis: Not the broken levees. They blow up the levee! That's why all that water come on like that.

Did you see that?

Curtis: I heard that.

What did you hear?

Cassandra: *Boom!* They set detonators. That Sunday afternoon, all you seen was the military riding the streets, coming from the levee. A friend of mine saw the military afternoon before Katrina hit, they was posted in the same area where the levee breaching. So, what coincidence is that? Ain no such thing! They blew the levees, they set detonators, the timing for it to go off. They thought we all was dead over here.

Curtis: They had to try to kill us in our sleep.

Cassandra: And they killed all them children. They drowned them. I said no, uh-uh, we had to come out this water.

Curtis: Water came up so fast you didn't have the chance to get nothing.

You went to your roof?

Cassandra: I was asleep. They had to wake me up. So when I did make it out and touched the sidewalk the water was up to my neck. And I looked back to Claiborne and you could see it steady making its way in. And with the grace of God the young neighbors stuck together. We made out. We had some orange extension cords and they hooked them over the power lines right there like ropes and we just held on to the ropes, and all pedaled through the water to the house over there. I'm not a swimmer.

And you made it to that house right there with the tall roof? That three-story one?

Curtis: That is the house that saved our lives!

Where have you guys been living?

Cassandra: Dallas.

You gonna come back to live here?

Cassandra: Ain nothing about coming back! Forty years from now they're gonna blow the fucking levee again! I'm thirty-one now. Thirty, forty more years from now, you think I'm going to go through this again? No indeed!

What did you guys take with you?

Cassandra: Nothing but the clothes on our backs. We ain had no kind of assistance.

Curtis: They ain gonna help you! The twenty-three hundred dollars they claim is just to pay your rent. I hadn't received the two thousand dollars head of household or nothing they talking about. The people that are coming and inspecting and all that silliness. What you need to inspect? We was underwater. You need to swim in it?

Cassandra: Yeah, we don't have nothing. Red Cross, they give you three hundred sixty dollars, but it's a one-time thing, you know what I'm saying? That's not no money to start over again. It's not.

Curtis: Ain tryin to help us no kind of way, ain tryin to do nothing for us.

Cassandra: FEMA got you on hold and you gotta wait on them. We didn't have to wait for them to send that water in.

Curtis: Ain got no problem dumping that water on us, so why they don't want to pay us?

Could I—Would it be okay to walk inside your home?

Cassandra: Go on ahead.

These people were not able to return to clean and gut their homes before it got bad, like Raul and Rooster and Bumm Steer. The walls are dark with mud, spotted with yellow and brown and black mold, dank and disgusting, horrible smelling, flies everywhere. I have no idea what I'm walking on, could be a couch or a mattress. The light stops dead at the doorway, comes no further. I don't see the woman beside me until she says, "Look at the television."

She's blond, looks like an overweight Kathleen Turner, wearing a large black muumuu. Black eyeliner runs down her red cheeks, blond hair back in a bun, a mask on. She's holding a large illustrated Bible caked with sediment. "See it up there, how it's wedged between the top of the kitchen door and the ceiling? And how—look—there's one corner of the television barely touching the ceiling and one barely touching the door? And yet it's wedged in there so hard we couldn't knock it out. You really should have a mask on, you know. This is real harmful."

"I just realized, this is the first flooded home in New Orleans I've stood inside," I say.

Cassandra ducks her head in. "That's Ms. Diane," she says. "She's been helping us a whole lot. Seems like God sent an angel our way in Dallas."

"They don't know me very well," Diane says, carefully making her way out of the house ahead of me.

Cassandra: She found us. She's been helping us the whole while. That's the only help we had. Ain't nobody else want to help us. FEMA don't want to help us.

You live in Dallas?

Diane: Yeah. I met them when I was working for the Salvation Army. We found out yesterday we could come down here and so we came. We left at eleven last night. We got here at daybreak. These things that are in the car here are exactly what we rescued from three houses so far. The things that were salvageable.

A TV, a vase, a couple boots, an illustrated Bible. Had you seen pictures of this neighborhood before you came over?

Diane: Yeah, we'd seen a lot of news coverage, you know, but news can't do it justice. It's even worse than looking at it from an airplane or a helicopter. You can't smell it. You can't really see it. It's just amazing, astonishing, what water can do. Who's that? Cassandra, that's your sister running up the street! That's Nadine! You know, the interesting thing about these people is they are so composed. They don't lose their cool, they don't get upset.

Nadine: Oh baby, FEMA got a nice thing to talk about now! I just made them NBC newspeople a scene outside my house. I was crying and everything! And I was saying why people that is staying in Metairie who can go home, and they got two thousand dollars and twenty-three hundred dollars?! They ain't nothing wrong with their house!

Cassandra: Ain no future here. It's over. They can rebuild, they can do whatever, but I don't want to see no more of this. This is a mass destruction. And I'm used to seeing it on TV, hitting other states. When it hit home, it's a whole pill to swallow. I guess we'll all meet up in another place. Not here. I been here all my life. All my life. All the neighbors know each other. You know who lives where. When we in Texas, we don't know nobody, but Ms. Diane. And she come by us every day and offer us rides and bring our children to school. That's all the help we have out there.

Curtis: Whatever reason for this . . . it was no reason. They was not prepared for nothing. The rescue team took us to the St. Claude Bridge in a boat and left us there on Wednesday. We couldn't get no cold water. They wouldn't give us a cracker. We hadn't ate since Sunday. All we wanted was some sense of help or something.

Where did you go to from there?

Cassandra: We just walked. We walked until we came upon a car. Once we got upon a car we made it to Baton Rouge.

A car that you owned?

Cassandra: A car that was just loaned . . . [laughing] It's not funny but we had to get out.

So, you all managed to hot-wire the car?

Cassandra: You ain gonna get us in any trouble . . . but yeah we managed to hot-wire a car. We had to do what we had to do. And we got outta there. Once we get up on that car we sayed our prayers, "Lord just help us get up out of this mess! Just get us to a drier safer ground." And that's what He did.

Y'all weren't able to get out before the flood?

Cassandra: Well, we was able, but we really didn't know it was gonna get like this. We didn't have no cars. Our family members was willing to take us, but you know we like, we thought we was gonna get a little bit of water and we was gonna be able to survive it out. But just from hearing the stories of our parents talk about this happening in the sixties and all that, you know, we really shoulda left.

We made it to Baton Rouge. Once we stopped at Baton Rouge at a Dollar Store the car died and we just thanked God, you know what I'm saying? They brought us to a shelter at Southern University and from there a church family came down and brought us to Louisville, Texas, and left us there. And, from there, we seek help at the shelters in Dallas and we met Ms. Diane and she helping us.

Curtis: We ain got nothing, but we got God, we got faith, He giving us strength. We gonna make it. Cause only the strong survive.

Cassandra: I've been living by this canal all my life. There was only the handful that left, evacuated, so it is a good toll that probably did die. Cause there's friends we haven't heard anything from, you know. It's a good number and I don't think the news is really being accurate with it.

Curtis: Wednesday, three days after the storm, we knew people were still home. But they gave up. The Wildlife people was saying if they wasn't on their roofs or in sight where they could see them they wasn't going to go back in the area.

Cassandra: Some of the dead bodies they had was people that was living to get on the boat. But once they got out and saw what was in the neighborhood they caught a heart attack or caught a stroke or whatever. They took them off in a boat and dumped them in the river. There was this fireman from Galveston. He was a redneck. I don't know his name but I know his face. He wouldn't give us nothing. He dumped them in the river.

Curtis: Everybody scattered around. We don't know where our family at. Everybody's a different place. North Carolina, Detroit, California. Alabama. What they want us to do? How we gonna see our people?

Cassandra: They thought a lot of us over here was dead. But God had us like this.

Curtis: They sho tried to kill us. God saved us, that's all I can say. By the grace of God. He wasn't ready for us yet.

Cassandra: I knew it was God, 'cause guess what? All the street lights was out, but you see that night when we was first on the roof, when the rain stop and the wind stop, I ain never seen the sky light up like that. Lord, they had some stars up there twinkling, letting you know, "Baaa*by*! Don't worry! *Huh.* We *got* you up here."

I leave Ride with them and head alone down Egania Street toward the Mississippi River levee, the floodlines slowly dropping, trees still in the ground, less and less things in the trees. This is where the men with the garbage bags full of champagne said they were from, the ones we met that Tuesday after the storm outside Molly's. A man is walking the opposite direction, empty-handed and laughing hysterically.

Yep, it's messed up pretty bad, we don't have nothing. It's all gone.

You gonna come back and live here?

No. We scared that if this happens again, we have to run again. We not planning on running again. We came eight hundred miles just to see this. We wasn't ready for this. Yep. I have to laugh, I have to get some fun out of this. You know, you work so hard to get things, and you think that at a age of fifty-five, you know, you're settled. And you go back and within your house there's nothing. I got to laugh!

He walks on, howling with laughter alone under the blue morning sky. Two blocks later I find a man standing in full scrubs who eagerly takes me inside his home just across Chartres Street from the river levee.

Anthony: And this's my little girl's room. Here, walk right here. Step on that bureau here. We tried to show it to a newsman earlier but he refused to walk inside with us. Said it was too dangerous to breathe this.

That's going to break.

Anthony: No, okay, then walk on the mattress.

Where?

Anthony: You standing on it.

You said you guys evacuated on Sunday right before the storm?

Anthony: Yeah. I mean, you smell this? And you ain even got a mask on. You must be smelling it.

Were you aware how vulnerable this neighborhood was to flooding?

Anthony: We wasn't going to take no chance, not me. You've got to look out for your family. And, look now. It's terrible, it's unlivable.

I see the waterline, where it settled down to, about chest level, about four and a half feet.

Anthony: This my wife, Danielle.

Danielle: The insurance man said nothing was wrong with the house, he say, "Oh, it's fine, it'll be okay, it's livable, the mold is not bad. Just knock down some Sheetrock and the house will be fine." We just talked on the phone with him yesterday, so we thinking our house is okay, and when we come in here it's like, "That guy is crazy."

What's the worst thing about all this?

Danielle: The worst thing is that Katrina happened August 29 and we've been out of our home until today, October 12. We was running down here three times already because they telling you you can get in the 9th Ward, and you get here, then Ray Nagin is saying you can't get in for one reason or another. So, we got to go all the way back. This happen three times. And it's so discouraging, because we in Hope, Arkansas now. That's like an eight-hour ride. And we don't have the money for the gas.

You got a cut on your head? Why do you keep scratching your head?

Danielle: No, he fine. His nerves is just shot.

What's the worst thing you lost?

Anthony: The worst thing is all your life-earned hard work. It's gone.

Danielle: To think that this is gonna be your home for the rest of your life. And now you don't want to be here no more.

Anthony: Look in there at the bedroom. That's just the front, but the back—oh, my man . . .

Danielle: You know, my husband is a wreck—

Anthony: It's history.

Danielle: I'm just so depressed.

Anthony: Man, I don't know how FEMA could say that this is livable. You think so?

If y'all come back, is there any chance of you living here?

Danielle: I doubt it very much. And we know if they wants to rebuild the neighborhood, it's not never gonna be the same. Never.

Anthony: I'm finished here. I'll make a new life in Hope.

How'd you all find Hope?

Anthony: We just drove until the truck run out of gas, and we just lay right there by the Super 8, in the parking lot. We ain plan it. We just did it. And so when we got there in Arkansas, the next morning, I went to Wal-Mart, because I've been at Wal-Mart fifteen years. I asked to talk to the manager and I told him the situation about us, and he called the main office, and the main office said, "Hire him." And he say, "Whenever you want to come, you're welcome. You got you a job."

Danielle: Talking about just put up a slab of Sheetrock? I wouldn't move my children back in here like that. I don't know where that mold went. That water went about eight foot of water, and they're telling people four and a half. That's a shame, that's how they doing to poor people.

So, this is it. Just dinge.

Joan Didion once wrote something that's stuck in my mind since: "You sit down to dinner and life as you know it ends. Confronted with sudden disaster we all focus on how unremarkable the circumstances were in which the unthinkable occurred, the clear blue sky from which the plane fell, the routine errand that ended on the shoulder with the car in flames, the swings where the children were playing as usual when the rattlesnake struck from the ivy."

This, here, did not start as an unremarkable day at summer's end like that other American tragedy four years earlier, unremarkable as most of the tragedies of our lives begin. Here, the ocean rose above the land. Here, the sky shook the very Earth. And yet, there's no shock, no glamour, no rhythm, no pattern to the aftermath. No visible beauty in its terror. You'd think it would be worthy of that, that they at least deserved that, something physical, powerful enough to reflect their destroyed lives here. But there's just mud and mold and a little explosion in every home and everything darker and grayer than it used to be. It can almost bore you now, if you did not suffer it.

It is afternoon. I lie on my back within the grass at the bottom of the levee, unmowed for two months now, spiking the clear blue October afternoon above me, a helicopter cutting through it. A monarch butterfly, perched on the top of a single blade. Opens and closes its wings above me, fanning them into the sun. Light. Here.

The in and out and in and out and dark and light of these homes below me now. Five hours now of giving people just enough time to see their homes alone, then me stepping in to catch the ends of their first reactions, early enough to feel like an asshole but late enough to feel human. The dark inside them so thick, even noon sun could only weep into it enough to barely tell the difference between a bathroom and a bedroom.

I'd keep looking for the little details, hooks that the newspaper people seize upon, pretend that they illustrate the whole: the tricycle, the Cabbage Patch Kid, the illustrated Bible, the photo of a newborn baby. They're there. But their essence is lost in the dinge. And then I'd cough to pretend I wasn't yawning, and wonder what to eat next—that breakfast burrito Ride made me that's still in the car or should I have one of those Honey Nut Cheerio cereal bars or should I go and get some Salvation Army food? And then I would realize I'm not even hungry. And I'll even have my routine back soon and then I won't have lost a single thing.

A couple of dragonflies hooked to each other, tail to head, had spun through Cassandra's legs, around her feet covered in black mud, over her photos and all the flies flying around the whole time. And when I asked if they would return, Danielle saying, "And we know if they wants to rebuild it, it's not never gonna be the same. Never."

"*They* wants to rebuild it . . ." They? Danielle's place in this world has been taken out of her hands. Perhaps long before Katrina. And I suppose we are all to blame. And I thought of Rose and that Lafitte mud. "*Our* mud," she had called it.

I stand up, walk back down Chartres Street, cannot find Ride. I get in the car, drive around looking for him. I find a familiar block. Where the noises had come from yesterday. I stop, get out. There it is. Like two birds chirping at each other, a few beats between each call and each response. There is no one on this street. I walk back around the house, up the steps. The door still swings in and out, slower now, too slow to be mistaken for the noises' cause any longer. I throw it open. The sounds, one after another, come out of the darkness at me like water. I walk inside, hands in front of me groping the thick decomposing air, a chair, a small table falls over soundless into the mud floor, and I see something black inside the dark, the sounds coming from it. My shadow? From what light I do not know. I reach into it. Empty. I move my hand around until broken glass cuts my wrist. A cupboard? Cabinet? Then something metal brushes through my fingers. I do not stop it, feel the bottom of the pendulum as it passes again, whines again at its bottom like a door wrenched open on rusty hinges, not loud enough that it should be heard from two blocks away. My other hand finds the face of the clock above it, level with my own face. A grandfather clock. Its hands are both at ten. I rest a finger there for a few minutes, gently, letting the pendulum creep though the fingers of my other hand, squealing back and forth, while the door behind me swings slowly shut, then open, shut, open, fanning light into the room. The hands do not move at all.

48

I tell Katherine I thought we were going to talk. She looks at me for the first time, her left brow swollen, eyes small, rimmed with pink thin as a razor. "So talk," she says.

I can still feel sediment between my toes. I want to hold her and not say anything, and just please start getting through this. I waited here tonight, on a bench by the river, a hundred feet from my front door, for an hour before she showed up with a friend of ours, Michael, who'd just gotten back to town. She had a drink in her hand and his arm around her. She'd been crying. We exchanged niceties until Michael went back to her car to get his cigarettes.

"What have you been doing?" she asks. "Where have you been all this time?"

"Been going out, seeing things. We went to the Lower 9th today."

"I was there. We were in a helicopter."

"With who?"

"This Condé Nast magazine I'm taking photos for."

"That's great, glad you're doing so well," I say. "So, what did it look like from up there?"

"Dirty. Though you could see there was a pattern to it all, like rose petals fanning out from the levee break. It was almost beautiful. I suppose up close it uglies up pretty quick, huh?"

"It's like there was a little explosion inside every home and it makes me tired. It makes me hungry too, being there. So when do you think we stop simply trying to get through this?" I ask. "When do we build the future and how's it going to be and what are we going to do to make things better?"

"This is, was, the future of us. This, Josh, is how you and I are going to be. You can't simply try to float through a time, and pretend it's not acting upon everything, pretend it's not creating the future until it is the future."

"I meant the city, not us."

She stares into the river, somewhere past all the city's lavender haze shimmering upon it. "Us," she says. "Down there, where the water has no reason to go anywhere. Quiet and peaceful and nobody bothers you. And yet that bottom is lost beneath so many currents. So many tiny explosions. Flattened with them until it's all just lightless dirt and you just can't clean that up. And that's us. And I don't think I can inhabit that anymore."

"You know, I don't come here enough," says Michael as he walks up to us. He lights his cigarette, sits on the bench beside me. "I lived here most my life and I never come down here to just sit like this and look at the river."

"Yeah," I say. "I'll see y'all later."

She looks up at me as I stand, says, "Josh, don't be distant." And she tries to touch my face.

The next afternoon we just keep going, turning away from the setting sun every time the road ends and a new one begins. We have not seen a person, not another car, for an hour. We were trying to drive to Violet, at the end of St. Bernard Parish, and we're doing a pretty shitty job. Like Lafitte, I once found it by driving to the end of the line, going east this time.

We had to drive through the Lower 9th to get here, showed them our press passes, had the National Guard move the city bus they'd been using as a barricade between rows of stacked, crushed cars into the parish. The destruction grew more violent the further into St. Bernard Parish we got. Now live oaks line both sides of the road, entwine above us in a cathedral ceiling spilling purple and blue light over us. The homes grow larger and further from the road. Telephone poles slant toward us, their ends crooked crucifixes just two feet off the ground, some lines still connected and sagging through the grass. Traces of Spanish moss cling dead to trees, small and white like icicles.

We stop in the middle of the road for no reason at all, get out of the car. Setting sun crawls blood red across shallow water in ditches on sides of the road around cypress knees. A black squirrel hops off a telephone pole, runs through the grass, and disappears into a turquoise house that has a birch tree growing out of its middle. The house and tree sit tangled in the middle of a field. The house appears to have collapsed long ago. The storm has thrown its insides up into the tree like toothpicks. And I wonder what it all looks like from the sky.

Beside this field is a larger, yellow house. I tear the weeds off the chest-high wrought iron sign in front of it. WELC ME T DUCROS M SEUM ND LIBRA Y. On the front porch lie two clean tables, covered with artifacts that have clearly been sorted and cleaned since the storm: bones, a cannonball, pottery, ancient cooking utensils. The door is open. Inside it smells like something burnt, nothing worse. All the walls are covered in bookcases. The books are ruined up to chest level, then they are fine. There is a copy of Josef Conrad's *The Secret Agent*, one of the books I had given Katherine, one of the books that had gotten wet in her apartment, just above the water level here. I open it. In it, Conrad posits that the source of terrorism is the desire to affect severe change—revolution even—without the labor and perseverance and tolerance of routine that it would otherwise take. Something like that. The reason this book is dear to me is this one line I will never forget: "All idealization makes life poorer. To beautify it is to take away its character of complexity—it is to destroy it."

I slide it back into its place. On the top shelf sits a Siamese kitten, watching me with eyes deep blue as the hole in a glacier I once peered down into. I turn to see another kitten walking out the door. It pays no attention to Ride filming the bones laid out on the table, but crosses the yard, then walks down the street until it vanishes into the violet haze hanging over everything and trees have become silhouettes. Here is the simplicity I long for . . . the butterfly opening and closing its wings, last light of evening scattered and shattered and shimmering upon the river, something to hold to, like Mars alone on a balcony the last night anything was certain. At the cost of all else, I clung to it, until it too slipped through my fingers like sun, and the world here peeled into layers of sediment and sentiment. From here on, finding beauty will be the complex thing.

49

Wednesday, October 19, we drive across Lake Pontchartrain on the Causeway Bridge, longest bridge across water in the world, to the North Shore, take a right in Mandeville, and hug the lake east toward Slidell.

Clayton Borne III stands in the lawn outside his perfectly intact 1840 house overlooking Lake Pontchartrain. Five years ago, FEMA told him his house needed to be fourteen feet above sea level to be safe from a hurricane surge. The sea wall extends six feet above the lake, so he raised the entire house eight feet above the ground. He shows us the water line, two inches below his front doorstep. His neighbors didn't fare so well.

Two miles east we find Max Smiley on his twenty-one-foot boat, *Fine Wine.*

Max: I was back in Bayou Castine just off the lake tied up with about fifteen ropes when the storm came. Water came up about fourteen feet. Water went up, water went down.

How long were you on the boat for?

Max: About three weeks. I lived on it for twenty years, so, no problem. I raised the boat after a hurricane. It sank off the coast back in '85, Hurricane Daniel. All the looters and stuff afterwards, you got to protect yourself. People were stealing fuel back here after the storm.

What was the worst thing you saw?

Max: Man's inhumanity to other man. To let people die of thirst and stuff up on the interstate for four or five days from lack of water. We can put troops on the ground anywhere in the world in twelve hours, how come we can't get people water? There's no reason for people to die from lack of water in the USA. My brother lives in Paris, and they're sitting over there watching it in Europe, just appalled. The biggest superpower in the world can't take care of their own people. It was pretty pathetic.

Where were you during the storm?

Max: Right up here in the cockpit. Why miss the adventure? The trees were all popping. You'd see the little mini tornado bursts that were coming through.

Were you having a cocktail?

Max: We're in Louisiana, aren't we? Myers with water and lime. It was exciting. Thank God it hit during the daytime though. It's worse at night when something comes, you can't see what's going on. You just miss all the excitement.

Max Smiley's friend Jerry Houston takes us to the nearest marina where his black sailboat is impaled on a piling, about six feet above the water.

Jerry: This cool looking or what? You know how you got the rooster on a weather vane? That's kind of like how this looks, huh?

Is this a good idea being in the boat?

Jerry: Well, you don't jump up and down.

What do you do?

Jerry: I'm a plumber. I tell you, I did fourteen calls out in Metairie yesterday and you see all those beautiful homes on the lakefront that flooded, and people are not saying, "Look what the water did." They all saying the exact same story: "Look what Aaron Broussard did to my house."

Because he's the mayor of Metairie and he ordered the water-pump workers to evacuate?

Jerry: "Look what Aaron Broussard done to my house." That's how they say it. It's not the water that did it. You know, being a service mechanic you meet everybody. I got ex-governors for customers, I got senators, got judges. One of the best mornings I ever had, first call I did was for a drug user. Second call I did for a drug dealer, third call was for a guy who flew the helicopter for the DEA, he's my regular customer, you know? The fourth guy, the fellow was a judge that does all the drug cases, you know, on a government level, he's my regular customer, too. I did all these people before noon one day. So, you meet everybody. I met Indian chiefs. Never met a president, though.

Man, all the dumbass shit I see every day. I'm not saying I'm the smartest guy in the world, but this lady had a big St. Bernard dog, and she said she had water on her floor, so I was laying on my side, you know being a mechanic, you're either laying on your side, you on your back, or on your knees. And I'm laying like this, looking at the lady's dishwasher. I stuck my head in the dishwasher, I couldn't see nothing wrong with it, but I felt hot water going down the side of my head. I pulled out my head, wiped it, sure enough there was water. I stuck my head back in, and I felt it again. Now I done this three times, sticking my head in this lady's dishwasher. By the third time I went to scratch my head like this, like I thought I had a bug on it or something, and I grabbed the dog's weenie. It was peeing on me. I stood up, it went down my ear, down my backbone, down on my tailbone, and it dripped down my pants. And you know what really pissed me off more than anything? The lady comes running in, looks at me, and starts yelling at me for peeing on her floor.

Jerry, you could make someone forget their problems.

Jerry: You know, I used to wear my pants where the crack of my ass shows, but I don't do that no more. See? I got bigger pants now, because I had a dog that fell in love with me. I did this call for this lady one day, she had a Doberman pinscher, you know. I had my head in the lady's oven, I was on my knees, and I had the carriage moved where I really couldn't get out. This big old dog, he bear hugged me, he fell in love with me. When I felt that cold nose between the crack of my ass, I said *oh shit*, then he just bear hugged me. I couldn't move, and I could feel his weenie touching me. *Arf arf arf arf* . . . you know, I couldn't get him off me. It took me and that lady to get that dog off of me. I kept kicking that dog and she kept pulling and he kept going *arf arf arf* . . . I kept screaming at her, "Would the dog put his dick back in his thing!" He fell in love with me.

There ain't nothing that surprises me, you know. You know I got bunches of them stories. Listen, tell your friends do not throw their refrigerator away. Get a pan, put some newspaper in it, and fill it up with some charcoal on top of that, shut it up, and turn your refrigerator on the coldest setting you can put it on, and in about four or five days, the smell just magically disappears. Works for your freezer, too. Smell just disappears.

50

At 1265 Louisiana Avenue, a little sign says COMMUNITY MEETING with an arrow pointing into Our Lady of Good Counsel Catholic Church. "Evacuees, families of evacuees, or lovers of Louisiana are invited."

"Where do we fit in?" I ask Ride.

Outside the church, uptown New Orleans is dingy and pruned but grinding back to normal. Cars roll down Louisiana Avenue, most power lines are back up, the median strips have been mowed, and the only debris lying there is in little piles stacked recently by returning home-owners.

Inside the big beautiful church are two dozen people all saying the same thing—they feel like they don't have any power to affect the rebuilding process and they're worried about the intentions of the organizations and big political figures. This is the first of many such meetings across the city. We listen to them prepare a report for the Planning Commission, then we drive down St. Charles Avenue through the Garden District, the Warehouse District, along the edge of the Quarter, into the Bywater, and finally over the St. Claude Bridge back down into the Lower 9th. They still won't let us north of Claiborne Avenue. There's two army soldiers sitting at every barricade, and each tells us the same thing: No one is getting in there. "They got to get all the bodies out before they let real people in," says the last soldier we ask.

We drive through the rest of the Lower 9th Ward into St. Bernard Parish again until we see the plywood sign outside the Dog House: OPEN— VIDEO POKER—POOL—DARTS—COLD BEER. "No way," I say, letting my eyes settle into the beer-sign-lit darkness. "How long y'all been open?"

"Almost two hours now," says the bartender. "We the high ground in St. Bernard. This is the only place didn't flood. Just a couple inches came in over the floor, that's bout it."

There's only two other guys in there, looking through some photos laid out on the bar, sipping Budweisers. I order one myself, Ride an orange juice, and sit next to them. In every photo, roofs just barely stick up out of endless water. There's a bunch of the guy sitting next to me, riding through the flooded streets carrying people in a little johnboat—about ten feet long, three wide, with a flat bottom and a motor hanging off the back. Says his name is Eric Colopy. And his friend tells me these are pictures of people he rescued. Eric's bashful, reluctant to talk about it at first. I ask if I could interview him outside. He eventually obliges, pours the remainder of his beer in an eight-ounce plastic cup, and follows us outside as the sun sets across the empty St. Bernard Highway.

A demolition shirt hangs over Eric's lean broad shoulders, short sandy hair curling at the edges out of a sun-bleached baseball cap above a face like those busts of Julius Caesar if Caesar had shrugged off the empire, let his land crease the corners of his eyes, and put dirt irreversibly far up his wide fingernails and slow his speech; but there it is, that same face—strong brow over deep, wide, brown eyes, hooked Roman nose, high cheekbones, hollow cheeks, strong chiseled jaw slanting into a thin chin. He takes out the first roll of photos, spreads them on the hood of his truck, nods back at the bar.

Eric: That's my favorite hangout. We shot darts here and pool. Worst part is that the teams I shot with, we was in first place, but now that they had the flood we don't get no trophies.

Where were you for the actual storm?

Eric: I wasn't gonna stay. But my wife took the kids and the credit cards and I was left with only twenty dollars in my pocket. I forgot what time it was, but the storm woke me up, went down to the kitchen, drank me a beer, listening to the radio. In about five minutes, my feet was getting wet. I said, "What the hell?" I looked toward the door and I see water seeping in through the cracks in the door. Hell, when I open up the door, the water was up to the door handle, and it just blew me back. I put both feet on the opposite wall and I got the door shut and I just started grabbing as much stuff as I could think of. Well, the ice chest first with the beer and all in it, I threw that in the laundry room. Then, I started grabbing all my dogs, and throwing them in the laundry room. Then, after that, I went and got the boat from my neighbor's yard, started throwing them in the boat. It was my third trip in the house, my front door blew in and that's when the water came in big time, and I had to climb over furniture and everything just trying to get my wife's dogs out of the house. I had to get them, because she would have killed me. Than the water was up over the gutters that fast. I didn't have time, you know, to go back and save a whole lot.

Well, me and my neighbor, the old man that used to live next door to me, Mr. Billy, when I come out throwing stuff in the boat, I saw him standing in his doorway with water up to his chest almost, and I told him, "What you waiting for? Get in the boat." "Well, I'm gonna go in the attic," he said. I said, "You ain't going in the attic; you're getting in the boat." Once I got him in the boat, the water came up over the gutters, so we just tried to find a house or something to get behind and get out of the wind. And as the water come up, we had to move to a different building because it went over our roofs. We found a three-story apartment, thinking we'd get out of the wind there, but we couldn't have nowhere to hold onto it. So, that's when we found Andrew Jackson High School, and the doors were all blown open, so we made that our shelter. As we were sitting there, unloading everything, I heard a shotgun going off, and I went out to the boat, and one of the guys in the apartment over there was shooting a shotgun in the water to get my attention. So, I went and got him, and then I got five people from another apartment right down the street, you know, a couple of apartments over. And after that, you know, it was getting dark, so, I mean, I wasn't planning on getting power lines tangled with the motor, so we stayed at the high school through that evening. The next morning, woke up and just started going around picking up people, you know?

The first street I went down I'm hollering, "Rescue. Anybody in their attics?" I'd turn my engine off and yell that. I heard banging on the roofs, people screaming. Just so happened the first house I went to, the guy had a big axe, so we knocked off the big vent fan, and the people were trying to climb out there. Once I got them out, you know, I kept going to more and more houses. But the people was on their roofs. I told them, you know, I got too many people trapped in their attics, I gotta get them out of the attics before I can get you off the roof. It was like that for the next four or five days. People that was trapped in the attics for maybe three, four days. After that I might have caught one house, two houses every block, where there was still people. Then I didn't hear nobody banging on any of the attics or nothing like that after about the fourth day. So, then I just started picking up whoever I found on the roofs.

How many people did you rescue?

Just in the attics, I don't know, at least a hundred fifty people I chopped out the attics, me and Mr. Billy. I just happened to know Mr. Billy from this bar here. And after that, it could have been in the thousands, people that was just on the roofs. I mean, I filled up the boat with as many people as I could get. He even had three full boats tied up behind me—I was just pulling them toward the highway, and then they all got out and started walking toward the ferry.

So, you really were the only one helping people in your whole area?

Me and Mr. Billy. The ones in the high school, after a few days passed, they started wondering where the outside world was. So—oh, there's Emeril in this picture. That's when we was frying the chicken Friday night.

Emeril?

Yeah. After we got tired of eating tuna fish and chips and cookies I broke into the cafeteria and found some chicken and there was Emeril hiding out. So, I said, "We're cooking fried chicken with Emeril tonight."

So, how did he get there?

I think he might have been teaching a cooking class and got stuck there.

We were all wondering where he was.

You'd have to look at the pictures to see the Emeril that I'm talking about. It's a life-size cardboard cutout poster.

Did he say "bam" a lot?

Well, I was saying the bam for him a lot. See, here, in this photo, I was asking him if the chicken was cooked yet or if it had enough seasoning on it. Here he is talking about his seasoning that he had. But I had the Zatarain's right here, you know. I told him, "I'm using Zatarain's." Well, we sitting there arguing about the seasoning, you know. He wanted to use his, I wanted to use mine. Anyway, after I rescued everybody, I left Emeril at the high school. He couldn't fit in my boat with me.

A lot of these pictures, I don't know—most of them are just of me riding around the neighborhoods. The first few days you're not thinking about taking photos, of course. This one, as I was coming down the street, I noticed a body floating over here in front of the house right here, and I just kinda snapped these as I was getting closer. It was an old man with gray hair, he was all bloated up, see. I don't know if he was stuck on the little fence, on the column or stuck in the weeds, but he was still just sitting there.

This old guy here, I found him on the roof. He punched his way out the attic. His hand all here was purple and blue from his knuckles to his wrist. He was all cut up on his back, his arms, his legs, because he punched a small hole and he squeezed through it.

Well, we made it, you know, we did what we had to do. We just tried not to panic. It was an experience. I mean, we organized all our stuff, we had plenty of drinks, food, water, we had our little propane tank, our coffee in the morning and stuff like that. Hey, we were happy. We had fun. We made the most of it, you know?

51

Ride and I continue searching different pockets of the city, and spend the days in between trying to normal up, feeling more and more estranged from these people living in New Orleans now. Every interaction inevitably turns awkward, and so I give up, do not return calls from even my oldest friends. I shut myself in my apartment, continue transcribing my interviews and promoting the reprint of *French Quarter Fiction.* I get in touch with an NOPD spokesperson. It takes her two weeks of culling through files to send me a list of every single injury suffered by police officers in the month after the storm. Thankfully, despite many of them telling me about being shot at every day, not a single officer was killed in the line of duty. And while several were injured helping others evacuate, the spokesperson could find only three accounts of officers receiving any kind of malicious injury in that entire period.

Meanwhile Katherine is couch-hopping, I don't know where. I can never get it out of her during our brief telephone conversations before she hangs up on me. But, finally, she agrees to meet me. She is at a friend's place at the end of St. Charles Avenue by the riverbend, as far uptown as one can get. She will be alone there tonight. She has to do an interview in the morning. For what, with whom, again, she will not tell me.

As I fill my radiator that evening, the water simply pours out of the bottom onto the street. I wait an hour and a half for a friend to pick me up, drive me all the way uptown, and leave me where Katherine's staying. I am here to have the conversation we should have had by the river the other day, but I don't know what that is, what those words are that will make things better. I only know I wanted to hug her that night, that was the plan before she showed up late, drunk, with a friend. Now, I do not even know that.

We sit on opposite ends of a couch, quiet, unmoving, our bodies warped around opposite edges of the blank television screen in front of us, until she suddenly bolts across the room to her suitcase, which has been lying open in the corner. She shoves in some T-shirts that were on the floor beside it, then her purse, the one that belonged to her great-grandmother, zips the suitcase shut, and pushes it quickly into a closet.

She turns to me from the closet door, breathes deep, and starts before I can even bring myself to look her in the eye for the first time. She claws at everything I am: my attitude, my work, my family, anything. And I do my best to throw it back at her threefold, wanting all the time to do nothing but hug her. She slips further from me in the room with every breath until we're in opposite corners, still not looking at each other, words falling before proper ones are thought, building between us, burning the air until I charge across the room at her and she backs into the wall behind a stereo speaker, crouches to the ground, puts her hand up, palms up against me, face turned, eyes clamped shut, thinking I am going to hit her.

It is the first time I have seen her shake. Her hair falls flat across her hidden face, the gray now dyed blond again. Her pajamas, the same she wore that night we walked through downtown after the storm, hang loose over bony shoulders, pieces of what she used to be, the rest washed away, brittle pieces held together for these last minutes only with the strength it took to claw at me, but silent and dry pieces hunched, crumpled, and cowering now below me. And I can't believe she thinks I am going to hit her. Then, I realize my arm is out, hand open, pointing at her.

"I was going to put my finger to your lips," I say. "I just wanted to touch you somewhere, reach inside you and stop this."

She stops trembling, but stays crouched to the floor, while that space in me that once loved her floods again, fills my ribs, and the anger at its desiccation stops. "Please, look at me," I say.

She turns her face to me, but her eyes stay on the ground, bloodshot and red-rimmed and dry, a crease down the middle of her brow, deflated cheeks sagging, and then I know what it is that has flooded that old space inside me. It is full of hate now. And I just leave it there, with her, right in her fucking lap, and walk out with nothing.

I walk home all the way across the city, downriver, down St. Charles Avenue from end to end, believing for the first time that there is a real chance we will not grow old together. I do not think: that night almost two months ago, the end of August, walking these same blocks, lost in stars now tumbled away and constellations shifted, tripping down the neutral ground with her cooler, the only's. There are lights on in some houses. The sidewalk is totally clear. No cars. There is still some sort of curfew but I'm not sure when. I just keep walking, three hours to get to my door, and not stopping when my head hits the pillow, still pushing downriver, river as dark as space as big as alone all alone with nothing holding me just me until bottom. I find the bottom. It is simple, the water familiar as my mother whispering my name above me in the dark and bottom soft beneath feet no longer fighting it, toes stroking the bones of de Soto who first glimpsed it a half millennium ago, Chickasaws and Chippewas and Choctaws who simply built mounds to stand on when river flooded and keep walking pushing the bones down deeper current and flow beating every side of me propping me straight up in place of Katherine's hand in mine is this force become of snowflakes in Montana and Minnesota where river begins, force falling like sunlight through my fingers as I continue downriver winding through land until land has been washed of man for now and the river is alone and full no emptiness burning no more, full of a country's sediment once making land, and they thought they could constrain me and Katrina come pushed me the wrong way back toward the lonely snowflake, Katrina's finger to my lips reached inside me to stop this momentum but nothing stops this nothing simply unload it onto the land onto Plaquemine falling easy as sunlight through my fingers but black as space as good and simple sleep and tasting the water saltier now like the Gulf feeling it coming to an end I reach out, try to keep myself in it, hold to land, hold it in my hand, and the end of the river comes loose in my hand.

I open my fist. Something about the size of an egg there but perfectly round and black and hard. There are more of them. They still cling to the tree. Black ornaments in a bleached world. Broken white branches from other trees coil through this one like snakes. I break open the thing in my hand, a black satsuma, rotted solid, sunken. It is empty. I drop it. It meets the ground soundless as shadow.

The floor is marked with leaves, large and flat and snow white on wet beige earth. Out of the earth come the black bases of trees, thin enough to fit my hands around, rows of them like the one before me. Their black bases fade up into ash gray, then into white as pure as the leaves which break up the ground.

Crows' cries shock the sky. I step back and see blood on the ground, soaking into a white leaf. My feet are bleeding. I am not used to walking this much. Blood is crusted to my heels, and it runs slow over my shoes and I wonder if I could ever make the walk back.

The ground is still wet in some places. I try to walk back to the road, but lose my footing, slide around, hold to the little satsuma branches too flimsy to snap. Some come off in my hands. They do not snap but just come right off. Not branches, but smooth sticks, curled and curved and furrowed with the river, driftwood. Then I pull a single wooden chair leg out of a tree and I take it with me, step over a pirogue, its rope still tied above my head to the top of another tree. There is a stuffed Santa Claus doll caught in its branches. On the other side of the road, on the ground, are what look like massive black tarps, each twisted like a quilt on a bed left unmade. But these are roofs.

I wear the same clothes as last night, moving through dreams, hugging the Mississippi River, awoke to RideofTwoFires hitting my buzzer for the fourth time, and in which I drove an hour and a half south, through the last puddles, over this ashen sediment now dried and hardened and split to pieces like a brittle leaf that's been stepped on, until I am here.

This is the town of Magnolia, Plaquemines Parish. The world divided between ash and shadow and me.

Ride's waiting in the truck. A Ford F-150 with dual cab. Enterprise finally got it in this morning and we took it for a month. I get some Band-Aids and paper towels out of the cab, clean the outsides of my shoes and bandage my heels. And we keep moving downriver. We have not seen another person for an hour.

Earlier, subdivisions had quickly given way to dead grass and slanting, shattered trees and a bloated deer a couple of miles before the checkpoint. We showed the U.S. marshals our fake press passes, and after looking through the truck they waved us on.

Over the last few weeks, I've heard widely varying stories of how the flooding happened here. One night I had a bartender on Bourbon Street, who'd snuck into Plaquemines illegally to find her home, give a tear-filled account of seeing an actual river levee breach; ten minutes later a friend of mine in the Coast Guard, who said he was the first into the parish after the storm, assured me he had driven down the entire river levee and it was only *marsh* water in Plaquemines.

Whatever it is, there's only a few inches of it left on the road. So far, we've seen nothing but a couple of pickup trucks zooming by us: no repaired levee breaches, no other cars, no people, nothing but the splinters of homes, if anything remained at all. Imagine the shelter of your bedroom, filled with warmth and memory, now a few dirty sticks caught in the branches of a dead satsuma tree that I've just peed on.

Despite it beginning only five miles southeast of the city, many New Orleanians have never set foot in Plaquemines Parish. Some have no idea where it is. The only thing it's on the way to is itself. There is no major suburb here, no interstate. Only one road winds along this last 100 miles of the Mississippi and dead-ends in its delta. The parish is the end of the longest river on the continent, the end of the valley of America.

About ten thousand lived in its northernmost town of Belle Chasse, which was the least affected part. The other seventeen thousand inhabitants of the parish stretched themselves through a couple dozen communities, not a single one incorporated, upon sediment barely above sea level, solid only a mile wide at most the whole way down, shooting crazily alone into the Gulf of Mexico, like a tail, eighty miles south of Waveland, Mississippi.

Katrina made landfall here, the parish went underwater, and yet, as ever, it has already been largely forgotten, both in the media and in New Orleans. The parish's seclusion, arguably voluntary, is mythological, and it is no stranger to flooding. During the Great Mississippi Flood of 1927, city and state leaders dynamited a levee, flooding Plaquemines in order to spare New Orleans. The destruction of the parish turned out to be unnecessary and remains unrewarded. The sacrifice left a bitter taste in residents' mouths for outside intervention. They didn't fool with the United States, including its taxes. The parish, with its oil, gas, and fishing industries, essentially functioned as a self-sufficient sovereign state for decades. Until recently, they saw no reason to let the outside world waste their money. And now, it would almost seem, the outside world is returning the favor.

I had only been here once before, just to see it. As soon as I crossed into it, the world became very simple. Everything, even the river, turned green but for the bright orange satsumas. The only signs were magic-markered posterboard, "Pick your own." Women fished off the side of the road while their husbands were out shrimping and the towers of distant oil refineries exhaled flames. "We live here because nobody fucks with you. You do what you want," said one of the women on the side of the road. "You can pretty much just put a stick in the water and the fish will bite it."

We keep moving downriver, my shoes cleaned of blood, heels bandaged, with roofs crumpled like cloth along the road, sometimes in the road, until the grand piano. It's just sitting there on the side of the road, at the base of the river levee to our left. There are four cars beside it, upright and clean. We park alongside them. And to our right, people, about a dozen of them, slowly shifting colors scattered amongst the debris.

The piano is ash gray like everything else, but seemingly unscathed. I lift the fallboard off the keys. They too are intact, gray. The air is empty of even the crows' cries I heard further north in the satsuma grove. Ride is putting a new tape in his camera, looks at me, says, "Don't." I hit the middle C key. The note rings clear across the landscape. The people stop moving. It takes me a while to separate them from the debris again. Ride and I walk across the street.

We pass a motorboat, its front end still connected to a trailer that is bent around a telephone pole that has snapped out of the ground, the telephone wires in turn wrapped around the boat's mangled engine. Two women sit nearest the side of the road, on a set of four cement steps that once led to a porch, the only thing still standing in its original place. One is holding a child that looks too young to fool with words. Beside them are several dirty porcelain roosters and a piece of cardboard with RIP written on it in black magic marker. The women are the same age, maybe late forties, a yellow hue to their river-brown skin. Ride and I introduce ourselves. Mary. Alcedia. They do not look at us. Both face the road, their land to their backs, as though they're waiting for something. Ride moves past them, films the others who have now turned away from us, begun shifting through the pieces again in the background.

I stand still, a couple of feet to the side of the two women, watching all behind them, waiting for them to speak, my tape recorder recording the nothing. It no longer unnerves me, the debris and sediment and tears, our new landscape. And that same silence I once expected at any moment to be filled with the bird's call or cricket's legs has become common as the ash that is everything but the blue October sky and us, and I will stand here until they say something.

Mary: No words could explain it. You have to walk into my shoes to understand.

Alcedia: Now you know. You watch it on the TV, and you see devastation in other countries. But I go back to my life. Now, you know.

You were here, forty years ago, for Betsy and Camille?

Mary: Yes, when we were young with my mom and dad, you know, and we were back home very soon. And then this. We're all grown up now, and we're dealing with this.

Alcedia: We're lost.

Whose foundation is this one? Whose porch is this?

Alcedia: This is where my daddy's house was. Don't know where that is. He built this community. This foundation was the first thing he ever built. His name was Rip.

These names, written in the cement on the side of these stairs you're sitting on, are these you guys?

Alcedia: Yeah. Well, this is my daughter. This is Kylie, that's my niece. This is Mary, this is me. And this is Lucy, my niece. Nadia, Jacinta, Nobu, Meghan, Fallon, my dad. His name was Louis, but they nicknamed him Rip. And Will and Big Boo right here, and—

Mary: This whole neighborhood is just our family. This whole community, everyone's just related to everybody. We're all in close proximity of my mom. Eighteen grandchildren, nine boys, nine girls. When we left, we all left together. We convoyed like nine, ten cars. We convoyed to Abbeville.

Alcedia: How do we, how do we get together again? We're all scattered, and it's how to start building, you know, the foundation. We can't even find a foundation yet with our family.

Were you prepared for this, before you came back? Did you see footage of the devastation here?

Alcedia: No, they hadn't showed us.

Mary: Our brother rode the storm north of here, near the city. We were not prepared for what he told us.

Alcedia: No.

Mary: We could not believe what he told us. We were underwater. He told us everything was underwater. My mom's house, they said they couldn't find it. "Everybody lost," he said. "Everybody lost."

When you were coming into town, did you just immediately break into tears?

Mary: Yes. I thought I could handle it, having heard all the rumors. But when I hit Point a la Hache, that took everything from me. There was nothing there.

Alcedia: Beyond tears . . .

Is this yours?

Mary: Grandson.

Hey, there, what's your name?

Alcedia: Tell him your name, tell the man your name, Corrin.

Corwin, is that right?

Alcedia: Corrin. He's almost two.

Corrin, I'm Josh. This is a tape recorder. How old are you, Corrin?

Corrin: Nine.

Nine? No you're not. You're not even two.

Corrin: Nine.

Corrin, you want to come back and live here?

Alcedia: Corrin, you want to come home? Tell the man with the recorder.

You want to go home?

Corrin: Yep.

Yeah?

Corrin: Yep.

You want to—

Corrin: I fix it.

Alcedia: You want to fix home?

Corrin: Yep.

You want to see? See, it's a little tape that goes around that records. You want to hear yourself? Okay, talk. Say something about your home.

Corrin: Hello.

[tape breaks]

[Corrin laughing]

Mary: It's like death.

Alcedia: The older folks is gonna grieve, I'm gonna tell you that, they gonna grieve.

Corrin: Hello.

Have any of them been back?

Alcedia: One came back and he caught a heart attack. My mom and my aunt, that's too hard for them to come down here. These are houses they built with their own hands. It wasn't something that other people did. And nobody knew about this place. We a little dot.

Mary: Since a day or so after the storm there's been no media coverage of Plaquemines at all. It's frustrating.

Are you going to try to rebuild?

Alcedia: We want to come back.

Mary: I can't vision it. I really can't.

Alcedia: I would like to, but being back with such devastation . . . but I really do want to come back. Home. This is home. This is home. This is—I cannot envision being anywhere else but here. I really can't do it. I've tried to, but . . . You know, we've been in Abbeville for five weeks, and it's a very nice place. Everything is, you know, at your hands, the restaurants, the grocery store, department stores are all there, but we're used to country living. We have one grocery store, we have one pharmacy, and this is what we're used to. We're not used to the fast-paced city and that's a lot of adjusting for us. And it's all just hitting us so, so bad. We're displaced. We're displaced with housing. We're displaced in ourselves. We don't know how to function right now. We're just living a day at a time. We just waking up in the morning, and opening our eyes and starting wherever we gotta start.

I guess what it was, we became so complacent, you know, that we weren't focusing on the outside. We had our own world here. We weren't focused on New Orleans, we weren't focused on other people, we were just focused on our little town, Diamond. I worked at the high school; I was the secretary there. Our high school's gone. My grandkids have to go somewhere else to school.

I just can't see—it's gonna be years, I can't see the—You hear on the news and the president and our senators and all, you know, yeah, they're saying we're gonna rebuild, we're gonna rebuild, but you know, I don't think reality really hit them.

Mary: Until they're here, to see.

Alcedia: You have to see. Our heart is here. Our heart is shape and then broken in half, that's the way it feels.

Mary: I don't think I'm gonna come back. I can't. This is my last time, my last trip. This is it for me. I saw enough. I don't need to see anymore. I praise the one that can see it happen, but me, I cannot see it. If you'd like, I'd like you to see my house.

I would like that.

Mary: We can take a walk if you want.

You haven't been back there yet?

Alcedia: No. We haven't been back there. We been sitting here, trying to get us something to hold to.

They rise, Corrin in Mary's arms, his legs straddling her hip, his eyes watching my tape recorder. They walk with their heads turned to the sky, as though the land is too much to bear. They tell me this used to be a pecan orchard right here, that they own all the land between the river levee where we stopped and the marsh half a mile ahead of us, that it has been in their family for almost a century.

Corrin reaches out for my tape recorder again. He wants to hear himself. I stub my toe. A Bible. It's heavy as brick, the open pages crusted with sediment. "My mama's Bible," says Mary. I try to turn the page but it tears off in my hand, exposing a few verses from *Ecclesiastes I* on the clean white page underneath it.

4 *Generations come and generations go, but the earth remains forever.*

5 *The sun rises and the sun sets, and hurries back to where it rises.*

6 *The wind blows to the south and turns to the north;*
round and round it goes, ever returning on its course.

7 *All streams flow into the sea, yet the sea is never full.*
To the place the streams come from, there they return again.

8 *All things are wearisome, more than one can say.*
The eye never has enough of seeing, nor the ear its fill of hearing.

⁹ *What has been will be again, what has been done will be done again;*
there is nothing new under the sun.

¹⁰ *Is there anything of which one can say, "Look! This is something new"?*
It was here already, long ago; it was here before our time.

It hits the new earth at my feet with a dull thud.

"My daddy's picture," says Alcedia. "I need to find his picture."

"I can't find my kitchen floor," says Mary's son Claude, the only man there.

"I think I saw one over there," I say. "Over there, that tile floor?"

"No, that's one of my walls," he says.

The only thing higher than me, still standing somewhat, is a single house. It is in one piece, about forty feet from its foundation. Mary stands in front of where the front door used to be. "Here," she says. "This is my home."

It's raised three feet off the ground. The stairs are gone, so I pull what's left of a stove over and Mary and I use it as a step. The roof is still attached, but the ceilings have all caved in and the walls have disappeared, leaving only two-by-fours holding it all together. There are three trees inside the house, branches, leaves, everything torn and caked with sediment. A Bambi doll is caught in the beams below the roof. Kitchen cabinet doors still hang from their hinges, but their contents are gone, replaced with two inches of wet mud. The doors hang open because the cabinets themselves all slope down to the ground. There are no right angles anymore. The floor is covered with thousands of small sticks, matted into each other, rising in humps over Mary's crushed furniture, flowing across the entire living room, down the hallway, into the other rooms like frozen waves. "These sticks, Mary, where did they come from?"

"These are river sticks. Look at the direction they come from. That's where the water come from. This was river water."

"Did the levee break?"

"Levee never broke. It overtopped. Katrina pushed the Gulf of Mexico up into the river, but this longest river in the world wasn't going nowhere so it climbed over the levee and came into my home instead."

Mary climbs across a bureau and a mattress, pulls something out of the sticks. A construction hat. It says BIG DOG in bold black letters around the top. "My husband's," she says. "Now, I need to find my diamond engagement ring." She climbs down the hallway into her bedroom.

"I wanna go home," says Corrin, in her arms.

I walk out the back door, jump down to the ground. The only thing holding up the roof on this side is a single beam thin enough to wrap my hand around, slanting at a thirty-degree angle to the ground.

"Mary, why don't you come out of there?" I say. "You sneeze, this house is going to come down on you."

She comes to the back door, sees the beam I'm talking about, how the whole roof is balancing impossibly on it. She hands Corrin down to me, then jumps out into the sun. "You see, you notice afterwards," she says. "When you look at it, you don't realize the danger. And we was inside of that."

She points to a small tractor lying on its side. "My husband died under that. He was forty-nine. Hydraulics got loose and smothered him. That was in 1998, May 13. After he died, everything, I mean everything, went down. I suppose it makes all this easier for me."

"Is his grave okay? Did you check on him?"

"Yes."

"We're thinking about wherever we move, you know, maybe we'll take his remains," says Alcedia coming around the house now. "Along with our father's."

Days later we will find their family graveyard just past their satsuma grove. The water lifted whole stone tombs out of their encasings in the ground and dropped them at the end of the cemetery. Most of the coffins are missing. There are no bones scattered about the base of a tree as in Lafitte, because the trees themselves are gone, holes in the earth where their roots were.

Mary's son Claude walks over and takes Corrin from me. "This was all family here," he says. "If you come to my gramma's house, and say, 'I want something to eat,' she'll feed you, you know what I'm saying? That's the type of people we was over here in Diamond. Everybody just get along, and you know, to see it all gone, you know . . ."

"I wanna go home," says Corrin.

"And that piano there, it was inside my grandmother's house," says Claude, pointing to the grand piano on the levee. "We had to take the legs off it just to fit it in the door. How it got out like that . . ."

It is the only thing that has not been washed further from the river, but toward it somehow, and it is the only thing whole I've seen since entering lower Plaquemines this morning.

For the next couple of hours we walk around the land separately, searching the ground, pulling up like seashells on a beach the physical things that once made up their lives. It's not hard to imagine these things. Just look around you. Right now. At the things in the space around you.

Then imagine any two of those things—maybe this book and whatever you're sitting on—after they have been underwater for weeks, then buried below a thin layer of ashen dirt 100 feet from each other over a wide open field where your neighborhood used to be. And all those other things that are on you, everything else that you see around you right now, are just gone.

So you pull this book out of the earth and it suddenly becomes a very rare thing. Maybe it reminds you of the light that's falling on it now, or the sounds around you you're not paying attention to, or anything else physical that makes up this time—the floor, your clothes, the things you take for granted, the things you would have forgotten, things that are normal. They are gone, and now you remember them because there is only dirt in their place.

Mary and Alcedia and the others move slowly, silently through the pieces, noticeably keeping their distance from some objects, touching others with hands steady in want to remember, lifting others. The family's skin ranges the colors of the river—coffee, gray like burnt charcoal, some have a hint of red like the clay earth further north, brown rich as swamp bottom, ochre dull as the river's sandbars, milky as its slow-breaking waves. They are now, quite literally, *sediment*: "a material eroded from preexisting rocks that is transported by water, wind, or ice and deposited elsewhere." But their skin is the sediment in the river, where it is alive and roiling, not this ashen residue on their land, that mottles their clothes, that dulls their skin now.

As the sun descends, mosquitoes cover my legs, burn like fire, and my stomach is growling. Alcedia still cannot find any pieces of her house, only the foundation. June, Alcedia's daughter, is the first to start openly weeping. She is crouched beside a roof. It lies like the carcass of some massive creature that gave up, crumpled, collapsed, a few flaps of roofing like skin, otherwise all bone. She is reaching out to it, petting it timidly as though it could still wake, and it's hurting her. Its edges lie on the ground and slope gently up to a tip as tall as me in the center.

Slowly the rest of the family draws in toward her, around the roof, about a football field away from the road, from the foundations. Alcedia ducks down, peers into the rafters. "That's Kalee's bedpost!" she says. "That's his house under there. Oh, my daddy's house. Oh, my God, my daddy's picture is in there."

The ten of them stand around it, silent but for June, staring vacantly into it, some of them holding photos, one a single sandal, one a Spider-man DVD. Corrin wants down. Claude puts him on the ground. He takes a few steps, stumbles, then sits in the dirt beside me, pulls a butterknife out of the ground, and starts banging it soundlessly against the earth.

"My daddy's picture," cries Alcedia. "Where his picture?"

June's whimpers grow longer, fading only for quick breath.

"Mary, is this the house that was up there?" I whisper. "Did those porch steps you were sitting on when I first started talking to you, did those belong to this house?"

"Yes," says Mary. "This was my daddy's house."

"Hello," says Corrin, still beating the ground with the butterknife. He is not understanding why his voice is not coming back out of the tape recorder as it did when I played it back for him earlier.

June puts a foot on one of the beams, finds steadiness there, steps up onto it. She climbs to the next one, and then the next, her hands pulling her along, nothing to wipe her face, until she is straddling the beam along the top of the gable roof like a jungle gym.

"Oh, look at my . . ." says Alcedia, crouched in front of a small hole in the roof. "Oh my, oh god . . . My daddy . . . My house . . . My daddy's house . . ." She squats down and puts her hands on two beams. "My daddy's picture. My daddy's picture . . . Oh, oh, God . . ." She pulls her head and shoulders into the hole.

"Alcie, don't you go in any further," says Mary. "That's not safe. Alcie!"

Mary grabs her waist as it goes into the hole, tries to pull Alcedia out. "Alcie! Don't you go in there!"

Alcedia pushes her hands away, then keeps pulling herself in, saying, "My daddy's picture . . . My daddy's picture . . ."

"Alcedia, please, get out of there," I say. "We'll come back with a chain saw or—Christ." Before I can stop her, her last Reebok disappears inside.

A double-prop Chinook helicopter roars overhead, flying low, carrying a sandbag the size of a car. Its roar mutes June, rocking back and forth, in and out of silhouette between the sun and me, flesh clinging to the skeleton of their daddy's home.

When the helicopter's propellers burn away, the house is moaning. It is Alcedia still inside it, like a slow, slow, slow children's bawl. And then, the others, all but Mary and Corrin and the man, reach out to the roof. I suppose their cries might have been faster, more explosive when they first drove in this morning, when they'd first taken it in. Then the lull for the last few hours. Now, they are giving it out, feeling it slip from them, high-pitched cries falling away into long, low moaning, groaning slower and slower, until maybe somehow they could wear it out. Corrin looks around at his family, bewildered, then says, "Hello!" He pushes at the buttons of the tape recorder in my hand. "Hello!"

"Corrin, look, it's you," says Mary. She has pulled a small framed picture out of the ground. The glass is missing. Iridescent stains ring the crumpled photograph in waves, like someone tossed a rock into an oil slick. A newborn's eye and nose lie beneath the stains, nestled into the curve of a man's arm, hardly anything human.

Corrin throws the butterknife, takes the photo, hands it to me, again tries to push the tape recorder's buttons. He is not smiling anymore, only frustrated that his voice is not echoing out of the recorder. "Hello!"

"Corrin, do you understand that this is you?" I whisper. He stares at the photo in my hand for a moment before reaching again for the tape recorder. "This picture is very important, Corrin." I hand it back to him. He starts scooping dirt with it. Mary is still the only one silent. "Mary, what's Alcedia looking for? I worry about her in there. There's not exactly any medical services around here if she gets hurt."

I stick my head between a couple of beams in the roof. "Alcedia?" I put my recorder down, kneel on the ground, push my shoulder under a beam into the house. "Alcedia? Please, you need to get out of there." I crawl into the thing on my belly, through the same hole Alcedia went into. June is rocking herself back and forth, moaning through the sun above me. Everything feels broken and dirty. "Alcedia?"

There is only the soft, dying wailing in the darkness all around me like coming into the consciousness of pain, not awake enough for vocalization, for screaming and crying, not for anything but moaning with your heart, your innards. This is not a cognitive response to what they see before them. It is simply what they see.

"Alcedia?" Everywhere I put my hands is sharp.

"Oh, my daddy's picture . . ." she whimpers. It's hard to hear her within the others' cries, hard to see her within the dark, sun casting blinding slants across it all. "My daddy's picture . . ."

"Alcedia?!"

"What? Who's that? What you want?"

"I want you to please for God's sake stop talking about that picture and get out of here right now."

"It was my picture. I kept it in his house after he passed last year." She's out of reach, somewhere ahead. "Oh, God. Where my daddy's picture?"

"Okay, you're never going to find it in here. You need to get out of here, now."

"Oh, God, his picture. My daddy's picture."

"We need get someone down here with a chainsaw, open it up, get some light in here."

"His picture . . ."

I grab the dark where I think she is. "Alcedia, are you hungry? We got some Cheetos in the truck."

Nothing. A smell smacks me in the face.

"Alcedia . . . did any of your family stay here? Did anyone try to make it through the storm?"

Her whimpers stop all of a sudden.

"Alcedia? Goddammit. Alcedia!"

June stops too, rocking silently above me now.

"Alcedia," I whisper with all the rage and volume whisper can carry, my hand over my nose. The helicopter is coming back now, shivering the slats of sun that fall through the roof. Its shadow pulls everything into darkness for an instant. I turn over. June is gone.

The helicopter's roar fades. Silence returns. From what I can tell, I'm in the middle of the house now. I feel hardened cushions, wood, more glass. I crawl to the nearest hole, barely manage to poke my head through a flap of roofing. There's Alcedia holding a large picture out with both hands, light from it shooting her entire body. Her face is scratched, her arms bleeding, river sticks in her hair. She looks down at me. "Oh, God, isn't it wonderful?" she says.

I pull my head back inside and start punching the roofing, opening it up, until I can squeeze my shoulders through. The others are walking away, back toward their cars, Ride keeping pace behind them, filming. "Oh, Lord, I got it," says Alcedia. "I found my daddy's picture."

"Will you help me out of here, please?" I ask.

She keeps hugging the picture to her chest with bleeding palms. "Oh, my daddy's picture . . ." It is almost half as long as her. An electric plug dangles from it onto the ground beside me. I'm still lying there with only my head and arms out when she holds the picture out.

That's the picture?" I ask.

"Yes," she says.

"That's not your father."

I pull my ribs, then hips through, finally get my ankles out and fall to the ground at her feet. My legs are covered in blood and mosquitoes.

Light from the setting sun's reflection flies over my face as she holds the picture above me. It is Manhattan's skyline at night, the Twin Towers highlighted with a gaudy pink glow. The sky portion is a mirror. It seems impossibly clean, doesn't share a bit of the dirt we have on us.

"It's in good condition still," she says. "And it lights up. See all the tiny dots around the buildings, they lights. You have to plug it in. That's my daddy's picture. He went to New York and brought this back for me. I treasure this, because I felt so sorry for them."

I stand, try to brush myself off, look into it, myself and the marsh behind me framed in the mirrored sky above New York, her family tiny in the distance over her shoulder, shut inside their cars to keep the mosquitoes off them. "Sorry for them?" I ask. "What about you? Your family?"

"Your life is, oh God . . . Even though we lost it all, we have our lives, our family. They didn't know it was the last. New York had lives. They lives is gone. We had a chance to get out. New York is more devastating to us."

The path of her belongings, which wound away from the river to where we are now, has stopped somewhere behind her. There is nothing more but sediment.

"You think there's someone in New York with a picture of Diamond?" I ask.

"Yes, I think so. And I think they relate what we going through." She turns the picture back toward her, looks into it. "But that's what I saved from my home," she says. "New York City."

After I help her put the picture into her otherwise empty trunk, Ride and I stand beside their cars for a while in the silence. Ash-white land holds its line against an amethyst sky. If you painted it no one would believe it. But we all know how the sky changes so quickly and harmlessly. Down here, change comes harder. Here, there was no chance for men like Eric Colopy to save a thousand neighbors. There was no one to save. The river itself fell upon this land.

"We're over in Belle Chasse now, we're not that far," says Alcedia. "You got our number. Y'all come over and meet the rest of the family and we'll have a dinner."

"Y'all do that," says Mary.

"Y'all come by," says Claude.

"I will never forget y'all," says Alcedia, as they're driving off. There is a breeze, the first chill since last March. Today was the first day I'd forgotten about the air, the heat, and Ride says it before I can.

"I just remembered," he says, "today's the first day of fall."

52

Her robes flow around her in waves, pooling down into the sediment on the floor, her raised wings arcing into a shelter over her head. And in her hand, a rose, its dusty red a tiny wrinkled heart to the place, the only color, trembling. The whole house is trembling. I look out the front door, straight down the yellow center lines of Highway 23. A convoy of army trucks is tearing down the middle of the highway at me. The noise is tremendous. Just when I think they're going to drive straight into the front door, the first one swerves off the road, swings around the house, then back into the highway, zooming off in the kitchen window. The others follow. There are about twenty soldiers sitting in the bed of each truck. Their roar fades and the dust settles over the road, through the house, me, the porcelain angel, her rose. The red disappears, at last fits in with everything else.

I jump out of the front door, down into 23, the only road through Plaquemines Parish. We get back in the truck, keep chasing the helicopters carrying sandbags. We don our construction hats, drive underneath a bridge in Empire, through construction cones, find a dirt road that takes us to the marsh, unlatch a gate there and drive onto the levee. There's cows grazing along the landside bottom of the levee. There's huge shrimp boats upside down all along it, some half sunken in the marsh to our left, a couple of computer monitors, a golden casket. A flock of egrets flies by. It's the kind of day that would be chilly in the shadows, but perfect in the sun. Only there are no shadows left here, nothing to make them.

We get up to the levee breach, one of several on the marsh side of these towns. Water came in from both sides, river and marsh, for Katrina, and then again through the marsh for Rita. A single army soldier in a green T-shirt and cargo pants stands there alone. We get out of the car wearing our construction hats and ID tags. He asks if we're here to fire him.

He explains that it breached just this morning. There's supposedly a Shell pipeline below this, the water is black, and he says it has killed a lot of fish and seagulls already. The bags are three thousand pounds apiece, all sand. Each round trip takes a helicopter about twenty-five minutes and they can only take one sandbag, two at most, at a time. And they don't always drop them in the right place. It's frustrating, he says. So far, about a dozen poke out of the water at the base of the levee where it caved into a broken wall of mud. The water flowing through has been reduced now to a stream.

A helicopter approaches, its load dangling about fifty feet below it, wrapped in a large white tarp, about the size of a car. The soldier rushes down the steep slope of the levee, jumps onto one of the sandbags in the water, and raises his arms straight overhead. The helicopter circles directly over us. Our helmets go flying. The soldier crosses his wrists over his head and the helicopter releases the bag from the cable and it falls in front of him. It seems to make no difference in the water flowing around it.

We drive back through Empire, where I had heard the storm was about to make landfall a couple of minutes before New Orleans lost power. Spray paint on a hardware store says, ~~Betsy~~ ~~Camille~~ ~~Katrina~~ ~~Rita~~ WE WILL BE BACK. Three of those could indeed properly be crossed out.

We find a man standing beside a boat on the side of the road, clip-board in hand. He says he works for the largest boat insurance company in the country. He's followed hurricanes for the last twenty years, but never seen anything like Plaquemines today. "The boats, they're everywhere, it's like they were just dropped from the sky," he says. "Forty percent of the boats claimed haven't been found. They just vanished."

We pass a barbecue on the side of the road. About a dozen men holding cans of Budweiser cheer as we roll by. "Whatcha gonna do?!" yells one. A barge, about two hundred feet long, and twenty-one feet tall, is sitting on top of the river levee, a shrimp boat from Venice crushed underneath its red belly, its stern sticking up into the air above us. A sign leaning up against it says, SLOW. SCHOOL AHEAD.

Landfall was actually just south, in Buras, where the only thing still in its place is Buras High School, shattered glass doors, ceilings hanging, wires, cords like tentacles wrapped around books and balls overhead, open lockers, an Algebra II textbook heavy as stone, solid with sediment and water that poured in from windows twenty feet up above the gymnasium bleachers. My footprints are the first into the mud on the second floor, into the library, paper everywhere, but every book still in its place, stepping around the broken glass peeking out of the floor, light slanting over it through shattered windows, sun paling into autumn, the clock on the wall ticking. 5:10. *Leatherneck* magazine, a whole booth, still upright, full of Marine pamphlets, Army, National Guard.

I find another set of stairs. Again, my footprints are the first, this time tracking dirt on clean carpet. I come into the band room. All by itself up here, a little third-floor room, white music sheets and shining trophies scattered in sunlight, a breeze through broken windows. But clean. This was only wind. One can pick up the pieces, put them back where they belong. I hit a bass drum with my open palm, leave a handprint of mud there.

The high school is built like my apartment building, a large, low, thick, brick fortress, and this room is about the same height as my own. I can see down into the river, as I can from my living room, then across the river to the wilderness on the other side of it. There are no towns on the other side of the river, just swamp and forest until the delta. I am told deer were overly abundant there, and that they are all gone now, like the rabbits in Lafitte. Natural instincts were no match for water. The humans here were the ones that survived. How opposite from the stories we heard after the south Asian tsunami on December 26, 2004, how the animals, cows, dogs, cats, everything went dashing up into the hills before the water came, while the humans walked out into the low tide. Here, the animals had no high ground. And these people knew to get out of the way. They had warning. Only three people were reported to have died in Plaquemines.

But those back in the 9th Ward, who stayed because they didn't know the storm was coming, because they were so out of touch with the water around them, above them on all sides, that they never learned to swim, never sat on the levee just feet from their doors, never watched the sun set behind the skyline and rise over the riverbend. They are the ones that tell me they will not come back. While the ones down here in Plaquemines lost every physical root of their family and yet remain tied to these waters and this untenable sliver of land. Nature let the river into Plaquemines. Man let water into the 9th Ward. Nature is forgiven. Man, in this case, only forgotten.

53

I stop checking e-mail and taking phone calls altogether. Day after day, we push the truck through the shrinking puddles of Plaquemines until there is no water but where it should be. We cannot find another resident. On our fifth day we finally make it to the last town in Louisiana, Venice, two and a half hours south of the city. The Curl Up and Dye hair salon has fallen on top of a house beside another house caught in a shrimp net. There are rusted and shattered bar coolers sitting alongside the highway outside Deuces Wild, a bar and dance hall I found on my first trip here years ago.

I spent that afternoon listening to hungover shrimpers, who'd come down to help rebuild after Hurricane Camille in '69 and stayed, complaining about NAFTA and describing the difference between the North and South Vietnamese who settled here. They explained the ecology of their waters by giving me the order of what would eat my decapitated head " . . . and finally, when you decompose to your natural elements, then shrimp'll eat what's left. Shrimps are the maggots of the sea."

We take a right at the last gas station in Venice, the end of Highway 23. The nameless road is cracked as if from millions of little earthquakes and lined with massive overturned shrimp boats, a red helicopter on its side, boatyards and refineries, until they thin out, and we're left only with cypress trees in the marsh to either side of us. And then Louisiana comes to an end.

We get out, walk to the edge of the dock. For the first time since August 29, there is not the slightest sting of sediment or rank water. It smells like it should. Like nothing for us. Like the world used to.

I pee off the dock as little fish jump through day's copper end. Though it sounds silly, they seem happy. The already rusting wreckage of boats spots the otherwise pristine marsh. The lower half of the cypress trees around me are still reddish brown, scarred from the flood, but the upper halves are raging green. They look like something off the cover of a travel guide. There's a road sign face down beside me in the dirt. I flip it over with my foot. DEAD END. The dead end of Louisiana, so alive. The sign seems irrevocably scratched, its pole twisted. We throw it in back of the truck. And we make our way up from the bottom of the Mississippi.

The sun sets as we drive through Diamond an hour later. There is a woman sitting on those same concrete steps where we found Alcedia and Mary five days ago, holding a small green street sign still attached to its metal pole: BARTHOLEME LANE.

"It's our family land," she explains. "Rip was my uncle. This is my second trip here. The first time I had to go back because I made a mistake, I took my grandchildren with me. My granddaughter was in my truck screaming because she saw my home. She could not believe what she saw."

She is living in a trailer in Baker, Louisiana. She is down here with her son, Little Joseph, who I see now is shifting through the debris behind her. "He's the one just had a baby," she says. "They evacuated to Lake Charles for the storm. She had the baby on the twenty-first of September, and the second they had the baby they had to be evacuated from there for Rita. But we have something to go on now. That granddaughter. And as of this November, I'm a great-great-grandmother. We gonna pick it up from there. I wanna see them raised up. I wanna be able to tell them, because one of them was just two months old when we had to leave from here. So, there's a lot of things we have to tell them."

"Is there any chance they're going to grow up here?"

"Oh yes, we're coming back home, we're coming back home, we're coming back home. This is home, we're coming back home. We're going to rebuild. We're gonna come back down. We're going to start over again."

When she and Little Joseph get back in their car and leave, Ride and I walk across the street, past the piano, just as we did five days earlier. But now, as we crest the river levee, noises come from the batture of broken trees between levee and river. They lift into the cobalt twilight in three tiers. First there are the frogs, what must be hundreds of them, heavy, belching. Beneath that a cicada cries and cries and cries until another joins it and another and another and they stumble into a shrill rhythm. And, below it all, holding these sounds and the twilight itself up, are the other insects, I will probably never know what they are, millions blending into a pulsing hum, rising and falling as imperceptibly as the susurrus of an occupied city.

I like to look up at the sky, especially now. There it is, always itself, always different, always recognizable, always beautiful. Evening blooms a billion billion exploding suns, such pinpricks for us we think there's some order to it all, constellations untouched by man unlike nature on earth, which always has the last say.

With every step the sounds, those three tiers, rise and fall in relation to one another, ease into new tones and rhythms. There is the piano below us, still at the base of the levee. Its fallboard is up, as I left it. I stand in front of it, reach my forefinger lazily down, put a stop to all these sounds.

They do not return before we get into the truck. On the way home we're listening to Clutch, the stereo screaming, *You would cry, you would scream if you knew half the things I've seen!* and I think of the things I've seen whole in Plaquemines Parish: an angel, a barge, a piano, and a band room. An owl, white belly, swoops out of the black down at the truck, across the windshield, missing us by inches. There are two fires along the levee, what's left of homes burning, we have no idea why. There are no other vehicles anywhere around, no other people. Ten minutes later two fire trucks pass us, roaring back down into the parish. Then a couple more. Then several more. We swing the truck around, chase them south. "We've become grave robbers and ambulance chasers," says Ride.

We follow them for twenty minutes, long past the fires, until a cop car pulls us over. He simply rolls his window down, pulls alongside. "There's a curfew! Get your ass outta here! Now! Now!!!"

We drive back to the high school. The flashlight guides us up to the third floor band room. I stick my head out of a broken window, back into rhythms pulsing from the dark earth while it glows with the distant fires along the levee and fire trucks' flashing lights and refineries twinkling and ships' lights sliding by us on their way into the Gulf toward Russia and Hong Kong and Amsterdam and anywhere else. I beat that same bass drum as yesterday, beat steady until my dried mud handprint crumbles off, over and over and over again until it is like breathing, heart beating, clock ticking, until I still hear it as we cruise over the Crescent City Connection bridge an hour and a half later, into our city blushing with light, where we can no longer be alone. Carnival Cruise ships line the banks, lit with tiny rooms being rented to police officers. Another place between our new horizons, northern and southern, Biloxi and Buras.

54

"So, you two, you go out to these edges of God's green Earth and just walk right up to these people and do interviews?" asks the Professor.

"Sure."

"Have you ever looked in the mirror at yourselves together?" he asks.

Ride and I shrug our shoulders as best we can while we're holding the Professor's armoire as he stands there in the entrance to his pod, blocking us from getting out. He holds his pipe in one hand, a sledgehammer in the other, wearing gardening gloves, his tweed elbow-patched jacket, paisley bow tie, safety goggles, and a surgical mask placed cockeyed and puny over that beard of his which has only grown wilder in the last two months while he was gone and is now speckled with molded paint particles. He plunges the pipe back into the side of his mask.

"Here's these people trying to come to terms with the fact that everything that was once familiar to them is now alien, and, all of a sudden, through their wreckage comes striding these two six-foot two-inch dudes, one wearing khaki shorts and flip-flops with albino hair shooting up all over the place like Flock of Seagulls and the other a long-hair Cheyenne biker with holes in his ears and spikes coming out of his eyebrows, charging at them with a tape recorder and a video camera? Dear God."

"Get out of the way, please?" I ask.

Ride and I carry the armoire out of the pod. The floodline on the Professor's house, like the others on his street, is up to my chest, though it's only about two feet above his raised porch. His neighbor walks out her front door carrying a large wooden sculpture of a black man wearing a loincloth, playing a bongo with a cigar in his mouth. She dumps it on top of a dirt-crusted flat-screen television. Outside her home, like all the others on this block, is a pile of debris as large as a couple SUVs. Where the Professor's pile should be is his pod—essentially the whole back of a truck—white and red and shiny, half unloaded already.

"Really wets your spleen, doesn't it boys? Seeing this? Wets it right up," he says, then tosses his Heineken bottle into his neighbor's pile. "So, what the hell good did staying do? What'd it teach you?"

"That warm Heineken isn't so bad after all," I say, carrying the bottom of the armoire up the stairs. We ease past Parker Junior, who's tearing insulation out of the hallway wall. Ride and I aren't wearing masks and the place stops burning with bleach only when we get upstairs. I'm not wearing the bandage anymore, yet still, every time I twist my left wrist, pain shoots my skull. "In the bedroom!" the Professor calls from outside.

When we get back downstairs he's telling Parker Junior he has to get running. "I'd love to help you sods destroy my house, but, you see, I need to get to a meeting. Seems they've got me on some sort of board to rebuild New Orleans or something like that," he says, handing me his sledgehammer which he has yet to use. "These rebuilding plans are multiplying faster than anyone can make sense of them. You know, the mayor's proposing we open the city up to gambling, let the casinos come in." My bent wrist flares with pain and I drop the sledgehammer on my foot. I hop up and down for a bit while the Professor tosses his gloves and mask into his Geo Metro, dusts his tweed jacket off, and wipes the paint particles around his beard so they look like snow, says, "You can leave the tools on the back porch once you get rid of the insulation downstairs and get all these boxes upstairs."

My phone rings as he drives off, weaving around piles of debris. It's a friend from New York. She wants to set up a benefit reading for KARES, wants me to come up in two weeks, stay with her on Long Island. "I think you need to get out of there," she says.

I tell her I'll think about it. Ride walks upstairs with another box.

"So, what do you call it?" she asks. "Is there a name yet?"

"Call what?"

"You know how like after the planes brought the Twin Towers down here it was a while before the event collectively became known as 9/11. What will you call this?"

I can only hear sledgehammers hitting concrete, further away, closer to the 17th Street Canal levee breach. "I think it already had a name before we'd even heard of it," I say. "Katrina." And I imagine flying toward Newark Airport, coming out of the clouds over the hills of New Jersey, green grass and turning leaves, the light and life of Manhattan, then Long Island, villages which would not burn my nostrils, my lungs, gut, the windows little squares of copper light at night, something I might like to see. "Okay," I say. "I'll see about flights tomorrow."

I call my mother in D.C., ask if she'll be around in two weeks, I could take the train down from New York and see her. Turns out she'll be in Las Vegas with my stepfather, who has work there the whole week before and that weekend too. I hang up, sit on the curb with my warm Heineken.

The longer I listen, the more of them I can hear inside their homes, clanging and prying and chipping away.

We heard none of this yesterday at this time. We were in Plaquemines, on the way to Venice. Unlike homes, you can't rebuild communities by clanging and prying and chipping away. By the time I lost power at 6:37 A.M., August 29, Katherine still sleeping in my bed, twenty-one feet of water had already erased most tangible evidence of Alcedia and Mary's existence. Two hours later, a twenty-eight-foot storm surge moved shattered casinos across the highway on the Mississippi Gulf Coast, and anything older was swept away. The surge went up to six miles inland, pushing Bumm Steer's jeep into his kitchen, flattening Jimmy James' house and cracking open his bathtub as it went through his wall. At 9:45 A.M., about the time Katherine woke up, the storm made its last landfall near Eden Isle on the state border.

These were expected consequences. Ocean storm surge, like wind, is inevitable with hurricanes. Gulf Coast towns always have and always will face potential obliteration every storm season. "Mother Nature," as Popcorn Junior called it. New Orleans, however, is not a coastal town. Its destruction, this destruction here in Lakeview, like most of the rest of Louisiana, including Lafitte, is the fault of man. It happened for two reasons. The first was that many levees were not built and maintained properly to withstand even the Category 3 storm they were supposed to. But more importantly, it happened because the hurricane plowed through the warm waters of the Gulf, feeding on them, where once there had been land that killed hurricanes. Man is destroying the wetlands that once buffered Louisiana. Mississippi suffered the storm's violence, while Louisiana suffered man's negligence, and therein lies the greater tragedy.

I had never even heard of the Mississippi River Gulf Outlet before the storm. Now I know they call it MR. GO. I notice its thin line on maps, flanking the towns of St. Bernard Parish to the Northeast, providing a seldom-used shortcut between the Intercoastal Waterway and the Gulf.

By five that morning, storm surge from the Gulf had pushed enough water over weakened wetlands, into the MR. GO, that its levee burst in places where it was no longer buffered by wetlands. As a result St. Bernard Parish flooded. Meanwhile, the Intercoastal Waterway levee also overtopped and breached, for the same reason, flooding New Orleans East. Then the two waterways converged, funneling water into the Industrial Canal, as though someone had designed them as the optimal way to get floodwater as quickly as possible into New Orleans.

By 7:30 A.M. a small section of the Industrial Canal's western wall gave way, flooding part of the Upper 9th Ward, where T-Nasty lived, drowning the kid who mowed his lawn and others, and water came down to St. Claude Avenue across the street from Robért's supermarket. About fifteen minutes later, a larger section of the eastern wall burst and water poured into the Lower 9th Ward—just as I watched it do during Rita—into Curtis and Cassandra's home, leaving whole only a television wedged between the kitchen door and the ceiling, forcing them and countless others onto third-story roofs for three days, and then to Texas for six weeks and maybe forever. This water kept going, through the entire Lower 9th, into St. Bernard Parish, toward the Dog House where it was met by other water from the breached MR. GO. The water covered that parish, made it above Eric Colopy's roof, into the Ducros Museum, up the bookcase, until it stopped at Joseph Conrad's *The Secret Agent.*

Meanwhile, still unabated by dimimished wetlands, the storm also shoved water from the Gulf into Lake Pontchartrain, swelling the lake until a fourteen-foot surge rose beneath Max Smiley on his boat drinking Myer's rum, up to Clayton Borne III's doorstep, over his neighbors, and left Jerry Houston the plumber's sailboat on top of a piling. On the Lake's south shore, water pushed into New Orleans' three drainage canals, until one by one their levees failed in quick succession. The 17th Street Canal was the worst. The water poured through Lakeview from John's, Katherine's schoolmate's, house—his children's photos, his new BMW, everything on the first floor gone—until it made it all the way to the Professor's house here, fourteen blocks away, near the Orleans Street Canal. Then that canal's levee overtopped, and, also parallel to the 17th, both sides of the London Street Canal had been breached by ten-thirty that morning, destroying Mahoney the dog's home. This water from the London Street Canal reached the western wall of the Industrial Canal levee and the circuit was complete. Only the sections along the river, some of Uptown down through the convention center, the Quarter, until the Bywater, remained dry.

There were other, smaller levee failures, too, and most of the levees that breached did so in more than one exact place and at more than one exact time. The lake spread out into the city until September 1, three days after the storm made landfall, three days after the storm surge had receded from the Gulf Coast. That was the day, while the other 80 percent of the city was trying to get *out* of the water, Katherine and I snuck into K.K.'s pool, knowing only what we could see and touch in front of us, holding tight to the river.

It wasn't until three weeks later that all breaches were repaired and most of the water was pumped out of the city and we were able to bike to the lake with Parker Junior. Then, Rita passed us in the Gulf, pushing water into Lafitte, lifting dumpsters and tombs, and reflooding the Lower 9th.

Now, the end of October, the water is all gone, and many are biding their time, waiting to see what the insurance companies, the government, and the weather have in store for them. New Orleans is filling with contractors and residents, numbers and talk. They say things like "Katrina means cleansing," sprouting *ooohs* and *ahhhs* from those listening. Best I could find from my own research, the name comes from a few Greek words: *hekateros*, meaning "each of two"; *aikia*, a word whose symmetrical beauty defies its meaning: "torture"; and yes, the verb *katharizein*, meaning to "purify"—the root of *katharos* or "catharsis." Take from all that what you will.

And too, they say things like "A city is only as resilient as its citizens"; "We are all one after the storm"; "We all suffered."

But the conditions were not the same. I, for example, was not trapped in an attic with my mother's corpse floating beside me. And even those who suffered the same circumstances, dealt with them differently. Regardless of age or sex or race, the storm and the flood drew us apart as much as they ever drew us together.

55

When I get home from the Professor's that afternoon, there's an e-mail from Katherine. Below the words "Call me" are our photos from the Claiborne Bridge immediately after Rita. Below Katherine is the breached levee, the Lower 9th full of sky. Then, there is me, the river in the distance, and between the river and me, all that land, our piece of the city, protected by its levee, sinking three feet a century.

Her clothes are still on my bedroom floor from that last Saturday night, the ones she wore to the Children's Museum fundraiser, the violet, silk, full-length skirt I had curled up in beside my pin-striped pants, which I'd used as a pillow while trying to ignore the phone calls that morning, friends telling me to get the hell out of the city, when I had already held her for the last time with certainty. Beside them, my miniature boom box is still tuned to 1460 AM. How the second that radio went on, we stopped hearing each other.

It has been two weeks since I last spoke to her, that night I left her, and walked the length of St. Charles Avenue, and kept on walking the river in dreams. I do not expect her to answer the phone, but she does. "Hey," she says.

My hand finds the single wooden chair leg I pulled from a satsuma tree the morning after, on our first day in Plaquemines, clutches it, dry and rough.

"Josh?"

"I'm just going to say this. I want to try," I say. "I am going so hard to try, Katherine. I want us to just to be together. Not to do anything, but just be together, maybe sit together, like on my futon, not touching, and just be quiet. I think we could do that. Do you think we can do that? Just be silent, deny the air between us words, listen to the city, and see what we can build from that. Just sit silent together for like fifteen minutes, some time? Maybe even this week? What's so funny?"

"Josh. Oh, God, Josh, I'm in Memphis. They offered me a job. I'm getting a grant to do research until I start teaching in the spring."

The chair leg still holds the colors of that day beneath slivers of varnish.

"Josh."

Black grooves thin as hair split apart striations of ash and white. The white is bone, Nova Scotia sand when the waves broke from it.

"Josh?"

"Sure."

"I was very lucky to get this. They're giving me a very good deal."

"What are you going to do about your apartment?"

"Oh, Josh. I cleaned it out a week ago. I mailed you your things. I have no idea when you'll get them, when mail will start working again, I'm sorry, it was the best way I could think of."

"Thank you."

"I'm in my office now. I can't really talk. I can see the river from here, you know. Not a whole lot of it, just a little piece of it between buildings, through trees. Some leaves are turning colors. I'm looking at it now, the river. Are you looking at it there?"

"What's it like?"

"It's a calmer thing. It just sits there, kind of. The sky's not so broken on it here . . ."

I put the phone down, pull its cord out, pick up the first bundle of mail that came today. They say it will be months before magazines and packages start arriving. For now it is only bills and a thick letter-sized envelope from K.K., my friend who manages the compound. Inside is over a dozen photocopied newspaper clippings, mostly from 1984. "Thought this might interest you," says her note. On the first page there is a man standing in a ditch, holding a half dozen bones out to the camera. The headline reads: CITY'S FIRST GRAVEYARD TO BE BURIED UNDER CONDO.

"Construction of the development was halted briefly in April when construction workers unearthed the remains of black laborers or slaves," it states. They discovered that this cemetery was the city's original burial site. The articles document the brief battle between preservationists and developers, but neither seemed to think it was a big deal, and work soon resumed: "Pilings have already been sunk through caskets, and bones were scattered by the backhoe on the site." Then they give the address. It's the Compound. The condos went up without even excavating the remains. The pool was built over the highest concentration of them.

A photocopy from *New Orleans Architecture,* also in the envelope, states, "For nearly seventy years the St. Peter Street Cemetery served the city. During that time, in 1762, Louisiana passed from the rule of France to Spain, and New Orleans grew from a village to a sizable little city. The year 1788 was one of calamity—the river overflowed, a great fire laid waste four-fifths of the city, followed by a serious epidemic that brought death to many people." And so, to accommodate the overflow of bodies and prevent another outbreak of pestilence, a new cemetery was built further away—St. Louis Cemetery #1, now a popular tourist attraction where voodoo priestess Marie Laveau lies and *Easy Rider* ended, commonly referred to as the city's oldest cemetery.

So, those bottles of Sauvignon Blanc and crates of Guinness rested inches above the centuries-old skulls of our city's lowest class. And so did I, cooling off in the water beneath starry nights, while their descendants, in class and no doubt some in blood, were floating face down in the water beneath the same stars a few blocks away, north of Rampart Street.

I know now we spent that first week skimming the surface of tragedy, just as those families skimmed the surface of the Quarter, along Rampart or Decatur Street, in their exodus to the convention center or the Superdome. Then there were those who never made the exodus, trapped fatally just across the Industrial Canal while we were barbecuing, while

I was holding a lamb chop in one hand, a steak in the other, and Katherine cried for her purse. And those who walked the wrong way when water crept under their door, away from the Quarter instead of toward us. Death, as always, just a breath away from life.

Geography, as ever in New Orleans, was no boundary. The boundaries were social. We could not of course feed and bathe forty thousand people here. But if I had known what waited a few blocks away for those families I saw walking through the Quarter, I would have gladly given them shelter and food and drink and a smile, as we did anyone who joined us, until they could securely evacuate. Instead they walked on by, from flooded homes to being dehydrated and homeless.

The horror that falls through my fingers. The screams a few blocks away you cannot hear. We spend most of our waking hours grasping what is out of reach, on the news, in books, on the phone. Yet it takes an explosion lighting and shaking the night sky to give us a hint of what is happening beside us. But then true fright comes not with explosions and screams and alarms but with their silence, when the things and people around us cannot scream, when even the insects do not call, when we must cry into the night instead.

And when civilization returned to our neighborhood, when the insects sang again, I went to those areas that tragedy did not miss, and groped at their experience, wanting to suffer it.

56

"When it's your time to die, it's gonna be your time to die. I was on a metal fishing boat for Hurricane Camille. We were scared. I don't care where yat, when the storm hits you gonna be scared. *But*, I'm still staying." That was what the man on the four-wheeler told his mayor the day before the storm. We saw it on television. They were in Grand Isle, our barrier island furthest south, typically ground zero for a hurricane coming out of the Gulf at New Orleans. The mayor pleaded with him to evacuate, to no avail.

I call the Grand Isle Town Hall. They know exactly who it was. Riley Lasseigne. And he's still alive and well, living in his raised house, laughing about his fifteen seconds of fame when I finally reach him. Upon realizing he'd be the only person left in town, he rode his four-wheeler into the bed of his Dodge pickup and bolted like the others. I can't help but be a little disappointed. He tells me he drove back into Grand Isle the next afternoon with the mayor and chief of police. There were not even slabs left on the north side of the island, he says. He went to the cemetery to make sure his tomb was still there. It was. "Glad I did leave, because now I'm brave again," he tells me. "If I had stayed and seen that wall of water I might have been too scared to stay here for the next one."

I tell him I don't understand that logic.

"You only could die once," he explains.

I give up, thank him, and say goodbye. Then I try to call Conrad, the 9th Ward man who was wandering Baton Rouge alone with his family right before Rita, pleading with WWL radio to help him find a new shelter because a girl had been raped in the last one. I want to know if he ever got in touch with the good Samaritan who offered to pay for a hotel room. But the line is no longer in use. And neither, still, is his neighborhood.

Yesterday, Ashley broke into her eye doctor's office with some guys from a SWAT team so she could find her contact-lens prescription. Today, she and Ty are on their way to Colorado for some R&R in the ambulance, pushing ninety miles per hour in the left lane watching everyone get out of their way for fifteen hundred miles. Meanwhile, Derek and Petrovski are on their way back down to the city in Ty's Volvo station wagon, to restore a little chaos. T-Nasty is gutting his house. Tayl is trying to get the keys back to BJ's bar for good. And we're getting back to America, as much as we ever were, at least.

It looks like the mule barn turned out okay, even though I forgot to check on it, because they're dragging shouting contractors sloshing cocktails in carriages underneath my balcony, while once again their drivers spout off flawed histories of what went on behind these French and Spanish colonial façades. And I search doorways' shadows for Bartender Bart and Possum. Every day I think I see one of them, from a distance, from my periphery, but it's always the face of some other nameless abandoned ghost that crouches there, meets my gaze like we know each other.

Trash is piled high on every corner. Parker Junior still pulls it into his kitchen and I into my living room. The wood chair I sit in, the wood table I write this on, are all mute witnesses, what remained when the waters subsided. It only takes an hour to clean each piece of furniture, scraping mold, bleaching, polishing. I do it on my balcony, listening for the susurrus of a city which is not there yet.

I haul the Ripley's sign, half the size of me, up the stairs, give it a good scrubbing in my bathtub, then hang it off my balcony. That should give them a reason to look up here for once, if they return. And if they do, they can have it back if they want it, bent and scratched and all.

I put fresh batteries in my matchbook-sized radio and put it back in my closet, where it sat between 9/11 and Katrina, ready for the next. I pick her clothes up off my floor, put them in a bag in the same closet. On my mantel, the cigar box, and inside a piece of a skyscraper's window I once pulled from my foot beside the shell of a dragonfly once emerald, now black, its crystalline body large as my middle finger. The candles from the Compound, about three dozen of them, lie around it, their wax other tombs for other insects. What remains after the rest has turned to smoke, sediment after the water has receded.

I leave the day after tomorrow. When I return, after I've settled into some semblance of routine—bent and scratched like the Ripley's sign—RideofTwoFires and I will continue to drive, to document these places, walk their deserts, for as many years as it takes, to see exactly what will grow from this new American landscape, to record it, and help it. And I will wait until June, the start of the next hurricane season, and the June after, and the one after, and the one after, and after and after and after and on until my grave remains patiently against them.

57

Rubbernecking is a widespread epidemic in New Orleans traffic, and today it takes about half an hour to get through the intersection of West End and Veterans boulevards because everyone's staring at the monolithic pile of debris on the neutral ground there. It is about three stories high and a football field long and wide. It's hard not to be hypnotized by the gore of it, all this viscera that was once people's stuff, from couches to coffee mugs just dumped here. Then, traffic eases and the flood lines along West End rise higher and higher, the 17th Street Canal two blocks to the left, until the road ends at the marina on the lake. This afternoon is the last sailing regatta of the season, the first and only since the storm. A friend invited me out to be part of his crew, a mistake on his part. We come in last.

Sailboats are piled three-deep on the small road to the Southern Yacht Club, so everyone needs to take a water taxi to get to the party after the race. There, I sit on the seawall alone for hours, watching people stand around in their Oakleys and Croakies and Polos and khakis and good tans, cocktails in hand, eating from the expensive buffet or just shoving the free bananas into their mouths as they talk about nothing. The grass is mowed short and raging green and the clubhouse stands tall beside them, a charred black frame of what it was two months ago. On its stone patio, which only suffered a few burn marks, a dozen black and Hispanic servers slice roast beef and spoon vegetables onto white people's plates.

One of the servers comes over, sits on the wall near me, black tie, white shirt, bronze Latino skin, high wide mestizo cheekbones and narrow eyes. He lights a cigarette with fingers that are even tinier than they should be for someone five feet tall. He came to New Orleans just two weeks ago for the first time, he tells me, and thinks he will bring his family soon. Of course, we start talking about the hurricane.

"These deaths, they are little," he says, frowning, waving his fingers toward the city on the other side of the burnt yacht club. "*Muy poquito*, you know? In Guatemala, where I am from, I watch the army put knifes in my mother and then my father and then my brother while I hide under a tree and ants bites my face until I cannot see nothing. So, then I am only to hear them burning when the army make them on fire. It was no problem for the government. It does not take them all this water to do that."

He frowns again, throws his cigarette into the lake, and stands, looking behind me into the same water that funneled into the neighborhoods just below us.

"I read that in the Democratic Republic of Congo, fifteen hundred people lose their lives every day from disease and hunger," I say. "That's about the number they say, so far, we lost here from the flooding. Doesn't make it any better though, you know?"

They're throwing fire in the middle of Frenchman Street. Ghosts and ghouls and goblins clutch cocktail cups and stomp the street to the throbbing thud and thunder of a drum circle. A Humvee tries to push through. A Viking steps onto its front fender, walks onto the hood, jumps up onto the roof and starts shaking his ass. Someone throws him some fire and he eats it. Jazz lifts out of the Spotted Cat, funk out of the Apple Barrel, rock out of DBA, all convulsing together here in the street, clobbering the shouts of the fatigued soldiers under the slightest sliver of moon and fire. The Chiquita banana girl balances a basket of bananas on her head, passes them out with a kiss to a SWAT team. The Viking skips over the soldiers' hands grabbing at his ankles, across the Humvee's canvas roof, jumps into a crowd of walking refrigerators with duct tape and flood lines around them, disappears.

I myself am an escaped convict, but I wanted to be a cow. When I went to the Sexy Beast this evening, my cow costume was no longer in my trunk. In its place was a pair of orange pajamas cut off into shorts, OPP stamped haphazardly across them, standard issue for Orleans Parish Prison inmates. So, that became my costume instead, with a pair of handcuffs dangling from one wrist, while I keep an eye out for an escaped convict in my cow costume. There are other cows, ones I recognize, and, as the evening wears on, other costumes fall away into faces and bodies I know, ones I have not seen since August.

That police officer, the mustachioed one who handcuffed Katherine and me outside my place, is sitting in his car talking to Elena, Mario's cousin, the reason he let us go. I walk up to him, wave hi, try to show off my genuine prison gear, but he tries to drive off soon as he sees me, though siren and lights are lost on the crowd, the only vehicle making ground a topless Bronco with Tayl at the helm. I climb up into the backbench seat and ride with him into the Quarter, to the truck Ride and I rented.

Ten minutes later, I drive alone across the St. Claude Bridge into the Lower 9th, and the world goes dark and dead. I turn the headlights off and idle through the starlit streets until I'm a couple blocks south of Claiborne Avenue, then park between two ruined cars. I wait for the patrol cars to pass twice down Claiborne, then creep to the intersection. There's no National Guard sitting there as there is during the day, telling us we can't enter no matter who we are because they're still doing body recovery.

Another patrol cruises slowly toward me, flashing its lights. I jump over a fence, hide behind a house until it passes. I hold my handcuffs so they don't clank, then wonder why I am still wearing handcuffs, and still dressed like an escaped convict while hiding from the police. When the car's a couple blocks past, I scurry across the intersection, through the barricades into the last piece of the city that is off-limits.

Ghosts I do not know watch from every broken doorway, every shattered window, every hole in the side of a house. I invite them out, offer them my bottle of Jim Beam, and, to the younger ones, I extend my hand, to touch, tug at my shorts, anything to see I'm real. None will show themselves, not in light not sound nor smell nor touch. So, I drink instead, toast the cars in houses, the houses on cars. A couple blocks in, the scenery starts breaking down, things become a little more unrecognizable with every step, I have no idea what is metal, what is wood, plastic, rubber, cement. In another couple blocks it disintegrates into nothing but dead grass between slabs of concrete, no place for ghosts no matter how little. I know how these people will deal with it, the ones who left, even the shadow of all they once had swept from the earth into the pieces of some other darkness. I am told they will be escorted through on buses in a few weeks, not allowed to get out and touch.

I run a hand along the red barge sitting across the street from the levee breach. It's about twice my height, maybe a hundred feet long, thirty wide. It must have sounded like some hell of an explosion when it broke through the levee wall. A small school bus sticks out of the barge's side, its front crushed flat beneath it. Behind the barge is a single, two-story, once-white house that seems to be on its original foundation, the only one I can see in the starlight. Though it cleared everything else on this block, the barge stopped just short of it, must have shielded it from the force of the water. I walk through what would have been the front garden, the things of lives crunching, breaking, sliding beneath my sandals. A painting of dark-skinned Jesus lies on the ground by the front door, tear-filled eyes cast skyward out of his golden halo, asking why. The floor inside is still wet with mud, I try to shrug the smell hanging on me, but it just keeps climbing back on. I take another drink against it, duck down into the room which is shorter than I am, climb over mounds, what must have been furniture. My hands find a rocking chair upright, small enough for a child, then another doorway, a sink, the kitchen. I open a cabinet, dinner plates still perfectly stacked, stick my finger an inch deep into the mud on top of them, wonder if someone was listening for the door last year this time, what kind of candy they gave trick-or-treaters.

A crane sits on the levee itself, a quarter mile of dark-brown dirt where it breached. There's a corrugated metal wall where the concrete levee wall used to be. The Claiborne Bridge looms above the Industrial Canal, its towers, from where Katherine and I watched water pour into the spot I'm standing on, look so thin and old and frail against downtown's lavender sky. Then, over me, this neighborhood, is our last slab of stars over this last dark place. I sit there on the levee, on the new dirt in my OPP shorts, lie back, and peer into Andromeda in the sky, nearly moon-less as it was when electricity returned, as it was when electricity went away and it all began. She is still there, still chained to her rock. The insects are back, making little noises in this space they have their own now.

Next thing I know, two National Guardsmen are telling me that I'm going back to jail. It's not quite dawn yet. I sit up, brush the dirt off my face, look up at them, tell them I can't really do that right now, I have a flight to catch. I show them the handcuffs are fake, it's all a costume. They escort me south along the canal, down a street I never set foot on before last night, and I look at the viscera of this place, the gray of predawn mixing with the gray of what was once a neighborhood to make everything once again like some dim reflection of a dream, and I want so badly to care, to ache, not from the head like we all do, but from the heart. But I just can't, no matter how hard I try, not now.

The National Guardsmen open the barricades on Claiborne Avenue and walk me back to the truck. I toss the Jim Beam in the back seat, take the handcuffs off, and thank them. It's six in the morning, three hours before my flight. I stay on that side of the canal, drive around with the windows down while day rises until I find the house.

The sounds are still there, like two birds chirping at each other, back and forth, back and forth. I walk around the house, the bench sticking out its side through broken century-old clapboards, the sounds gaining weight, seemingly slowing as I get nearer. I push the back door in, walk across the room, around the chair, the table I knocked over last time, and stand before the grandfather clock, as tall and wide as me. I feel its hands, still pointed to ten, its body, an old shell holding a tired creaking heart, the pendulum groaning back and forth, back and forth. I reach inside it, let the cold metal disk fall to my forefinger, where it stops.

EPILOGUE

Colors. The clouds burn off and there are colors. Late afternoon, copper sun, long shadows, low hills, goldenrod and Indian red and ochre and sienna and mauve and still green in dying leaves, the hills of New Jersey, ten minutes from Newark Airport, and another tear burning down my cheek.

She leans over in her violet silk skirt, looks out the window at these same colors that for two months now existed only on Señor Petucci's walls, her eyes trembling depthless as a little water over Nova Scotia, says, "Sure are a lot of swimming pools." She laughs. It is a deep laugh. Her breath is full of whiskey and bacon. I lose the dream, open my eyes, and the man says it again, "Sure looks like they got a lot of swimming pools in New Orleans," his face leaning into mine, staring at me, chins trembling with laughter, wanting an acknowledgment of his joke.

I look out the window. We've just left the airport. We're flying over the suburbs of New Orleans, blue tarps on a good portion of the roofs sparkling in noon sun. "Oh, I get it," I say, "the tarps." His chins stop trembling and he goes back to his USA Today. The headline nearest me reads, "LACK OF FEMA DATA SLOWS RELIEF."

I make very sure I am awake now. It appears so. I pick dirt out of my ear from the Industrial Canal levee where I slept this morning. I barely had time to change, threw jeans on over the Orleans Parish Prison shorts which are giving me a wedgie now. I look back out the window, the river's currents one by one lighting white with sun tearing away from the calmer water, winding into the horizon through flat gray land, the Gulf just barely beyond, out of sight; and the other way, framed in the opposite window, it goes up the country, past Memphis into all those snowflakes on mountain tops that begin it. From here, there is so much land, seemingly so little water. And then clouds.

When we leave the clouds five hours later, I'm on my third leftover banana from the Chiquita girl last night, and the man beside me is on his fifth Dewar's and water, every twenty minutes or so pretending it's someone else who just passed gas. I realize he's still talking at me. He's bringing me up to date right now on what he's been doing the last couple months, how the storm affected him up in northern Louisiana, and some of the stories he's heard from people in New Orleans and I cannot believe he's been going on all this time. Who on Earth does he think he is that someone would want to hear about him for five hours? I nod my head again as contours of the naked Earth splay open below us. A hundred crests descend in soft ridges to the floor of the desert, like cloth draped over the backbones and ribs of sleeping animals. And then, without warning, a city emerges. The highest casino resorts sparkle clear above it all and it makes me want to hop on the first return flight. But I don't. I walk down to the Budget rental car desk, stand in the long line, and call my mother, who thinks I'm still in New Orleans.

"Listen, Mom, what hotel are you staying at in Vegas? . . . No, I know you're not in Vegas yet. But you'll be here in three days, right? . . . No, I just wanted to know, in case I need to reach you. I hope y'all have fun. I might not have my phone on for a few days. . . . Yeah. . . . I'll be in New York in a week, sorry I'll miss you when I'm there. . . . Okay. Okay, me too."

At the rental car counter, the woman asks for my credit card and driver's license. She starts jamming numbers into her computer, then stops abruptly. "Oh," she says, looking at my license. "So, how is it?"

"It is," I say.

"Have you been back there yet?" Her lips curl into a small smile while her eyes arch downward like she might cry.

"Any chance you could upgrade me to a convertible?" I ask her. "I'd really love one, but the last couple months have been kind of tough, you know, financially."

Outside, the sun is brittle, the shadows too cool, and nothing looks old or used, not the slightest piece of this city. I put the Sebring's top down and try three different ways to get out of town, but I just keep winding back to the Strip. I'm at a light on the corner of Flamingo and Las Vegas Boulevard, looking at my map, when I realize there are about a hundred people standing on the sidewalk beside me, looking over a low fence at what appears to be a big pond in front of the Bellagio Hotel.

I recognize these people. They are the ones who once walked by Ripley's across the street from my apartment, the ones who once stumbled down Bourbon Street at night after another day in the convention center, some still wearing their lanyards, poking their heads into Déjà Vu, daring each other to go in. And then I hear it, beneath all their sounds, beneath the traffic—the breath of a city. Until all of a sudden a fountain stabs a hundred feet into the sky from the middle of the Bellagio's pond. The cameras come out as a hundred other strings of water arc out of the pond around the first, continuous jets of water swaying back and forth, perfectly identical in flawless symmetry. I drive through the red light, but it doesn't stop the acidic taste, like pennies, on the sides of my tongue.

When I break out of the city, when the buildings end entirely, the wind chills, and I'm tempted to pull over and put on a sweatshirt but I don't want to stop. An hour later, I turn onto Highway 93 and billboards and other cars disappear. Mountains and plateaus rise in the distance, bringing into sharp relief the emptiness of the land spreading impossibly vast before them. I've always thought that if Earth is a god, the American desert is where it might lay quietly with the other gods. Horizontal lines run through the mountains, lavender, white, ash, black, and every shade of brown, something familiar. I turn onto a road not on the map, trying to make the fences disappear, something nearly impossible in America now. The pavement ends half a mile later. Three more turns I'll never remember, and forty-seven miles later, I beat the fences too. Ten minutes further I cannot imagine a man having a larger visible space to his own. I stop and start walking through the low bushes, mostly just brittle balls of brown sticks, searching the ground for the human details, until I am content that there are none here. I walk until I can't see the car anymore, until it is my own strange planet.

Sun spills between two mountain ridges over me. It is winter sun, thin-skinned and light sweet as satsuma. The mountain's blue shadow is turning purple. I am tired. So tired I almost step on it.

A little speck of pink, almost flourescent. Damn. A piece of candy? Paper? Plastic? A bead? I'll have to keep driving now. I reach down to pick it up but it doesn't want to come out of the ground. I kneel down and put my face up to it. A flower, tiny as a drop of water.

I lie down on my side next to the flower, below the whisper of the wind, smile. My ears invent hollow sound again within the silence, stillness. Vega, faint, is already showing. Earth tilts me away from the sun until it hits the mountain, pulling cold violet shade over me. I curl my knees into my chest, push my fingers—fingernails still lined with new dirt from the 9th Ward levee—into the dry, hard ground. I push my entire hand in, palm up beneath the flower, then lift that handful of land out of the ground, still warm from day in my palm, the coming night cold on the back of my hand, until something hot runs through it.

My knuckle is bleeding, the blood a single line rolling down my fore-arm now. I reach my other hand into the hole and feel. A cold shard. Glass. It too does not want to come out of the ground. I work my finger into the bottle, pull it out by its broken neck, blow it off. It is full of dirt, a half pint, glass the color of honey, almost a quarter-inch thick. The only mark on it is raised lettering across the top of its body: FEDERAL LAW FORBIDS SALE OR RE-USE OF THIS BOTTLE. It was made from a two piece mold with bulging joint lines that end just below the broken lip. It was here already, long ago; it was here before our time. I tip it upside down, let earth pour from it as the earth in my other hand cools beneath the lit-tle pink flower on its top.

ACKNOWLEDGMENTS

I'm deeply grateful to my editor at Free Press, Amber Qureshi, for being there anytime, for anything; for her own love of this place; and for her tireless, not-a-second-to-spare effort at helping me take much needed scissors to the text. The only thing better than Amber I could possibly imagine would have been more time itself—"always the best editor" as my dear friend and mentor Lee Grue puts it—which might have granted us the distance to further hone what I agonizingly think of as a rough draft.

My agent, Anna Stein, who too was always there to lead me by the hand, with editing, encouragement, direction, and some big balls when they were needed.

All those who helped me get the historical and scientific details right (big shout to Mark Fernandez at Loyola University and Mark Davis at the Coalition to Restore Coastal Louisiana).

Stafford Scott for understanding, for letting me spend so many days and nights in another world, far away from her.

My mother for staying calm, trusting and believing in me through it all.

Those whose names lie on these pages. And to all those others who were here with us, and who shared their words with me, but do not appear on these pages. I will never forget you.

Lastly, to brother Ride for tireless help and heart every step of the way.

This is not a book I ever wanted to have to write. Not one I can take great pleasure in, despite the fun we sometimes had, the fragile smiles on our faces, in my words. And this is a book we can avoid ever having to write again. I only hope we will. Please read the Afterword to learn how.

AFTERWORD

"I got the Gulf a Mexico in my backyard and holes in the heavens over my trampoline," said Loon.

He'd just whupped me at pool for the seventh time. I didn't need to drive all the way to Lafitte, a half hour south of New Orleans, for this. I said the whole damn state of Louisiana was on the Gulf if you looked at it that way. He said no. "Not swamp. The Gulf. C'mon, show you."

We were down at Fuzzy's Bar, and Peggy Sue was working that night. This had nothing to do with any storm. This was five years before Katrina, five years before Peggy Sue would stare into those bones of once-impenetrable swamp, and tell me, "I was born here and I got my feet in this sloppy mud, and they ain't gonna go nowhere. Nothin like Lafitte mud."

Loon bought a twelve-pack of Milwaukee's Best from her and we started walking. The sun had long set, the air and water and sky were deepest blue, all the land violently green. I followed him for what seemed like miles, until all that was left of the visible universe was a mess of stars, among frogs and cicadas and grasshoppers and crickets and an owl or two and creatures I did not know but needed to hear. By the time I asked myself what the hell I was doing, following a man named Loon—I'd never seen that variety of bird anywhere in Louisiana—just to have him point to some puddle in the swamp and pretend it's the Gulf, we'd gone so far that I had no idea how to get back.

The road ended, and I tried to follow his footsteps, muted now upon that Lafitte mud. Eventually, we crossed a drawbridge, one at a time, over some black formless pit, wound through some more cypress until I saw lights and then his house, half clapboard and half trailer. How the hell he got a trailer there I had no idea.

Three of his daughters were in the sky. "See, told you—holes in the heavens," said Loon. They seemed to fight their fall back to Earth, back to the trampoline, the biggest one I'd ever seen, bigger than the trailer even. Then all three would bounce back up, arms raised, poking holes in the star-clouded blue-black sheet of night over them. Lime-green Spanish moss hung from gnarled oaks, tickled the edges of the trampoline-like curtains sheltering the yard and house from the surrounding jungle. Loon's oldest, Julia, who looked about twelve, sat cross-legged eating popcorn on a cypress's roots. The roots spanned out from the tree's trunk into a platform three feet above the ground before reaching their honey-colored fingers straight down into the burnt-umber mud.

All these years later the evening seems a fairytale dream. We jumped into the heavens and ate popcorn and Loon and I drank Milwaukee's Best until my stomach cramped. He insisted I spend the night—not the first such invitation I'd had from the people in Lafitte, easily some of the kindest I'd ever met in the four continents I'd lived on. I had to accept his offer because I'd never find my way back. I decided I wouldn't embarrass him about his claiming to have the Gulf in his backyard. Holes in the heavens were a bit easier to believe. I knew my maps well enough. The Gulf was hidden from Louisiana behind thousands of square miles of swamp and marsh. Unless you're on a barrier island, you're not on the Gulf, and we were far from any barrier island.

It was some hours later when Loon's two youngest daughters, twins barely up to my waist, took my hands and yanked me up off the ground where I was lying, exhausted. They led me away from the house, away from the lights, between two cypress, into total darkness. Jungle pulsed, the thick air eclipsed the sky. I could barely hear the others' footsteps behind us. The blades of palmetto leaves scraped my legs. A spiderweb wrapped around my face. I let go of one of their hands, wiped it away, upon the muscles of vine and tree entwined against my passing fingers, Spanish moss delicate as the worn sinew of the blanket I clung to in the nights of my childhood. Then all of a sudden the path went downwards, curved, and ended in twin skies, the stars above shimmering upon the open water. No land, no marsh, no swamp in sight. "Told ya," said Loon, already standing there at water's edge.

Julia walked past us, down into the water in her clothes until outer space gathered around her waist, its stars flickering in her wake, points stubbornly rooted to their original places, the night behind us filled with all those sounds I did not know but needed to be heard, sounds that once upon a time used to be in front of us as well.

Now, five years later, I finally get it. It took Katrina to make me understand why Loon had the Gulf of Mexico in his backyard, why this water is not here on the maps beside me in my office. And why it is the reason so many died in our city.

Through natural and man-made disasters, many other countries have seen it, the destruction that lies now between Biloxi and Buras, but this is a new American landscape. It will be a long time before we know what we can grow from it. In the meantime, we better learn to live in and love it, because before we know it, this mess we made will never be over.

As they have for the last three centuries, our city's demographics will again shift. Our people and their culture, like our sediment, will take many years to resettle. I pray that those who have not returned find fertile ground elsewhere, and that new people will make this home and add to our cultural gumbo.

Bienville founded the settlement La Nouvelle-Orléans here, at this river bend outside my window, because it was the most viable port. (To think that almost three hundred years later it took five days to get bottled water to those stranded here . . .) Two hurricanes leveled the settlement before 1730. They rebuilt after each. Three centuries of floods and fires and plagues and ten wars followed and New Orleans, with the French Quarter at its heart, always rebuilt. It has never been a place for the faint of heart.

The loss of our having the city alone is now overbalanced with hope for her future. But, finally, after she's been through so damn much already, there may not be a future for New Orleans, because Loon has the Gulf of Mexico in his backyard.

The coast is moving closer and closer. Someday, the Gulf will lie on the horizon for us, as it does for Waveland. Remember Waveland after the storm. Desert of cracked white mud. Immaculate nothing but for the sounds of insects over concrete slabs. This will be New Orleans. And it's not far off.

Homes will literally vanish. Instead of a demolished casino barge lying on top of a Holiday Inn, like in Mississippi, there will be downtown offices, the Hyatt, the Superdome, lying in rubble blocks from where they once stood. Addresses spray-painted on pieces of broken plywood will let the insurance people know where skyscrapers, music clubs, and landmarks used to be. And, unless every single last person evacuates successfully, he, too, vanishes.

All of the levee repairs, the $100 billion already spent in recovery after Katrina, this gutting and rebuilding of homes, every nail being driven into roofing right now will matter very little if New Orleans becomes a Gulf Coast town in fifty years.

Louisiana's coast is unlike any other in the United States. It contains America's Wetlands. These thousands of square miles of marsh and barrier islands lying between New Orleans and the Gulf, created over millennia from the Mississippi's sediment, have always buffered the region from hurricane surge. Hurricanes feed on water. Every three miles of wetlands knocks the storm surge down one foot and begins the slow death of incoming storms, typically reducing a hurricane to diminished winds and rainfall by the time it reaches New Orleans.

But the wetlands are disappearing. Starting in the early 1900s, in order to expand oil and gas infrastructure, they were dredged for pipelines and navigation. Now, a web of ten thousand miles of channels crisscrosses them, funneling salt water from the Gulf into the back marshes and killing the vegetation that holds the marshes together. In addition, the current Mississippi River levees, completed after the Great Flood of 1927, keep the river's sediment from reaching its deltaic plain and replenishing these wetlands as it once did through natural flooding. This also causes the region to sink, because the natural process of subsidence is going unchecked by the addition of new sediment. All this sediment, drained from most of the states in America, is now dumped into the Gulf of Mexico. It is ironic that Katrina became such a disaster not because the canal levees failed, but because the river levees held for so long before that.

Since 1928, almost one third—over 2000 square miles—of Louisiana's coast has eroded, fallen into the Gulf of Mexico. How would we feel if some other country came and annexed Rhode Island? I imagine we'd be pissed. Well, Louisiana's already lost more land than that. And our country's doing it to itself.

Over 80% of all coastal wetlands loss in the U.S. occurs in Louisiana. *It is the fastest disappearing landmass on the planet.* More than 30% of the state's shoreline may be gone by 2050, while New Orleans continues to sink. At this moment, we are losing one football field of land every 30 minutes. While we once lost 40 square miles a year, now we're losing 25, more than the size of Manhattan, every year, simply because there's less to lose. The numbers go on and on and on. And they only get worse as time passes.

I once thought there would always be a settlement here, even if it's me alone with a few boxes of Deet and a fishing pole. But the land is eroding. In the not too distant future, Lafitte will be gone. "God's country," as Popcorn Junior called it, will be water. The mud that Peggy Sue got her feet born into will be the bottom of the sea. There will not be a flood every twenty years, as Barbara, holding her pet nutria, told me she could handle, but a permanent one. The Gulf will creep over Lafitte, up to New Orleans.

Then, it is only a matter of time until a hurricane's storm surge levels the city—not flooding, but, for the first time, a *surge* directly from the Gulf—extinguishing it as a functioning city forever.

Finally, the last step is a slow, gradual one. The Gulf will creep through the last levees, to the city's concrete doorsteps, all that was left standing of our homes, over the slabs of foundations long abandoned, relieving them of the hum of insects and calls of birds. Yes. Atlantis. Silent as the water in Loon's backyard.

This is not some fantastic doomsday scenario. If we do not restore our wetlands, it is a sure thing.

This begs the question: Do you give a shit?

Disregarding the unique cultures of our city and its surrounding parishes (home to two-thirds of Louisiana's residents), or this massive habitat for endangered and threatened species, or that our wetlands are the largest and most significant coastal ecosystem in North America (40% of America's salt marshes, 28% of coastal wetlands in the lower forty-eight states), a good percentage of the things you use every day, whether you're a farmer or an investment banker, probably came through our waterways, the world's largest port system. One-fifth of all America's imports and exports go through here.

In addition, southern Louisiana boasts 28% of the entire U.S. fisheries annual catch, 20% of all domestic oil production, 25% of natural gas, and 88% of our offshore oil and gas. Do you think we use this to heat *our* homes in winter?

Wetlands shield pipelines, platforms, and other oil infrastructure from storms and corrosion. Their loss leaves this infrastructure extremely vulnerable. Largely because the wetlands had been eroded, damage caused by Katrina and Rita shut down 90% of crude oil production in the Gulf of Mexico, and gasoline prices soared nationwide.

I could go on and on about how we fuel the country, whether it's your car or your tummy. As America attempts to shift toward a self-sufficient energy policy, the fate of that fuel hangs in the balance. Six countries' flags have flown over southern Louisiana, and it might be argued that those countries have always used us more than we used them, but if America wants to continue doing so, we need our wetlands. And we can have them.

The disappearance of New Orleans can be stopped. There is a solution. We've spent three centuries trying to conquer the natural forces that created this region. We must now begin to work with river floods and ocean tides instead of against them, in order to rebuild and nurture coastal land, through multifaceted approaches. Barrier shoreline projects and hydrological restoration must be applied together to replicate the natural river processes that originally built and sustained the wetlands. It is called the Coast 2050 plan.

The plan would cost about $14 billion over two decades, less than the price tag of Boston's Big Dig. Like the Big Dig, this cost would have to be split between federal and state funds. Anyone who's sat in mind-numbing gridlock during Boston's rush hour can attest to the worth of building an underground tunnel through that city. However, I don't think its benefits quite measure up to saving America's Wetlands, which affect virtually every living soul in the United States and much of the world. Not to mention that, if we don't enact this plan, well, that'll be one way to solve our own traffic problems down here in New Orleans, for-ever. And doing nothing will cost more than $150 billion just to restore the infrastructure that will be lost in the coming decades—far, far more than the Coast 2050's price tag, even if it increases twofold, like so many other public works.

Part of this cost to rebuild the wetlands will have to come from a greater amount of state funding in an already poor state, but the federal government must, in turn, step up. For starters, we need our fair share of what the federal government takes from the oil and gas industry here, as other states commonly receive. In 1995, for example, the federal govern-ment received $2.8 billion from mineral reserves alone here, while Louisiana got $16 million, and, as always, bore the environmental burden.

Unlike revenues from land-based drilling, which are split evenly between the states and federal government, most revenues from offshore drilling are not yet allocated to states. While our coast supplies the rest of the country with oil and gas, and immense federal tax revenues, our ecosystem and homes face obliteration as a consequence.

Restoring the coast is possible and practical, as is the survival of New Orleans. People have been living below sea level practically since people existed. Choctaws were here long before Europeans arrived and built lev-ees. Today, Amsterdam, for example, is twelve feet below sea level. In fact, half of the Netherlands, a land mass forty-five times larger than all of Orleans Parish, lies below sea level. And, contrary to popular belief, only about half of New Orleans is actually below sea level.

New Orleans is *not* in the natural path of destruction by a future hur-ricane. Katrina does not, and should not, have to ever happen again. We created this situation. While it is true that the levees were not maintained properly, ultimately they failed because of our weakened coast.

The first levees to fail were along the Mississippi River Gulf Outlet (MR. GO). Those levees breached only where the wetlands, which armor the levees, had eroded, and St. Bernard Parish flooded. Water from the MR. GO then went into the Industrial Canal, subsequently causing those levees to breach as well, destroying the Lower 9th Ward and flooding much of the Upper 9th. Had the wetlands not been so eroded they would have also greatly diminished the massive surge into Lake Pontchartrain, which caused the city's three drainage canals to fail, flooding most of New Orleans, from Lakeview to downtown to the Industrial Canal, completing the circuit.

At least thirteen hundred people died because of this. And we will be murdering thousands and thousands more if we don't restore America's Wetlands. This cannot wait.

The time is now. If Katrina's eye had hit ground a nudge further west, over Lafitte and the weakened wetlands directly south of the city (instead of the weakened wetlands in St. Bernard and Plaquemines parishes), all of Jefferson Parish and probably New Orleans, too, would have been underwater.

So, here's the funny thing: Though I spent the weeks after Katrina ignoring our federal government and avoiding its threats and catastrophes, for this, I know we need them. There is no other way.

Certain small measures over the last two decades have been implemented. Most recently, Congress insured that some Gulf-wide offshore oil revenue sharing will begin in 2017, but that will be too little too late. The choice is between a relatively small cost over twenty years, or $100 billion in fifteen months and thousands of lives like after Katrina.

This is not about politics. It is about policy. We are not constrained by science and engineering. Unlike Kennedy announcing travel to the moon within a decade, the science is *here, now*, but the *policy* is not.

So, make this an issue. If someone wants your vote, especially if you live outside Louisiana, make sure they know this is important to you. Join an organization, any organization, that fits your politics and makes this an issue, and add your voice. If you can, support those organizations that make this cause their mission. As Americans, we cannot afford to make Louisiana's land loss a fleeting interest, some fun facts, fodder for party conversation. Learning about it is not enough. It must become an avocation. It is our survival. It is sad that it took Katrina to force this upon me.

We need to think big—big questions and big answers. Sure, levees are in our faces and provide immediately visible security, but they are short-term solutions that, as we've seen all too clearly, can provide long-term suffering.

Some countries are millennia ahead of us at screwing up their environment. Russia almost drained the whole Aral Sea. Now, they've adapted and learned to reverse the process. We're new at this. This is the first time we've ruined our own soil to such an extent. Let's take Katrina's fatal hint. This is *not* a debatable political issue. It's *fact*. It's already happened, and in the time it took you to read the last page we lost a further 2,500 square feet of land.

For heaven's sake, if we can send a spaceship to Pluto, we should be able to stop destroying our wetlands. We want to be here for a long time to come, here for you to come down and see how much there is to save.

Loon would probably let you crash at his place. Only it's not there anymore.

—Joshua Clark
January, 2007

For more ways to help save the wetlands, and for further information, please visit:

www.AmericasWetland.com
www.crcl.org